Retracing the Past

Readings in the History of the American People

VOLUME ONE • TO 1877

Third Edition

EDITORS

Gary B. Nash

University of California, Los Angeles

Ronald Schultz

University of Wyoming

 HarperCollinsCollegePublishers

Acquisitions Editor: Bruce Borland
Developmental Editor: Carol Einhorn
Project Coordination, Text and Cover Design: Proof Positive/
    Farrowlyne Associates, Inc.
Cover Illustration: Theodore de Bry, *America*, Frankfort, 1591
Photo Researcher: Leslie Coopersmith
Production Manager: Kewal Sharma
Compositor: Proof Positive/Farrowlyne Associates, Inc.
Printer and Binder: Malloy Lithographing, Inc.
Cover Printer: Malloy Lithographing, Inc.

Retracing the Past: Readings in the History of the American People, Volume One,
To 1877, Third Edition

Library of Congress Cataloging-in-Publication Data

Retracing the past : readings in the history of the American people /
    editors, Gary B. Nash, Ronald Schultz. — 3rd ed.
        p. cm.
        Contents: v. 1. To 1877 — v. 2. Since 1865.
        ISBN 0-06-501060-4 (v. 1). — ISBN 0-06-501061-2 (v. 2)
        1. United States—History. I. Nash, Gary B. II. Schultz,
    Ronald, 1946– .
    E178.6.R45 1993
    973—dc20
                                                                93-27282
                                                                    CIP

93 94 95 96 9 8 7 6 5 4 3 2 1

CONTENTS

Preface **v**

PART ONE
A COLONIZING PEOPLE 2

PART TWO
A REVOLUTIONARY PEOPLE 88

PART THREE
AN EXPANDING PEOPLE 170

PREFACE

This two-volume reader has been constructed to accompany the third edition of *The American People: Creating a Nation and a Society* (New York: HarperCollins, 1993), but we hope it will also prove a useful supplement to other books in American history. The essays have been selected with three goals in mind: first, to blend political and social history; second, to lead students to a consideration of the roles of women, ethnic groups, and laboring Americans in the weaving of the nation's social fabric; and third, to explore life at the individual and community levels. The book is also intended to introduce students to the individuals and groups that made a critical difference in the shaping of American history or whose experience reflected key changes in society.

A few of the individuals highlighted are famous—Benjamin Franklin, Abraham Lincoln, and Jackie Robinson, for example. A number of others are historically visible but are not quite household names—Squanto, Anne Hutchinson, Tecumseh, and John Muir. Some will be totally unknown to students, such as George Robert Twelves Hewes, a Boston shoemaker who witnessed some of the most important events of the American Revolution, and Absalom Jones, who bought his way out of slavery and became a leader of Philadelphia's free African-American community after the Revolution. Often the focus is on groups whose role in history has not been adequately treated—the Chinese in the building of the transcontinental railroad, the grassroots black leaders during Reconstruction, and the Hispanic agricultural workers of this century.

Some of these essays take us inside American homes, farms, and factories, such as the essays on working women in New York City before the Civil War and the families of Butte, Montana, who welcomed the radio into their lives during the 1920s and 1930s. Such essays, it is hoped, convey an understanding of the daily lives of ordinary Americans, who collectively helped shape their society. Other essays deal with the vital social and political movements that transformed American society: the debate over the Constitution in the 1780s; reform in the antebellum period; populism and progressivism in the late nineteenth and early twentieth centuries; and the rise of political conservatism in our own time.

Readability has been an important criterion in the selection of these essays. An important indicator of readability, in turn, is how vividly and concretely the authors have brought the past to life. The main objective of these readers is a palpable presentation of the past—one that allows students to sense and feel the forces of historical change and hence to understand them.

Gary B. Nash
Ronald Schultz

ACKNOWLEDGMENTS

In developing this volume of readings, the editors have been well advised by the following academic colleagues, who reviewed the previous edition and read preliminary tables of contents:

Rosemary Abend
El Camino College

Gregg Andrews
Southwest Texas State University

Ron Aquila
Ball State University

Sidney Bland
James Madison University

James D. Bolton
Coastline Community College

Catherine C. Catalfano
St. Vincent College

Gene Clanton
Washington State University

David Edmunds
Indiana University

James Fell
Metropolitan State College

Gretchen Harvey
North Dakota State University

Frances S. Hensley
Marshall University

Jerrold Hirsch
Northeast Missouri State University

M. Paul Holsinger
Illinois State University

Thomas B. Jones
Metropolitan State University

Tim Lehman
Rocky Mountain College

Sylvia W. McGrath
Stephen F. Austin State University

David Moore
Loyola University

Ian Mylchreest
University of Nevada

W. R. Swagerty
University of Idaho

In addition, Ronald D. Schultz of the University of Wyoming played a major role in preparing the introductory notes and in readying the manuscript for publication.

GBN

Retracing
the
Past

PART ONE

A COLONIZING PEOPLE

The expansion of Europe westward across the Atlantic during the sixteenth and seventeenth centuries brought together peoples from Africa, Western Europe, and the Americas to create a new form of multiracial and multiethnic society. The local societies created by this unprecedented mixing of peoples were among the most complex in recorded human history. Reflecting this complexity, the history of colonization in North and South America was largely a story of conflict and accommodation in which people with different cultures and divergent ways of life struggled to create stable patterns of everyday life in a world of constant change.

The early experiences of people in the colonial era were decisively shaped by biological interactions between the Old World and the New. In "Metamorphosis of the Americas," Alfred W. Crosby asks us to consider the vital importance of flora, fauna, and disease on the early history of the Americas. This theme is continued in the poignant story of "Squanto: Last of the Patuxets," in which the kidnapped Native American leader returns to his native Massachusetts to find that his people have been decimated by European disease. His attempt to restore some measure of stability to his society and to elevate his personal position through his actions as a cultural and political broker reminds us that Native Americans were not passive victims of European conquest, but sought to maintain the integrity of their social world in ways that paralleled those of the English settlers.

The realization of a stable social life was no easier for the English than for the Patuxets, as T. H. Breen reveals in his survey of life in the early Chesapeake, "Looking Out for Number One." The single-minded pursuit of individual interest that marked the first generations of Virginia settlers made even the most rudimentary forms of social and political life difficult to achieve. Although faced with mounting conflict with Native Americans and the threat of Spanish invasion, early Virginians refused to put aside their pursuit of profit long enough even to serve in their local militia units.

Individualism was a problem in New England as well as in Virginia. Although settled by established family groups rather than young, unattached men—as was the case in the tobacco colonies—Massachusetts Bay experienced a series of intense struggles between the formal corporate ethic of the colony and the individualistic propensities of many of its settlers. In his essay "The Case of the American Jezebels," Lyle Koehler recounts one of the most revealing of these conflicts, the battle between the Boston establishment and Anne Hutchinson for the spiritual soul of the Puritan colony.

By 1700, English settlers had achieved a substantial measure of social and political stability. Yet the new century would bring new challenges to colonists living in a changing world. Slavery was one of the most important legacies of the colonial era, creating divisions in American society that would lead to a civil war in 1861 and to distorted social relations for much of our nation's history. In "Patterns of Black Resistance," Peter H. Wood takes us into the private world of South Carolina slaves, showing us the many, often subtle, ways in which African bondspeople resisted the control of their masters and in the process reaffirmed their basic humanity and their own countervailing power. Labor was the heart of slave life, just as it was for colonial women. In tracing "The Small Circle of Domestic Concerns," Mary Beth Norton provides us with an intimate look at the everyday lives of American women, whose experiences ranged from the drudgery faced by frontier wives to the more genteel—but no less demanding—duties of the plantation mistress.

Beginning in the early eighteenth century, the combined effects of imperial warfare and economic change began to transform America into a recognizably "modern" society. In asking the question "Who Was Benjamin Franklin?" John William Ward invites us to examine an important part of this rising modernity: the ability of some men to manipulate their public image for personal gain. Much like public figures today, Franklin's reputation rested less on his community's intimate knowledge of his character than on his own public image-making and self-advertisement. While much of American society remained traditional in Franklin's time, by midcentury unmistakable signs of change existed as well.

1

METAMORPHOSIS OF THE AMERICAS

ALFRED W. CROSBY

The quincentenary of Columbus's landing in the Americas has prompted many historians to reevaluate the meaning of the "discovery" of the "New World." Unlike traditional accounts that focus on the expansion of Europe, the voyages of discovery, and Columbus as a heroic explorer, these reconsiderations take a broader perspective both by incorporating the indigenous peoples (whom Columbus misnamed "Indians") into the process of trans-Atlantic contact and by tracing the long-term consequences of the events of 1492. Influenced by the disciplines of social anthropology, medical history, and agronomy, these new accounts emphasize the interaction between peoples and cultures and the contribution that both Europeans and Native Americans made to the creation of a new American culture in the sixteenth and seventeenth centuries.

These new accounts of cross-cultural contact have been especially sensitive to the impact that the arrival of Europeans had on the indigenous peoples of the Americas. Although few in number during the initial phases of contact, the Europeans nonetheless had a profound effect on native societies, often altering them in ways that were neither anticipated nor fully understood by the early explorers. In this essay, Alfred W. Crosby adopts an ecological perspective to explore this hidden history of European–Native American interaction. Drawing upon the biological concepts of ecosystems, biota (the totality of living organisms in an ecosystem), and epidemiology (the study of the life cycles and transmission of diseases), Crosby explains how European crops, weeds, animals, and—especially—diseases affected New World societies. Reflecting historians' increasing recognition of environmental influences on human society, Crosby portrays a complex process of biological exchange that changed European and Native American societies alike.

Crosby's perspective, focusing as it does on the long-range human and environmental effects of 1492, has decidedly tragic overtones, especially because European diseases ravaged Indian populations in what amounted to a biological holocaust. Moreover, this essay obliges us to see the arrival of Europeans in the Americas from the viewpoint of the indigenous peoples.

"Metamorphosis of the Americas" reprinted from Seeds of Change: A Quincentennial Commemoration, *eds. Herman J. Viola and Carolyn Margolis (Washington, D.C.: Smithsonian Institution Press, 1991), pp. 70–89, by permission of the publisher. Copyright © 1991 by The Smithsonian Institution. All rights reserved.*

Chimalpahin Cuauhtlehuanitzin, one of our best sources of information on Mexico in the years immediately before and after the Spanish conquest, was an Indian historian whom the invaders trained in the reading and writing of the Roman alphabet in the sixteenth century. His writings (in Nahuatl) inform us that the year 13-Flint before the invasion was a grim one in the Valley of Mexico. There was sickness, hunger, an eclipse of the sun, an eruption of some sort between the volcanoes Iztaccíhuatl and Popocatépetl, "and many ferocious beasts devoured the children." But 13-Flint, Chimalpahin makes clear, was an exception in what was an era of triumph for the Aztecs. They, who within recorded memory had been wanderers from the savage north, now exacted tributes of food, gold, quetzal feathers, and human hearts from vassal states all the way from the remote dry lands from which they had emerged to the rain forests of the south and east. The stiff-necked Tarascos, at the cost of perennial war, retained their independence, as did—precariously—the anciently civilized Mayas, and there were a few others who survived in the chinks of the Aztec empire. Otherwise central Mexico lay under the hegemony of the Aztecs.

Lord Ahuitzotl, who was ruler of the Aztecs in 13-Flint, used the legions and wealth under his command to improve and adorn his capital, the incomparable Tenochtitlán. He built a new aqueduct to bring fresh water to its scores of thousands of inhabitants. He rebuilt and reconsecrated the gigantic temple to the Aztec tribal deities, Huitzilopochtli and Tezcatlipoca. He did not—how could he have?—see in the strange events of 13-Flint portents of the end of his empire and of his world.

A decade later, in 10-Rabbit, his nephew Motecuhzoma Xocoyotzin, known to us as Montezuma, succeeded him as a leader of the Aztecs. His subjects numbered in the millions, and, so far as he or they knew, the empire had no equal in power and riches under the sky. Montezuma made plans to rebuild the great temple once more, higher and more extravagantly than any of his predecessors.

Reports drifted in from the eastern coast of pale, hairy visitors in boats "like towers or small mountains." There were only a few of them, and invaders traditionally came from the north, as had the Aztecs themselves, not from the east and never from the sea. Gods, however, might come from the sea.

In the year 1-Reed the visitors came to invade and to stay forever. The invaders proved to be humans, not gods, but they were incomprehensibly alien and powerful. They had light skin and much hair on their lips and chins, and some of them had yellow hair. They dressed in metal and brought weapons of metal. They had huge animals allied with them. The invaders had at their sides dogs bigger and fiercer than any seen before: "The color of their eyes is a burning yellow; their eyes flash fire and shoot off sparks." They had, also, man-animals that ran faster than any man and were more powerful than any creature the Aztecs had ever known. Then these creatures divided, and the Aztecs saw that the invaders had "deer to carry them on their backs wherever they wish to go. These deer, our lord, are as tall as the roof of a house."

Most hideous of all the invader's allies was a pestilence, a *hueyzahuatl,* that swept all the land immediately after the Aztecs, quickened by atrocities, turned on the invaders, killing half of them as they fought their way out of Tenochtitlán. The pestilence spared the invaders but was a thing of agony, disfigurement, and death for the peoples of Mexico. There was no defense against it nor cure for it. Sahagún learned how it struck in the month of Tepeilhuitl and

spread over the people as great destruction. Some it quite covered on all parts—their faces, their heads, their breasts, and so on. There was a great havoc. Very many died of it. They could not walk; they only lay in their resting places and beds. They could not move; they could not stir; they could not change position, nor lie on one side; nor face down, nor on their backs. And if they stirred, much did they cry out. Great was its destruction.

Covered, mantled with pustules, very many people died of them.

A third, a half—no one knows how many—of the Aztecs and the other peoples of Mexico died.

Then the invaders and their human allies, the Aztecs' former vassals and enemies, diminished by the epidemic but emboldened by the presence of the invaders, fought their way down the causeways and across Lake Texcoco into Tenochtitlán. Seventy-five days later, on the day 1-Serpent of the year 3-House, the siege of Tenochtitlán ended. Aztec poets expressed the grief of those who, somehow, had survived:

> *Weep my people:*
> *know that with these disasters*
> *we have lost the Mexica nation.*
> *The water had turned bitter,*
> *our food is bitter.*

The invaders' chief, Hernán Cortés, ordered that stones from the temple of which Lord Ahuitzotl had been so proud should be gathered up, and that a Christian cathedral should be made of them in the center of what had become, by his victory, Mexico City. The vanquished learned that the ominous year 13-Flint was more properly designated as the year 1492 of a deity both more imperialistic and more merciful than Huitzilopochtli or Tezcatlipoca, and that Tenochtitlán had fallen in the year 1521, not 3-House.

The fall of Tenochtitlán in the year 3-House was the worst discrete event in the Aztecs' history. Worse, however, was this: 3-House was the beginning of the worst century of their history. Their civilization suffered massive amputations and survived at the root only by accepting alien graftings in the branch, as the conquistadores and the friars replaced their ancient noble and priestly classes. There were advantages that came with the defeat: an alphabet, a more supple instrument for expression than their own logosyllabic system of writing; the true arch to replace the corbel; tools with an iron edge that did not shatter like an obsidian edge when it struck the rock hidden in the leaves. But the magnitude of the change, good and bad, was almost greater than the mind could encompass or the heart endure. The metamorphosis was more than political or religious or intellectual or technological; it was biological. The biota of Mexico—its *life*—and, in time, that of the entire Western Hemisphere changed.

If Lord Ahuitzotl had returned to Mexico (now New Spain) a hundred years after 13-Flint he would have found much the same as in his lifetime. He would have recognized the profiles of the mountains, all the wild birds, and most of the plants. The basic and holy food of his people was still maize. But he would have been stunned by the sight of plants and creatures he had never seen or dreamed of during his days on earth. Alien plants grew alongside the old plants in Mexico, and its 1592 fauna, in its large animals, was as different from that of 1492 as the native fauna of Zimbabwe differs from that of Spain.

The invaders had brought in wheat and other Eurasian and African grains; peach, pear, orange, and lemon trees; chick-peas, grape vines, melons, onions, radishes, and much more. A Spanish nobleman come to America could require his *indios* to furnish his table with the foods of his ancestors. Along with the Old World crops had come Old World weeds. European clover was by now so common that the Aztecs had a word of their own for it. They called it Castilian *ocoxochitl*, naming it after a low native plant that also prefers shade and moisture.

Of all the new sights of 1592—the cathedrals, the fields of wheat, wheeled vehicles, brigantines with sails and lounging sailors on Lake Texcoco where there had once been only canoes and sweating paddlers—nothing could have amazed Ahuitzotl more than the new animals: pigs, sheep, goats, burros, and others. Now there were cattle everywhere, and ranches with more than a hundred thousand each in the north. Now there were thousands upon thousands of horses, and they were available to any European (and, despite the law, the Indian, too) with a few coins or the skill to rope them. The horsemanship of the Mexican vaquero was already legendary on both sides of the Atlantic.

During Lord Ahuitzotl's lifetime the best way to move four hundred ears of maize in Mexico was on the bent back of a man, and the fastest means to deliver a message was by a runner. Now the bent man loaded four thousand ears onto a wheeled wagon pulled by a burro, and the messenger vaulted onto a horse and set off at several times the fastest pace of the fastest sprinter.

But Lord Ahuitzotl was an Aztec, an *indio,* and what would have put a catch in his breath a century after 13-Flint was not so much the new animals, for all their number, but his own kind of people, in their meager number. War, brutality, hunger, social and family disarray, loss of farmland to the invading humans and their flocks, and exploitation in general had taken their toll, but disease was the worst enemy. The *hueyzahuatl* of 1520–21, like the fall of Tenochtitlán, may have been the worst of its kind, but, more important, it was the beginning of a series of pestilential onslaughts. The worst of the worst of times of *cocoliztli* were 1545–48, a time of bleeding from the nose and eyes, and 1576–81, when, again, many bled from the nose and windrows of Indians fell, but few Spaniards. If Lord Ahuitzotl had returned a century after his death, he would have found one for every ten or even twenty *indios* who had lived in his time.

Some of the survivors were *mestizos,* children of European men and Indian women. The mestizo, with his Indian skin and Visigothic eyes, proffering a cup of cocoa, a mixture of *chocolatl* and Old World Sugar; the wild Chichimec on his Berber mare; the Zapotec herder with his sheep; the Aztec, perhaps the last of the line of Ahuitzotl, receiving the final rites of the Christian faith as he slipped into the terminal coma of an infection newly arrived from Seville—in so many ways New Spain was *new,* a combination, crossing, and concoction of entities that had never before existed on the same continent.

To understand the complexity of that concoction, we have to look far back in the history of our planet, farther back than Europeans of the age of exploration could imagine. They believed that God had created the world a cozy six thousand years earlier, a colossal underestimation that forestalled comprehension of the causes of the differences between biotas on opposite sides of the Atlantic. Columbus and his contemporaries had no inkling that two hundred million years ago the continents of the earth were part of one immense world continent in which physical contiguity minimized the development of biological diversity. That is to say, the world's land biota, though it varied from one region or even neighborhood to another, was more homogeneous than at any time since, because true geographical isolation was very rare, except for oceanic islands.

Then slow and unimaginably powerful tectonic forces tore the supercontinent into several, eventually six, masses and shouldered them to the positions where they were in 1492, where they are today, with a few centimeters difference. During the interval of more than 150 million years the dinosaurs disappeared, birds appeared, and mammals advanced from minor status to dominance over most of the terrestrial globe. In the large Eurasian-African mass, most of the species of mammals that are most widely distributed in the world today originated or evolved into their present forms. In the other land masses, life evolved divergently, and thus Australia's biota is very different from Eurasia-Africa's.

Columbus wrote of the West Indies that the trees were "as different from ours as day from night, and so the fruits, the herbage." He was so surprised by the differences in the plants, and animals too, that he even claimed the rocks were different.

In Africa a few geological eras ago arboreal mammals with binocular eyesight and prehensile hands and feet moved down from the trees and out on to the grasslands. The toes of some of them shortened and the palms of their feet flattened and rose into arches for walking, and two of their ten fingers developed into thumbs. They developed bigger and better brains to compensate for the puniness of their teeth and claws and their slowness in pursuit and flight. They learned how to live and to hunt in teams, how to make and use tools, how to make clothing, how to control fire, and how to teach their young these skills. Their numbers increased; they began to migrate, first throughout Africa-Eurasia and even into the blue shadows of the retreating glaciers, and then to Australia, and across from Siberia to Alaska and the Western Hemisphere.

That was, for the geologist or paleontologist, barely yesterday, but for the anthropologist or historian it was a long time ago. The most recent common ancestor of Native Americans, whose ancestors crossed from the eastern extreme of Eurasia into America, and of Europeans, who sailed from the western extreme in 1492, lived tens of thousands and perhaps even more years ago. The Tainos and Spaniards who met in the Greater Antilles were products of physical and, more significantly, of cultural evolutions that had been diverging for a very long time. The Tainos reached out to feel the Spaniards "to ascertain if they were flesh and bones like themselves." For the Spaniards, the Tainos were the most exotic people they had ever met, with their hair not tightly curled like the Africans' "but straight and coarse like horsehair." Columbus wrote of them that "the whole forehead and head is very broad, more so than any other race that I have ever seen." They did not have the wheel or wheat or rice or iron or bronze. They did have a few trinkets of gold.

The contrasts continued to astonish Native Americans and Europeans after the latter reached the mainland. And no wonder: these two peoples had migrated in opposite directions around the world and for millennia before they met each other. The duration of their period of separation ensured that not only their physical appearance but their cultures had developed divergently. In the crude test of confrontation, one would be likely to have, at least for the short run, material advantages over the other. History makes clear that it was the Europeans who had the edge.

But to exploit their advantages, they had to get them across the Atlantic. Europeans could no more have successfully invaded the Americas from Europe in the sixteenth century than the Allies could have invaded Normandy from North America in 1944. Large offshore bases were

essential in both cases, the British Isles in the latter, the Greater Antilles in the former. The Allies needed the British Isles as a center from which to gather intelligence about the mainland and as a storage, training, and staging area. The conquistadores needed the Antilles for all that and—much more importantly—for the seasoning and propagation of their biological allies.

Except for the Tainos and bats, the only land mammal in the Greater Antilles in 1492 was the hutia, a tasty rabbit-sized rodent. There was a profusion of birds and many reptiles, including the large, extravagantly ugly but tasty iguana. The Tainos, whom Columbus noted as "very unskilled with arms" and fit to be servants and even slaves, were numerous, at least three million on Española (Hispaniola) alone, said an eyewitness.

Columbus returned to Española and the Antilles in 1493 with seventeen ships; twelve hundred men; seeds, cuttings, and stones for wheat, chick-peas, melons, onions, radishes, salad greens, grape vines, sugarcane, and fruit trees; and horses, dogs, pigs, cattle, chickens, sheep, and goats. That he also brought weeds, vermin such as rats, and germs is certain: there was no such entity then (or now) as a sack of truly clean seed, an absolutely clean ship, or a horse, pig, or man without microorganisms in its feces, fluids, and breath.

European crops, though they eventually prospered in both Americas, did not thrive in the tropical Antilles; the conquistadores were obliged to substitute the Taino staple, manioc, for wheaten bread. But their livestock did well, some fabulously well, in the Antilles, where the large carnivores were rare, where there were no local equivalents of rinderpest or hoof-and-mouth disease, and where, at first, the quantity of nourishment was immense and its quality splendid. Most of the imported animals prospered, most notably for the purposes of Cortés, Pizarro, and the like, the horses, cattle, and swine. They increased so fast that soon the backcountry of the Antilles swarmed with feral livestock. When the time came for launching invasions of the mainland, good mounts, pack animals, pork, beef, and hides were cheap—free, if you were willing to go get them yourself. Cortés did not invade Mexico with horses emaciated from weeks crossing the Atlantic, but with horses fresh from Cuba. Hernando de Soto traveled amid herds of hundreds of succulent pigs, all probably descendants from the eight Columbus brought from Spain to Española in 1493. The masters of America's first *haciendas* did not begin with bulls too weak to mount cows too frail to carry calves to full term, but with healthy beasts selected from the avant-garde herds of the Antilles.

The conquistadores' most powerful ally of all, the smallpox virus, also incubated in the Antilles. Smallpox had been a common affliction in the more densely populated regions of Europe in the Middle Ages, but it was not commonly a killer. Then, around 1500 it added to its ease of transmission a tendency to kill its hosts. It was so common in the cities facing west across the Atlantic that nearly all urban children caught it and were soon dead or immune—either way, no longer media for its propagation. Not for two more decades did chance provide the virus with a way to cross to the Americas. However it came, either by means of a few smallpox scabs in bale of waste cloth or the serial infection of a few immunologically virgin hidalgos from rural Castile who decided to gamble their futures in the colonies, it arrived not long before or after Christmas of 1518.

It seared through the Tainos like a fire driven through the dry brush by the wind they called *hurakán*. Their number had been falling precipitously since the 1490s, and now came the worst single blow of all. Bartolomé de las Casas recorded that the smallpox left no more than one thousand alive on Española "of that immensity of people that was on this island and which we have seen with our own eyes."

Within thirty years of Columbus's first landfall in the West Indies those islands contained all that the conquistadores needed for the successful invasion of the mainland: considerable numbers of their ambitious selves, livestock in cheap abundance, and at least one highly infectious and deadly disease to which almost every adult invader was immune and for which Native Americans

were kindling. This team of invaders conquered the Aztecs within two years of first penetrating their empire. In the following decade the same team, pushing south from the Spanish settlements in Central America, achieved an equally dramatic conquest of the Inca empire. There were no more such magnificent conquests because there were no more such empires in the Western Hemisphere; but whenever the Spaniards—Soto, Coronado, Valdivia—made their spectacular *entradas* into unknown lands, and wherever they founded permanent settlements—Buenos Aires, Guatemala City, Florida's Saint Augustine—their successes were as much due to their biological allies as to their abilities. The feats of the conquistadores seem to us, four or five centuries later, superhuman precisely because they were just that—the triumphs of teams that included more than humans.

The reputations of the conquistadores and their Portuguese, French, Dutch, British, and Russian equivalents need no more burnishing than historians have already afforded them, but the other large creatures of the invading team have been relatively neglected. In the long run, such species as chickens, sheep, and goats were crucially important, particularly for the Native Americans, but let us focus on the imported organisms that were most important in the short run, particularly to the invaders: pigs, cattle, horses, and pathogens.

First, the noble swine who accompanied the conquistadores were not the pampered, paunchy Neros of our barnyards, but the lean, fast, tusked boars and sows of medieval Europe. They were intolerant of direct sunlight and high temperatures, but there were shade and wallows in plenty in the American tropics. More food was immediately available for these omnivorous beasts in the areas first settled by Europeans in the Americas than there was for any other immigrant animal. In the Antilles they rooted the Tainos' manioc tubers and sweet potatoes out of the ground, stole their guavas and pineapples, gobbled lizards and baby birds—everything went down their maws. Within a few years of their debarkation in Española they were running wild there in numbers *infinitos.* Swine explosions of commensurate magnitude took place in the other islands of the Greater Antilles.

Pigs adapted similarly everywhere in continental America. In New England they thrived on the shellfish they rooted out of the tidal flats; in Virginia they did "swarm like Vermaine upon the Earth." In the open pampas the sun was hostile, but they adapted and went wild along the watercourses; and in Brazil, according to a visitor in 1601, "they beginne to have great multitudes, and heere [pork] is the best flesh of all." Much of the meat in the first European colonists' diet, from Nova Scotia to Patagonia, was American green turtle or venison or other game, but after that it was usually pork—plentiful, tasty, nourishing, cheap in the market, and free to the hunter.

Cattle do not have the swine's sensitivity to sunlight and heat, but neither are they as good at crawling under logs as pigs nor are they omnivorous. In other words, they were not as ready to seize the opportunity for independence in so wide a variety of American environments as pigs. Jungles, for instance, are not to their liking, and they often require a period of several generations to adapt to hot, wet grasslands. On the other hand, they were agile, swift, and formidably equipped for survival. They were more like their Pleistocene ancestors or Texas longhorns than upholstered Guernseys and Holsteins.

The Spanish cattle took to the meadows and savannas of the Antilles like Adam and Eve returning to Eden. The cows were soon dropping calves two and three times a year, and the first American bulls were massively bigger than those back in Spain, a report confirmed by modern archaeology. In 1518 Alonzo de Zuazo informed his king that thirty or forty strays would grow to three or four hundred in as little as three or four years. Feral cattle were roaming the hinterlands of Española by the 1520s and, soon after, the other Antilles. Stray men could and did live off these stray herds. When these humans became pirates, they were called buccaneers, a name probably derived from the wooden grate, the *boucan,* on which they smoked their wild beef.

Historians have recounted in detail the prodigious propagation of the cattle throughout the Western Hemisphere, a story mirrored in several respects in the drama of the horse. Columbus brought horses, essential to almost every European endeavor in the Americas, across the Atlantic in 1493. Many of these large animals, awkward to care for and difficult to feed properly on shipboard, died during the crossings, and the West Indian environment was not ideal for them; but by 1501 there were twenty or thirty on Española and two years later no fewer than sixty or seventy. Horses, good ones, were available when the conquistadores set off for the mainland. They were slow in adapting to the tropical lowlands of the continents but achieved population explosion when they reached the temperate grasslands of the Western Hemisphere.

At the end of the sixteenth century the horses roaming free in Durango were beyond possibility of counting. Taken to New Mexico and California, beyond the great deserts, by Spanish explorers and settlers, they inspired the covetousness of the northern Indians, who rustled them and traded some to Indians further north. That process repeated itself until horses reached Alberta by the mid-eighteenth century. When the Aztecs first saw horses they called them deer; the Mayas called them tapirs; and Indians to the west of the Great Lakes called them moose. Mounted upon these wonderful animals, the Indians moved on to the plains to live off the buffalo and became light cavalry nonpareil. They were the last Native Americans north of Mexico to wage war against the invaders from the eastern ocean.

On the pampas the drama of the horse of Mexico was matched and surpassed. As in North America, Indians swung up onto their backs and moved into the grasslands to live off the herds of wild quadrupeds, which here were not indigenous buffalo but exotic horses and cattle. Native American resistance on the pampas would not be broken until the nineteenth century, at approximately the same time as the Great Plains Indians were defeated. The differences between the new kings of the great grasslands of the Americas—vaqueros, gauchos, cowboys—were not discernible at more than a few hundred meters, nor were the differences between their lightly tamed mounts.

The impact of the animals the Europeans brought with them on the Americas transformed whole ecosystems. For example, cattle and horses were so numerous on the pampas early in the seventeenth century that there were reports that they were destroying the ground cover. That is quite plausible, considering their density and the fact that, in time, Eurasian and North African grasses and forbs took over much of the pampas, a usurpation which could have taken place only along with the destruction of the native flora. Similar usurpations took place in Mexico and Texas in the first post-Columbian centuries.

The first Euro-Americans paid little attention to the impact of the smaller creatures they brought with them, but it may have been as great as that of the larger animals, even as great as that of the close-cropping sheep and goats. Old World rats swarmed in and around European colonies from Quebec to Patagonia, decimating the native small animals and minor flora and enhancing the importation and spread of disease. Imported domestic cats and dogs threw off their allegiances to humanity and went wild everywhere the environment allowed, living off whatever creatures they could pounce upon or drag down. Nothing, however, that crossed from the Eastern to the Western Hemisphere made as much difference in the first or any other post-Columbian century as disease.

Native Americans are not native to the Americas, if by the adjective you mean in possession of a pedigree that goes back forever in association with a particular geographical region. Tapirs qualify as native Americans, but Indians are descendants of immigrants from Asia who crossed through the Arctic into the Western Hemisphere a phylogenetically short time ago. Human beings are not native to the Americas, nor are their direct ancestors and near relatives, the chimps, gorillas, and such.

This has not only zoological but great historical importance, because it means there could have been no microorganisms or parasites adapted and predisposed to preying on humans when those clever bipeds came down through the glaciers into America. These immigrants were not free of infections, of course. They brought some infections with them, but not those informally known as the "crowd diseases." The Proto-Indians were hunters and gatherers and traveled and lived in small bands, not crowds. The microorganisms of diseases like smallpox or measles disappear in small populations of hosts. These viruses have no animal hosts to circulate among while not circulating among humans; they quickly die outside living bodies; and they race through small populations, either killing or producing permanent immunity as they go. That is, they swiftly burn up all their fuel and disappear like a forest fire that has run out of trees. As for the germs of long-lasting infections like tuberculosis or syphilis, the Proto-Indians could have and doubtlessly did bring some in that category with them, but perhaps not as many as you might think. The Proto-Indians came as nomads through the climatically hostile Arctic, where the chronically ill could not have lasted for long: they either died or were, for the sake of the band, left behind to perish.

To put it in a nutshell, a medical officer in Alaska at the end of the Pleistocene epoch would have given most of these Asian immigrants a clean bill of health. They were entering a Western Hemisphere free of specifically human infections, but not a totally wholesome Eden. A few American microorganisms and parasites managed in the brief interval (i.e., thousands, but not millions, of years) between the first entry of humans into the Americas and the appearance of Christopher Columbus in the West Indies to adapt to living in and off the newcomers. Chagas' disease, for instance, is natively American. But most of what were in 1492 and have since been the leading causes of morbidity and mortality among the world's communicable diseases were not present in the Western Hemisphere.

The world's leading infections were the by-products of the rise of agricultural and pastoral peoples in not the Western but the Eastern Hemisphere, where humans began living in dense, often sedentary, and usually unhygienic concentrations before even the most advanced American Indians. Many Eurasians and Africans lived, as well, in close proximity with their live-stock, exchanged infections with their herds, and, one might almost say, cultivated pathogens and parasites.

There is much debate about which historically important infectious diseases were present in the Eastern but *not* in the Western Hemisphere at the beginning of 1492. A truly definitive list may never be made, but most paleopathologists, epi-demiologists, and scholars who have perused the early records of Europe's first American empires agree that the list should include smallpox, measles, whooping cough, bubonic plague, malaria, yellow fever, diphtheria, amoebic dysen-tery, and influenza. The list should probably be longer, but this one is long enough to indicate what devastation the arrival of Europeans could visit upon an immunologically naive population.

The densest populations of the Eastern Hemisphere from China and Java to western Europe and Africa (the natives of the last two never long out of contact with America after 1492) were also the sickest, especially the city dwellers. They caught all the endemic or com-monly epidemic infections long before advancing to adulthood, hence the name given to many his-torically significant infections, the "childhood dis-eases." Those who survived had efficiently adapt-ed to their environments, and they often had long and productive lives. Children who died were quickly replaced by means of what was, over the years, a very high birth rate.

When the Europeans and Africans carried their diseases to America, "virgin soil epidemics" followed, infecting the great majorities of all pop-ulations at risk and killing adults as often as chil-dren. These epidemics were as effective in breaking resistance to the invaders as the air raids on civilian targets were intended to be in World War II, but were not. That is to say, they

slaughtered great numbers, especially in the cen-ters of population where the leadership elites lived; they paralyzed normal economic, religious, and political functions; and they terrorized sur-vivors.

We cannot be sure when the first post-Columbian virgin soil epidemic detonated in America. The decline of the Antillean Tainos in the first quarter century after 1492 seems to have been steeper than can be attributed to Spanish brutality. The swarms of pigs certainly provided a medium for an influenza epidemic, but the early chroniclers did not mention one, and whether anything as explosive as an influenza epidemic could have escaped their attention is doubtful. The fact is that the record does not mention any unambiguously epidemic infection until the end of 1518 or the very beginning of 1519.

The Spaniards in Española, where the infec-tion struck first, identified the disease as small-pox. Bartolomé de las Casas said it was from Castile. It rarely affected the Europeans but dev-astated the Indians, killing one-third to one-half, a death rate not far out of line with what the pop-ulation at risk in European ports—that is, the children—suffered. The affliction quickly spread throughout the Antilles, reaching Cuba just late enough for the Cortés expedition to the Mexican mainland to embark without it. In the next year a following expedition to Mexico included a man who carried smallpox. He infected the household in Cempoala where he was quartered, and the infection "spread from one Indian to another, and they, being so numerous and eating and sleeping together, quickly infected the whole country."

This, America's first recorded pandemic, spread far beyond the Antilles and Mexico. It rolled ahead of the Europeans and reached the lands of the advanced peoples of South America before the conquistadores' invasion of the fabu-lous Inca empire. It slaughtered the Inca's sub-jects, killed the Inca himself, disrupted the suc-cession, and set off a civil war. The people whom Pizarro conquered were the survivors of one of the worst periods of their history. How much fur-ther south and east the smallpox spread we can only guess, but if fire spreads in tinder, then why would this infection have stopped at the far boundaries of the Inca empire?

To the north of Mexico the record on the subject is blank, but again we must grant that there was little reason for disease not to have spread. A decade after the fall of the Inca empire a veteran of Pizarro's invasion of Peru, Hernando de Soto, led an expedition on a long maraud through what is now the southeastern part of the United States in search of other Tenochtitláns and Cuzcos. He found hierarchical societies, village complexes, dense populations, pyramid temples, but nothing as attractively lootable as Mexico or Peru. He also found evidence of the passage of epidemic disease. In Cofachiqui, somewhere in present-day Georgia, he came upon recently emptied villages and large funereal houses filled with the drying cadavers of people who had perished in an epidemic. What he saw in Georgia may have, should have, reminded him of what he had seen in Peru.

Onslaughts of the new diseases swept over the Native American peoples throughout the sixteenth century and for all the generations since. It may be that we distort reality if we try to count epidemics, plucking them up out of the surmounting tide of infection, but for the sake of getting some idea of the dimensions of the flood, let us take the chance. About fifty epidemics swept through the valley of Mexico between 1519 and 1810. Peru underwent twenty between the arrival of the Spaniards and 1720, Brazil perhaps forty of smallpox alone between 1560 and 1840.

The epidemiology of England's beginnings in America was similar to Iberia's. When Sir Francis Drake raided Saint Augustine in the 1580s, he brought an epidemic with him. The local Florida Indians "died verie fast and said amongst themselves, it was the Inglisshe God that made them die so faste." Another (conceivably the same) epidemic swept the coastal tribes of Carolina and Virginia before the end of that decade, "the like by report of the oldest men in the countrey never happened before, time out of mind." The Pilgrim settlement to the north at Plymouth was preced-

ed by an epidemic that began in 1616 and, said contemporary sources, killed 90 percent of the coastal Indians.

The material effect of these tidal waves of infection is one that we can at least crudely apprehend even at a distance of many years. The psychological effect—that is to say, the interpretations the invaders and the invaded placed on these epidemics—is not as apparent to people like ourselves, who blame infections on germs, not on the supernatural. Consider for a moment a statement made by an early nineteenth-century clergyman on the precipitous decrease of New England Indians since the first coming of the English: "Must we not ascribe it to the sovereign pleasure of the Most High, who divides to the nations their inheritance; who putteth down one and raiseth up another?" Both invaders and the invaded may have found this idea plausible.

And on and on to the present day. Alaska's and Canada's most remote Eskimos and Indians and South America's last tribes of hunter-gatherers and horticulturalists have been decimated by tuberculosis, measles, and influenza within living memory. Ninety-nine percent of the native people of Ungava Bay in northern Quebec came down with measles in a brief period of 1952, and about 7 percent died, even though some had the benefit of modern medicine. In 1954 measles broke out among the Native Americans of Brazil's Xingu National Park: the death rate was 9.6 percent for those who had modern medical treatment and 26.8 for those who did not. In 1990 the Yanomamos of the borderland of Brazil and Venezuela were decreasing rapidly under the attack not only or even primarily of the encroaching gold miners, but of malaria, influenza, measles, and chicken pox. The best ally of the invaders continues to be disease.

An avalanche of exotic organisms from the eastern Hemisphere has been pouring onto the shores of the Americas for five hundred years. It continues, altering the ecosystems in all parts of the Western Hemisphere and the fates of Americans of every ethnicity and generation. The more recent immigrant organisms have often, like the wheat and peach trees that arrived in the sixteenth century, had positive effects. The Far East's soybean, for instance, has become a major crop and source of nourishment in the Americas since World War II, but the nastiest newcomers, like the Japanese beetle and Dutch elm disease, are the ones that get the most attention. Kudzu, a vine introduced from the Far East about a hundred years ago, was a decorous sort of plant until the 1930s; since then it has been spreading cancerously through the Gulf and southern Atlantic states. The notorious "killer bees," aggressive African bees first released in Brazil in 1957, have spread in spite of every effort to hold them back and in 1990 were nearly at the border of the United States. Flying Asian cockroaches, newly arrived, infest Florida. Significant and infamous above all recent imports is the AIDS virus, which probably first appeared in the Western Hemisphere in the 1970s. By sea and by air, by mammoth container ship and by jet aircraft, by diplomatic pouch and by impromptu encounter, the homogenizing process accelerates.

Native Americans often object to the name "New World," a European term for the lands of the Western Hemisphere. They point out that those lands were familiar to them long before Christopher Columbus was born, and their argument is one the rest of us owe respectful consideration. But we all are justified in the use of the title for the Americas since 1492. Until Columbus found his way across the Atlantic the biota of the two sets of continents on either side were markedly different, the products of what, through time, had usually been divergent evolution. Since then the biota of both, most undeniably of the Americas, have in significant part been the product of revolution, that is, the abrupt addition and explosive propagation of exotic species from the lands on the other side of the waters that Columbus crossed in 1492. The great Genoese navigated, administered, crusaded, enslaved, but above all he mixed, mingled, jumbled, and homogenized the biota of our planet.

2

SQUANTO: LAST OF THE PATUXETS

NEAL SALISBURY

By the beginning of European colonization in the seventeenth century, Native American tribes had inhabited the eastern seaboard of North America for more than 6000 years. Until recently, historians have paid little attention to the contributions of the Powhatans, Mahicans, Abenaki, and many other tribes to American history. In this essay, Neal Salisbury recasts the familiar story of Squanto in light of this new scholarship and in the process reveals the complex interaction between the original inhabitants and the Europeans who explored and settled along the New England coast.

The central event of Squanto's life was the virtual destruction of his people by European diseases. From the time of Columbus's landing in the New World, Native American peoples, who had lost their immunities to Euro-Asian diseases through centuries of geographic isolation, were devastated by the introduction of smallpox, cholera, and even such relatively minor European diseases as measles and chicken pox. As Salisbury points out, the horrible decimation of the Native American population that followed European contact had profound effects upon those who, like Squanto, survived. With mortality rates as high as 80 percent in a single generation, normal social relations became impossible, the mixed economy of hunting and planting was disrupted, political alliances were shattered, and long-standing cultural systems were destroyed. Survivors were left vulnerable to the designs of European settlers and to the new economic system that they brought with them.

In spite of this devastation and cultural dislocation, the history of early European–Native American contact was more than a tale of death and destruction. It was also the story of the many ways in which early settlers depended on the Native Americans: for the sites of their settlements, for their crops, and for the pelts of indigenous animals with which the colonists paid for their imported goods. As this essay reveals, successful interaction between Native Americans and Europeans depended on the skills of cultural mediators who worked to bring the disparate cultures together. Without these mediators, New England might have developed very differently.

As every American schoolchild knows, a lone Indian named Squanto rescued the Pilgrims from the wilderness by teaching them how to plant corn and introducing them to friendly natives. In so doing, the textbooks imply, he symbolically brought about the union of the European colonizers and the American land. Though contemporary events and critical historical inquiry are now undermining this myth, Squanto's story retains some significance. For when placed in its historic and cultural context, it reveals the range of truly human, if prosaic, qualities called forth among Native Americans during the early colonization of New England.

As befits a mythic hero, the time and circumstances of Squanto's birth are unknown. His birth date can only be inferred from what the sources say and do not say. The firsthand descriptions of him, written between 1618 and his death in 1622, do not suggest that he was strikingly young or old at that time. All we can safely conclude is that he was probably in his twenties or thirties at the time he was forcibly taken to Europe in 1614.

Though Squanto's early years are obscured by a lack of direct evidence, we know something of the cultural milieu that prepared him for his unexpected and remarkable career. Squanto and his fellow Patuxet spoke an Algonquian dialect that they shared with the other natives around Plymouth Bay and west as far as the near shore of Narragansett Bay. Moreover, its differences from other dialects in what is now southern New England were minimal, so that the Patuxet could communicate with the natives throughout this region. Like other coastal villages below the mouth of the Saco River, Patuxet was positioned to allow its inhabitants to grow crops, exploit marine resources, and have easy access to wild plants and animals. In accordance with the strict sexual division of labor maintained by virtually all eastern North American Indians, Squanto's major activities would have been to hunt game and to engage in certain kinds of fishing. He would also have fashioned a wide variety of tools and other material items and participated in the intensely ritualized world of trade, diplomacy, religious ceremonies, recreation, warfare, and political decision making that constituted a man's public life.

The training of young men in precontact southern New England was designed to prepare them for that world. Of the Pokanoket, closely related to the Patuxet, the Plymouth leader Edward Winslow wrote, "a man is not accounted a man till he do some notable act or show forth such courage and resolution as becometh his place." A New Netherland official noted that young Pokanoket men were left alone in the forest for an entire winter. On returning to his people in the spring, a candidate was expected to imbibe and vomit bitter [poisonous] herbs for several days. At the conclusion of his ordeal, he was brought before the entire band, "and if he has been able to stand it all well, and if he is fat and sleek, a wife is given to him."

As a result of such training, young Algonquians learned not only how to survive but also how to develop the capacities to withstand the severest physical and psychological trials. The result was the Indian personality type that Euroamericans came to characterize as stoic, the supreme manifestation of which was the absolute expressionlessness of prisoners under torture. Though the specific content of such training did little to prepare Squanto for his later experiences in Malaga, London, or Newfoundland, it imparted a sense of psychological independence and prepared him for adapting to the most demanding environments and situations.

Patuxet men such as Squanto also exercised their independence in making political judgments and decisions. As elsewhere in southern New England, the band, consisting of one or more villages, was the primary political unit. Its leader, the sachem, was drawn from one of a select group of lineages elevated in prestige above the rest. The sachems distributed garden plots to families and exercised certain judicial prerogatives. They also represented the band on diplomatic and ceremonial occasions. But a sachem's power was derived directly from the band members. To secure economic and political support he or she needed leadership ability as well as a family name. Band members could oblige a faltering sachem to share the office with a relative or step down altogether. Moreover, major political decisions were reached through a consensus in meetings attended by all adult males. Squanto came from a world, then, where politics was a constant and integral component of a man's life.

Squanto was even better prepared for his unusual career if, as seems probable, he was a *pniese* in his band. In preparation for this position, young men were chosen in childhood and underwent unusually rigorous diets and training. The purpose of this preparation was not simply to fortify them and develop their courage but to enable them to call upon and visualize Hobbamock, a deity capable of inflicting great harm and even death on those he did not favor. Hobbamock appeared in many forms to "the chiefest and most judicious amongst them," in Winslow's words, "though all of them strive to attain to that hellish height of honor." It is clear that those who succeeded in the vision quest had developed the mental self-discipline demanded of all Indians to an extraordinary degree. By calling on Hobbamock, the *pnieses* protected themselves and those near them in battle and frightened their opponents. They constituted an elite group within the band, serving as counselors and bodyguards to the sachems. They were universally respected not only for their access to Hobbamock and for their courage and judgment but for their moral uprightness. Because of his psychological fortitude, his particularly astute grasp of Indian politics and protocol, and his continued sense of duty to his band after its demise, it is quite likely that Squanto was a *pniese*.

The few recorded observations of Patuxet during Squanto's early years show that it was a very different place from the "wilderness" the Plymouth colonists later found there. Both Samuel de Champlain, in 1605 and 1606, and John Smith, in 1614, noted that most of the coast between Massachusetts and Plymouth bays was under cultivation. The colonists were told, probably by Squanto himself, that in Plymouth Bay "in former time hath lived about 2000 Indians." The population of the surrounding area—that is, of

the Indians with whom the Patuxet maintained the closest relations—was probably between twenty and twenty-five thousand in 1615. Most of these natives were concentrated in village communities ranging in size from five hundred to fifteen hundred individuals. Squanto was thus accustomed to a more densely settled environment that we might expect and was probably as comfortable in the European cities he later visited as in the tiny colonies.

Though no one could have known it at the time, Squanto was born at a turning point in the history of his people and his region. For a century Europeans had been trading and skirmishing with, and sometimes kidnapping, Indians along the coast. At the time of Squanto's birth, however, these activities had not been extended south of Canada on a regular basis. Infrequent visits from European explorers and traders and the natives' own well-established exchange routes brought some iron tools and glass beads to Patuxet. But these were too scattered to induce any economic or cultural changes of a substantive nature. Unlike the fur-trading Indians to the north, the Patuxet and their neighbors had not become dependent on European trade items for their survival.

The turn of the century marked an intensification of French and British interest in New England's resources. The differing economic goals of the colonizers from the two countries gave rise to differing attitudes and policies toward the natives. The French were concerned primarily with furs. Following Champlain's explorations of the New England coast in 1605 and 1606, French traders using his descriptions and maps began to visit the Indians annually and to cultivate an extensive trade as far south as Cape Cod. Their goals encouraged the maintenance of friendly relations with stable Indian bands and even the development of broad regional ties among the natives.

For the English, however, furs were at best a useful by-product of more pressing interests. Beginning with Bartholomew Gosnold's expedition in 1602, they showed a preference for resources such as fish and sassafras that did not require the cooperation of the natives. Moreover, they thought in long-range terms of making Indian land available to Englishmen for farming, a goal that virtually guaranteed eventual conflict with the natives. Indian allies were cultivated, but only for purposes of assisting the English in establishing themselves, and the methods used were generally more coercive than those of the French. Nearly every English expedition from Gosnold's to that of the Mayflower generated hostility with the Indians. By 1610 taking captured Indians to England had become routine. Would-be colonizers such as Sir Ferdinando Gorges hoped to impress their captives with the superiority of English culture, to learn as much as they could about the lay of the land, and to acquire mediators with the local Indians. They also displayed their captives prominently in order to attract financial and public support for their projected colonies.

John Smith, the former Virginia leader, witnessed the results of the competition between the two colonial strategies when he explored the coast from the Penobscot River to Cape Cod in 1614. Smith found that he had arrived at the end of an active trading season. Aside from one Englishman's cozy monopoly at the mouth of the Pemaquid River, all the ships were French. Though the better-endowed region north of the Pemaquid had yielded twenty-five thousand skins that year, Smith judged the south capable of producing six to seven thousand annually. He himself had retrieved thirteen hundred pelts, mostly beaver, in the wake of the French departure. He also found that all Indians in the region he visited were friendly with one another through three loose regional alliances. Ostensibly formed to resist incursions from the Micmac in eastern Canada, the friendship chain had an economic function as well, for Smith noted that some primarily horticultural Indians in southern New England traded corn to Abenaki hunting groups farther north whose concentration on the fur trade was apparently leading to food shortages. In return the horticulturalists obtained some of the Abenaki's supply of European trade goods. Though only minimally developed by 1614, this trade was already fostering a specialized division of labor among France's clients in New England.

The extent of Patuxet's participation in the corn trade is unknown. But Squanto and his people were producing substantial fur surpluses by the time of Smith's visit in 1614 and had gained at least some acquaintance with the Europeans. From the visits of Champlain, Smith, and the traders, Squanto had learned something of European approaches to trade, diplomacy, and military conflict and had witnessed some of their technological accomplishments. But the regularized trade was less than a decade old. And the ease with which groups of Patuxet men were manipulated by Smith and his officer, Thomas Hunt, in 1614 suggests that they had not developed the wariness toward Europeans, particularly the English, of the more experienced Indians to the north.

Squanto's life reached a sudden and dramatic turning point with Hunt's visit. Smith had returned to England, leaving Hunt in charge of his fishing crew to complete the catch and carry it to Malaga, Spain. Before departing, Hunt stopped at Patuxet. Using his association with Smith, who had left on friendly terms, he lured about twenty natives, including Squanto, aboard. Quickly rounding Cape Cod, he drew off seven more from Nauset and then turned east for Malaga. Hunt's action indelibly marked the English as an enemy of all the Indians in the Patuxet–Cape Cod region. In the words of Sir Ferdinando Gorges, Hunt's action resulted in "a warre now new begunne betweene the inhabitants of those parts and us," and John Smith condemned Hunt for moving the Indians' "hate against our Nation, as well as to cause my proceedings to be more difficult."

Native outrage at Hunt's action was reinforced by the near-simultaneous return of an earlier Indian captive, Epenow, a sachem of Capawack (Martha's Vineyard). Epenow had been seized three years earlier and taken to Gorges in England. On constant public display, he learned English well and impressed Gorges and others as "a goodly man of brave aspect, stout and sober in his demeanour." Thus his tales of gold on

Capawack were eagerly seized upon, and in 1614 Gorges commissioned a voyage under Nicholas Hobson, accompanied by Epenow as a guide. Epenow had apparently planned his escape all along, but the news of Hunt's deed hardened his desire for revenge. As the ship drew near his island, Epenow escaped under a cover of arrows from the shore. A fierce battle ensued with heavy casualties on both sides. Among the injured was Hobson himself, who returned to England empty-handed. Epenow thereafter constituted one source for the anti-English sentiment that would persist in the region to the founding of Plymouth colony six years later.

Meanwhile Squanto and his fellow captives reached Malaga, where Hunt tried to sell them as slaves. A few had already been sold when, according to Gorges, "the Friers of those parts took the rest from them and kept them to be instructed in the Christian faith." What happened to Squanto in the next three years is not clear. Particularly intriguing are questions about the extent and influence of his Catholic instruction and the means by which, in William Bradford's words, "he got away for England." We know only that by 1617 he was residing in the London home of John Slany, treasurer of the Newfoundland Company, where he learned or at least improved his English and his understanding of colonial goals. In the following year he went to Newfoundland itself, presumably at Slany's instigation. Here he met for the second time Thomas Dermer, an officer with Smith in 1614 who now worked for Gorges. Dermer was so impressed with Squanto's tales of Patuxet that he took him back to England to meet Gorges. Though the strategy of employing captive Indians as guides had backfired several times, Gorges was ready to try again. He saw in Squanto the key to countering the recent successes of the French and reestablishing England's reputation among the Indians. For his part Squanto knew, as had earlier captives, how to tell Gorges what he wanted to hear in order to be returned home. In March 1619 he and Dermer were bound for New England.

Moving in the circles he did, Squanto undoubtedly knew something of the epidemic that had ravaged New England, including Patuxet, during his absence. A Gorges expedition under Richard Vines had witnessed what Vines called simply "the plague" at Sagadahoc in 1616 and reported on its effects. Most notable was the immunity of the English; while most of the Indians were dying, Vines and his party "lay in the Cabins with those people, [and] not one of them ever felt their heads to ake." This immunity and the 75 to 90 percent depopulation among the Indians make it clear that a virgin soil epidemic of European origin had been planted in New England's isolated disease environment. Though the specific instigator cannot be identified because of the frequency with which Europeans were visiting New England, it is noteworthy that the stricken zone, as reported by Dermer in 1619, was the coast from the Penobscot to Cape Cod—precisely the area encompassing the loose coalition of Indian groups engaged in trade with the French and each other. At its southern extremity the epidemic spread west to the Patuxet's allies, the Pokanoket, at the head of Narragansett Bay, but not to their Narragansett rivals on the western side. Such an outline suggests that the epidemic spread via established exchange routes that were shaped to a great extent in response to the fur trade and the accompanying developments.

Squanto found his own village completely vacated. Most of its inhabitants had died, but some had fled inland to other villages. He surely noticed, as did others, the undergrowth that had overtaken the formerly cultivated fields and the vast numbers of unburied dead whose "bones and skulls," in one Englishman's words, "made such a spectacle . . . it seemed to me a new found Golgotha." The depopulation was so great that the Narragansett were able to force the weakened Pokanoket to abandon their position at the head of Narragansett Bay and to retain only the eastern shore.

The Narragansetts' avoidance of the epidemic gave them a greater advantage than that derived from numbers alone. In the view of their stricken neighbors, the Narragansetts' good health reflected their faithful sacrifices to the deity, Cautantowwit. The ritual worlds and belief systems of the stricken Indians, however, had been badly shaken by the epidemic. The usual practice of gathering with the *pow-wow* (shaman) in a sick person's wigwam could only have served to spread the disease more rapidly. With even the *pow-wows* succumbing, the Indians could only conclude that their deities had aligned against them. And being unable to observe the proper burial rituals, the survivors had to fear the retribution of the dead. The Indians' perception that they had lost touch with the sources of power and that others controlled the access to them would be a critical factor in facilitating Squanto's later political success.

As Dermer's expedition traveled overland from Patuxet in the summer of 1619, Squanto's presence and diplomatic skill enabled the English to break through the antagonisms toward them and to make friendly contacts at Nemasket (near Middleboro) and Pokanoket (near Bristol, Rhode Island). For once an Indian captive had performed as Gorges hoped. But as Dermer returned to his ship and prepared to sail around Cape Cod, Squanto took his leave to search for surviving Patuxets. On his own, Dermer was unable to persuade the Indians at Monomoy (now Pleasant Harbor) of his good intentions. He was captured and barely succeeded in escaping. After a seemingly cordial meeting on Martha's Vineyard with Epenow, the former Gorges captive, Dermer was attacked off Long Island and again managed to escape. Returning to New England in the summer of 1620, he was captured by his newly made friends at Pokanoket and Nemasket and released only after Squanto interceded on his behalf. Dermer, with Squanto, then proceeded to Martha's Vineyard, where they were attacked by Epenow and his followers. Most of the crew was killed this time, while the luckless captain escaped with fourteen wounds and died in Virginia. Squanto was again made a captive, this time of the Indians.

In a letter written after his release at Nemasket, Dermer attributed his reception there to his hosts' renewed desire for revenge. He noted that another English crew had just visited the area, invited some Indians on board their ship, and then shot them down without provocation. The incident could only have revived the Indians' suspicions of the English that had prevailed before Squanto's return. These suspicions were now focused on Squanto himself, as Dermer's accomplice, and led to his being turned over to the Pokanoket with whom he remained until he was ransomed by the Plymouth colonists in March 1621.

The Patuxet–Pokanoket–Cape Cod region was vastly different in the autumn of 1620 from a decade earlier when French traders had begun to frequent it regularly. Fewer than 10 percent of its twenty thousand or more former inhabitants were still living, and they were now consolidated into a few bands. The region was vulnerable as never before to exploitation by outsiders. The once-powerful Pokanoket and their sachem, Massasoit, had been subjected to a humiliating tributary relationship with the Narragansett, who were emerging as the most powerful aggregation in New England because of their size and their control of Indian–European trade links east of Long Island. Moreover, the decimated Indians could no longer count on the fur trade as a means of compensating for other weaknesses. Always limited in both the quality and quantity of its fur resources, the region's loss of most of its hunters now made it an unprofitable stop for traders.

Though a captive, Squanto was able to capitalize on the Pokanokets' despair. "He told Massasoit what wonders he had seen in England," according to a future settler, "and that if he could make English his friends then Enemies that were too strong for him would be constrained to bow to him." He did not have to wait long to be proved right. In December 1620, less than six months after Dermer's departure, word reached Pokanoket that a shipload of English colonists had established a permanent settlement at Patuxet.

Like the other Puritans who later settled New England, the group at Plymouth (for so they renamed Patuxet) was motivated by a combination of religious and economic motives that shaped their attitudes toward the natives. Their experience with persecution in England and exile to the Netherlands had sharpened their desire to practice their exclusionary, intolerant separatism without external inference. Moreover, though seeking distance from English ecclesiastical authorities, the settlers were attempting to reinforce their English identities. They had abandoned their Dutch haven for fear that their children would be assimilated there. Finally, though ostensibly migrating to fish and trade for furs, the colonists sought land to improve themselves materially and, they supposed, spiritually. Though Plymouth lacked the sense of divine mission of the later nonseparatist Puritan colonies, its goals of religious and ethnic exclusivity and an abundance of land had obvious implications for its relations with the natives.

These implications were apparent in Plymouth's early policies and attitudes toward the Indians. In a major promotional pamphlet published in 1622, Robert Cushman restated what had already become a familiar justification for dispossession of native lands:

> Their land is spacious and void, and there are few and do but run over the grass, as do also the foxes and wild beasts. They are not industrious, neither have art, science, skill, or faculty to use either the land or the commodities of it, but all spoils or rots, and is marred for want of manuring, gathering, ordering, etc. As the ancient patriarchs therefore removed from straiter places into more roomy . . . so is it lawful now to take a land which none useth, and make use of it.

Cushman's statement was consistent with the emerging European doctrine of *vacuum domicilium,* by which "civil" states were entitled to the uncultivated lands of those in a "natural" state. Though Plymouth's own "civility" was formalized by the hastily contrived *Mayflower* Compact, its financial backers had anticipated its need for more than an abstract principle to press its claim—among its own people as well as among any natives they might encounter. Accordingly, they had hired Miles Standish, a soldier of for-

tune fresh from the Dutch wars, to organize the colony militarily. It was Standish who would shape Plymouth's Indian policy during its first generation.

Standish began to execute this policy even before the *Mayflower* arrived at Patuxet. Landing first at Cape Cod, the settlers aroused native hostilities by ransacking Indian graves, houses, and grain stores. At Patuxet they also stirred suspicions during the first four months of their stay. But their own situation grew desperate during their first New England winter. They lost half their numbers to starvation and disease, and as inexperienced farmers they were ill-prepared for the approaching planting season. In this condition they could no longer expect to alleviate their shortages through pilferage with impunity. The impasse was broken one day in March 1621 by the appearance of Samoset, a sachem of the Pemaquid River band, which had been trading with the English for more than a decade. Samoset learned the needs and intentions of the colony and returned a few days later with Squanto.

The Pokanoket had been watching the Plymouth group throughout the winter. With Samoset and the newly useful Squanto offering advice and experience, they concluded that the time was ripe to befriend the settlers instead of maintaining a hostile distance. Such an alliance would enable them to break from the hold of the Narragansetts, whose haughty demeanor stung even more than that of the English. Nevertheless, the decision was not to be taken lightly. Bradford wrote that the Indians did first "curse and execrate them with their conjurations" before approaching the settlers. But this description betrays his fear of witchcraft as it was understood by Europeans, rather than his comprehension of Indian rituals. More likely the Pokanoket were ritually purging themselves of their hostilities toward the English.

Samoset and Squanto arranged the meeting between the Pokanoket and Plymouth colony that resulted in their historic treaty. In it each side agreed to aid the other in the event of attack by a third party, to disarm during their meetings with each other, and to return any tools stolen from the other side. But in addition to these reciprocal agreements, several others were weighted against the natives. Massasoit, the Pokanoket sachem, was to see that his tributaries observed the terms; the Indians were to turn over for punishment any of their people suspected of assaulting any English (but no English had to fear being tried by Indians); and, the treaty concluded, "King James would esteem of him [Massasoit] as his friend and ally." The meaning of the last honor was made explicit by the colony's annalist, Nathaniel Morton, who wrote that by the treaty Massasoit "acknowledged himself content to become the subject of our sovereign lord the King aforesaid, his heirs and successors, and gave unto them all the lands adjacent to them and theirs forever." Morton made clear that among themselves the English did not regard the treaty as one of alliance and friendship between equals but as one of submission by one party to the domination of the other, according to the assumptions of *vacuum domicilium.*

For the Pokanoket, however, the meaning of a political relationship was conveyed in the ritual exchange of speeches and gifts, not in written clauses or unwritten understandings based on concepts such as sovereignty that were alien to one party. From their standpoint, the English were preferable to the Narragansett because they demanded less tribute and homage while offering more gifts and autonomy and better protection.

The treaty also brought a change in status for Squanto. In return for his services, the Pokanoket now freed him to become guide, interpreter, and diplomat for the colony. Thus he finally returned to his home at Patuxet, a move that had, as we shall see, more than sentimental significance. Among his first services was the securing of corn seed and instruction in its planting, including the use of fish fertilizer, which he learned from his own people or from the Newfoundland colonists.

Squanto also enabled Plymouth to strengthen its political position in the surrounding area. He helped secure peace with some bands on Cape Cod and guided an expedition to Massachusetts Bay. His kidnapping by anti-English Indians at Nemasket and subsequent rescue by a heavily armed Plymouth force speaks compellingly of his importance to the colony. Moreover, this incident led to a new treaty, engineered in part by Squanto, with all the Indian groups of Massachusetts Bay to the tip of Cape Cod, including even Epenow and his band. By establishing a tributary system with the surrounding Indian bands, the colony was filling the political vacuum left by the epidemic and creating a dependable network of corn suppliers and buffers against overland attack. But it also incurred the resentment of the Narragansett by depriving them of tributaries just when Dutch traders were expanding their activities in the bay. The Narragansett challenged Plymouth's action in January 1622 by sending a snakeskin filled with arrows. On Squanto's advice Plymouth's leaders returned the skin filled with powder and shot. The Narragansett sachem, Canonicus, refused to accept this counterchallenge, in effect acknowledging the colony's presence and political importance.

However effective in appearance, Plymouth's system of Indian diplomacy was fraught with tensions that nearly destroyed it. A Pokanoket *pniese,* Hobbamock (named for his patron deity), became a second advisor to Plymouth in the summer of 1621. Whether the English thought that Hobbamock would merely assist Squanto or would serve to check him is unclear. In any event, Squanto was no longer the only link between the colony and the Indians; indeed, as a Pokanoket, Hobbamock had certain advantages over him. As one whose very life depended on the colony's need for him, Squanto had to act decisively to check this threat to his position. His most potent weapon was the mutual distrust and fear lingering between English and Indians; his most pressing need was for a power base so that he could extricate himself from his position of colonial dependency. Accordingly, he began maneuvering on his own.

Squanto had been acting independently for several months before being discovered by the

English in March 1622. As reconstructed by Edward Winslow:

> his course was to persuade [the Indians] he could lead us to peace or war at his pleasure, and would oft threaten the Indians, sending them word in a private manner we were intended shortly to kill them, that thereby he might get gifts to himself, to work their peace; . . . so that whereas divers were wont to rely on Massasoit for protection, and resort to his abode, now they began to leave him and seek after Tisquantum [Squanto].

In short, he sought to establish himself as an independent native political leader. At the same time he endeavored to weaken the Pokanoket's influence on Plymouth by provoking armed conflict between the two allies. He circulated a rumor that Massasoit was conspiring with the Narragansett and Massachusett to wipe out the colony. The English quickly verified the continued loyalty of the Pokanoket but, though angry at Squanto, were afraid to dispense with him. Instead they protected him from Massasoit's revenge, which brought tensions into the Pokanoket–Plymouth relationship that were only finally assuaged when Squanto died later in the year.

In seeking to establish his independence of Plymouth, Squanto was struggling for more than his survival. As Winslow put it, he sought "honor, which he loved as his life and preferred before his peace." What did honor mean to Squanto? For one thing, of course, it meant revenge against the Pokanoket, not only for threatening his position at Plymouth but for his earlier captivity. But it meant more than that. Squanto appears to have made substantial inroads among Indians loyal to Massasoit in a short period of time. Winslow indicated, unknowingly and in passing, the probable key to this success. The news of Massosoit's alleged treachery against Plymouth was brought, he said, by "an Indian of Tisquantum's family." Contrary to the Plymouth sources (all of which were concerned with establishing the colony's unblemished title to the land around Plymouth Bay), there were certainly a few dozen Patuxet survivors of the epidemic at Pokanoket, Nemasket, and elsewhere. Though Squanto undoubtedly sought the loyalty and tribute of others, it was to these relatives and friends that he would primarily have appealed. The honor he sought was a reconstituted Patuxet band under his own leadership, located near its traditional home.

Squanto's hopes were shattered when his plot collapsed. With Massasoit seeking his life, he had, in Bradford's words, "to stick close to the English, and never durst go from them till he dies." This isolation from other Indians and dependence on the colonists helps explain the latter's willingness to protect him. In July, Squanto again engineered an important breakthrough for Plymouth by accompanying an expedition to Monomoy, where suspicion of all Europeans persisted. The Indians here had attacked Champlain's party in 1606 and Dermer's in 1619. Standish's men had taken some of their corn during their stop at Cape Cod in November 1620. Now, as Winslow phrased it, "by Tisquantum's means better persuaded, they left their jealousy, and traded with them." The colony's take was eight hogsheads of corn and beans. But as the expedition prepared to depart, Squanto "fell sick of an Indian fever, bleeding much at the nose (which the Indians take for a symptom of death) and within a few days died there."

By the time of Squanto's death, Plymouth colony had gained the foothold it had sought for two and a half years. The expedition to Monomoy marked the establishment of firm relations with the last local band to withhold loyalty. Moreover, the trade in corn was no longer an economic necessity, remaining important primarily as a means of affirming tributary relationships. These accomplishments would have been infinitely more difficult, if not impossible, without Squanto's aid. But it is questionable whether his contributions after the summer of 1622 would have been as critical. Thereafter, the colony's principal dealings were with the hostile Massachusett and Narragansett Indians beyond Patuxet's immediate environs. Moreover, the world in which Squanto had flourished was vanishing. A rationalized wampum trade had begun to transform Indian–European relations in southern New England. And the end of the decade would bring a mighty upsurge in English colonization that would surround and dwarf Plymouth. Within the restrictions imposed by his dependence on Plymouth's protection. Squanto would have adapted to these changes. But his knowledge and skills would no longer have been unique nor his services indispensable.

It is difficult to imagine what direction the life of this politically and historically isolated man, who valued "honor" above all else, might have taken in the coming decades. It is in this light that we should read his well-known deathbed conversion wherein he requested Bradford "to pray for him that he might go to the Englishmen's God in Heaven; and bequeathed sundry of his things to sundry of his English friends as remembrances of his love." He was acknowledging that after eight years of acting with honor in alien settings, he had been cornered. Dying so ignominiously, the last Patuxet would have found it ironic that later generations of Americans celebrated him as a hero.

3

LOOKING OUT FOR NUMBER ONE: CONFLICTING CULTURAL VALUES IN EARLY SEVENTEENTH-CENTURY VIRGINIA

T. H. BREEN

Emigration to the New World in the seventeenth century was an arduous undertaking. The journey required two to six months at sea, with passengers huddled in cramped quarters with little provision for privacy. During the long voyage one could expect minimal—and at times rotten—provisions. Seasickness, fevers, contagious diseases, and boredom afflicted most sojourners. Death itself often awaited the very young, the old, and the infirm. For those who set sail for the Chesapeake, the voyage was only the first part of the ordeal. Once ashore, virtually every immigrant contracted yellow fever, malaria, or some other parasitic disease from the mosquitoes that thrived in the low-lying tidewater swamps. Contemporary records suggest that up to half of all English immigrants died of disease within a few years of reaching Virginia or Maryland.

Yet despite the rigors and dangers of such a crossing, thousands of English men and women left their homeland for the Chesapeake in the first half of the seventeenth century. In this essay, T. H. Breen explores the character of those who made this fateful choice. What drew these people to the Chesapeake, most of them as indentured servants? And what about these people inspired them to risk disease and death to come to a region with so little in the way of typical English social and family life?

The answer, Breen suggests, is a simple one. Wave after wave of immigrants came to the Chesapeake to make money from the tobacco crop that was the sole reason for colonization of the region. The well-off and poor alike arrived in Virginia with the hope of obtaining the land and labor that would enable them to rise in the expanding economic world of the seventeenth century. The stakes and risks were both high, Breen concludes, and those who attempted to follow the Chesapeake's quick way to wealth were "adventurers"—atypically individualistic, competitive, and materialistic Englishpeople with few concerns other than their own advancement.

Despite their common English background, the thousands of European men and women who migrated to Barbados, Virginia, and New England during the seventeenth century created strikingly different societies in the New World. As one historian, Thomas J. Wertenbaker, explained of Virginia, it "developed a life of its own, a life not only unlike that of England, but unique and distinct." Certainly, for anyone analyzing the founding of these colonies a major problem is accounting for the appearance of diverse social forms.

This essay examines the creation of a distinct culture in Virginia roughly between 1617 and 1630. Although early Virginians shared certain general ideas, attitudes, and norms with other English migrants, their operative values were quite different from those that shaped social and institutional behavior in places such as Massachusetts Bay. Virginia's physical environment, its extensive network of navigable rivers, its rich soil, its ability to produce large quantities of marketable tobacco, powerfully reinforced values which the first settlers carried to America. The interplay between a particular variant of Jacobean culture and a specific New World setting determined the character of Virginia's institutions, habits of personal interaction, and patterns of group behavior that persisted long after the early adventurers had died or returned to the mother country.

An ethnographic reconstruction of Virginia between 1617 and 1630 begins with an analysis of the values that the settlers carried with them to the New World. Here the distinction that social anthropologists make between "dominant" and "variant" values becomes relevant. The men and women who sailed for the Chesapeake Bay in the early seventeenth century were certainly part of a general English culture. They shared a set of views, customs, and expectations with other Jacobeans, with New Englanders and Barbadians, with those persons who remained in the mother country. Historians of colonial America have closely analyzed this common cultural background, and there is no need to repeat their findings in detail.

From these accounts we learn that the crucial formative values transferred to Virginia were religious and political. Their constitutional heritage provided the colonials with civil and legal imperatives; their religion with a world view that structured their daily lives. Perry Miller has reminded us that the Virginians were products of the English Reformation. Both Virginians and New Englanders, he argued, were "recruited from the same type of Englishmen, pious, hard-working, middle-class, accepting literally and solemnly the tenets of Puritanism—original sin, predestination, and election—who could conceive of the society they were erecting in America *only* within a religious framework." Miller claimed that without knowledge of this theological system, the history of Virginia was no more than "a bare chronicle." Other writers, without denying the importance of Calvinistic Protestantism, have stressed the role of English legal and political precedents in shaping institutional behavior. Wesley Frank Craven explained that the Chesapeake migrants brought "their identification with the traditions of the Common Law, a decentralized system of local administration, and parliamentary usages of government for the development of the colony's political institutions."

Early Virginians undoubtedly subscribed to these general constitutional and religious values and, whenever feasible, attempted to translate them into action. Anyone who has read the colony's history knows the first settlers saw God's hand behind human affairs, marched to church to the beat of a drum, and formed a representative legislative body called the House of Burgesses. But this sort of analysis does not carry us very far in understanding why Virginia society was unlike those formed by English migrants in other parts of the New World, or why despite the presence of common dominant values various groups of settlers created distinctive patterns of social and institutional behavior.

Such problems are reduced when we realize that the early settlers in Virginia were an unusual group of Jacobeans. In no way did they represent a random sample of seventeenth-century English society or a cross section of English values. While little is known about the specific origins or back-grounds of most settlers, we do have a fairly clear idea of what sort of inducements persuaded men and women to move to Virginia. The colony's promotional literature emphasized economic opportunity, usually quick and easy riches. In his "True Relation of the State of Virginia" written in 1616, for example, John Rolfe pitied England's hard-working farmers who barely managed to make ends meet. "What happiness might they enjoy in Virginia," Rolfe mused, "where they may have ground for nothing, more than they can manure, reap more fruits and profits with half the labour." And in 1622 Peter Arundle, over-looking the colony's recent military setbacks at the hands of the Indians, assured English friends that "any laborious honest man may in a short time become rich in this Country." It was a com-pelling dream, one which certain Englishmen were all too willing to accept as truth. Indeed, so many persons apparently risked life and posses-sions in the illusive search for the main chance that John Harvey, a future Royal Governor of Virginia, begged men of integrity on both sides of the Atlantic to control "the rumors of plenty to be found at all tyme[s] in Virginia."

The lure of great wealth easily obtained held an especially strong appeal for a specific type of seventeenth-century Englishman, individuals who belonged to a distinct subculture within Jacobean society. By all accounts, early Virginia drew a disproportionately large number of street toughs, roughnecks fresh from the wars in Ireland, old soldiers looking for new glory, naive adventurers, mean-spirited sea captains, marginal persons attempting to recoup their losses. If con-temporaries are to be believed, Virginia found itself burdened with "many unruly gallants packed thether by their friends to escape ill des-tinies." Even Sir Thomas Dale, himself a recent veteran of English military expeditions in Holland, was shocked by the colony's settlers, "so prophane, so riotous, so full of Mutenie and trea-sonable Intendments" that they provided little "testimonie beside their names that they are Christians."

Even if Dale exaggerated, there is no reason to question that the colonists were highly individ-ualistic, motivated by the hope of material gain, and in many cases, not only familiar with violence but also quite prepared to employ it to obtain their own ends in the New World. By and large, they appear to have been extremely competitive and suspicious of other men's motives. Mutiny and anarchy sometimes seemed more attractive than obeying someone else's orders. Few of the colonists showed substantial interest in creating a permanent settlement. For the adventurer, Virginia was not a new home, not a place to carry out a divine mission, but simply an area to be exploited for private gain. It was this "variant" strain of values—a sense of living only for the present or near future, a belief that the environ-ment could and should be forced to yield quick financial returns, an assumption that everyone was looking out for number one and hence that cooperative ventures of all sorts were bound to fail—that help to account for the distinctive pat-terns of social and institutional behavior found in early Virginia.

The transfer of these variant values, of course, only partially explains Virginia's cultural develop-ment. The attitudes, beliefs, and ideas that the founders brought with them to the New World interacted with specific environmental condi-tions. The settlers' value system would certainly have withered in a physical setting that offered no natural resources capable of giving plausibility to the adventurers' original expectations. If by some chance the Virginians had landed in a cold, rocky, inhospitable country devoid of valuable marketable goods, then they would probably have given up the entire venture and like a defeated army, straggled home. That is exactly what happened in 1607 to the unfortunate men who settled in Sagadohoc, Maine, a tiny outpost that failed to produce instant wealth. Virginia almost went the way of Sagadohoc. The first decade of its history was filled with apathy and disappointment, and at several points, the entire enterprise seemed doomed. The privatistic val-ues that the colonists had carried to Jamestown, a tough, exploitive competitive individualism were dysfunctional—even counter-productive—in an environment which offered up neither spices nor gold, neither passages to China nor a subject population easily subdued and exploited. In fact, before 1617 this value system generated only political faction and petty personal violence, things that a people struggling for survival could ill afford.

The successful cultivation of tobacco altered the course of Virginia's cultural development. Clearly, in an economic sense, the crop saved the colony. What is less obvious but no less true, is that the discovery of a lucrative export preserved the founders' individualistic values. Suddenly, after ten years of error and failure, the adventurers' transported values were no longer at odds with their physical environment. The settlers belatedly stumbled across the payoff; the forests once so foreboding, so unpromising, could now be exploited with a reasonable expectation of quick return. By 1617 the process was well-advanced, and as one planter reported, "the streets, and all other spare places planted with Tobacco . . . The Colonie dispersed all about, planting *Tobacco.*"

The interplay between the settlers' value system and their environment involved more than economic considerations. Once a market for tobacco had been assured, people spread out along the James and York Rivers. Whenever possible, they formed what the directors of the Virginia Company called private hundreds, small plantations frequently five or more miles apart which groups of adventurers developed for their own profit. By 1619 forty-four separate patents for private plantations had been issued, and by the early 1620's a dispersed settlement pattern, long to be a characteristic of Virginia society, was well established. The dispersion of the colony's population was a cultural phenomenon. It came about not simply because the Virginia soil was unusually well suited for growing tobacco or because its deep rivers provided easy access to the interior, but because men holding privatistic values regarded the land as an exploitable resource, and within their structure of priorities, the pursuit of private gain outranked the creation of corporate communities.

The scattering of men and women along the colony's waterways, their self-imposed isolation, obviously reduced the kind of ongoing face-to-face contacts that one associates with the villages of seventeenth-century New England. A migrant to Virginia tended to be highly competitive and to assume that other men would do unto him as he would do unto them—certainly an unpleasant prospect. Dispersion heightened this sense of suspicion. Because communication between private plantations was difficult, Virginians possessed no adequate means to distinguish the truth about their neighbors from malicious rumor, and lacking towns and well-developed voluntary organizations, without shared rituals, ceremonies, even market days, they drew increasingly distrustful of whatever lay beyond the perimeter of their own few acres.

The kind of human relationships that developed in colonial Virginia graphically reveal the effect of highly individualistic values upon social behavior. In this settlement only two meaningful social categories existed: a person was either free or dependent, either an exploiter or a resource. There was no middle ground. Those men who held positions of political and economic power treated indentured servants and slaves not as human beings, but as instruments to produce short-run profits. As a consequence of this outlook, life on the private plantations was a degrading experience for thousands of men and women who arrived in Virginia as bonded laborers. Whatever their expectations about the colony may have been before they migrated, the servants' reality consisted of poor food, meager clothing, hard work, and, more often than not, early death. The leading planters showed little interest in reforming these conditions. The servants were objects, things to be gambled away in games of chance, beaten or abused, and then replaced when they wore out.

But dependence has another side. In Virginia dominance went hand in hand with fear, for no matter how tractable, how beaten down, the servants may have appeared, both masters and laborers recognized the potential for violence inherent in such relationships. In the early 1620's several worried planters complained that Captain John Martin, a long-standing troublemaker for the Virginia Company, "hath made his owne Territory there a receptacle of Vagabonds and bankerupts & other disorderly persons." Whether the rumors of Martin's activities were accurate is not the point. In such a society a gathering of "Vagabonds" represented a grave threat, a base from which the exploited could harass their former masters. The anxiety resurfaced in 1624 when the Virginia Company lost its charter and no one in the colony knew for certain who held legitimate authority. In shrill rhetoric that over the course of a century would become a regular feature of Virginia statute books, the colony's Assembly immediately ordered that "no person within this Colonie upon the rumor of supposed change and alterations [may] presume to be disobedient to the presente Government, nor servants to theire privatt officers masters or overseers, at their utmost perills."

The distrust that permeated Virginia society poisoned political institutions. Few colonists seem to have believed that local rulers would on their own initiative work for the public good. Instead, they assumed that persons in authority would use their office for personal gain. One settler called Governor George Yeardley, a man who grew rich directing public affairs, "the right worthy statesman for his own profit." William Capps, described simply as an old planter, referred to the governor as an "old smoker" and claimed that this official had "stood for a cypher whilst the Indians stood ripping open our guts." Cynicism about the motives of the colony's leaders meant that few citizens willingly sacrificed for the good of the state. In fact, Virginia planters seem to have regarded government orders as a threat to their independence, almost as a personal affront. William Strachey, secretary of the colony, condemned what he labeled the general "want of government." He reported, "every man overvaluing his owne worth, would be a Commander: every man underprising anothers value, denied to be commanded." Other colonists expressed agreement with Strachey's views. During the famous first meeting of the House of

Burgesses in 1619, the representatives of the various plantations twice commented upon the weakness of Virginia's governing institutions. Toward the end of the session, they declared that whatever laws they passed in the future should go into immediate effect without special authorization from London, "for otherwise this people . . . would in a shorte time grow so insolent, as they would shake off all government, and there would be no living among them."

The colonists' achievements in education and religion were meager. From time to time, Virginians commented upon the importance of churches and schools in their society, but little was done to transform rhetoric into reality. Church buildings were in a perpetual state of decay; ministers were poorly supported by their parishioners. An ambitious plan for a college came to nothing, and schools for younger children seem to have been nonexistent. The large distances between plantations and the pressure to keep every able-bodied person working in the fields, no doubt discouraged the development of local schools and parish churches, but the colony's dispersed settlement plan does not in itself explain the absence of these institutions. A colonywide boarding school could have been constructed in Jamestown, a Harvard of Virginia, but the colony's planters were incapable of the sustained, cooperative effort that such a project would have required. They responded to general societal needs as a individuals, not as groups. Later in the seventeenth century some successful planters sent their sons at great expense to universities in England and Scotland, but not until the end of the century did the colonists found a local college.

An examination of Virginia's military policies between 1617 and 1630 provides the clearest link between social values and institutional behavior. During this important transitional period, military affairs were far better recorded than were other social activities, and the historian can trace with a fair degree of confidence how particular military decisions reflected the colonists' value system. And second, in any society military efforts reveal a people's social priorities, their willingness to sacrifice for the common good, and their attitudes toward the allocation of community resources. Certainly, in early Virginia, maintaining a strong defense should have been a major consideration. Common sense alone seemed to dictate that a group of settlers confronted with a powerful Indian confederation and foreign marauders would, in military matters at least, cooperate for their own safety. But in point of fact, our common sense was not the rule of the seventeenth-century Virginian. The obsession with private profits was a more compelling force than was the desire to create a dependable system of self-defense. This destructive individualism disgusted John Pory, at one time the colony's secretary of state. In 1620 he reported that Governor Yeardley asked the men of Jamestown "to contribute some labor to a bridge, and to certaine platformes to mounte great ordinance upon, being both for the use and defense of the same Citty, and so of themselves; yet they repyned as much as if all their goods had bene taken from them."

Virginians paid dearly for their failure to work together. On March 22, 1622, the Indians of the region launched a coordinated attack on the scattered, poorly defended white settlements, and before the colonists could react, 347 of them had been killed. The details of this disaster are well known. The Massacre and the events of the months that followed provide rare insight into the workings of the Virginia culture. The shock of this defeat called into question previous institutional policies—not just military ones—and some colonists even saw the setback as an opportunity to reform society, to develop a new set of values.

Virginia's vulnerability revealed to some men the need to transform the privatistic culture into a more tightly knit, cooperative venture. Local rulers bravely announced that "this Massacre will prove much to the speedie advancement of the Colony and much to the benefitt of all those that shall nowe come thither." No longer would the planters live so far apart. Shortsighted dreams of tobacco fortunes would be laid aside, and the people would join together in the construction of

genuine towns. And most important, the settlers would no longer evade their military responsibilities. As the members of the Virginia Council wrote only a month after the Massacre, "our first and princypall care should have beene for our safetie . . . yet its very necessarie for us yett at last, to laye a better and surer foundation for the tyme to come." But despite the death and destruction and despite the bold declarations about a new start, the colonists proceeded to repeat the very activities that contemporary commentators agreed had originally caused the people's immense suffering.

Even though the Indians remained a grave threat to security throughout the 1620's, the settlers continued to grumble about the burden of military service. Each person seemed to assess the tragedy only in personal terms—how, in other words, had the Indian Massacre affected his ability to turn a profit. By the end of the summer of 1622, there were unmistakable signs that many people no longer regarded the defeat of the Indians as a community responsibility. Few men talked of the common good; fewer still seemed prepared to sacrifice their lives or immediate earning power in order to preserve the colony from a second disaster.

Even as the governor and his council were weighing the various military alternatives, colonists were moving back to their isolated frontier plantations. The dispersion of fighting men, of course, seemed to invite new military defeats. But the danger from the Indians, although clearly perceived, was not sufficient to deter Virginians from taking up possessions which one person declared were "larger than 100 tymes their Number were able to Cultivate." In a poignant letter to his parents in England, a young servant, Richard Frethorne, captured the sense of doom that hung over the private plantations. "We are but 32 to fight against 3000 [Indians] if they should Come," he explained, "and the nighest helpe that Wee have is ten miles of us, and when the rogues overcame this place last [Martin's Hundred], they slew 80 Persons how then shall wee doe for wee lye even in their teeth, they may easily take us but that God is mercifull." Frethorne wrote this letter in March 1623, just twelve months after the Massacre had revealed to all the survivors the consequences of lying in the Indians' teeth.

The Virginia Council protested to colonial administrators in England, "It is noe smale difficultie and griefe unto us to maintaine a warr by unwillinge people, who . . . Crye out of the loss of Tyme against their Commanders, *in a warr where nothing is to be gained.*" By contrast, the village militia in Massachusetts Bay provided an effective fighting force precisely because the soldiers trusted those persons who remained at home. In theory, at least, most New Englanders defined their lives in terms of the total community, not in terms of private advancement, and the troops had no reason to believe that their friends and neighbors would try to profit from their sacrifice. But in Virginia long before the massive enslavement of black Africans, human relationships were regarded as a matter of pounds and pence, and each day one man chased the Indians through the wilderness or helped build a fortification, another man grew richer growing tobacco. When William Capps in 1623 attempted to organize a raiding party of forty men to go against the Indians, he was greeted with excuses and procrastination. Almost in disbelief, he informed an English correspondent of the planters' train of thought, "take away one of my men, there's 2000 Plantes gone, thates 500 waight of Tobacco, yea and what shall this man doe, runne after the Indians. . . . I have perhaps 10, perhaps 15, perhaps 20, men and am able to secure my owne Plantacion; how will they doe that are fewer? let them first be Crusht alittle and then perhaps they will themselves make up the Nomber for theire own safeties." Perhaps Frethorne's anxiety grew out of the knowledge that no one beyond Martin's Hundred really cared what the Indians might do to him and his comrades.

Such foot-dragging obviously did nothing to promote colonial security. Regardless of the planters' behavior, however, Virginia leaders felt compelled to deal with the Indians. After all, these appointed officials did not want to appear incompetent before the king and his councillors. But the Virginians soon discovered that in the absence of public-spirited citizen soldiers, their range of military responses was effectively reduced to three. The governor and his council could make the business of war so lucrative that Virginians would willingly leave the tobacco fields to fight, entrust private contractors with the responsibility of defending the entire population, or persuade the king to send English troops at his own expense to protect the colonists from their Indian enemies. Unfortunately, each of these alternatives presented specific drawbacks that rendered them essentially useless as military policies.

The first option was to make the conditions of service so profitable that the planters or in their place, the planters' servants, would join in subduing the common enemy. In times of military crisis, such as the one following the Great Massacre, both Company and Crown officials tried their best to persuade the settlers that warfare was not all hardship and sacrifice—indeed, that for some men, presumably not themselves, Indian fighting could be an economic opportunity. For the majority, however, such arguments apparently rang hollow. The colonists had learned that local Indians made poor slaves, and in a spacious colony like Virginia, the offer of free land was an inadequate incentive for risking one's life. The promise of plunder drew few men away from the tobacco fields, and with typical candor, Captain John Smith announced in 1624, "I would not give twenty pound for all the pillage . . . to be got amongst the Salvages in twenty yeeres."

A second possible solution for Virginia's military needs was to hire someone to defend the colonists. The merits of this approach seemed obvious. The state could simply transfer public funds to groups enterprising individuals who in turn might construct forts along the rivers, build palisades to ward off Indian attacks, and even in some cases, fight pitched battles along the frontier. Unlike the New Englanders, who generally regarded matters of defense as a community responsibility, much like providing churches and schools, Virginians accepted the notion that private contractors could serve as an adequate substitute for direct popular participation in military affairs.

In this belief the Virginians were mistaken. A stream of opportunists came forward with schemes that would compensate for the colony's unreliable militia. Without exception, however, these plans drained the public treasury but failed to produce lasting results. Indeed, Virginia's social values spawned a class of military adventurers—perhaps military profiteers would be a more accurate description—who did their best to transform warfare into a profitable private business.

Some of the private military schemes of the 1620's were bizarre, others humorous, almost all misallocations of public revenues. In the summer of 1622 a sea captain named Samuel Each, whose military qualifications remain obscure, offered to construct a fort of oyster shells to guard the mouth of the James River. Each's project seemed a convenient way to secure the colony's shipping from possible foreign harassment. For his work, the captain was promised a handsome reward, but as was so often to be the case in the history of seventeenth-century Virginia, the contractor disappointed the settlers' expectations. The proposed site for the fortification turned out to be under water at high tide and "at low water with everie wynd washed over by the surges." One colonist sardonically described Each's pile of sea shells as "a Castle in the aire" and suggested that the captain had wisely died on the job "to save his Credit."

During the 1620's other adventurers followed, but their performance was no more impressive than Each's had been. These men sometimes couched their proposals in rhetoric about the common good. There was no question, however, about what considerations motivated the contractors. In 1628, for example, two of the colony's most successful planters, Samuel Mathews and William Claiborne, presented the king of England with what they called "A Proposition

Concerning the Winning of the Forest." They humbly informed Charles I that their plan grew "not out of any private respects, or intent to gaine to our selves, but because in our own mindes wee perceive [?] our selves bound to expend both our lives and fortunes in so good a service for this Plantation." One may be justly skeptical about the extent of their anticipated personal sacrifice, for in the next paragraph, the two Virginians demanded 1200 pounds "in readie monye" and 100 pounds sterling every year thereafter. Governor Francis Wyatt gave the project begrudging support. He explained that because of the planters' "too much affection to their private dividents" and their unwillingness to alter their pattern of settlement in the interest of defense, Mathews and Claiborne should be encouraged to construct a fortified wall running six miles between the Charles and James Rivers. The two men promised to build a palisade and staff it with their own armed servants. There is no record of what happened to this particular plan, but if it had been accepted, the servants most likely would have spent their days planting tobacco for two men already quite wealthy.

The reliance on military adventurers held dangers of which the Virginians of the 1620's were only dimly aware. As long as the price of tobacco remained relatively high, the colonists ignored much of the waste and favoritism associated with lucrative military contracts. But high taxes caused grumbling, even serious social unrest. In the early 1620's the members of the Virginia Council reported that when it came time to reimburse Captain Each, there was "a general unwillingness (not to say an opposition) in all almost but ourselves." As tobacco profits dropped over the course of the seventeenth century, small planters and landless freemen showed an increasing hostility to private military contractors, and a major precipitant of Bacon's Rebellion was Governor William Berkeley's expensive frontier forts which appeared to do little good except for a few of the Governor's friends engaged in the Indian trade.

A second difficulty with the adventurers was no bigger than a man's hand during the 1620's. The colony needed every able-bodied defender that could be found, and no one seems to have worried much about arming indentured servants and poor freemen. But in later years, Virginians would have cause to reconsider the wisdom of creating mercenary bodies composed largely of impoverished recruits. The leading planters discovered, in fact, that one could not systematically exploit other human beings for private profit and then expect those same people to risk their lives fighting to preserve the society that tolerated such oppressive conditions. As privatism became the way of life, the colony's leading planters were less and less certain whether internal or external enemies posed a greater threat to Virginia's security.

A third possible solution to the settlement's early military needs lay in obtaining direct English assistance. During the 1620's Virginia leaders frequently petitioned the mother country for arms, men, and supplies. In 1626—four years after the Massacre—the royal governor informed the Privy Council that the security of Virginia required "no less nombers then five hundred soldiers to be yearly sent over." On other occasions officials in Virginia admitted that as few as 50 or 100 troops would do, but however many men England provided, the colonists expected the king to pay the bill. Free protection would remove the necessity for high taxes. Understandably, the English administrators never found the settlers' argument persuasive, and royal policy makers may well have wondered what several thousand colonists were doing to defend themselves.

Before the 1670's not a single English soldier was dispatched to Virginia. Nevertheless, despite repeated failures in gaining English assistance, the dream of acquiring a cheap, dependable military force remained strong. Had the colony's own citizens been more involved in Virginia's defense, more willing to live closer together, there would have been no reason to plead for outside support. But the spirit of excessive individualism ironically bred a habit of dependence upon the mother country, and as soon as internal problems threatened the peace, someone was sure to call for English regulars.

Virginia's military preparedness was no more impressive in 1630 than it had been a decade earlier. The colony's rulers still complained that the planters "utterly neglected eyther to stand upon their guard or to keepe their Armes fitt." The Council admitted helplessly that "neyther proclamations nor other strict orders have remedied the same." The settlers were incorrigible. Forts remained unbuilt; the great palisade neither kept the colonists in nor the Indians out. And in 1644 the local tribes launched a second, even more deadly attack, revealing once again the fundamental weakness of Virginia's military system.

Virginia's extreme individualism was not an ephemeral phenomenon, something associated only with the colony's founding or a peculiar boom-town atmosphere. Long after the 1620's, values originally brought to the New World by adventurers and opportunists influenced patterns of social and institutional behavior, and instead of providing Virginia with new direction or a new sense of mission, newcomers were assimilated into an established cultural system. Customs became statute law, habitual acts tradition.

The long-term effects of these values upon society are too great to be considered here. It should be noted, however, that seventeenth-century Virginians never succeeded in forming a coherent society. Despite their apparent homogeneity, they lacked cohesive group identity; they generated no positive symbols, no historical myths strong enough to overcome individual differences. As one might expect, such a social system proved extremely fragile, and throughout the seventeenth century Virginians experienced social unrest, even open rebellion.

Nor should the grand life style of the great eighteenth-century planters, the Byrds, the Carters, the Wormeleys, mislead one into thinking that their value system differed significantly from that of Virginia's early settlers. These first families of the early eighteenth century bore the same relationship to Captain John Smith and his generation as Cotton Mather and his contemporaries did to the founders of Massachusetts Bay. The apparent political tranquility of late colonial Virginia grew not out of a sense of community or new value-orientations, but out of more effective forms of human exploitation. The mass of tobacco field laborers were now black slaves, men and women who by legal definition could never become fully part of the privatistic culture. In Byrd's Virginia, voluntaristic associations remained weak; education lagged, churches stagnated, and towns never developed. The isolation of plantation life continued, and the extended visits and the elaborate balls of the period may well have served to obscure the competition that underlay planter relationships. As one anthropologist reminds us, "in a society in which everyone outside the nuclear family is immediately suspect, in which one is at every moment believed to be vulnerable to the underhanded attacks of others, reliability and trust can never be taken for granted." In the course of a century of cultural development, Virginians transformed an extreme form of individualism, a value system suited for soldiers and adventurers, into a set of regional virtues, a love of independence, an insistence upon personal liberty, a cult of manhood, and an uncompromising loyalty to family.

4

THE CASE OF THE AMERICAN JEZEBELS: ANNE HUTCHINSON AND THE ANTINOMIAN CONTROVERSY

LYLE KOEHLER

One of the most revealing ironies of early American history was the transformation of Puritanism from an English protest movement into an established orthodoxy in seventeenth-century New England. The Puritans had been staunch critics of the established Church of England since the late sixteenth century, believing that the English church was insufficiently reformed in structure and doctrine. Drawing on the ideas of the French Protestant reformer John Calvin, the Puritans criticized not only the doctrines of the established church but its elaborate ceremonies and its close connections with the monarchy as well. By the 1620s, the spread of Puritanism to a growing number of English communities became a threat to the established church as well as to Charles I's ambition to make England into an absolutist state. Under the policy of William Laud, Archbishop of Canterbury and titular head of the national church, Puritan ministers and their congregations were harshly persecuted as heretics and as enemies of the state. In the minds of many Puritans, the only hope lay in migration to the wilderness of New England, where they hoped to create the kind of pure and religiously cohesive communities that English conditions prevented them from achieving at home.

Moving to the New World, however, created a new set of problems. As Massachusetts Governor John Winthrop and leading Puritan ministers attempted to impose doctrinal uniformity on the newly founded colony, they encountered resistance from ordinary colonists and dissident clergymen alike. Less than five years after the founding of the Puritan colony, one English-trained minister, Roger Williams, publicly accused Winthrop and his clerical allies of attempting to create a state church in New England much like the Anglican Church they had so recently left behind. When Winthrop moved to have Williams deported in 1636, the separatist minister fled south to live among the Narragansett people and eventually helped to create the colony of Rhode Island. Williams's departure gave Winthrop and his allies little relief, however, for just as the dissident minister fled Boston a new threat to New England orthodoxy arrived in the person of Anne Hutchinson.

As Lyle Koehler details in this essay, Hutchinson not only attacked Boston's established clergy for abandoning strict predestination—the cornerstone of Calvinist doctrine—but challenged deep-seated notions about women's proper place as well. By speaking her mind about Puritan theology, a universally male domain in this era, Hutchinson stepped out of the subordinate role traditionally prescribed for seventeenth-century women and placed herself on an equal footing with the university-trained clergy of the colony. Hutchinson's call for a strict interpretation of Calvinist doctrine was thus more than a doctrinal squabble. As Koehler demonstrates, Hutchinson also challenged the established notions of male superiority on which New England society rested.

In reading this essay, it is important to remember that Anne Hutchinson's concerns were those of a seventeenth-century woman and not those of her twentieth-century counterparts. Koehler's view has been criticized by some historians for reading modern-day feminism back into the past, thereby ignoring the historical context in which the Antinomian controversy took place.

Between 1636 and 1638 Massachusetts boiled with controversy, and for more than three centuries scholars have attempted to define and redefine the nature, causes, and implications of that controversy. Commentators have described the rebellious Antinomians as "heretics of the worst and most dangerous sort" who were guilty of holding "absurd, licentious, and destructive" opinions, as "a mob scrambling after God, and like all mobs quickly dispersed once their leaders were dealt with," and as the innocent victims of "inexcusable severity and unnecessary virulence." Other narrators have called the most famous Antinomian, Anne Hutchinson, a "charismatic healer, with the gift of fluent and inspired speech," another St. Joan of Arc, a rebel with a confused, bewildered mind, and a woman "whose stern and masculine mind . . . triumphed over the tender affections of a wife and mother."

Almost without exception, these critics and defenders of Ms. Hutchinson and the Antinomians have dealt specifically with Antinomianism as a religious movement and too little with it as a social movement. Emery Battis has traced the occupational status of 190 Antinomians and Antinomian sympathizers to examine the secular as well as the religious aspects of the controversy, but his work suffers from one major oversight: only three of his rebels are female. As Richard S. Dunn has rightly observed, "The role of women in colonial life continues to be neglected," and only one colonial specialist, Michael J. Colacurcio, has been much concerned with women as Antinomians. Colacurcio has argued that sexual tensions were central to the Antinomian controversy, but it is not his primary concern to describe the nature of those tensions. Rather, he focuses on Anne Hutchinson as a "type" of Hawthorne's scarlet lady, Hester Prynne. Dunn's appeal, "We need another view of Ms. Hutchinson," still entices.

That Anne Hutchinson and many other Puritan women should at stressful times rebel, either by explicit statement or by implicit example, against the role they were expected to fulfill in society is readily understandable, since that role, in both old and New England, was extremely limiting. The model English woman was weak, submissive, charitable, virtuous, and modest. Her mental and physical activity was limited to keeping the home in order, cooking, and bearing and rearing children, although she might occasionally serve the community as a nurse or midwife. She was urged to avoid books and intellectual exercise, for such activity might overtax her weak mind, and to serve her husband willingly, since she was by nature his inferior. In accordance with the Apostle Paul's doctrine, she was to hold her tongue in church and be careful not "to teach, nor to usurp authority over the man, but to be in silence."

In their letters, lectures, and historical accounts many of the Bay Colony men and some of the women showed approval of modest, obedient, and submissive females. Governor John Winthrop's wife Margaret was careful to leave such important domestic matters as place of residence to her husband's discretion, even when she had a preference of her own. She was ashamed because she felt that she had "no thinge with in or with out" worthy of him and signed her letters to him "your faythfull and obedient wife" or "your lovinge and obedient wife." Lucy Downing, Winthrop's sister, signed her chatty letters to her brother, "Your sister to commaund." Elizabeth, the wife of Winthrop's son John, described herself in a letter to her husband as "thy eaver loveing and kinde wife to comande in whatsoever thou plesest so long as the Lord shall bee plesed to geve me life and strenge."

Winthrop himself was harshly critical of female intellect. In 1645 he wrote that Ann Hopkins, wife of the governor of Connecticut, had lost her understanding and reason by giving herself solely to reading and writing. The Massachusetts statesman commented that if she "had attended her household affairs, and such things as belong to women, and not gone out of her way and calling to meddle in such things as are proper for men, whose minds are stronger, etc. she had kept her wits, and might have improved them usefully and honorably in the place God had set her." Earlier he had denounced Anne Hutchinson as "a woman of a haughty and fierce carriage, of a nimble wit and active spirit, and a very voluble tongue, more bold then a man, though in understanding and judgement, inferiour to many women."

Winthrop echoed the expectations of the male-dominated society in which he lived, in much the same way as the New England propagandist William Wood and Anne Hutchinson's ministerial accusers did. In 1634 Wood praised the Indian women's "mild carriage and obedience to their husbands," despite his realization that Indian men were guilty of "churlishness and inhumane behavior" toward their wives. Reverend John Cotton arrived in Boston in 1633 and soon requested the women desiring church membership be examined in private since a public confession was "against the apostle's rule and not fit for a women's modesty." At a public lecture less than a year later Cotton explained that the apostle directed women to wear veils in church only when "the custom of the place" considered veils "a sign of the women's subjection." Cambridge minister Thomas Shepard, one of Anne Hutchinson's most severe critics, commended his own wife for her "incomparable meekness of spirit, toward myself especially," while Hugh Peter, a Salem pastor and another of Ms. Hutchinson's accusers, urged his daughter to respect her feminine meekness as "Womans Ornament."

The female role definition that the Massachusetts ministers and magistrates perpetuated severely limited the assertiveness, the accomplishment, the independence, and the intellectual activity of Puritan women. Bay Colony women who might resent such a role definition before 1636 had no ideological rationale around which they could organize the expression of their frustration—whatever their consciousness of the causes of that frustration. With the marked increase of Antinomian sentiment in Boston and Anne Hutchinson's powerful example of resistance, the distressed females were able—as this article will attempt to demonstrate—to channel their frustration into a viable theological form and to rebel openly against the perpetuators of the spiritual and secular status quo. Paradoxically enough, the values the Antinomians embraced minimized the importance of individual action, for they believed that salvation could be demonstrated only by the individual feeling God's grace within.

The process of salvation and the role of the individual in that process was, for the Puritan divines, a matter less well defined. The question of the relative importance of good works (i.e., individual effort) and grace (i.e., God's effort) in preparing man for salvation concerned English Puritans from their earliest origins, and clergymen of old and New England attempted to walk a broad, although unsure, middle ground between the extremes of Antinomianism and Arminianism. But in 1636 Anne Hutchinson's former mentor and the new teacher of the Boston church, John Cotton, disrupted the fragile theological balance and led the young colony into controversy when he "warned his listeners away from the specious comfort of preparation and re-emphasized the covenant of grace as something in which God acted alone and unassisted." Cotton further explained that a person could become conscious of the dwelling of the Holy Spirit within his soul and directed the Boston congregation "not to be afraid of the word *Revelation*." The church elders, fearing that Cotton's "Revelation" might be dangerously construed to invalidate biblical law, requested a clarification of his position.

While the elders debated with Cotton the religious issues arising out of his pronouncements, members of Cotton's congregation responded more practically and enthusiastically to the notion of personal revelation by ardently soliciting converts to an emerging, loosely-knit ideology which the divines called pejoratively Antinomianism, Opinionism, or Familism. According to Thomas Weld, fledgling Antinomians visited new migrants to Boston, "especially, men of note, worth, and activity, fit instruments to advance their designe." Antinomian principles were defended at military trainings, in town meetings, and before the court judges. Winthrop charged the Opinionists with causing great disturbance in the church, the state, and the family, and wailed, "All things are turned upside down among us."

The individual hungry for power could, as long as he perceived his deep inner feeling of God's grace to be authentic, use that feeling to consecrate his personal rebellion against the contemporary authorities. Some Boston merchants used it to attack the accretion of political power in the hands of a rural-dominated General Court based on land instead of capital. Some "ignorant and unlettered" men used it to express contempt for the arrogance of "black-coates that have been at the Ninneversity." Some women, as we will see, used it to castigate the authority of the magistrates as guardians of the state, the ministers as guardians of the church, and their husbands as guardians of the home. As the most outspoken of these women, Anne Hutchinson diffused her opinions among all social classes by means of contacts made in the course of her profession of midwifery and in the biweekly teaching sessions she held at her home. Weld believed that Ms. Hutchinson's lectures were responsible for distributing "the venome of these [Antinomian] opinions into the very veines and vitalls of the People in the Country."

Many women identified with Ms. Hutchinson's rebellious intellectual stance and her aggressive spirit. Edward Johnson wrote that "the weaker Sex" set her up as "a Priest" and "thronged" after her. John Underhill reported he daily heard a "clamor" that "New England men usurp over their wives, and keep them in servile subjection." Winthrop blamed Anne for causing "divisions between husband and wife . . . till the weaker give place to the stronger, otherwise it turnes to open contention," and Weld charged the Antinomians with using the yielding, flexible, and tender women as "an Eve, to catch their husbands also." One anonymous English pamphleteer found in Antinomianism a movement "somewhat like the Trojan horse for rarity" because "it was covered with womens aprons, and bolstered out with the judgement and deep discerning of the godly and reverent."

From late 1636 through early 1637 female resistance in the Boston church reached its highest pitch. At one point, when pastor John Wilson rose to preach, Ms. Hutchinson left the congregation and many women followed her out of the meetinghouse. These women "pretended many excuses for their going out," an action which made it impossible for the authorities to convict them of contempt for Wilson. Other rebels did, however, challenge Wilson's words as he spoke them, causing Weld to comment, "Now the faithfull Ministers of Christ must have dung cast on their faces, and be no better than Legall Preachers, Baals Priests, Popish Factors, Scribes, Pharisees, and Opposers of Christ himselfe."

Included among these church rebels were two particularly active women, Jane (Mrs. Richard) Hawkins and milliner William Dyer's wife Mary, both of whom Winthrop found obnoxious. The governor considered the youthful Ms. Dyer to be "of a very proud spirit," "much addicted to revelations," and "notoriously infected with Mrs. Hutchinson's errors." Ms. Dyer weathered Winthrop's wrath and followed Anne to Rhode Island, but her "addictions" were not without serious consequence. Twenty-two years later she would return to Boston and be hanged as a Quaker. The other of Hutchinson's close female associates, Jane Hawkins, dispensed fertility portions to barren women and occasionally fell into a trance-like state in which she spoke Latin. Winthrop therefore denounced her as "notorious for familiarity with the devill," and the General Court, sharing his apprehension, on March 12, 1638, forbade her to question "matters of religion" or "to meddle" in "surgery, or phisick, drinks, plaisters, or oyles." Ms. Hawkins apparently disobeyed this order, for three years later the Court banished her from the colony under the penalty of a severe whipping or such other punishment as the judges thought fit.

Other women, both rich and poor, involved themselves in the Antinomian struggle. William Coddington's spouse, like her merchant husband, was "taken with the familistical opinions." Mary Dummer, the wife of wealthy landowner and Assistant Richard Dummer, convinced her husband to move from Newbury to Boston so that she might be closer to Ms. Hutchinson. Mary Oliver, a poor Salem calenderer's wife, reportedly exceeded Anne "for ability of speech, and appearance of zeal and devotion" and, according to Winthrop, might "have done hurt, but that she was poor and had little acquaintance [with theology]." Ms. Oliver held the "dangerous" opinions that the church was managed by the "heads of the people, both magistrates and ministers, met together," instead of the people themselves, and that anyone professing faith in Christ ought to be admitted to the church and the sacraments. Between 1638 and 1650 she appeared before the magistrates six times for remarks contemptuous of ministerial and magisterial authority and experienced the stocks, the lash, the placement of a clef stick on her tongue, and imprisonment. One of the Salem magistrates became so frustrated with Ms. Oliver's refusal to respect his authority that he seized her and put her in the stocks without a trial. She sued him for false arrest and collected a minimal ten shillings in damages. Her victory was short-lived, however, and before she left Massachusetts in 1650 she had managed to secure herself some reputation as a witch.

Mary Oliver and the other female rebels could easily identify with the Antinomian ideology because its theological emphasis on the inability of the individual to achieve salvation echoed the inability of women to achieve recognition on a sociopolitical level. As the woman realized that she could receive wealth, power, and status only through the man, her father or her husband, so the Antinomian realized that he or she could receive grace only through God's beneficence. Thus, women could have found it appealing that in Antinomianism *both* men and women were relegated vis-á-vis God to the status that women occupied in Puritan society vis-á-vis men, that is, to the status of malleable inferiors in the hands of a higher being. All power, then, emanated from God, raw and pure, respecting no sex, rather than from male authority figures striving to interpret the Divine Word. Fortified by a consciousness of the Holy Spirit's inward dwelling, the Antinomians could rest secure and self-confident

in the belief that they were mystic participants in the transcendent power of the Almighty, a power far beyond anything mere magistrates and ministers might muster. Antinomianism could not secure for women such practical earthly powers as sizable estates, professional success, and participation in the church and civil government, but it provided compensation by reducing the significance of these powers for the men. Viewed from this perspective, Antinomianism extended the feminine experience of humility to both sexes, which in turn paradoxically created the possibility of feminine pride, as Anne Hutchinson's dynamic example in her examinations and trials amply demonstrated.

Anne Hutchinson's example caused the divines much frustration. They were chagrined to find that she was not content simply to repeat to the "simple Weomen" the sermons of John Wilson, but that she also chose to interpret and even question the content of those sermons. When she charged that the Bay Colony ministers did not teach a covenant of grace as "clearly" as Cotton and her brother-in-law, John Wheelwright, she was summoned in 1636 to appear before a convocation of the clergy. At this convocation and in succeeding examinations, the ministers found particularly galling her implicit assertion that she had the intellectual ability necessary to judge the truth of their theology. Such an assertion threatened their self-image as the intellectual leaders of the community and the spokesmen for a male-dominated society. The ministers and magistrates therefore sharply criticized Anne for not fulfilling her ordained womanly role. In September 1637 a synod of elders resolved that women might meet "to pray and edify one another," but when one woman "in a prophetical way" resolved questions of doctrine and expounded Scripture, then the meeting was "disorderly." At Anne's examination on November 7 and 8, Winthrop began the interrogation by charging that she criticized the ministers and maintained a "meeting and an assembly in your house that hath been condemned by the general assembly as a thing not tolerable nor comely in the sight of God nor fitting for your sex." Later in the interrogation, Winthrop accused her of disobeying her "parents," the magistrates, in violation of the Fifth Commandment, and paternalistically told her, "We do not mean to discourse with those of your sex." Hugh Peter also indicated that he felt Anne was not fulfilling the properly submissive, nonintellectual feminine role. He ridiculed her choice of a female preacher of the Isle of Ely as a model for her own behavior and told her to consider "that you have stept out of you place, *you have rather bine a Husband than a Wife and a preacher than a Hearer; and a Magistrate than a Subject.*"

When attacked for behavior inappropriate to her sex, Ms. Hutchinson did not hesitate to demonstrate that she was the intellectual equal of her accusers. She tried to trap Winthrop when he charged her with dishonoring her "parents": "But put the case Sir that I do fear the Lord and my parents, may not I entertain them that fear the Lord because my parents will not give me leave?" To provide a biblical justification for her teaching activities, she cited Titus's rule (2:3–4) "that the elder women should instruct the younger." Winthrop ordered her to take that rule "in the sense that elder women might instruct the younger about their business, and to love their husbands." But Anne disagreed with this interpretation, saying, "I do not conceive but that it is meant for some publick times." Winthrop rejoined, " "We must . . . restrain you from maintaining this course," and she qualified, "If you have a rule for it from God's word you may." Her resistance infuriated the governor, who exclaimed, "We are your judges, and not you ours." When Winthrop tried to lure her into admitting that she taught men, in violation of Paul's proscription, Anne replied that she thought herself justified in teaching a man who asked her for instruction, and added sarcastically, "Do you think it not lawful for me to teach women and why do you call me to teach the court?"

Anne soon realized that sarcastic remarks would not persuade the court of the legitimacy of her theological claims. Alternatively, therefore, she affected a kind of modesty to cozen the authorities at the same time that she expressed a kind of primitive feminism through double-entendre statements and attacked the legitimacy of Paul's idea of the nonspeaking, nonintellectual female churchmember. When the Court charged her with "prophesying," Anne responded, "The men of *Berea* are commended for examining *Pauls* Doctrine; wee do no more [in our meetings] but read the notes of our teachers Sermons, and then reason of them by searching the Scriptures." Such a statement was on one level an "innocent" plea to the divines that the women were only following biblical prescription. On another level it was an attack on the ministers for presuming to have the final word on biblical interpretation. On yet a third level, since she focused on "Pauls Doctrine" and reminded men that they should take another look at that teaching, her statement was a suggestion that ministerial attitudes toward women ought to be reexamined.

At another point Anne responded to Winthrop's criticism with a similar statement having meaning on three levels. The governor had accused her of traducing the ministers and magistrates and, when summoned to answer this charge, of saying that "the fear of man was a snare and therefore she would not be affeared of them." She replied, "They say I said the fear of man is a snare, why should I be afraid. When I came unto them, they urging many things unto me and I being backward to answer at first, at length this scripture came into my mind 29th Prov. 15. The fear of man bringeth a snare, but who putteth his trust in the Lord shall be safe." Once again, her response was phrased as an "innocent" plea to God to assuage her fears, while at the same time it implied that God was on her side in opposition to the ministers and magistrates. Her statement also told women that if they trusted in God they need not fear men, for such fear trapped them into being "backward" about reacting in situations of confrontation with men.

Anne, although aware of the "backwardness" of women as a group, did not look to intensified group activity as a remedy for woman's down-trodden status. Her feminism consisted essentially of the subjective recognition of her own strength and gifts and the apparent belief that other women could come to the same recognition. A strong, heroic example of female self-assertiveness was necessary to the development of this recognition of one's own personal strength. Anne chose the woman preacher of the Isle of Ely as her particular heroic model; she did, Hugh Peter chided, "exceedingly magnifie" that woman "to be a Womane of 1000 hardly any like to her." Anne could thus dissociate herself from the "divers worthy and godly Weomen" of Massachusetts and confidently deride them as being no better than "soe many Jewes," unconverted by the light of Christ. Other Bay Colony women who wished to reach beyond the conventional, stereotypic behavior of "worthy and godly Weomen" attached themselves to the emphatic example of Anne and to God's ultimate power in order to resist the constraints which they felt as Puritan women.

Fearful that Ms. Hutchinson's example might be imitated by other women, the divines wished to catch her in a major theological error and subject her to public punishment. Their efforts were not immediately successful. Throughout her 1637 examination Anne managed to parry the verbal thrusts of the ministers and magistrates by replying to their many questions with questions of her own, forcing them to justify their positions from the Bible, pointing out their logical inconsistencies, and using innuendo to cast aspersions upon their authoritarianism. With crucial assistance from a sympathetic John Cotton, she left the ministers with no charge to pin upon her. She was winning the debate when, in an apparently incautious moment, she gave the authorities the kind of declaration for which they had been hoping. Raising herself to the position of judge over her accusers, she asserted, "I know that for this you goe about to doe to me, God will ruine you and your posterity, and this whole State." Asked how she knew this, she explained, "By an immediate revelation." With this statement Anne proved her heresy to the ministers and they then took steps to expose her in excommunication proceedings conducted before the Boston church. The divines hoped to expel a heretic from their midst, to reestablish support for the Puritan way, to prevent unrest in the state and the family, and to shore up their own anxious egos in the process.

The predisposition of the ministers to defame Ms. Hutchinson before the congregation caused them to ignore what she was actually saying in her excommunication trial. Although she did describe a relationship with Christ closer than anything Cotton had envisioned, she did not believe that she had experienced Christ's Second Coming in her own life. Such a claim would have denied the resurrection of the body at the Last Judgment and would have clearly stamped her as a Familist. Ms. Hutchinson's accusers, ignoring Thomas Leverett's reminder that she had expressed belief in the resurrection, argued that if the resurrection did not exist, biblical law would have no validity nor the marriage covenant any legal or utilitarian value. The result would be a kind of world no Puritan could tolerate, a world where the basest desires would be fulfilled and "foule, groce, filthye and abominable" sexual promiscuity would be rampant. Cotton, smarting from a psychological slap Anne had given him earlier in the excommunication proceedings and in danger of losing the respect of the other ministers, admonished her with the words "though I have not herd, nayther do I thinke, you have bine unfaythfull to your Husband in his Marriage Covenant, *yet that will follow upon it.*" By referring to "his" marriage covenant Cotton did not even accord Anne equal participation in the making of that covenant. The Boston teacher concluded his admonition with a criticism of Anne's pride: *"I have often feared the highth of your Spirit and being puft up with your owne parts."*

Both the introduction of the sexual issue into the trial and Cotton's denunciation of Ms. Hutchinson must have had the effect of curbing dissent from the congregation. Few Puritans would want to defend Anne in public when such a defense could be construed as supporting promiscuity. Since Cotton had earlier been sympathetic to the Antinomian cause and had tried to save Anne at her 1637 examination, his vigorous condemnation of her must have confused her following. Cotton even went so far as to exempt the male Antinomians from any real blame for the controversy when he characterized Antinomianism as a women's delusion. He urged that women, like children, ought to be watched, reproved Hutchinson's sons for not controlling her theological ventures, and called those sons "Vipers . . . [who] *Eate through the very Bowells of your Mother,* to her Ruine." Cotton warned the Boston women "to looke to your selves and to take heed that you reaceve nothinge for Truth which hath not the stamp of the Word of God [as interpreted by the ministers] . . . for you see she [Anne] is but a Woman and *many unsound and dayngerous principles are held by her.*" Thomas Shepard agreed that intellectual activity did not suit women and warned the congregation that Anne was likely "to seduce and draw away many, Espetially simple Weomen of her owne sex."

The female churchmembers, who would have had good reason to resent the clergy's approach, could not legitimately object to the excommunication proceedings because of Paul's injunction against women speaking in church. Lacking a clearly defined feminist consciousness and filled with "backward" fear, the women could not refuse to respect that injunction, even though, or perhaps because, Anne had been presented to the congregation as the epitome of despicableness, as a woman of simple intellect, and as a liar, puffed up with pride and verging on sexual promiscuity. This caricature of Anne did not, however, prevent five men, including her brother-in-law Richard Scott and Mary Oliver's husband Thomas, from objecting to her admonition and excommunication. Cotton refused to consider the points these men raised and dismissed their objections as rising out of their own self-interest or their natural affection for Anne.

In Anne's excommunication proceedings the ministers demonstrated that they had found the means necessary to deal effectively with this rebellious woman and a somewhat hostile congregation. At her examination and her excommu-

nication trial Anne attempted to place the ministers on the defensive by questioning them and forcing them to justify their positions while she explained little. She achieved some success in the 1637 trial, but before her fellow churchmembers she found it difficult to undercut the misrepresentation of her beliefs and the attack on her character. Perhaps fearing the banishment which had been so quickly imposed on her associate, John Wheelwright, she recanted, but even in her recantation she would not totally compromise her position. She expressed sorrow for her errors of expression but admitted no errors in judgment and assumed no appearance of humiliation. When Wilson commanded her "*as a Leper to withdraw your selfe out of the Congregation,*" Anne rose, walked to the meetinghouse door, accepted Mary Dyer's offered hand, and turned to impugn her accusers' power: "The Lord judgeth not as man judgeth, better to be cast out of the Church then to deny Christ."

During the year and a half following Ms. Hutchinson's excommunication, the Massachusetts ministers and magistrates prosecuted several other female rebels. In April 1638 the Boston church cast out Judith Smith, the maidservant of Anne's brother-in-law, Edward Hutchinson, for her "obstinate persisting" in "sundry Errors." On October 10 of the same year the Assistants ordered Katherine Finch to be whipped for "speaking against the magistrates, against the Churches, and against the Elders." Less than a year later Ms. Finch again appeared before the Assistants, this time for not carrying herself "dutifully to her husband," and was released upon promise of reformation. In September 1639 the Boston church excommunicated Phillip(a?) Hammond "as a slaunderer and revyler both of the Church and Common Weale." Ms. Hammond, after her husband's death, had resumed her maiden name, operated a business in Boston, and argued in her shop and at public meetings "that Mrs. Hutchinson neyther deserved the Censure which was putt upon her in the Church, nor in the Common Weale." The Boston church also excommunicated two other women for partially imitating Anne Hutchinson's example: Sarah Keayne was found guilty in 1646 of "irregular prophesying in mixed assemblies," and Joan Hogg nine years later was punished "for her disorderly singing and her idleness, and for saying she is commanded of Christ so to do."

The Salem authorities followed Boston's example in dealing with overly assertive women. In late 1638 the Salem church excommunicated four of Roger Williams's former followers: Jane (Mrs. Joshua) Verin, Mary Oliver, servant Margery Holliman, and widow Margery Reeves. These women had consistently refused to worship with the congregation, and the latter two had denied that the churches of the Bay Colony were true churches. Yet another woman, Dorothy Talby, who was subject to a different kind of frustration, troubled the Essex County magistrates by mimicking Anne Hutchinson's proclamation of "immediate revelation" to justify her personal rebellion. In October 1637 the county court ordered her chained to a post "for frequent laying hands on her husband to the danger of his life, and contemning the authority of the court," and later ordered her whipped for "misdemeanors against her husband." Later, according to Winthrop, she claimed a "revelation from heaven" instructing her to kill her husband and children and then broke the neck of her three-year-old daughter, Difficult. At her execution on December 6, 1638, Ms. Talby continued her defiance by refusing to keep her face covered and expressing a desire to be beheaded, as "it was less painful and less shameful."

Dorothy Talby was one of an increasing number of women to appear before the General Court and the Court of Assistants, an increase which seemed to reflect both a greater rebelliousness in women and a hardening of magisterial attitudes. In the first five years of Puritan settlement only 1.7 percent of the persons convicted of criminal offenses by the Deputies and the Assistants were women. During and after the years of the Antinomian controversy the percentage of female offenders was significantly higher—6.7 percent from 1635 to 1639 and 9.4 percent from 1640 to 1644. If Charles E. Banks's

enumeration of 3,505 passengers from ship lists is representative of the more than 20,000 persons who came to Massachusetts between 1630 and 1639, it can be assumed that the number of women did not increase proportionately to the number of men. Banks's ship lists reveal that 829 males and 542 females came to Massachusetts between 1630 and 1634, a number which increased in the next five years to 1,279 males and 855 females. The percentage of females increased only 0.6 percent, from 39.5 percent between 1630 and 1634 to 40.1 percent between 1635 and 1639. These comparative figures suggest that by 1640 the magistrates could no longer afford to dismiss with verbal chastisement females found guilty of drunkenness, cursing, or premarital fornication.

The magistrates not only used the threat of a humiliating courtroom appearance and possible punishment to keep female rebels quiet but also levied very stringent penalties on male Antinomian offenders. Anne Hutchinson's son-in-law William Collins was sentenced to pay a £100 fine for charging the Massachusetts churches and ministers with being anti-Christian and calling the king of England the king of Babylon. Anne's son Francis, who had accompanied Collins to Boston in 1641, objected to the popular rumor that he would not sit at the same table with his excommunicated mother and, feeling that the Boston church was responsible, called that church "a strumpet." The church excommunicated Francis and the Assistants fined him £40, but neither he nor Collins would pay the stipulated amounts (even when those fines were reduced to £40 and £20) and therefore spent some time in jail.

Besides prosecuting Antinomian sympathizers in church and court, the Massachusetts ministers and magistrates carefully watched new ministers, lest they deliver "some points savoring of familism," and justified the emergent orthodox position in their sermons and publications. Of these publications, which were directed at audiences both in New and old England, John Cotton's *Singing of Psalmes a Gospel-Ordinance* most significantly asserted the traditional feminine role-response. The Boston teacher, apparently with Ms. Hutchinson in mind, told his readers that "the woman is more subject to error than a man" and continued, "It is not permitted to a woman to speak in the Church by way of propounding questions though under pretence of desire to learn for her own satisfaction; but rather it is required she should ask her husband at home. For under pretence of questioning for learning sake, she might so propound her question as to teach her teachers; or if not so, yet to open a door to some of her own weak and erroneous apprehensions, or at least soon exceed the bounds of womanly modesty." Cotton explained that a woman could speak in church only when she wished to confess a sin or to participate in singing hymns.

Other Bay Colony leaders popularized the idea that the intellectual woman was influenced by Satan and was therefore unable to perform the necessary functions of womanhood. Weld described Mary Dyer's abortive birth as "a woman child, a fish, a beast, and a fowle, all woven together in one, and without an head," and wrote of Anne Hutchinson's probable hydatidiform mole as "30 monstrous births . . . none at all of them (as farre as I could ever learne) of the humane shape." According to Winthrop's even more garish account of Mary Dyer's child, the stillborn baby had a face and ears growing upon the shoulders, a breast and back full of sharp prickles, female sex organs on the rear and buttocks in front, three clawed feet, no forehead, four horns above the eyes, and two great holes upon the back. Wheelwright wrote from his new home in Exeter to attack the governor's far-fetched description of these births. That clergyman called Winthrop's monsters "a monstrous conception of his brain, a spurious issue of his intellect," and told that governor that he should know better *then to delude the world with untruths.* [For] I question not his learning, etc. but I admire his certainty or rather impudence: did the man obtestricate [obstetricate]?"

Despite Wheelwright's effort, Weld's opinion that "as she had vented mishapen opinions, so she must bring forth deformed monsters"

impressed the people of the Bay Colony, a people who believed that catastrophic occurrences were evidences of God's displeasure. Some Massachusetts residents viewed the births as the products of both the women's "mishapen opinions" and their supposed promiscuity. Edward Johnson and Roger Clap lamented the "phantasticall madnesse" of those who would hold "silly women laden with their lusts" in higher esteem than "those honored of Christ, indued with power and authority from him to Preach." A rumor reached England that Henry Vane had crossed the Atlantic in 1637 with Ms. Dyer and Ms. Hutchinson and had "debauched both, and both were delivered of monsters." It was also widely rumored that three of the Antinomian women, Anne Hutchinson, Jane Hawkins, and Mary Oliver, had sold their souls to Satan and become witches. Anne in particular "gave cause of suspicion of witchcraft" after she easily converted to Antinomianism one new male arrival in Rhode Island.

The promotion of the belief that the Antinomian female leaders were witches filled with aberrant lusts and unable to live as proper women was accompanied by an attack on the masculinity of some of the Antinomian men. Although Anne's husband, William, had been a prosperous landowner, a merchant, a deputy to the General Court, and a Boston selectman, Winthrop described him as a "man of very mild temper and weak parts, and wholly guided by his wife." Clap also felt that William Hutchinson and the other Antinomian men were deficient in intellect and judgment. He expressed surprise that any of the men in the movement had "strong parts."

While Massachusetts gossip focused on disordered Antinomian births, lusty Antinomian women, and weak Antinomian men, Winthrop and Cotton tried to convince their English and New England readers that public opinion had been solidly behind Ms. Hutchinson's excommunication. Winthrop contended that "diverse women" objected to this rebel's example and would have borne witness against her "if their modesty had not restrained them." Cotton supported the governor's claim by construing the relative silence at Anne's church trial to mean that the "whole body of the Church (except her own son) consented with one accord, to the publick censure of her, by admonition first, and excommunication after." By asserting this falsehood and ignoring Leverett's admission that many churchmembers wished to stay Anne's excommunication, Cotton made it appear that any person who complained about her censure was contradicting the near-unanimous opinion of the congregation.

The effort to discredit the Antinomians and Antinomian sentiment in the Bay Colony was quite successful. By the late 1640s Antinomianism, in a practical sense, was no longer threatening; the ministers and magistrates had managed to preserve a theological system they found congenial. "*Sanctification* came to be in some Request again; and there were *Notes* and *Marks* given of a good Estate." The position of Massachusetts women within the religious system remained essentially unchanged, while in Rhode Island and nearby Providence Plantations the status of women was somewhat improved. In Providence and Portsmouth the men listened to the wishes of the women and protected the "liberty" of women to teach, preach, and attend services of their choosing. When Joshua Verin, one of the original settlers at Providence, restrained his wife Jane from attending religious services at Roger Williams's home, a town meeting considered the matter. John Greene argued before the townsmen that if men were allowed to restrain their wives, "all the women in the country would cry out." William Arnold rejoined that God had ordered the wife to be subject to her husband and that such a commandment should not be broken merely to please women. According to Winthrop, the townsmen "would have censured Verin, [but] Arnold told them, that it was against their own order, for Verin did that he did out of conscience; and their order was, that no man should be censured for his conscience." Winthrop neglected to record that the town meeting did disfranchise Verin until he declared that he would not restrain his wife's "libertie of

conscience," nor did Winthrop mention that Verin had "trodden" his wife "under foot tyrannically and brutishly," endangering her life. After his censure, Verin returned to Salem, and Roger Williams urged Winthrop to prevent this "boisterous and desperate" young man from hauling "his wife with ropes to Salem, where she must needs be troubled and troublesome."

After Anne Hutchinson's arrival and throughout the remainder of the century, women taught and preached in public in Rhode Island. Johnson wrote that in 1638 "there were some of the female sexe who (deeming the Apostle Paul to be too strict in not permitting a room [woman] to preach in the publique Congregation) taught notwithstanding . . . having their call to this office from an ardent desire of being famous." According to Johnson, Anne Hutchinson, "the grand Mistresse of them all, . . . ordinarily prated every Sabbath day, till others, who thirsted after honour in the same way with her selfe, drew away her Auditors." This prating was more purposive than Johnson might have been willing to admit, for Anne soon involved herself in a new controversy, this one springing out of the resentment of many of the poorer inhabitants of the settlement toward Judge (Governor) William Coddington's autocratic rule, his land allotment policy, and his efforts to establish a church resembling closely the Massachusetts example. Allying herself with Samuel Gorton, a religious freethinker and a defender of justice for all men, "rich or poore, ignorant or learned," Anne began to attack the legitimacy of *any* magistracy. Together, she and Gorton managed to foment the rebellion of April 28, 1639, in which the Portsmouth inhabitants formed a new body politic, ejected Coddington from power, and chose William Hutchinson to replace him. William, however, also did not believe in magistracy and soon refused to occupy the office of judge. Coddington, who had fled south with his followers to found Newport, then claimed the judgeship by default, was recognized by the Massachusetts authorities, and proceeded to administer the affairs of Rhode Island. Gorton and at least eleven others responded to

Coddington's resumption of power by plotting armed rebellion against him and were ultimately banished from the colony. Anne broke with the Gortonists over that issue, and she and William joined the Newport settlement.

William Hutchinson died at Newport in 1640, and for much of that year Anne was silent. By 1641, however, she had come out of mourning and, according to Winthrop, turned Anabaptist. She and "divers" others supported passive resistance to authority, "denied all magistracy among Christians, and maintained that there were no churches since those founded by the apostles and evangelists, nor could any be." Such opinions achieved enough popularity in Rhode Island to contribute to the dissolution of the church at Newport, although not enough to remove Coddington from power. Disgruntled and fearing that Massachusetts would seize the Rhode Island settlements, Anne sought refuge in the colony of New Netherland in 1642, but her stay there was not long. In August 1643 she, William Collins, two of her sons, and three of her daughters were killed by Indians who had quarreled with her Dutch neighbors.

The Massachusetts clergy rejoiced. Not only had God destroyed the "American Jesabel," but the Lord's vengeance had descended upon her sons and daughters, the poisoned seed. Peter Bulkeley spoke for all the Massachusetts ministers when he concluded, "Let her damned heresies shee fell into . . . and the just vengeance of God, by which shee perished, terrifie all her seduced followers from having any more to doe with her leaven." But her "seduced followers" were horrified only at the reaction of the Puritan clergy. Anne's sister, Katherine Scott, commented that the Bay Colony authorities "are drunke with the blod of the saints," and Anne's former Portsmouth neighbor, Randall Holden, blamed those same authorities for forcing Anne first to Rhode Island and ultimately to her death. He reminded them of her partially successful struggle against authority: "you know . . . your great and terrible word magistrate is no more in its original, than masterly or masterless which hath no great lustre in our ordinary acceptation."

Impervious to such protests, the Bay Colony divines considered Anne Hutchinson's death to be the symbolic death of Antinomianism. To these divines she had been the incarnation of the Antinomian evil, and her accounts of the Antinomian stress in Boston accented *her* beliefs, *her* activities, and *her* rebelliousness. The ministers were not as concerned with the important roles played by Coddington, Wheelwright, Vane, and the other male Antinomian leaders because none of these men threatened the power and status structure of society in the concrete way that Anne Hutchinson did. Anne was clearly not, as the ministers might have wished, a submissive quiet dove, content to labor simply in the kitchen and the childbed. She was witty, aggressive, and intellectual. She had no qualms about castigating in public the men who occupied the most authoritative positions. She claimed the right to define rational, theological matters for herself and by her example spurred other women to express a similar demand. Far from bewildered, she thwarted her accusers with her intellectual ability. Perceiving her as a threat to the family, the state, the religion, and the status hierarchy, the Puritan authorities directed their antagonism against Anne's character and her sex. By doing so, they managed to salve the psychological wounds inflicted by this woman who trod so sharply upon their male status and their ministerial and magisterial authority. Their method had a practical aspect as well; it helped restore respect for the ministry and curb potential dissent.

Anne's ability to attract large numbers of women as supporters caused the ministers and magistrates some worry but little surprise, since they believed that women were easily deluded. They chided Anne for choosing a female preacher as a role model and refused to attribute any merit to her at times subtle, at times caustic intellectual ability. They could see only the work of Satan in Anne's aggressiveness and not the more human desire for equal opportunity and treatment which this rebel never hesitated to assert by example in the intellectual skirmishes she had with her accusers throughout her trials. The double oppression of life in a male-dominated society, combined with biological bondage to her own amazing fertility, could not destroy her self-respect. Because of the theologically based society in which she lived, it was easy for her to ally herself with God and to express her self-confidence in religious debates with the leading intellectual authorities. Neither Anne's rebellion nor the rebellion of her female followers was directed self-consciously against their collective female situation or toward its improvement. Specific feminist campaigns for the franchise, divorce reform, female property ownership after marriage, and the like would be developments of a much later era. For Anne Hutchinson and her female associates Antinomianism was simply an ideology through which the resentments they intuitively felt could be focused and actively expressed.

5

PATTERNS OF BLACK RESISTANCE

PETER H. WOOD

As English colonists gained a foothold on the mainland of North America and began the process of establishing permanent communities, the need for labor became increasingly acute. The small farmers of New England and the Middle Atlantic colonies needed labor to clear land, harvest crops, and maintain livestock. In the South, large plantations required flocks of fieldhands to tend labor-intensive crops such as tobacco and rice. And in the growing seaport cities, labor was needed to handle a growing volume of goods, to build houses for a burgeoning population, and to augment the production of local artisans. During the colonial period, much of this labor was supplied by indentured servants, who exchanged four to seven years of their labor for passage to America.

But by the end of the seventeenth century, colonists began to turn to a new source of labor: African slaves. Slavery was not new to the Americas: Spain and Portugal had been conducting a profitable slave trade since the sixteenth century. English mainland colonists could also draw upon the experiences of their West Indian counterparts, whose sugar plantations depended on a constant supply of slaves for their operation. By the early eighteenth century, southern plantation owners as well as northern artisans and merchants had turned to large-scale importations of slaves in order to maintain their tobacco and rice plantations, their shops, and their homes.

While the importance of early American slavery has long been recognized, historians have only recently turned their attention to the lives of the slaves themselves. One of the most important outcomes of this research is our growing understanding of the African-American response to enslavement. In this essay, Peter H. Wood explores one aspect of this response, the subtle and varied ways in which slaves resisted their bondage. Slave resistance was continuous, he suggests, and took place along a continuum that ranged from collective violence at one extreme to individual acts of defiance and dissimulation on the other. While America witnessed no successful large-scale rebellions, African-American slaves nonetheless engaged in a continuous struggle with their owners and overseers throughout the colonial and antebellum periods.

It is by no means paradoxical that increasingly overt white controls met with increasingly forceful black resistance. The stakes for Negroes were simply rising higher and the choices becoming more hopelessly difficult. As the individual and collective tensions felt by black slaves mounted, they continued to confront the immediate daily questions of whether to accept or deny, submit or resist, remain or flee. Given their diversity of background and experience, it is not surprising that slaves responded to these pressures in a wide variety of ways. To separate their reactions into docility on the one hand and rebellion on the other, as has occasionally been done, is to underestimate the complex nature of the contradictions each Negro felt in the face of new provocations and new penalties. It is more realistic to think in terms of a spectrum of response, ranging from complete submission to total resistance, along which any given individual could be located at a given time.

As in any situation overladen with contradictory pulls, there were those few persons who could not be located on such a spectrum at all; that is, their personalities "dis-integrated" in the face of conflicting pressures—internal and external—and their responses became unpredictable even to themselves. The Negro Act of 1751 made provision for local parishes to relieve poorer masters of the cost of confining and maintaining "slaves that may become lunatic." This category of individuals is not easy to define, for mental illness, like physical illness, became an element in the incessant game of deception developing between masters and slaves; Negroes pretended outright insanity upon occasion, and owners readily called such bluffs, perhaps more frequently than they occurred. Deception aside, it is no easy matter to define rational behavior within an arbitrary social system. Certain acts of resistance such as appropriating goods and running away, usually involved prior calculation by their very nature, as did poisoning, arson, and conspiracy, which will be examined [here]. Many other actions represented impromptu responses to trying situations, but even reactions which seemed most irrational in terms of straightforward appearances and consequences rested upon a rational appraisal of the slave environment.

At one end of the spectrum of individual resistance were the extreme incidents of physical violence. There are examples of slaves who, out of desperation, fury, or premeditation, lashed out against a white despite the consequences. Jemmy, a slave of Capt. Elias Ball, was sentenced to death in 1724 "for striking and wounding one Andrew Songster." The master salvaged the slave's life and his own investment by promising to deport Jemmy forever within two months. For others who vented individual aggression there was no such reprieve. In August 1733 the *Gazette* reported tersely: "a Negro Man belonging to Thomas Fleming of Charlestown, took an Opportunity, and kill'd the Overseer with an Axe. He was hang'd for the same yesterday." An issue during 1742 noted: "Thursday last a Negro Fellow belonging to Mr. Cheesman, was brought to Town, tried, condemn'd and hang'd, for attempting to murder a white lad."

Such explosions of rage were almost always suicidal, and the mass of the Negro population cultivated strict internal constraints as a means of preservation against external white controls. (The fact that whites accepted so thoroughly the image of a carefree and heedless black personality is in part a testimony to the degree to which black slaves learned the necessity of holding other emotional responses in outward check.) This essential lesson of control, passed on from one generation to the next, was learned by early immigrants through a painful process of trial and error. Those newcomers whose resistance was most overt were perceived to be the least likely to survive, so there ensued a process of conscious or unconscious experimentation (called "seasoning" or "breaking" by the whites) in which Africans calculated the forms and degrees of resistance which were most possible.

Under constant testing, patterns of slave resistance evolved rapidly, and many of the most effective means were found to fall at the low (or invisible) end of the spectrum. For example, for those who spoke English, in whatever dialect, verbal insolence became a consistent means of resistance. Cleverly handled, it allowed slaves a way to assert themselves and downgrade their masters without committing a crime. All parties were aware of the subversive potential of words (along with styles of dress and bearing), as the thrust of the traditional term "uppity" implies, and it may be that both the black use of this approach and the white perception of it increased as tensions grew. In 1737 the Assembly debated whether the patrols should have the right "to kill any resisting or saucy Slave," and in 1741 the Clerk of the Market proposed that "if any Slave should in Time of Market behave him or herself in any insolent abusive Manner, he or she should be sent to the Work-house, and there suffer corporal Punishment."

At the same time traits of slowness, carelessness, and literal-mindedness were artfully cultivated, helping to disguise countless act of willful subterfuge as inadvertent mistakes. To the benefit of the slave and the frustration of the historian, such subversion was always difficult to assess, yet considerable thought has now been given to these subtle forms of opposition. Three other patterns of resistance—poisoning, arson, and conspiracy—were less subtle and more damaging, and each tactic aroused white fears which sometimes far exceeded the actual threat. All three are recognized as having been methods of protest familiar in other slave colonies as well, and each is sufficiently apparent in the South Carolina sources to justify separate consideration.

African awareness of plants and their powers [was widespread], and it was plain to white colonists from an early date that certain blacks were particularly knowledgeable in this regard. In 1733 the *Gazette* published the details of a medicine for yaws, dropsy, and other distempers "for the Discovery whereof, a Negroe Man in Virginia was freed by the Government, and had a Pension of Thirty Pounds Sterling settled on him during his Life." Some of the Negroes listed by the name "Doctor" in colonial inventories had no doubt earned their titles. One South Carolina slave received his freedom and £100 per year for life from the Assembly for revealing his antidote

to poison; "Caesar's Cure" was printed in the *Gazette* and appeared occasionally in local almanacs for more than thirty years.

In West Africa, the obeah-men and others with the herbal knowledge to combat poisoning could inflict poison as well, and use for this negative capability was not diminished by enslavement. In Jamaica, poisoning was a commonplace means of black resistance in the eighteenth century, and incidents were familiar on the mainland as well. At least twenty slaves were executed for poisoning in Virginia between 1772 and 1810. In South Carolina, the Rev. Richard Ludlam mentioned "secret poisonings" as early as the 1720s. The administering of poison by a slave was made a felony (alongside arson) in the colony's sweeping Negro Act of 1740. No doubt in times of general unrest many poisoning incidents involved only exaggerated fear and paranoia on the part of whites, but what made the circle so vicious was the fact that the art of poisoning was undeniably used by certain Africans as one of the most logical and lethal methods of resistance.

The year 1751 was striking in this regard. The Rev. William Cotes of Dorchester expressed discouragement about the slaves in St. George's Parish, a "horrid practice of poisoning their Masters, or those set over them, having lately prevailed among them. For this practice, 5 or 6 in our Parish have been condemned to die, altho 40 or 50 more were privy to it." In the same year the assemblymen attempted to concoct a legal antidote of their own. They passed an addition to the existing Negro Act, noting that "the detestable crime of poisoning hath of late been frequently committed by many slaves in this Province, and notwithstanding the execution of several criminals for that offence, yet it has not been sufficient to deter others from being guilty of the same." The legislation declared that any Negroes convicted of procuring, conveying, or administering poison, and any other privy to such acts, would suffer death. A £4 reward was offered to any Negro informing on others who had poison in their possession, and a strict clause was included against false informers.

Three additional clauses in the measure of

1751 suggest the seriousness with which white legislators viewed the poisoning threat. They attempted belatedly to root out longstanding Negro knowledge about, access to, and administration of medicinal drugs. It was enacted "That in case any slave shall teach or instruct another slave in the knowledge of any poisonous root, plant, herb, or other poison whatever, he or she, so offending, shall, upon conviction thereof, suffer death as a felon." The student was to receive a lesser punishment. "And to prevent, as much as may be, all slaves from attaining the knowledge of any mineral or vegetable poison," the act went on, "it shall not be lawful for any physician, apothecary or druggist, at any time hereafter, to employ any slave or slaves in the shops or places where they keep their medicines or drugs." Finally, the act provided that "no negroes or other slaves (commonly called doctors,) shall hereafter be suffered or permitted to administer any medicine, or pretended medicine, to any other slave; but at the instance or by the direction of some white person," and any Negro disobeying this clause was subject to "corporal punishment, not exceeding fifty stripes." No other law in the settlement's history imposed such a severe whipping upon a Negro.

A letter written years later by Alexander Garden, the famous Charlestown physician, sheds further light on the subject of poisonings. The outspoken Garden was forthright in criticizing his own profession, observing to his former teacher in Edinburgh that among South Carolina's whites, "some have been actually poisoned by their slaves and hundreds [have] died by the unskilfulness of the practitioners in mismanaging acute disorders." He claimed that when local doctors confronted cases

> proving both too obstinate and complicated for them, they immediately call them poisonous cases and so they screen their own ignorance, for the Friends never blame the doctors neglect or ignorance when they think that the case is poison, as they readily think that lies out of the powers of medicine. And thus the word *Poison* . . . has been as good a screen to ignorance here as ever that of *Malignancy* was in Britain.

Nevertheless, actual instances of poisoning intrigued Garden, and he put forward a scheme "To examine the nature of vegetable poisons in general." He took the association with Africa most seriously and requested from his colleague "assistance in giving me what information you could about the African Poisons, as I greatly and do still suspect that the Negroes bring their knowledge of the poisonous plants, which they use here, with them from their own country." Perhaps most conclusive of all is the fact that Garden listed explicitly as part of his plan "To investigate the nature of particular poisons (chiefly those indigenous in this province and Africa)."

But apparently neither strict legislation nor scientific observation could be effective in suppressing such resistance, for in 1761 the *Gazette* reported that "The negroes have again begun the hellish practice of poisoning." Eight years later several more instances were detected, and although the apparent "instigator of these horrid crimes," a mulatto former slave named Dick, made good his escape, two other Negroes were publicly burned at the stake. According to the account in a special issue of the *Gazette*, Dolly, belonging to Mr. James Sands and a slave man named Liverpool were both burned alive on the workhouse green, "the former for poisoning an infant of Mr. Sands's which died some time since, and attempting to put her master out of the world the same way; and the latter (a Negro Doctor) for furnishing the means." The woman was reported to have "made a free confession, acknowledged the justice of her punishment, and died a penitent," but the man denied his guilt until the end.

In 1770 the colony of Georgia passed a law similar to South Carolina's, but the practice was not curtailed. The Rev. Muhlenberg, living in the region in 1774, entered in his journal for October 1: "Visit from Mr. J[acob] M[ack], a neighbor of the Rev. Mr. Rabenhorst, who told me with sorrow that some time ago a household negress had given poison to Pastor Rabenhorst and his wife." The next week Muhlenberg recorded (October 10):

He also told me the circumstances of the poisoning of Mr. Rabenhorst and his wife. One evening about six weeks ago an old, sullen house negress had taken some arsenic, which she had been using to kill rats, and put it into the coffee, seeking to kill her master and mistress. As soon as Mr. Rabenhorst drank the first cup of it he became dizzy and sick and had to vomit. Mrs. R, supposing it to be caused by something else, also drank a cup, whereupon she immediately suffered the same violent effects. When the contents of the coffee-pot were examined, the poison was discovered in the grounds. They were in extreme peril of death, but by God's grace were saved by the use of powerful medicines. The negress is said to have betrayed herself by saying to the other negress [an informer?], "I thought my master and mistress would get enough, but it was not sufficient." The negress fell into the hands of the authorities, was condemned, and after several weeks burned alive.

The act of arson, highly destructive and difficult to detect, provided another peculiarly suitable means of subversion. Early in the century, with considerable forced labor being used to produce naval stores, the governor urged the Assembly "to make it ffelony without benefitt of Clergy, willfully to Sett ffire to any uncovered Tarrkiln or Pitch and Tarr in Barrells, as in like cases, ffiring Houses and Barnes." In later decades arsonists also fired stores of rice, and the Negro Act of 1740 was explicit in declaring death for "any slave, free negro, mulattoe, Indian or mustizoe, [who] shall wilfully and maliciously burn or destroy any stack of rice, corn, or other grain."

Indeed, as rice production intensified, the number of barns which burned between the months of October and January (when the majority of slaves were being pressed to clean and barrel the annual crop) increased suspiciously. A telling to the *Gazette* in October 1732 reads:

Sir,
I Have taken Notice for Several Years past, that there has not one Winter elapsed, without one or more Barns being burnt, and two Winters since, there was no less than five. Whether it is owing to

Accident, Carelessness, or Severity, I will not pretend to determine; but am afraid, chiefly to the two latter. I desire therefore, as a Friend to the Planters, that you'll insert the following Account from Pon Pon, which, I hope, will forewarn the Planters of their Danger, and make them for the future, more careful and human.

About 3 Weeks since, Mr. James Gray work'd his Negroes late in his Barn at Night, and the next Morning before Day, hurried them out again, and when they came to it, found it burnt down to the Ground, and all that was in it.

Several years later, just after Christmas, "the Barn of Mr. John Fairchild at Wassamsaw, with all his Crop was burnt down to the Ground," and in November 1742, "a Barn, belonging to Mr. Hume, at Goose-Creek, was burnt in the Night, and near 70 Barrels of Rice consumed."

Undoubtedly Negroes were occasionally made the scapegoats for fires which occurred by chance. The Rev. Le Jau relates vividly how a woman being burned alive on the charge of setting fire to her master's house in 1709 "protested her innocence . . . to the last." But as with accusations of poisoning, numerous Negroes charged with burning their masters' homes had actually resorted to such sabotage. Moreover, arson could occur in conjunction with other offenses, serving to cover evidence or divert attention. Runaways sometimes resorted to setting fires, and arson was occasionally linked to crimes of violence as well. The following news item from South Carolina appeared in Ireland's *Belfast News Letter,* May 10, 1763:

Charlestown, March 16. A most shocking murder was committed a few weeks ago, near Orangeburg by a Negro fellow belonging to one John Meyer, who happened to come to Charlestown; the cruel wretch murdered Mrs. Meyer, her daughter, about 16 years of age, and her sucking infant; he then dressed himself in his Master's best cloaths and set fire to the house, which was burnt to the ground; three other children of Mr. Meyers made their escape and alarmed the neighbors, some of whom did not live above half a mile distant. The murderer was taken up next day and by a Jury of

Magistrates and Freeholders condemned to be burnt alive at a stake which was accordingly executed. The unfortunate husband and father, we are told, is almost, if not entirely distracted by his misfortunes; it is said both he and his wife used the barbarous destroyer of their family and substance with remarkable tenderness and lenity.

It was fires within the town limits which aroused the greatest concern among white colonists, for not only were numerous lives and buildings endangered, but the prospect of subsequent disorder and vandalism by the city's enslaved residents was obvious. A fire engine was purchased by public subscription in the 1730s. But it proved of little use in 1740, when the Carolina colony, having experienced several epidemics and a series of slave conspiracies in rapid succession, added a severe fire to its "Continued Series of misfortunes." On the afternoon of Tuesday, November 18, flames broke out near the center of Charlestown, and whipped by a northwest wind, burned out of control for six hours, consuming some three hundred houses, destroying crucial new fortifications, and causing property losses estimated at £250,000 sterling.

Even though 2 P.M. seemed an unlikely hour for slave arson, there were strong suspicions about the origin of the holocaust. Not long before, in the strained atmosphere following the Stono Uprising, a slave had been accused of setting fire to the home of Mr. Snow and had been burned to death for the crime. Officials suspected the Spanish of instigating arson by Negroes as one form of resistance, for an act passed the previous April charged the Spaniards in St. Augustine with, "encouraging thither the desertion of our Slaves and . . . exciting them to rise here in Rebellion and to commit Massacres and Assassinations and the burning of Houses in divers parts of this Province of which practices there have of late been many proof[s]."

Word of the November fire reaching northern ports was accompanied by rumors of arson and insurrection. In January a Boston paper had to print a revised account of the fire, saying the story "that the Negroes rose upon the Whites at the same Time, and that therefore it was sup-

posed to be done by them, turns out to be a Mistake, it happening by some Accident." The story finally reaching London was that the flames were "said to have begun among some Shavings in a Saddler's Shop."

Whatever the actual cause of the fire, the white minority feared Negro violence in the aftermath of the blaze. "It is inexpressible to relate to you the dismal Scheme [scene?] . . . ," Robert Pringle wrote to his brother in London, "the best part of this Town being laid in Ashes." He blamed his "Incorrect Confus'd Scrawl" on the fact that he had hardly slept in the three days since the fire. He cited as an explanation "the great Risque we Run from an Insurrection of our Negroes which we were very apprehensive off but all as yet Quiet by the strict Guards & watch we are oblig'd to keep Constantly night & Day." In a letter the next week he mentioned that much property had been stolen and concealed, apparently by freemen and slaves alike. But large-scale disorder was prevented, and Negro labor was soon at work "pulling down the Ruins of Charles Town" and clearing away rubble for the arduous task of rebuilding.

Regardless of its true origins, the November fire could only have confirmed to slaves the effectiveness of arson. Moreover, there was word the following spring of Negro incendiaries at work in the northern colonies, supposedly with Spanish connections. On July 30, 1741, the *Gazette* contained a front-page story about a rash of barn-burnings in Hackensack, New Jersey. The next page was given over to details of an arson plot in New York City, for which nine Negroes had already been burned at the stake. The conspiracy, stated the report from New York,

was calculated, not only to ruin and destroy this City, but the whole Province, and it appears that to effect this their Design was first to burn the Fort, and if Opportunity favoured to seize and carry away the Arms in store there, then to burn the whole Town, and kill and murder all the Male Inhabitants thereof (the Females they intended to reserve for their own Use) and this to be effected by seizing their Master's Arms and a general

Rising, it appears also as we are informed, that these Designs were not only carried on in this City, but had also spread into the country. . . . And so far had they gone that the particular Places to be burnt were laid out, their Captains and Other Officers appointed, and their places of general Rendezvous fixed, and the Number of Negroes concern'd is almost incredible, and their barbarous Designs still more so. . . .

It may not be coincidence that within five days after these lurid reports appeared in Charlestown several slaves attempted to kindle another fire in the city. After dark a mulatto slave woman named Kate and a man named Boatswain entered Mrs. Snowden's house in Unity Alley, climbed to the roof, and placed a small bundle of straw on the shingles so that it rested under the gables of the adjoining house, belonging to Moses Mitchell and fronting on Union Street. They lit the tinder with a brand's end, and the fire they started might have been capable "of burning down the remaining Part of the Town," had not Mrs. Mitchell, walking in her yard, spotted the blaze so promptly that it could be dowsed with several pails of drinking water.

An old Negro woman who heard one of the arsonists stumble descending the stairs testified against Kate, and within forty-eight hours she had been tried, convicted, and sentenced to die. At the eleventh hour, upon promise of pardon, Kate named Boatswain as a co-conspirator, and he in turn was sentenced to burn alive. According to the *Gazette*'s account, "On his Tryal after much Preverication and accusing many Negroes, who upon a strict Examination were found to be innocent, he confessed that none but he and *Kate* were concerned." Since Boatswain "looked upon every white Man he should meet as his declared Enemy," his prosecutors concluded that the incident stemmed from "his own sottish wicked Heart," and that there was probably no larger plot. The same people may have been somewhat less sanguine several months later, when two slaves were found guilty of attempting to set fire to the city's powder magazine.

Arson, real and suspected, remained a recurring feature in eighteenth-century South Carolina. In 1754, for example, a slave named Sacharisa was sentenced to burn at the stake for setting fire to her owner's house in Charlestown. Two years later a suspicious fire started on a town wharf in the middle of the night. In 1797 two slaves were deported and several others were hanged for conspiring to burn down the city. In some ways the protracted Charleston Fire Scare of 1825 and 1826, which came four years after the Denmark Vesey Plot, was reminiscent of the concern for arson which followed in the wake of the Stono Uprising of 1739.

While poisoning and arson rarely involved more than one or two compatriots, organized forms of resistance, which involved greater numbers (and therefore higher risks), were not unknown in the royal colony. In fact uprisings appear to have been attempted or planned repeatedly by slaves. For obvious reasons, published sources are irregular on these matters—the *South Carolina Gazette* refrained from mentioning the Stono incident, which occurred within twenty miles of Charlestown—but a number of conspiracies were recorded. In these instances it is sometimes difficult to categorize the objectives of the insurgents, since often a will to overpower the Europeans and a desire to escape from the colony were intertwined in the same plot. The province's first major conspiracy, uncovered in 1720, provides a case in point. "I am now to acquaint you," wrote a Carolina correspondent to the colony's London agent in June, "that very lately we have had a very wicked and barbarous plott of the designe of the negroes rising with a designe to destroy all the white people in the country and then to take the town in full body." He continued that through God's will "it was discovered and many of them taken prisoners and some burnt some hang'd and some banish'd." At least some participants in the scheme "thought to gett to Augustine" if they could convince a member of the Creek tribe to guide them, "but the Savanna garrison tooke the negroes up half starved and the Creeke Indians would not join them or be their pylott." A party of whites and Indians had been dispatched to

"Savanna Towne," where fourteen captives were being held, and it was planned that these rebels would "be executed as soon as they came down."

This incident, or perhaps another similar one, was mentioned in an official representation sent to the king late in 1721. His majesty was informed that the "black slaves . . . have lately attempted and were very near succeeding in a new revolution, which would probably have been attended by the utter extirpation of all your Majesty's subjects in this province." Not surprisingly, the Negro Act of the following year spelled out more fully than ever the punishments to be inflicted on any slaves attempting to rebel or conspiring together or gathering up "arms, powder, bullets, or offensive weapons in order to carry on such mutiny or insurrection." A minister's letter from Goose Creek Parish in 1724 ascribed "secret poisonings and bloody insurrection" to certain Christian slaves.

Another scantily documented incident occurred in mid-August 1730. A letter written five days after the episode and published in Boston conveyed the initial shock and fatalism felt by many whites. It mentioned the prominent causes of failure in such attempts—divided leadership, insufficient recruitment, and premature discovery.

I shall give an Account [the correspondent wrote from Charlestown] of a bloody Tragedy which was to have been executed here last Saturday night (the 15th Inst.) by the Negroes, who had conspired to Rise and destroy us, and had almost bro't it to pass: but it pleased God to appear for us, and confound their Councils. For some of them propos'd that the Negroes of every Plantation should destroy their own Masters; but others were for Rising in a Body, and giving the blow at once on surprise; and thus they differ'd. They soon made a great Body at the back of the Town, and had a great Dance, and expected the Country Negroes to come & join them; and had not an overruling Providence discovered their Intrigues, we had been all in Blood. . . . The Chief of them, with some others, is apprehended and in Irons, in order to a Tryal, and we are in Hopes to find out the whole Affair.

What few details came to light may have been embroidered with time, for it seems likely that this foiled rebellion provided the basis for the tale told during the Revolution concerning a narrowly averted "Sicilian Vespers." Although the Hessian officer, named Hinrichs, who recorded the story mistakenly placed it in 1736, the scheme he described, like the one narrated in the Boston letter, unfolded in August and involved conflicting plans for plantation murders and an attack on Charlestown. Moreover, it took the form of a large gathering several miles outside the city two days before the intended coup and ended only "when fate was merciful and betrayed the horrible plot." Sine all these details conform with the letter sent to Boston, there seems little doubt that Hinrichs was referring to the incident of 1730. There is probably substance to his concluding remark that "Through torture and punishment their leaders were found out . . . and . . . tortured to death, while many others were subjected to severe bodily punishment."

Despite harsh reprisals, however, secret gatherings of slaves, sometimes exceeding one hundred people, were again reported within several years. In February 1733 the Assembly urged the slave patrols to special watchfulness and ordered a dozen slaves brought in for questioning, but there is no sign that any offense was uncovered. Late in 1736 a white citizen appears to have sought a reward for uncovering a Negro plot. Early in the following year the provost marshal took up three Negroes "suspected to be concerned in some Conspiracy against the Peace of this Government," and although the Assembly cleared and released the most prominent suspect, it did not deny the existence of a plot.

By September 1738 the government had completed "An Act for the further Security and better Defence of this Province" and given instructions that the two paragraphs relating to slaves were to be reprinted in the *Gazette*. The paper complied several days later by publishing the section which ordered that within a month every slaveowner in the colony was to turn in to the militia captain of his local precinct "a true and faithful List, in Writing, of all the Slaves of such

Persons, or which are under their Care or Management, from the Age of 16 Years to the Age of Sixty Years." Each list was required to specify "the Names, Ages and Country of all such Slaves respectively, according to the best of the Knowledge and Belief of the Persons returning the same."

The statute imposed a heavy fine of £100 upon any master who neglected or refused to comply, so that the required local lists (if collected and sent to the governor annually as authorized) must have constituted a thorough census of the colony's adult slaves. The unlikely reappearance of even a portion of these lists would be a remarkable boon to historians, in light of the unique request for the original country of all slaves. This detail appears to bear witness to the fact that masters were generally interested and informed as to the origins of the Negroes they owned. It may also reflect the belief, commonly accepted in the Carolinas as elsewhere, that new slaves from Africa posed the greatest threat to the security of the white settlers. John Brickell explained at this time, "The Negroes that most commonly rebel, are those brought from Guinea, and who have been inured to War and Hardship all their lives; few born here, or in the other Provinces have been guilty of these vile Practices." When country-born slaves did contemplate rebellion, Brickell claimed, it was because they were urged to it by newcomers "whose Designs they have sometimes discovered to the Christians" in order to be "rewarded with their Freedom for their good Services."

The thought that newcomers from Africa were the slaves most likely to rebel does not appear to have been idle speculation, for the late 1730s, a time of conspicuous unrest, was also a time of massive importation. In fact, at no earlier or later date did recently arrived Africans (whom we might arbitrarily define as all those slave immigrants who had been in the colony less than a decade) comprise such a large proportion of South Carolina's Negro population. By 1740 the black inhabitants of the colony numbered roughly 39,000. During the preceding decade more than 20,000 slaves had been imported from Africa. Since there is little evidence that mortality was disproportionately high among newcomers, this means that by the end of the 1730s fully half of the colony's Negroes had lived in the New World less than ten years. This proportion had been growing steadily. In 1720 fewer than 5 per cent of black adults had been there less than a decade (and many of these had spent time in the West Indies); by 1730 roughly 40 per cent were such recent arrivals. Heavy importation and low natural increase sent the figure over 50 per cent by 1740, but it dropped sharply during the nearly total embargo of the next decade, and after that point the established black population was large enough so that the percentage of newcomers never rose so high again.

Each of the lowland parishes must have reflected this shift in the same way. In St. Paul's for example, where the Stono Uprising originated, there were only 1,634 slaves in 1720, the large majority of whom had been born in the province or brought there long before. By contrast, in 1742 the parish's new Anglican minister listed 3,829 "heathens and infidels" in his cure, well over 3,000 of whom must have been slaves. Of these, perhaps as many as 1,500 had been purchased in Charlestown since 1730. A predominant number of the Africans reaching the colony between 1735 and 1739 have been shown to have come from Angola, so it is likely that at the time of the Stono Uprising there were close to 1,000 residents of St. Paul's Parish who had lived in the Congo-Angola region of Africa less than ten years before. While this figure is only an estimate, it lends support to the assertion in one contemporary source that most of the conspirators in the 1739 incident were Angolans. The suggestion seems not only plausible, but even probable.

European settlers contemplating the prospects of rebellion, however, seem to have been more concerned with the contacts the slaves might establish in the future than with experience that came from their past. White colonists were already beginning to subscribe to the belief that most Negro unrest was necessarily traceable to outside agitators. Like most shibboleths of the slave culture, this idea contained a kernel of truth, and it is one of the difficult tasks in considering the records of the 1730s and 1740s to separate the unreasonable fears of white Carolinians from their very justifiable concerns.

Numerous anxieties were intertwined. It was all too clear, for example, that internal and external threats to white security were likely to coincide and reinforce each other, if for no other reason than that the militia with its dual responsibilities for defense and control was divided and thereby weakened in times of trouble. Even if not linked beforehand, hostile elements inside and outside the colony could be expected to join forces during any alarm, so Europeans were as anxious about foreign infiltration as domestic conspiracy. For this reason Indians often appeared to be the slaves' likeliest allies. For example, suspicion of a Negro plot had scarcely died in 1733, when an Indian slave was brought before the Assembly. He testified "that an Indian Woman had told him that all the Indians on the Continent design'd to rise and make War, against the English." Had such word contained any substance it might have triggered slave impulses to rise against the English as well, but this particular rumor apparently lacked foundation, and the informant was dismissed.

The following spring the Assembly sent a memorial to the king, outlining the threats posed by the Indians, Spanish, and French and asking assistance in defense. This document from 1734 stressed that white colonists faced "many intestine Dangers from the great Number of Negroes" and went on to observe, "Insurrections against us have been often attempted, and would at any time prove very fatal if the French should instigate them by artfully giving them [the Negroes] an Expectation of Freedom." The next ten years were filled with enough dangers—real and imagined—from these various quarters to keep the English in a constant state of agitation. In 1748 James Glen, thinking back to this period, summarized the sea of anxieties which had beset white Carolinians:

Sometime ago the People of this Province were Annually alarmed with accounts of intended Invasions, & even in time of profound Peace they were made believe that the Spaniards had prepared Embarkations for that purpose at St. Augustine & the Havanna, or that the French were marching by Land from Louisiana with more Men than ever were in that Country to drive us into the Sea. Sometimes the Negroes were to rise & cut their Masters Throats at other times the Indians were confederating to destroy us.

Of the various sources of outside agitation none seemed so continually threatening after 1720 as St. Augustine, for the abduction and provocation of slaves by the Spanish were issues of constant concern. While London and Madrid were reaching a peace settlement in 1713, Charlestown and St. Augustine had renewed their agreement concerning the mutual return of runaways, but Spanish depredations continued long after the conclusion of the Yamasee War. During the 1720s Spanish ships, "stiling themselves Guarda-Costas on Pretence of searching," plundered or captured English vessels bound for southern ports. Often Africans were aboard these boats, as in the case of the sloop *Ann*, seized in 1721 coming form Barbados to South Carolina with a cargo of sugar, rum, and Negroes. The disappearance to the southward of slaves owned in South Carolina continued also. In December 1722 a committee of both Houses concerned with the return of slaves from St. Augustine urged higher rewards for taking up runaways. To guard against infiltrators who might encourage such defections, the committee also suggested that "a Law be passed to Oblige all Persons possessing Spanish Indians and Negroes to transport them off the Country." A mission sent to Florida in 1726 to confirm that agreement about returning fugitives seems to have accomplished little, for the Assembly soon received a petition from Thomas Elliott and several other planters near Stono seeking government action since they had "had fourteen Slaves Runaway to St. Augustine."

In June 1728 Acting Gov. Arthur Middleton sent a formal complaint to authorities in London that not only were the Spanish "receivieing and harbouring all our Runaway Negroes," but also,

"They have found out a New way of sending our own slaves against us, to Rob and Plunder us;— They are continually fitting out Partys of Indians from St. Augustine to Murder our White People, Rob our Plantations and carry off our slaves," Middleton stated, "soe that We are not only at a vast expence in Guarding our Southern Frontiers, but the Inhabitants are continually Allarmed, and have noe leizure to looke after theire Crops." The irate leader added that "the Indians they send against us are sent out in small Partys . . . and sometimes joined wth Negroes, and all the Mischeife they doe, is on a sudden and by surprize."

These petty incursions soon subsided. Nevertheless, rumors reached South Carolina in 1737 from the West Indies of a full-scale Spanish invasion intended, in the words of Lt. Gov. Thomas Broughton, to "unsettle then colony of Georgia, and to excite an Insurrection of the Negroes of this Province." He reported to the Lords of Trade that the militia had been alerted, "and as our Negroes are very numerous An Act of the General Assembly is passed, to establish Patrols throughout the Country to keep the Negroes in order."

The threatened assault never materialized, but in the meantime a new element was added to the situation. Late in 1733 the Spanish king issued a royal *cédula* granting liberty to Negro fugitives reaching St. Augustine from the English colonies. The edict was not immediately put into effect, and incoming slaves continued to be sold, but in March 1738 a group of these former runaways appealed successfully to the new governor for their freedom and obtained it. Seignior Don Manuel de Montiano established them on land two and a half miles north of St. Augustine at a site called the Pueblo de Gracia Real de Santa Terese de Mose, which soon became known as "Moosa." With the approval of the Council of the Indies, the governor undertook to provision this settlement of several dozen families until its first harvest and arranged for a Catholic priest to offer them instruction. He may also have urged other slaves to join them, for the captain of an English

coasting schooner returning to Beaufort the folowing month testified that "he heard a Proclamation made at S[t] Augustine, that all Negroes, who did, or should hereafter, run away from the English, should be made free." As a result, according to the captain, "several Negroes who ran away thither, and were sold there, were thereupon made free, and the Purchasers lost their Money."

In November 1738 nineteen slaves belonging to Capt. Caleb Davis "and 50 other Slaves belonging to other Persons inhabiting about Port Royal ran away to the Castle of St. Augustine." Those who made it joined the Negro settlement at Moosa. It was apparently at this time that the Catholic king's edict of 1733 was published (in the words of a South Carolina report)

> by Beat of Drum round the Town of St. Augustine (where many Negroes belonging to English Vessels that carried thither Supplies of Provisions &c. had the Opportunity of hearing it) promising Liberty and Protection to all Slaves that should desert thither from any of the English Colonies but more especially from this. And lest that should not prove sufficient of itself, secret Measures were taken to make it known to our Slaves in general. In consequence of which Numbers of Slaves did from Time to Time by Land and Water desert to St. Augustine; and the better to facilitate their Escape carried off their Master's Horses, Boats &c. some of them first committing Murder; and were accordingly received and declared free.

When Capt. Davis went to St. Augustine to recover his slaves he was pointedly rebuffed, a sign for Carolina's legislature that this difficulty might grow worse in the coming year. Any premonitions which colonial officials might have felt were to prove justifiable, for the year 1739 was a tumultuous and decisive one in the evolution of South Carolina. Only the merest twist of circumstances prevented it from being remembered as a fateful turning point in the social history of the early South.

6

THE SMALL CIRCLE OF DOMESTIC CONCERNS

MARY BETH NORTON

Throughout the colonial period, American women lived their lives in a world dominated by men. Subject to the will of their fathers from birth until marriage, once married they became wards of their husbands with no legal rights of their own. Yet despite their subordinate status, women formed a vital and indispensable part of the family economy, as Mary Beth Norton reveals in this essay. Whether their fathers and husbands farmed, traded, or crafted manufactured goods, women spent their days near the household, cooking, cleaning, rearing children, making cloth and clothing, tending vegetables, and maintaining the pigs, chickens, and cows that supplemented the family diet.

But while domestic concerns dominated the lives of all early American women, the character of their lives varied considerably, depending upon their race and class as well as the region in which they lived. Thus Norton shows that while everyday life on the frontier was dominated by an unremitting round of daily and weekly chores with little chance for recreation and sociability, the markets and density of urban life permitted middling-class women a much greater measure of leisure and conviviality. Equally, while northern wives might have overseen the work of apprentices or household servants as part of their family duties, the wives of southern planters were veritable managers of households that extended far beyond the Great House to encompass the welfare of all those who lived on the estate. Domesticity, this essay demonstrates, took many different forms in seventeenth- and eighteenth-century America.

From Liberty's Daughters *by Mary Beth Norton (Glenview, IL: Scott, Foresman and Company, 1980). Coyright © 1980 Scott, Foresman and Company. Reprinted by permission.*

The household, the basic unit of eighteenth-century American society, had a universally understood hierarchical structure. At the top was the man, the lord of the fireside; next came the mistress, his wife and helpmate; following her, the children, who were expected to assist the parent of their own sex; and, finally, any servants or slaves, with the former taking precedence over the latter. Each family was represented in the outside world by its male head, who cast its single vote in elections and fulfilled its obligations to the community through service in the militia or public office. Within the home, the man controlled the finances, oversaw the upbringing of the children, and exercised a nominal supervision over household affairs. Married men understandably referred to all their dependents collectively as "my family," thereby expressing the proprietary attitude they so obviously felt.

The mistress of the household, as befitted her inferior position, consistently employed the less proprietary phrase "our family." Yet she, and not her husband, directed the household's day-to-day activities. Her role was domestic and private, in contrast to his public, supervisory functions. As the Marylander Samuel Purviance told his teenaged daughter Betsy in 1787, "the great Province of a Woman" was "Economy and Frugality in the management of [a] Family." Even if the household were wealthy, he stressed, "the meanest Affairs, are all and ought to be Objects of a womans cares." Purviance and his contemporaries would have concurred with the position taken in an article in Caleb Bingham's *The American Preceptor*, a textbook widely used in the early republic: "[N]eedle work, the care of domestic affairs, and a serious and retired life, is the proper function of women, and for this they were designed by Providence."

Of course, such statements applied only to whites, for no eighteenth-century white American would have contended that enslaved black women should work solely at domestic tasks. But the labor of female slaves too was affected by their sexual identity, for they were often assigned jobs that differed from those of male slaves, even though such tasks were not exclusively domestic. Appropriately, then, an analysis of black and white women's experiences in eighteenth-century America must begin with an examination of their household responsibilities.

I

"I have a great and longing desire to be very notable," wrote a Virginia bride in 1801, declaring her allegiance to the ideal of early American white womanhood. In this context, the adjective "notable" connoted a woman's ability to manage her household affairs skillfully and smoothly. Thus the prominent clergyman Ezra Stiles asked that his daughter be educated in such a way as to "lay a founda[tion] of a notable Woman," and a Rhode Islander wrote of a young relative that she "Sets out to be a Notable house Wife." When the Virginian Fanny Tucker Coalter exuberantly told her husband, John, "I'm the picture of bustling notability," he could have had no doubt about her meaning.

The characteristics of the notable wife were best described by Governor William Livingston of New Jersey in his essay entitled "Our Grand-Mothers," which was printed posthumously in two American magazines in the early 1790s. Decrying his female contemporaries' apparent abandonment of traditional values, Livingston presented a romanticized picture of the colonial women of the past. Such wives "placed their renown" in promoting the welfare of their families, Livingston asserted. "They were strangers to dissipation; . . . their own habitation was their delight." They not only practiced economy, thereby saving their husbands' earnings, but they also "augmented their treasure, by their industry." Most important, "they maintained good order and harmony in their empire" and "enjoyed happiness in their chimney corners," passing on these same qualities to the daughters they carefully raised to be like themselves. Their homes, in short, were "the source of their pleasure; and the foundation of their glory."

Although other accounts of the attributes of notable housewives were couched in less sentimental form, their message was the same. Ministers preaching funeral sermons for women often took as their text Proverbs 31, with its description of the virtuous woman who "looketh well to the Ways of her Household and eateth not the Bread of Idleness." So too drafters of obituaries and memorial statements emphasized the sterling housewifely talents of the women they eulogized. Such a model of female perfection did not allow a woman an independent existence: ideally, she would maintain no identity separate from that of her male-defined family and her household responsibilities. A man like James Kent, the distinguished New York lawyer, could smugly describe himself as "the independent . . . *Lord of my own fireside,*" while women, as William Livingston had declared, were expected to tend the hearth and find "happiness in their chimney corners."

These contrasting images of autonomy and subordination were translated into reality in mid-eighteenth-century American household organization. Although the mistress directed the daily life of the household, her position within the home was secondary to that of her husband. She was expected to follow his orders, and he assumed control over the family finances. In 1750, the anonymous author of *Reflections on Courtship and Marriage,* a pamphlet long erroneously attributed to Benjamin Franklin, told men that it "would be but just and prudent to inform and consult a wife" before making "very important" decisions about monetary matters, but evidence drawn from a variety of sources indicates that few colonial husbands followed this advice. Instead, they appear to have kept the reins of financial management firmly in their own hands, rarely if ever informing their wives about even the basic details of monetary transactions.

The most comprehensive evidence of this phenomenon comes from an analysis of the claims for lost property submitted by 468 white loyalist refugee women after the Revolution. The claims procedure as established by Parliament and carried out by a commission appointed for the purpose required that American loyalists prepare detailed written statements of their losses of property and testify orally about those statements. Because each claimant wanted to receive the maximum possible return on her claim, there was no reason for her to withhold any information from the commission or to feign ignorance of a particular item of property that had belonged to her family. As a result, claims prepared by female refugees, the vast majority of them widows of loyalist men, accurately depict the dimensions of the world in which they had lived prior to the war. If they had participated in economic decision making, the claims documents would demonstrate that fact by revealing their knowledge of their families' financial status. But instead the claims uniformly disclose loyalist women's insulation from the external affairs of the household and their confinement to a wholly domestic realm.

The evidence of women's ignorance of financial affairs takes a variety of forms in the claims records. Rural wives often were unable to place a precise value on tools, lands, or harvested grain, even if they knew a farm's total acreage or the size of the harvest. Urban women frequently did not know their husbands' exact income or the cost of the houses in which they lived. The typical wealthy female was not aware of her husband's net worth because she did not know the amount of his outstanding debts or what was owed to him, and poor women occasionally failed to list any value at all for their meager possessions. Women of all descriptions, moreover, shared an ignorance of legal language and an unfamiliarity with the details of transactions concerning property with which they were not personally acquainted. The sole exceptions to their rule were a few widows who had already served several years as executrices of the family estates; some wives of innkeepers, grocers, or other shopkeepers who had assisted their husbands in business; and a small number of single women who had supported themselves through their own efforts.

Loyalist husbands, then, did not normally discuss economic decisions with their wives. The women lacked exactly that information which their husbands alone could have supplied, for they were able to describe only those parts of the property with which they came into regular contact. That the practice in these loyalist homes was not atypical is shown when one looks at patriot families as well.

American wives and widows alike repeatedly noted their lack of information about their husbands' business dealings. "I don't know anything of his affairs," a Virginian resident in London wrote in 1757; "whether his income will admit of our living in the manner we do, I am a stranger to." Elizabeth Sandwith Drinker, a Philadelphia Quaker, commented years later, "I am not acquainted with the extent of my husband's great variety of engagements," quoting an apposite poem that began, "I stay much at home, and my business I mind." To such married women, their spouses' financial affairs were not of immediate import. But widows, by contrast, had to cope with the consequences of their ignorance. On his deathbed, a New England cleric surprised his wife with the news that she would have "many debts to pay that [she] knew nothing about," and her subsequent experience was replicated many times over—by the Marylander whose husband left no records to guide her administration of his estate, by the Virginian who had to tell her husband's employer that he had evidently neglected to maintain proper rent rolls, by the New Yorker who admitted to her son-in-law that she had known "very little" of her spouse's affairs before his death.

It might seem extraordinary that colonial men failed to recognize the potential benefits—to their children and their estates, if not to themselves—of keeping their wives informed about family finances. Yet the responsibility was not theirs alone. Married women rarely appear to have sought economic information from their husbands, whether in anticipation of eventual widowhood or simply out of a desire to understand the family's financial circumstances. On the contrary, women's statements reveal a complete acceptance of the division of their world into two separate, sexually defined spheres.

"Nature & Custom seems to have destined us for the more endearing & private & the Man for the more active & busy Walks of Life," remarked Elizabeth Willing Powel, a leader of Philadelphia society, in 1784. A similar sense of the character of the difference between male and female realms shone through the 1768 observation of a fellow Philadelphian of Mrs. Powel, the teenager Peggy Emlen, who described the men she saw hurrying about the city streets: they "all seem people of a great deal of business and importance, as for me I am not much of either." Men shared this same notion of the dichotomy between male public activity and female private passivity. In 1745, an essayist warned women that they were best "confined within the narrow Limits of Domestick Offices," for "when they stray beyond them, they move excentrically, and consequently without grace." A New Englander twelve years later worried that women might want "to obtain the other's Sphere of Action, & become Men," but he reassured himself that "they will again return to the wonted Paths of true Politeness, & shine most in the proper Sphere of domestick Life."

If women were accordingly out of place in the world beyond the household, so men were not entirely at home in the female realm of domestic affairs. The family property may have been "his" in wives' terminology, but at the same time the household furnishings were "hers" in the minds of their spouses. Wartime letters from American husbands confirm the separation of male and female spheres, more because of what they do not contain than as a result of what they do. When couples were separated by the Revolutionary War, men for the most part neglected to instruct their wives about the ordinary details of domestic life. Since they initially sent explicit directions about financial affairs, their failure to concern themselves with household management would seem to indicate that they had been accustomed to leave that realm entirely to their wives. Only if they had not previously issued orders on domestic subjects would they have failed to include such directives in their correspondence.

The evidence, then, suggests that female whites shared a universal domestic experience that differentiated their world from that of men. Their lives were to a large extent defined by their familial responsibilities, but the precise character of those obligations varied according to the nature of the household in which they resided. Although demographic historians have concentrated upon determining the size of colonial households, from the standpoint of an American woman, size—within a normal range—mattered less than composition. It meant a great deal to a housewife whether she had daughters who could assist her, whether her household contained a helpful servant or demanding elderly relative, or whether she had to contend with a resident mother-in-law for control of her own domestic affairs.

But ultimately of greater significance were differences in the wealth and location of colonial households. The chief factors that defined a white woman's domestic role arose from the family's economic status, which determined whether there would be servants or slaves, and from the household's location in a rural or urban setting. With a similarity of household roles as a basis, one can divide eighteenth-century women into four groups: poor and middling white farm women, north and south; white urban women of all social ranks; wealthy southerners who lived on plantations; and the female blacks held in bondage by those same wealthy southerners.

II

A majority of white women in eighteenth-century America resided in poor or middling farm households, and so it is reasonable to begin a discussion of female domestic work patterns with an assessment of their experience. Their heavy responsibilities are revealed most vividly in accounts left by two city families who moved to rural areas, for farm women were so accustomed to their burdensome obligations that they rarely remarked upon them.

Christopher Marshall and his wife abandoned Philadelphia when the British occupied the city in the fall of 1777, shifting their large family to Lancaster, Pennsylvania. There Marshall mar-

veled at his wife's accomplishments, at how "from early in the morning till late at night, she is constantly employed in the affairs of the family." She not only did the cooking, baking, washing, and ironing, all of which had been handled by servants in their Philadelphia home, but she also milked cows, made cider and cheese, and dried apples. The members of the Palmer family of Germantown, Massachusetts, had a comparable experience when they moved in 1790 to Framingham, about twenty miles west of Boston. Mary Palmer, who was then fifteen and the oldest daughter in the home, later recalled that her father had had difficulty in adjusting to the change in his womenfolk's roles. "It took years to wean him from the idea that we must be ladies," she wrote, "although he knew that we must give up all such pretensions." Mary herself thrived in the new environment. "Kind neighbors" taught her mother how to make butter and cheese, and the girls "assisted in the laborious part, keeping churn, pans, cheese-hoops and strainers nice and sweet." After she married Royall Tyler and set up housekeeping in Brattleboro, Vermont, Mary continued to practice the skills of rural housewifery she had gained as a teenager. Between managing her dairy in the summer and supervising spinning and weaving in the winter, not to mention raising five children, she observed, "I never realized what it was to have time hang heavy."

Mary Palmer's recollections disclose the seasonal nature of much of farm women's labor. Such annual rhythms and the underlying, invariable weekly routine are revealed in the work records kept by farm wives like Sarah Snell Bryant, of Cummington, Massachusetts, and Mary Cooper, of Oyster Bay, Long Island. Each week Mrs. Bryant devoted one day to washing, another to ironing, and a third at least partly to baking. On the other days she sewed, spun, and wove. In the spring she planted her garden; in the early summer she hived her bees; in the fall she made cider and dried apples; and in mid-December came hog-killing time. Mary Cooper recorded the same seasonal round of work, adding to it spring housecleaning, a midsummer cherry harvest, and a long stretch of soapmaking, boiling "souse," rendering fat, and making candles that followed the hog butchering in December. In late 1769, after two weeks of such work, she described herself as "full of freting discontent dirty and miserabel both yesterday and today."

Unlike the laconic Mrs. Bryant, who simply noted the work she had completed each day, Mrs. Cooper frequently commented on the fatiguing nature of her life. "It has been a tiresome day it is now Bed time and I have not had won minutts rest," she wrote in November 1768. One Sunday some months later she remarked, "I hoped for some rest but I am forst to get dinner and slave hard all day long." On those rare occasions when everyone else in the household was away, Mary Cooper understandably breathed a sigh of relief. "I have the Blessing to be quite alone without any Body greate or Small," she noted in late October 1768, and five years later another such day brought thanks for "some quiate moments which I have not had in weeks."

Perhaps one of the reasons why Mrs. Cooper seemed so overworked was her obsession with cleanliness. Since travelers in rural America commented frequently upon the dirt they encountered in farmhouses and isolated taverns, it seems clear either that cleanliness was not highly valued or that farm wives, fully occupied with other tasks, simply had no time to worry about sweeping floors, airing bedding, or putting things away. Mary Cooper's experience suggests that the latter explanation was more likely. Often describing herself as "dirty and distrest," she faithfully recorded her constant battle against filth. "We are cleaning the house and I am tired almost to death," she wrote in December 1768; the following spring, after seven straight days of cleaning, she complained, "O it has been a week of greate toile and no Comfort or piece to Body or mind." Another time she noted with satisfaction, "I have got some clean cloths on thro mercy some little done to clean the house," and again, "Up very late But I have got my Cloths Ironed." Obviously, if a farm woman was not willing to invest almost superhuman effort in the enter-

prise, keeping her household clean was an impossible task.

Mary Cooper's diary is unique in that it conveys explicitly what is only implicit in other farm wives' journals: a sense of drudgery and boredom. Sarah Snell Bryant would record that she had engaged in the same tasks for days on end, but she never noted her reaction to the repetition. This sameness was the quality that differentiated farm women's work from that performed by their husbands. No less physically demanding or difficult, men's tasks varied considerably from day to day and month to month. At most—during planting or harvest time, for example—men would spend two or three weeks at one job. But then they would move on to another. For a farmer, in other words, the basic cycle was yearly; for his wife, it was daily and weekly, with additional obligations superimposed seasonally. Moreover, men were able to break their work routine by making frequent trips to town or the local mill on business, or by going hunting or fishing, whereas their wives, especially if they had small children, were tied to the home.

Rural youngsters of both sexes were expected to assist their parents. "Their children are all brought up in industry, and have their time fully employed in performing the necessary duties of the house and farm," remarked a foreign visitor to a western Pennsylvania homestead in 1796. His inclusion of both sons and daughters was entirely accurate, for although historians have tended to emphasize the value of boys' labor to their fathers, extensive evidence suggests that girls were just as important as aides to their mothers. The fifteen-year-old Elizabeth Fuller, of Princeton, Massachusetts, for example, recorded occasionally baking pies, making candles, scouring floors, mincing meat for sausages, making cheese, and doing laundry, in addition to her primary assignments, spinning and weaving. Nabby and Betsy Foote, sisters who lived in Colchester, Connecticut, likewise noted helping their mother with housework, again in conjunction with their major chores of sewing, spinning, and weaving. When the parents of Ruth Henshaw, of Leicester, Massachusetts, called her home in mid-July 1789 after she had been visiting a relative for four days, saying, she recounted, that they "could not Subsist with out me any longer," they were only expressing what is evident in all these diaries: the labor of daughters, like that of wives, was crucial to the success of a farm household.

Brissot de Warville, an astute foreign traveler, recognized both the value of women's work and the clearly defined gender role distinctions visible in rural life in his observations upon a fellow Frenchman's Pennsylvania farm in 1788. It is a "great disadvantage," Brissot remarked, that "he does not have any poultry or pigeons and makes no cheese; nor does he have any spinning done or collect goose feathers." The reason: he was a bachelor, and "these domestic farm industries . . . can be carried on well only by women." Brissot's friend had two women indentured servants, so he did not lack female labor as such; what was missing was a wife or daughters to supervise the servants. Significantly, neither he nor Brissot seems to have considered the possibility that he could himself keep poultry or learn enough about cheesemaking to direct the servants. That was clearly "woman's work," and if there was no woman present, such work was not done, no matter how pressing the need or how great the resulting loss of potential income.

Yet in some frontier areas the gender role divisions so apparent in more settled regions did blur, although they did not break down entirely. Farmers' wives and daughters occasionally worked in the fields, especially at harvest time. Travelers from the East were unaccustomed to the sight of white female fieldworkers and wrote about it at length. In 1778, for example, a doctor from Dorchester, Massachusetts, told his wife in some amazement that he had seen Pennsylvania German women "at work abroad on the Farm mowing, Hoeing, Loading Dung into a Cart." A New Hampshire farmer, by contrast, matter-of-factly recorded in his diary his use of female relatives and neighbors for field work. In that same colony in the early 1760s the pendulum swung the other way, and men helped with women's work. In the winters, recalled one woman many

years later, "the boys did as much Knitting as the Girls, and the men and boys also did the milking to spare the women."

Backcountry women had to cope with a far more rough-and-ready existence than did their counterparts to the east and south. The log cabins in which many of them lived were crudely built and largely open to the elements. Even the few amenities that brightened the lives of their poor contemporaries in areas of denser settlement were denied them; the Reverend Charles Woodmason, an Anglican missionary in western South Carolina, commented in 1768 that "in many Places they have nought but a Gourd to drink out off Not a Plate Knive or Spoon, a Glass, Cup, or any thing—It is well if they can get some Body Linen, and some have not even that." Later in the century, one woman on the Ohio frontier, lacking a churn, was reduced to making butter by stirring cream with her hand in an ordinary pail. Under such circumstances, simple subsistence would require most of a woman's energies.

How, then, did frontier women react to these primitive conditions? At least one group of pioneer men termed their wives "the greatest of Heroines," suggesting that they bore such hardships without complaint, but other evidence indicates that some women, especially those raised in genteel households, did not adapt readily to their new lives. Many, like a Pennsylvanian, must have vetoed their husbands' plans to move west because of an unwillingness to exchange a civilized life for a residence in "what she deems a Wilderness." Others must have resembled the Shenandoah Valley woman, a mother of eight, who descended into invalidism shortly after her husband moved her and their children to what their son described as a "valuable Farm but with a small indifferent house . . . & almost intirely in woods." Perhaps, like a female traveler in the west, the Virginian "felt oppress'd with so much wood towering above . . . in every direction and such a continuance of it." This was not a unique reaction: a Scottish immigrant, faced with his wife's similar response to the first sight of their new home, comforted her by promising, "[W]e would get all these trees cut down . . . [so] that we would see from house to house."

At least in this case the husband knew of his wife's discontent and reacted to it. In other instances, the lack of communication between spouses resulting from their divergent roles appears to have been heightened on the frontier, as wives deliberately concealed their unhappiness from their husbands, revealing their true feelings only to female relatives. Mary Hooper Spence, who described herself as having been beset by "misfortunes" ever since the day of her marriage, lived with her husband on the "dreary & cold" island of St. Johns (now Prince Edward Island) in the 1770s. In letters to her mother in Boston she repeatedly told of her loneliness and depression, of how she found a primitive, isolated existence "hard to bear." By contrast, her husband characterized their life as "happy" and reported to a relative that they were "comfortably" settled. Likewise, Mrs. Joseph Gilman, said by her husband to be pleased with living in the new settlement of Marietta, Ohio, in 1789, later recounted that on many occasions while milking their cows she would think of her New England home, "sob and cry as loud as a child, and then wipe her tears and appear before her husband as cheerful as if she had nothing to give her pain."

To point out the apparent dissatisfaction of many frontier women with their lives in the wilderness is not to say that they and others did not cope successfully with the trials they encountered. To cite just one example: Mrs. Hutchens, a Mississippi woman whose husband was kidnapped and whose slaves were stolen, pulled her family together in the face of adversity almost by sheer force of will alone. Her son subsequently recalled that she had told her children they could survive if they were willing to work. Accordingly, she and her three sons cultivated the fields while her daughters did the housework, spun cotton, and wove the fabric for their clothing. By the time her husband returned seven years later, she had prospered sufficiently to be able to replace all the slaves taken by the robbers.

The fact that Mrs. Hutchens put her daughters to work spinning and weaving is significant, for no household task was more time-consuming or more symbolic of the female role than spinning. It was, furthermore, a task quintessentially performed by young, single women; hence, the use of the word "spinster" to mean an unmarried female and the phrase "the distaff side" to refer to women in general. Farm wives, and especially their daughters, spent a large proportion of their time, particularly in the winter months, bending over a flax wheel or loom, or walking beside a great wheel, spinning wool. No examination of the domestic sphere can be complete without detailed attention to this aspect of household work.

Before 1765 and the subsequent rise in home manufacturing caused by colonial boycotts of British goods, spinning and weaving as ordinary chores were largely confined to rural areas of the northern and middle colonies and the backcountry South. Planters and even middling farmers who lived along the southeastern coast and city residents throughout America could usually purchase English cloth more cheaply than they could manufacture it at home, and so they bought fabric rather than asking their wives, daughters, or female slaves to spent the requisite amount of time to produce it. But rural women outside the plantation South spent much of their lives spinning. They began as girls, helping their mothers; they continued after their marriages, until their own daughters were old enough to remove most of the burden from their shoulders; and they often returned to it in old age or widowhood, as a means of supporting themselves or making use of their time. Not all farm women learned weaving, a skill open to men as well, but spinning was a nearly universal occupation among them.

Rural girls understood at an early age that spinning was "a very proper accomplishment for a farmers daughter," as the New Jersey Quaker Susanna Dillwyn put it in 1790. Susanna's niece Hannah Cox began trying to spin on an "old wheel which was in the house" when she was only seven, so her mother bought her a little new wheel, upon which Hannah soon learned to spin "very prettily." Similarly, the tutor on Robert Carter's Virginia plantation observed that his small pupils would tie "a String to a Chair & then run buzzing back to imitate the Girls spinning." Such playful fascination with the process of cloth production later turned for many girls into monotonous daily labor at wheels or looms during the months between December and May. The normal output of an experienced spinner who carded the wool herself was four skeins a day, or six if an assistant carded for her. Teenaged girls like Elizabeth Fuller, who were less practiced than their mothers, produced on the average two or three skeins a day. After a long stint of spinning tow (short coarse linen fibers) in January and February 1792, Elizabeth exploded in her diary, "I should think I might have spun up all the Swingling Tow in America by this time." Later that same year, she switched to weaving, at last completing her annual allotment on June 1. In three months she had woven 176 yards of cloth, she recorded, happily inscribing in her journal, "Welcome sweet Liberty, once more to me. How have I longed to meet again with thee."

But clothwork, which could be a lonely and confining occupation, as Elizabeth Fuller learned, could also be an occasion for socializing. Rural girls sometimes attended "spinning frolics" or quilting bees, many of which lasted for several days and ended with dancing. Even more frequently farm women "changed work," trading skills with others experienced in different tasks. Mary Palmer recalled that after her family moved to Framingham her mother would change work with other women in the area, "knitting and sewing for them while they would weave cotton and flax into cloth" for her, since as a city dweller she had never learned that skill. In a similar way Ruth Henshaw and her mother repaid Lydia Hawkins, who warped their loom for them, by helping her quilt or making her a pair of stays. Ruth regularly exchanged chores with girls of her own age as well; in December 1789, for example, she noted, "Sally here Spining Changeing works with Me," while ten days later she was at Sally's house, carding for her.

From such trading of labor farm women could easily move on to work for pay. By 1775 Betsy and Nabby Foote had taken that step. Nabby, like Lydia Hawkins of Leicester, specialized in warping webs and making loom harnesses; her sister Betsy worked in all phases of cloth production, carding wool, hatcheling flax, and spinning, as well as doing sewing and mending for neighbors. In the rural North and South alike white women spun, wove, and sold butter, cheese, and soap to their neighbors, participating on a small scale in the market economy long before the establishment of textile factories in New England and the consequent introduction of widespread wage labor for young northern women.

Given the significance of spinning in women's lives, it is not surprising that American men and women made that occupation the major symbol of femininity. William Livingston had declared that "country girls . . . ought to be at their spinning-wheels," and when Benjamin Franklin sought a wedding present for his sister Jane, he decided on a spinning wheel instead of a tea table, concluding that "the character of a good housewife was far preferable to that of being only a pretty gentlewoman."

Compelling evidence of the link between spinning and the female role in the eighteenth-century American mind comes from the observations of two visitors to Indian villages. Confronted by societies in which women did not spin but instead cultivated crops while their husbands hunted and fished, both the whites perceived Indian sex roles as improper and sought to correct them by introducing the feminine task of spinning. Benjamin Hawkins, United States agent for the Creek tribe, admired the industrious Creek women and encouraged them to learn to spin and weave. This step, he believed, would lead to a realignment of sex roles along proper lines, because the women would be freed from dependence upon their hunter husbands for clothing, and they would also no longer have time to work on the crops. The men in turn would therefore be "obliged to handle the ax & the plough, and assist the women in the laborious task of the fields." A similar scheme was promoted by the Quaker woman Anne Emlen Mifflin, who traveled in the Seneca country as a missionary in 1803. Men should work in agriculture, she told her Indian audience, so that women would be able to learn spinning and dairy management, which were "branches suited to our sex," as opposed to "drudging alone in the labors of the field."

As Mifflin's comment shows, women, too, found spinning a necessary component of femininity, a fact best illustrated by reference to Elizabeth Graeme Fergusson's poem "The Contemplative Spinner." In 1792, Mrs. Fergusson, one of the leaders of intellectual life in republican Philadelphia, composed a poem in which she compared her spinning wheel to a wheel of fortune, leading her to a series of observations on life, death, and religion. But the wheel did more: it also reminded her of other women, linking her inextricably to "a train of Female Hands/Chearful uniting in Industrious Bands." And so, she wrote:

> In such Reflections I oft passed the Night,
> When by my Papas solitary Light
> My Wheel I turned, and thought how others
>   toild
> To earn a morsel for a famishd Child.

To Elizabeth Graeme Fergusson, spinning symbolized her tie to the female sisterhood, just as to Benjamin Hawkins and other eighteenth-century men that occupation above all somehow appertained to femininity. It is consequently ironic that the one factor that differentiated the lives of urban women most sharply from those of their rural counterparts was the fact that they did not have to engage in cloth production. Women who had access to stores saw no point in spending hour after tedious hour at the wheel or loom. Not, at least, until doing so came to have political significance in the late 1760s, as Americans increasingly tried to end their dependence on British manufactured goods.

III

Although urban women did not have to spin and weave, the absence of that time-consuming occu-

pation did not turn their lives into leisured ones. Too often historians have been misled by the lack of lengthy work entries in urban women's diaries, concluding therefrom that city "ladies" contributed little or nothing to the family welfare. Admittedly, white urban women of even moderate means worked shorter hours and at less physically demanding tasks than did their rural counterparts, but this did not mean that their households ran themselves. Women still had the responsibility for food preparation, which often included cultivating a garden and raising poultry. The wives of artisans and shopkeepers also occasionally assisted their husbands in business. Furthermore, their homes were held to higher standards of cleanliness—by themselves and by their female friends—than were the homes of farm women like Mary Cooper. Even if they could afford to hire servants, they frequently complained that supervising their assistants took almost as much time and effort as doing the work themselves.

Middling and well-to-do urban women who described their daily routines in letters or diaries disclosed a uniform pattern of mornings devoted to household work, a late dinner at about two o'clock, and an afternoon of visiting friends, riding, or perhaps reading quietly at home. Although some women arose as late as eight o'clock (which one female Bostonian termed "a lazy hour"), others, including Abigail Adams, recorded that they habitually rose at five. A Pennsylvanian summed up the common practice in a poem:

> Like a notable house wife i rise with the sun
> Then bustle about till the business is done,
> Consult with the Cook, and attend to the
>   spiting [sic]
> Then quietly seat myself down to my
>   knitting—
> Should a neighbour step in we talk of the
>   weather
> Retail all the news and the scandle
>   together, . . .
> The tea things removed our party disperses,
> And of course puts an end to my very fine
>   verses.

The chores that city women performed in the mornings resembled those of farm wives. Their diaries noted hours devoted to washing and ironing, cooking and baking, sewing and knitting. Like that of their rural counterparts, their labor was affected by the seasons, although less consistently so: in the autumn they preserved fruit and stored vegetables, and early in the winter they salted beef and pork and made sausage. Yet there were differences. Most notably, urban dwellers made daily trips to large markets, where they bought most of their meat, vegetables, cheese, and butter. Rebecca Stoddert, a Marylander who had moved to Philadelphia, marveled that her neighbors quickly killed chickens they had purchased without "think[ing] of fattening them up," a practice she deplored as wasteful and short-sighted.

Although urban women were not burdened with the major stock-tending and clothmaking chores that devolved upon farm wives, some of the time thus saved was devoted to cleaning their homes. Many of the travelers in rural areas most horrified by dirty farmhouses and taverns were themselves urban women, who had adopted standards of cleanliness for their homes, clothes, and beds that were utterly alien to farm wives. Certainly no rural woman except Mary Cooper would have written a journal entry resembling that of a Philadelphian in 1781: "As we were whitewashing & cleaning house this day I seemed anxious, I fear over anxious to have every thing clean, & in order." Another Philadelphia resident, the Quaker Sally Logan Fisher, seems to have painted, whitewashed, or wallpapered her house each spring, even though she remarked in April 1785 that it was "troublesome work indeed, the pleasure afterwards of being nice, hardly pays for the trouble." Other wives in smaller towns similarly recorded their commitment to keeping their homes neat and clean.

Cleaning, though, was perhaps the only occupation at which city dwellers of moderate means expended more energy than women living in agricultural regions. One of the benefits of residing in a city or a good-sized town was the availability of a pool of female workers who could be hired at relatively low rates. If a woman decided that she could not afford even a minimal payment, she could take a girl into her home as a sort of apprentice in housewifery, compensating her solely with room, board, and clothes. . . .

The mistresses of such [middling and wealthy] homes felt caught in a dilemma. On the one hand, servants were impertinent, lazy, untrustworthy, careless, and slovenly (to list just a few of their complaints), but on the other hand it was impossible to run a household without some help. The women who offered themselves for hire were usually either single girls or elderly widows; only in rare cases can one identify white females who spent their entire lives as servants. Instead, girls worked as maids, cooks, or laundresses for a few years before marriage, often for a series of employers. From the diaries and letters of mistresses of urban households one gains the impression of a floating population of "young Giddy Headed Girls" who did largely as they pleased, knowing that with the endemic American shortage of labor they could always find another position. Few seem to have stayed in the same household for more than a few months, or a year at most, before moving on to another post. For example, in just the five years from 1794 to 1799, Deborah Norris Logan, Sally Logan Fisher's sister-in-law, employed at least ten different female servants in fairly rapid succession. Among them were two widows, some immigrants from Ireland and Germany, a pair of sisters, and several girls.

Deborah Logan had no daughters to assist her in the home, but even if she had, she, like other urban mothers, would not have expected them to contribute as much work to the household as did their rural counterparts. City daughters from well-to-do homes were the only eighteenth-century American women who can accurately be described as leisured. The causes of their relative lack of employment have already been indicated: first, the work of an urban household was less demanding than that of a farm, so that mothers and perhaps one or two servants could do all that was necessary; and, second, city girls did not have to produce the cloth supply for the family.

Accordingly, they could live at a relaxed pace, sleeping late, learning music and dancing, spending hours with male and female friends, and reading the latest novels.

This is not to say, as some historians have argued, that these young women were entirely idle and decorative, for they did extensive amounts of sewing for their families. Girls began to sew at an early age—Hannah, Sally Logan Fisher's daughter, was only eight when she made her first shirt—and they thereafter devoted many hours each day to their needles. Most of their tasks were mundane: mending and altering clothes; making shirts for their fathers and brothers; and stitching apparently innumerable aprons, caps, and shifts for themselves, their mothers, and their aunts. Such "common sewing" won a girl "no great Credit," the New Englander Pamela Dwight Sedgwick admitted in 1789, but at the same time, she pointed out to her daughter, "[I]t will be thought unpardonable negligence . . . not to doe it very nicely." Sometimes girls would work samplers or make lace, but even the wealthiest among them occasionally felt apologetic for spending a considerable amount of their time on decorative stitchery. Betsy DeLancey, a daughter of the prominent New York family, defended such evidently frivolous employment to her sister Anne in 1768 by referring to Proverbs: "I must be industrious and make myself fine with my own Hands, and who can blame me for spending some of my time in that manner when it is part of the virtuous Womans Character in the Bible."

In poor households, daughters' sewing skills could contribute significantly to family income, as may be demonstrated by reference to the Banckers of New York City. Christopher Bancker was an alcoholic, and his wife Polly tried to support the family by working as a seamstress. Yet she alone could not "du the whole," as she wrote in 1791, and so her two oldest daughters, Peggy and Betsy, also sought employment as seamstresses. Even with the girls' help the family experienced severe economic difficulties, yet the combined income of wife and daughters, coupled with charity proffered by reluctant relatives, kept the Banckers out of the poor house. Peggy and Betsy—and, by implication, other urban girls as well—thus proved to be economic assets to their families in a way that sons were not. The best that could be done with the two oldest Bancker boys was to send them out of the household to learn trades, so that they would no longer be a drag on family resources. Not until they had served apprenticeships of several years, with the expenses being borne by relatives, could they make positive contributions to the support of their parents and siblings. But their sisters had been "apprenticed" to their mother, and so they had developed salable skills at an early age. The other side of the coin was the fact that the Bancker boys' advanced training eventually paid off in higher wages, whereas the girls had little hope of ever improving their position, except through a good marriage.

Because sewing was readily portable, and because they lived so close to each other, well-to-do urban girls frequently gathered to work in sizable groups. While one of their number read, usually from a popular novel, the others would pass the afternoon or evening in sewing. Like farm girls, they created an opportunity for socializing out of the necessity for work, but as a result of their proximity they were able to meet more often, more regularly, and in greater numbers. One sewing group called itself the "Progressive Society" and confined its reading to edifying tracts. "Our design is to ameliorate, by every probable method, the morals, opinions, manners and language of each other," one of the members wrote, explaining why they excluded cardplaying, gossip, and men from their meetings.

In addition to sewing, city girls, like their rural counterparts, were taught what one of them termed "the mysteries of housewifery" by conscientious mothers. Sally Logan Fisher began to instruct her daughter Hannah in "Family affairs" when she was just ten, so that she would become "a good Housewife & an active Mistress of a Family." Daughters did some cooking, baking, and cleaning, helped to care for younger siblings, and on occasion took charge of the household. Sometimes they acquired this responsibility only when their mothers became ill, but in other cases adults deliberately adopted it as a training device. Abigail Adams, who believed it "an indispensable requisite, that every American wife, should herself know, how to order, and regulate her family," commented approvingly in 1788 that her son-in-law William Stephens Smith's four sisters were "well educated for wives as well as daughters" because "their Mamma had used them to the care of her Family by Turns. Each take it a week at a Time."

The words chosen by Mrs. Adams and Mrs. Fisher revealed a key difference in the domestic roles of urban and rural girls. Farm daughters learned to perform household tasks because their family's current well-being required their active involvement in daily work, whereas city girls acquired domestic skills primarily so that they could eventually become good wives and mothers. The distinction was crucial. Urban daughters participated sporadically in household tasks as a preparation for their own futures, but farm girls worked regularly at such chores as a direct contribution to their family's immediate welfare. The difference points up the overall contrast between the lives of urban and rural white women. In both city and farm, women made vital contributions to the success and survival of the household, but in rural areas those contributions were both more direct and more time-consuming.

IV

Wealthy southern women were directly responsible for even fewer household tasks than northerners with comparable means. But northerners who moved south soon realized the falsity of an initial impression that "a mrs of a family in Carolina had nothing to doe but be waited on as their was so many negros." Anna Bowen, a young Rhode Island woman who first went to South Carolina to visit a married sister and subsequently married a planter herself, told another sister in 1790 about the problems of running a large household. Required to "think incessantly of a thousand articles of daily supply," she sometimes did not know "which way to turn," Bowen admit-

ted, but, she added confidently, "I shall learn in time."

The daily schedules of mistresses of large plantations resembled those of wealthy urban women in the North, with the exception of the fact that social visits were confined to one or two afternoons a week because of the distance between plantations. The mornings were devoted to household affairs, although white southerners spent their time supervising the work of slaves instead of doing such chores themselves. The day began, sometimes before breakfast, with what one southern man termed "Grand Rounds from the Kitchen to the Larder, then to the Poultry Yard & so on by the Garret & Store Room home to the Parlour." After she had ascertained that the daily tasks were proceeding as planned, the mistress of the household could spend some time reading or playing music before joining her husband for dinner in early to mid-afternoon. Afterward, she would normally turn to needlework until evening, and then again to reading and writing.

The supervision of what were the largest households on the north American continent involved plantation mistresses in varied activities, almost always in the role of director rather than performer. What were small-scale operations on northern farms—running a dairy, raising poultry, tending a garden—were magnified many times on southern plantations, but they remained within the female sphere. Chores that northern women could do in a day, such as laundry, took nearly one week of every two on at least one South Carolina plantation. Food management, easily accomplished in small northern urban families with access to markets, occupied a significant amount of time and required much forethought on large plantations, where each year's harvest had to feed perhaps one hundred or more people for months. White women, it is true, did not usually make the decisions about how many hogs to kill or how many barrels of corn to set aside for food and seed, but they did manage the distribution of food once it had been stored, not to mention the supervision of its initial preservation. Furthermore, they coordinated the manufacture of the slaves' clothing, spending many hours cutting out garments or superintending that work, in addition to making, altering, and mending their families' clothes.

Such women invariably aroused the admiration of observers, who regularly commended their "industry and ingenuity," their "very able and active manner," or their character as "worthy economists" and "good managers." Surviving correspondence indicates that the praise could be completely deserved. A prime example is provided by the Marylander Hannah Buchanan, who in August 1809 returned alone to Woburn plantation while her husband remained in Baltimore on business. She reported to him in anger that the white couple they had left in charge did not have "the smallest idea of the proper economy of a Farm." Among the abuses she discovered were a misassignment of slave women to nonessential tasks, a lack of planning for the slaves' winter clothing, and extremely poor handling of food supplies, including such errors as allowing the slaves to have wheat flour, consuming all the pork, and having no vegetables at all. "This is miserable management," she declared, and set herself to correct the situation. A month later the work on winter clothes was coming along "Wonderfully," and she was filled with ideas on how to prepare and distribute the food more efficiently. Although she expressed a desire to rejoin her husband in the city, she proposed, "[L]et me direct next year and you will spend less believe me and the people will live much better."

Appropriately, then, the primary task of girls from wealthy southern families was to gain expertise in running large estates. Like their northern counterparts, they did some cooking and baking and a fair amount of sewing, but their household roles differed from those of both farm and city girls. Whereas one New England father told his daughter, "[L]earn to work as fast as you can to make Shirts etc & assist your Mother," Thomas Jefferson advised his younger daughter, Maria, who was usually called Polly, that she should know how to "manage the kitchen, the dairy, the garden, and other appendages of the hous[e]hold." Teenaged girls like Eleanor Parke

(Nelly) Custis accordingly served as "deputy Housekeeper" to the mistress of the family, who in her case was her grandmother Martha Washington. If this training was successful, parents could look with pleasure upon the accomplishments of such excellent managers as Martha Jefferson Randolph, who assured her father in 1791 that at Monticello under her direction "there is as little wasted as possible," or Harriott Pinckney Horry, whose fond mother, Eliza Lucas Pinckney, had herself managed three South Carolina plantations in the 1740s while she was still a teenager. "I am glad your little wife looks well to the ways of [her] hou[se]," Mrs. Pinckney told her new son-in-law within a month of his marriage, especially remarking upon her daughter's ability to run a "perfectly neat" dairy.

In the end, being a good plantation mistress involved very different skills from those of the usual notable housewife of northern communities. Most importantly, the well-to-do southern white woman had to know how to command and direct the activities of others, often a great many others, not just the one or two servants common to northern households. It was less essential for a wealthy female southerner to know how to accomplish tasks herself than it was for her to know how to order blacks to perform them, and to ensure that her orders were carried out. Thus when the Virginian Elizabeth Foote Washington, who feared that she would not survive until her baby daughter reached maturity, decided to leave her a book of household advice, she devoted most of its pages to hints on the management of slaves. A mistress should behave with "steadiness," she advised; she should show the servants that she would not be "impos'd upon." The most important goal was to maintain "peace & quietness" in the household, and to this end a mistress should be careful not to complain about the slaves to her husband or her friends. Such a practice would make the servants grateful and perhaps encourage their industry, she wrote.

As it happened, both the daughters born to Mrs. Washington died in infancy, and so her detailed delineation of the way to handle house servants was not passed on as she had hoped. But other white southern girls early assumed the habit of command. A telling incident involved Anne, the daughter of James Iredell, the North Carolina attorney and eventual associate justice of the Supreme Court. At the early age of four, she showed how well she had learned her lessons by "strutting about in the yard after Susanna (whom she had ordered to do something) with her work in her hand & an Air of as much importance as if she had been Mistress of the family."

The story of Anne Iredell's behavior inevitably forces one to confront a difficult question: how did Susanna, a mature black woman, react to being ordered about by a white child? Or, to broaden the issue, what sort of lives were led by the black women who, with their husbands and children, constituted the vast majority of the population on southern plantations? Many female slaves resided on small farms and presumably worked in both field and house, but the discussion here will concentrate upon larger plantations, for it was in such households that most black women lived, since the relatively small proportion of white families who possessed slaves tended to own large numbers of them.

Significantly, the size of these plantations allowed the specialization of domestic labor. White northern farm wives had to be, in effect, jills-of-all-trades, whereas planters often assigned slave women more or less permanently to particular tasks. A wide variety of jobs were open to black women, jobs that demanded as much skill as those performed by such male artisans as blacksmiths and carpenters. The slave list prepared by Thomas Middleton for his Goose Creek, South Carolina, plantation in 1784 included a dairymaid, a nurse, two laundresses, two seamstresses, and three general house servants. On other plantations women were also employed as cooks, spinners and weavers (after the mid-1760s), midwives, and tenders of poultry and livestock.

Female blacks frequently worked at the same job for a number of years, but they were not necessarily restricted to it for a lifetime, although practices varied from plantation to plantation. Thomas Jefferson used children of both sexes

under ten as infant nurses; from the ages of ten to sixteen he assigned girls to spinning and boys to nailmaking; and then either put them into the fields or had them learn a skilled occupation. Even as adults their jobs might be changed: when Jefferson went to France as ambassador in 1784, his "fine house wench" Dinah, then twenty-three, began to work in the fields, continuing at that assignment at least until 1792. The descriptions of slaves bought or sold on other plantations likewise showed women accustomed to different occupations. Colonel Fitzgerald's Nell, aged thirty-four, was "a stout able field wench & an exceeding good Washer and Ironer"; her daughter Sophy, eighteen, was a "Stout Wench & used to both field & [hou]se Work."

All field work was not the same, of course, and women who labored "in the crop" performed a variety of functions. Evidence of work assignments from both the Jefferson and Washington plantations shows that there were some field jobs reserved for men, most notably cradling wheat and cutting and hauling timber for fences, but that women sometimes built fences. Women plowed, hoed and grubbed the land, spread manure, sowed, harrowed, and at harvest time threshed wheat or husked corn. At Landon Carter's Sabine Hall plantation in Virginia two women, Grace and Maryan, each headed a small gang of female fieldworkers.

On outlying quarters, most women were agricultural laborers, with the occasional exception of a cook or a children's nurse. But female slaves raised at the home plantation could sometimes attain a high level of skill at conventionally "feminine" occupations. White masters and mistresses frequently praised the accomplishments of their cooks, seamstresses, and housekeepers. In a typical passage, Alice DeLancey Izard, a wealthy South Carolinian returning home after a long absence, commended her dairymaid Chloe because she found "the Dairy in excellent order, & plentifully supplied with Milk, & Butter," further observing that Chloe "has made little Chloe very useful in her line."

Mrs. Izard thereby called attention to the transmission of skills among generations of female blacks. Thomas Jefferson's censuses of his plantations demonstrate that women who were house servants tended to have daughters who also worked in the house, and the inventory of a Pinckney family plantation in 1812 similarly included a mother-daughter midwife team. Indeed, midwifery, which was most likely an occupation passed on from woman to woman rather than one taught deliberately by a master, was one of the most essential skills on any plantation. Slave midwives were often called upon to deliver white children as well as black, and masters recognized the special demands of their profession. In 1766, the midwife at Landon Carter's Fork Quarter, who was also the poultry tender, left her post to deliver a baby, an act resulting in the death of four turkeys. Even the petulant Carter realized that her midwifery duties came first, and so he did not punish her.

In this case, a conflict arose between the midwife's divergent duties within her master's household. More commonly, slave women must have had to contend with contradictory demands placed upon them by their plantation tasks and the needs of their own husbands and children. Only a few aspects of the domestic lives led by black women within their own families can be traced in the records of white planters, for masters and mistresses did not, on the whole, concern themselves with the ways in which female slaves organized their homes. Yet occasional comments by slaveowners suggest that black women carefully made the most of what little they had and were even able to exercise some entrepreneurial initiative on occasion. Slave families occasionally maintained their own garden plots and supplemented their meager food and clothing allowances through theft or guile. Further, black women established themselves as the "general Chicken Merchants" in the plantation South. Whites often bought fowls from their female slaves instead of raising chickens themselves, as a means, Thomas Jefferson once explained, of "drawing a line between what is theirs & mine."

That some black women had a very strong sense indeed of what was "theirs" was demonstrated on Nomini Hall plantation in the summer of 1781. Robert Carter had authorized two white overseers to begin making salt, and in order to accomplish that task they commandeered an iron pot from its two female owners. Joan and Patty, the aggrieved slaves, awaited their chance and then removed the pot from the saltworks. After the whites repossessed it, the women dispatched Patty's husband, Jesse, to complain to Carter about the treatment they had received. Carter sided with the women, agreeing that their pot had been taken in an "arbitrary" manner, and he ordered it returned to them.

One could argue that Joan and Patty were emboldened to act as they did because they anticipated that Carter, a well-meaning master who eventually emancipated his slaves, would sympathize with their position. But bondwomen less favorably circumstanced also repeatedly displayed a desire to control as much of their lives as was possible under the conditions of servitude. Robert Carter's relative Landon was quick to anger, impatient with his servants and children. He frequently had recalcitrant slaves whipped, a tactic to which Robert rarely resorted, yet the women at Sabine Hall were no less insubordinate than those at Nomini. If Robert Carter's "Young & Stout" Jenny deliberately had fits "upon her being reprimanded," Landon Carter's Sarah pretended to be pregnant for a full eleven months so that she could avoid work, and Criss sent her children to milk his cows in the middle of the night in retaliation for a whipping. Similarly ingenious was James Mercer's Sall, who in August 1777 convinced her master that she had consumption and persuaded him to send her to the mountain quarter where her parents lived. That summer he ordered that she should be well fed and allowed to ride six or seven miles on horseback each day until she recovered her health, but by the following year, Mercer had concluded she was faking and directed that "she must turn out at all events unless attended with a fever."

The same willful spirit asserted itself when masters and mistresses attempted to move female slaves from their accustomed homes to other locations. A North Carolina woman who was visiting Boston wanted to have her servant Dorinda sent north to join her, but learned from a relative that Dorinda "would by no means go to Boston or North Carolina, from Cape Fear." Some years later a Pennsylvanian who had sent a slave woman to Cuba to be sold learned that she had managed to convince the white woman accompanying her that she should be returned to her Philadelphia home, because she was "Very Unhappy and always Crying." And "Miss Charlotte," an East Florida black, demonstrated her autonomy by her reaction to a dispute over who owned her. One of the two whites involved reported that she lived with neither of them, but instead "goes about from house to house," saying "now she's a free woman."

Charlotte, Sall, Dorinda, and the others gained at least a little freedom of movement for themselves, but they were still enslaved in the end. All their victories were minor ones, for they could have only limited impact upon the conditions of their bondage. White women were subject to white men, but black women had to subordinate themselves to all whites, men, women, and children alike. The whites demanded always that their needs come first, before those of black women's own families. Female slaves' work lives were thus complicated by conflicting obligations that inflicted burdens upon them far beyond those borne by most whites.

V

White Americans did not expect their slaves to gain satisfaction from their work, for all that masters and mistresses required of their bond servants was proper behavior and a full day's labor. But white women, as already indicated, were supposed to find "happiness in their chimney corners," to return to William Livingston's striking phrase. Men certainly believed that women should enjoy their domestic role. As a Georgian told his married sister in 1796, "I am sure that those cares which duty requires to your husband, and your child—must fill up every moment of time—and leave you nothing but those sensations of pleasure—which invariably flow—from a

consciousness of having left no duty unperformed." Women too anticipated happiness from achieving the goal of notable housewifery. "Domestick oeconomy . . . is the female dignity, & praise," declared Abigail Adams's younger sister, Elizabeth Smith, in the late 1760s, and a Virginian observed to a friend nearly forty years later that she had "always been taught, that within the sphere of domestic life, Woman's chief glory & happiness ought to consist."

The expectation, then, was clear: domesticity was not only a white American woman's inevitable destiny, but it was also supposed to be the source of her sense of pride and satisfaction. Regardless of the exact shape of her household role—whether she was a rural or an urban wife, or the mistress of a southern plantation—she should find fulfillment in it, and she should take pleasure in performing the duties required of her as mistress of the home.

Unsurprisingly, women rarely found the ideal as attractive in reality as it was in theory. But the reasons for their dissatisfaction with the restrictions of notable housewifery, which required them to be consistently self-effacing and constantly employed at domestic tasks, are both illuminating and unanticipated.

First, it must be noted that Mary Cooper was alone among her contemporaries in emphasizing the difficult, fatiguing nature of housework as the primary source of her complaints. Only she wrote of "the continnel cross of my famaly," only she filled her diary with accounts of weariness and endless drudgery. Women's unhappiness with their domestic lives, in other words, stemmed not from the fact that the work was tiring and demanding. Their husbands' labor was also difficult, and in eighteenth-century America there were few models of a leisured existence for either men or women to emulate. Rather, women's expressed dissatisfaction with their household role derived from its basic nature, and from the way it contrasted with their husbands' work.

As has been seen, farmers' lives were much more varied than those of their wives, not only because they rarely repeated the same chore day after day in immediate succession, but also because they had more breaks from the laboring routine. The same was true of southern planters and or urban husbands, regardless of their occupation. The diaries of planters, professional men, and artisans alike demonstrate that their weeks were punctuated by travel, their days enlivened not only by visits with friends—which their wives also enjoyed—but also by a variety of business activities that took them on numerous errands. It was an unusual week, for example, when Thomas Hazard, a Rhode Island blacksmith, worked in his shop every day without any sort of respite from his labors, or when Ebenezer Parkman, a New England clergyman, did not call on parishioners, confer with neighbors about politics, or meet with other ministers.

Against the backdrop of their husbands' diverse experiences, the invariable daily and weekly routines of housewifery seemed dull and uninteresting to eighteenth-century women, especially those who lived in urban areas, where the housework was less varied and their spouses' opportunities for socializing simultaneously greater. "The same cares and the same wants are constantly returning in domestic Life to take up my Time and attention," Pamela Dwight Sedgwick told her husband, Theodore, the Massachusetts Federalist, in words that reappeared in other women's assessments of their lives. "A continual sameness reigns throughout the Year," wrote Christian Barnes, the wife of a Marlborough, Massachusetts, merchant, and Mary Orne Tucker, a Haverhill lawyer's wife, noted in her diary that she did not record her domestic tasks in detail because "each succeeding day with very little variety would present a compleat history of the last."

New England city dwellers were not the only women who made such observations about the unchanging character of their experiences. The transplanted Rhode Islander Anna Bowen Mitchell reported from her new South Carolina home in 1793, "[T]he detail of one day . . . would be the detail of the last six months of my life," while hastening to add that her days were not "insipid," but rather filled with "heart-soothing

tranquility." A Virginia planter's wife was more blunt about her situation in 1785, describing herself and her friends as "almost in a State of vegitation" because of their necessary attention to the "innumerable wants" of their large households.

She thus touched upon yet another source of housewives' discontent with their lot: the fact that their all-encompassing domestic responsibilities left them little time to themselves. In 1755, a New England woman remarked longingly to a correspondent, "[T]he little scraps of time that can be rescued from Business or Company, are the greatest cordials to my tired Spirits that I meet with." Thirty years later Pamela Sedgwick echoed her sentiments, telling her unmarried friend Betsy Mayhew, "[W]e that have connected ourselves in the famely way, find the small circle of domestic concerns engross almost all our attention." Sally Logan Fisher too commented, "[I] find so much to do in the Family that I have not all the time for retirement and improvement of my own mind in the best things that I wish," revealingly referring to her domestic duties as "these hindering things." Again, such complaints were not confined to northerners. A young Virginia wife observed in 1769 that "Domestic Business . . . even deprives thought of its Native freedom" by restricting the mind "to one particular subject without suffering it to entertain itself with the contemplation of any thing New or improving." A wry female poet made the same point in verse: "Ah yes! 'tis true, upon my Life! / No *Muse* was ever yet a *Wife*," she wrote, explaining that "Muses . . . in *poultry yards* were never seen," nor were they required "from Books and Poetry to Turn / To mark *the Labours of the Churn.*"

The point of all these remarks was the same, despite their divergent geographical and chronological origins. White American women recognized not only that their domestic obligations were never-ending, but also that their necessary concentration upon those obligations deprived them of the opportunity to contemplate "any thing New and improving." So Elizabeth Smith Shaw told her oldest sister, Mary Cranch, in 1781, several years after her marriage to the clergyman John Shaw, "[I]f Ideas present themselves to my Mind, it is too much like the good seed sown among Thorns, they are soon erased, & swallowed up by the Cares of the World, the wants, & noise of my Family, & Children." Abigail Adams in particular regretted her beloved younger sister's preoccupation with domestic concerns during her second marriage, to another clergyman, who boarded a number of students. In February 1800 she told Elizabeth (then Mrs. Stephen Peabody) that her "brilliant" talents were "encumbered" and "obstructed" by her household chores, lamenting "that the fire of imagination should be checked, that the effusions of genious should be stifled, through want of leisure to display them." Abigail's characterization of the impact of domestic responsibilities on her sister's life bore little resemblance to William Livingston's glorification of those same activities: "The mind which is necessarily imprisoned in its own little tenement: and fully occupied by keeping it in repair: has no time to rove abroad for improvement," she observed. "The Book of knowledge is closely clasped against those who must fullfil there [sic] daily task of manual labour."

Even with their expressed dissatisfaction at the endless, unchanging nature of housework, one might theorize that late eighteenth-century American women could nevertheless have found their domestic lives meaningful if they and their husbands had highly valued their contributions to the family well-being. But such was not the case. Women revealed their assessments of the importance of their work in the adjectives they used to describe it: "my Narrow sphere," my "humble duties," "my little Domestick affairs."

Always the words belittled their domestic role, thereby indicating its low status in contemporary eyes. Modern historians can accurately point to the essential economic function of women within a colonial household, but the facts evident from hindsight bear little relationship to eighteenth-century subjective attitudes. In spite of the paeans to notable womanhood, the role of the household mistress in the family's welfare was understood only on the most basic level. Such minimal recognition did not translate itself into an awareness that women contributed to the wider society. Instead, just as a woman's activities were supposed to be confined to the domestic sphere, so, too, was any judgment of her importance. Americans realized that a successful household needed a competent mistress, but they failed to endow that mistress with an independent social standing or to grant to her domestic work the value it deserved. Notable housewifery was conceived to be an end in itself, rather than as a means to a greater or more meaningful goal. As such, it was an inadequate prop for feminine self-esteem.

Accordingly, it comes as no surprise to learn that women generally wrote of their household work without joy or satisfaction. They spoke only of "the discharge of the necessary duties of life," of "perform[ing] the duties that are annex'd to my Station." Even the South Carolinian Martha Laurens Ramsay, described by her husband, David, as a model wife, regarded her "self denying duties" as "a part of the curse denounced upon Eve," as a penalty to be endured, instead of as a fulfilling experience. The usage was universal and the message unmistakable: their tasks, with rare exceptions, were "duties," not pleasures. The only Americans who wrote consistently of the joys of housewifery and notable womanhood were men like William Livingston. In contrast, Christian Barnes found the household a prison that offered no intellectual stimulation, describing it as a place where women were "Chain'd down to domestic Dutys" that "Stagnate[d] the Blood and Stupefie[d] the Senses."

Yet still women did not question the overall dimensions of the ideal domestic role. Sometimes, to be sure, they inquired about its details, as when Esther Edwards Burr, Jonathan Edwards's daughter, and her close friend Sarah Prince carried on a learned discussion about the precise meaning of the parts of Proverbs 31 that outlined the virtuous woman's daily routine. But ultimately they saw no alternative to domesticity. Many were simply resigned to the inevitable, for they had few options. Certainly some expressed the philosophy that "the height of happiness is

Contentment" with one's lot, that although their life had "no great veriety . . . custom has made it agreeable . . . and to desire more would be ungreatfull." More probable, though, is the fact that the household duties women found unsatisfying were intertwined in their own minds with responsibilities from which they gained a great deal of pleasure. Their role as mistress of the household, in the end, constituted but a third of their troika of domestic duties. They were wives and mothers as well as housekeepers, and these components of domesticity gave them the emotional and psychological rewards they did not receive from running their households efficiently.

7

WHO WAS BENJAMIN FRANKLIN?

JOHN WILLIAM WARD

Much like his contemporary George Washington, Benjamin Franklin has become one of the staples of American mythology. As John William Ward makes clear, however, Franklin was in reality no mythological being but a very complex and even contradictory man. The essence of Franklin, according to Ward, was his existence as a symbol of upward mobility. Beginning life as an apprentice printer, Franklin achieved business success before he was 30, earned an international reputation in science through his experiments in electricity, became influential in politics at the state and national levels, and served as one of the new nation's most successful diplomats in the Revolutionary era. The key to Franklin's rise, Ward contends, was his ability to separate appearance and reality: to appear to conform to community norms in public life while following his own desires in private affairs. It was this ability, Ward argues, that accounts for the seeming contradictions in Franklin's character.

"Who Was Benjamin Franklin?" Reprinted by permission from Mrs. John William Ward.

Benjamin Franklin bulks large in our national consciousness, sharing room with Washington and Jefferson and Lincoln. Yet it is hard to say precisely what it means to name Franklin one of our cultural heroes. He was, as one book about him has it, "many-sided." The sheer variety of his character has made it possible to praise him and damn him with equal vigor. At home, such dissimilar Yankees as the laconic Calvin Coolidge and the passionate Theodore Parker could each find reason to admire him. Abroad, David Hume could say that he was "the first great man of letters" for whom Europe was "beholden" to America. Yet D. H. Lawrence, brought up, he tells us, in the industrial wastelands of midland England on the pious saws of "Poor Richard," could only "utter a long, loud curse" against "this dry, moral, utilitarian little democrat."

Part of the difficulty in comprehending Franklin's meaning is due to the opposites he seems to have contained with complete serenity within his own personality. He was an eminently reasonable man who maintained a deep skepticism about the power of reason. He was a model of industriousness who, preaching the gospel of hard work, kept his shop only until it kept him and retired at forty-two. He was a cautious and prudent man who was a revolutionist. And, to name only one more seeming contradiction, he was one who had a keen eye for his own advantage and personal advancement who spent nearly all his adult life in the service of others. Small wonder that there have been various interpretations of so various a character.

The problem may seem no problem at all. Today, when we all know that the position of the observer determines the shape of reality, we observe the observer. If Franklin, seeing to it that the streets of Philadelphia are well lit and swept clean at a moderate price, that no fires rage, does not appeal to D. H. Lawrence, we tend not to think of Franklin. We think of Lawrence; we remember his atavistic urge to explore the dark and passionate underside of life and move on. Franklin contained in his own character so many divergent aspects that each observer can make the mistake of seeing one

aspect as all and celebrate or despise Franklin accordingly. Mr. I. Bernard Cohen, who has written so well on so much of Franklin, has remarked that "an account of Franklin . . . is apt to be a personal testament of the commentator concerning the America he most admires." Or contemns.

Yet there still remains the obstinate fact that Franklin could mean so many things to so many men, that he was so many-sided, that he did contain opposites, that he was, in other words, so many different characters. One suspects that here is the single most important thing about Franklin. Rather than spend our energies trying to find some consistency in this protean, many-sided figure, trying to resolve who Franklin truly was, we might perhaps better accept his variety itself as our major problem and try to understand that. To insist on the importance of the question, "Who was Benjamin Franklin?" may finally be more conclusive than to agree upon an answer.

The place to begin to ask the question is with the *Memoirs*, with the *Autobiography*, as we have come to call them, and the place to begin there is with the history of the text. Fascinating in and of itself, the history of the text gives us an initial lead into the question of the elusiveness of Franklin's personality.

The *Autobiography* was written in four parts. The first part, addressed by Franklin to his son, William, was begun during some few weeks in July and August, 1771, while Franklin was visiting with his friend, Jonathan Shipley, the Bishop of St. Asaph, in Hampshire, England. Franklin was then sixty-five years old. As he wrote the first part he also carefully made a list of topics he would subsequently treat. Somehow the manuscript and list fell into the hands of one Abel James who eleven years later wrote Franklin, returning to him the list of topics but not the first part of the manuscript, urging him to take up his story once again. This was in 1782, or possibly early in January, 1783. Franklin was in France as one of the peace commissioners. He wrote the second part in France in 1784, after the achievement of peace, indicating the beginning and the ending of this short second part in the manuscript itself.

In 1785, Franklin returned to America, promising to work on the manuscript during the voyage. Instead he wrote three of his utilitarian essays: on navigation, on how to avoid smoky streetlamp chimneys, and on his famous stove. He did not return to his life's story until 1788. Then, after retiring from the presidency of the state of Pennsylvania in the spring, Franklin, quite sick, made his will and put his house in order before turning again to his own history. This was in August, 1788. Franklin was eighty-three years old, in pain, and preparing for death. The third part is the longest part of the autobiography, less interesting than the first two, and for many years was thought to conclude the manuscript.

In 1789, Franklin had his grandson, Benjamin Franklin Bache, make two fair copies of Parts I, II, and III in order to send them to friends abroad, Benjamin Vaughan in England and M. le Veillard in France. Then, sometime before his death in April, 1790, Franklin added the last and fourth part, some seven and one-half manuscript pages, which was not included, naturally, in the fair copies sent abroad. For the rest, Mr. Max Farrand, our authority on the history of the text:

> After [Franklin's] death, the publication of the autobiography was eagerly awaited, as its existence was widely known, but for nearly thirty years the reading public had to content itself with French translations of the first and second parts, which were again translated from the French into other languages, and even retranslated into English. When the authorized English publication finally appeared in 1818, it was not taken from the original manuscript but from a copy, as was the preceding French version of the first part. The copy, furthermore, did not include the fourth and last part, which also reached the public in a French translation in 1828.
>
> . . . The complete autobiography was not printed in English from the original manuscript until 1868, nearly eighty years after Franklin's death.

The story is, as I have said, interesting in and of itself. The tangled history of one of our most important texts has its own fascination, but it also

provides us the first clue to our question. Surely, it must strike any reader of the *Autobiography* as curious that a character who speaks so openly should at the same time seem so difficult to define. But the history of the text points the way to an answer. All we need to do is ask why Franklin wrote his memoirs.

When the Quaker Abel James wrote Franklin, returning his list of topics and asking "kind, humane, and benevolent Ben Franklin" to continue his life's story, "a work which would be useful and entertaining not only to a few but to millions," Franklin sent the letter on to his friend, Benjamin Vaughan, asking for advice. Vaughan concurred. He too urged Franklin to publish the history of his life because he could think of no "more efficacious advertisement" of America than Franklin's history. "All that has happened to you," he reminded Franklin, "is also connected with the detail of the manners and situation of a rising people." Franklin included James's and Vaughan's letters in his manuscript to explain why he resumed his story. What had gone before had been written for his family; "what follows," he said in his "Memo," "was written . . . in compliance with the advice contained in these letters, and accordingly intended for the public. The affairs of the Revolution occasioned the interruption."

The point is obvious enough. When Franklin resumed his story, he did so in full self-consciousness that he was offering himself to the world as a representative type, the American. Intended for the public now, his story was to be an example for young Americans, as Abel James would have it, and an advertisement to the world, as Benjamin Vaughan would have it. We had just concluded a successful revolution; the eyes of all the world were upon us. Just as America had succeeded in creating itself a nation, Franklin set out to show how the American went about creating his own character. As Benjamin Vaughan said, Franklin's life would "give a noble rule and example of self-education" because of Franklin's "discovery that the thing is in many a man's private power." So what follows is no longer the simple annals of Franklin's life for the benefit of his son. Benjamin Franklin plays his proper role. He becomes "The American."

How well he filled the part that his public urged him to play, we can see by observing what he immediately proceeds to provide. In the pages that follow James's and Vaughan's letters, Franklin quickly treats four matters: the establishment of a lending library, that is, the means for satisfying the need for self-education; the importance of frugality and industriousness in one's calling; the social utility of religion; and, of course, the thirteen rules for ordering one's life. Here, in a neat package, were all the materials that went into the making of the self-made man. This is how one goes about making a success of one's self. If the sentiments of our Declaration were to provide prompt notes for European revolutions, then Franklin, as the American Democrat, acted them out. Family, class, religious orthodoxy, higher education: all these were secondary to character and common sense. The thing was in many a man's private power.

If we look back now at the first part, the opening section addressed by Franklin to his son, William, we can see a difference and a similarity. The difference is, of course, in the easy and personal tone, the more familiar manner, appropriate to a communication with one's son. It is in these early pages that Franklin talks more openly about his many *errata*, his "frequent intrigues with low women," and displays that rather cool and calculating attitude toward his wife. Rather plain dealing, one might think, at least one who did not know that William was a bastard son.

But the similarity between the two parts is more important. The message is the same, although addressed to a son, rather than to the world: how to go about making a success. "From the poverty and obscurity in which I was born and in which I passed my earliest years," writes the father to the son, "I have raised myself to a state of affluence and some degree of celebrity in the world." A son, especially, must have found that "some" hard to take. But the career is not simply anecdotal: "my posterity will perhaps be desirous of learning the means, which I employed, and which, thanks to Providence, so well succeeded with me. They may also deem them fit to be imitated." The story is exemplary, although how the example was to affect a son who was, in 1771, about forty years old and already Royal Governor of New Jersey is another matter.

The story has remained exemplary because it is the success story to beat all success stories: the runaway apprentice printer who rose to dine with kings; the penniless boy, walking down Market Street with two large rolls under his arms, who was to sit in Independence Hall and help create a new nation. But notice that the story does not deal with the success itself. That is presumed, of course, but the *Autobiography* never gets to the later and more important years because the *Autobiography* is not about success. It is about the formation of the character that makes success possible. The subject of the *Autobiography* is the making of a character. Having lifted himself by his own bootstraps, Franklin described it that way: "I have raised myself." We were not to find the pat phrase until the early nineteenth century when the age of the common man made the style more common: "the self-made man." The character was for life, of course, and not for fiction where we usually expect to encounter the made-up, but that should not prevent us from looking a little more closely at the act of creation. We can look in two ways: first, by standing outside the *Autobiography* and assessing it by what we know from elsewhere; second, by reading the *Autobiography* itself more closely.

A good place to begin is with those years in France around the end of the Revolution. It is so delicious an episode in plain Ben's life. More importantly—as Franklin said, one can always find a principle to justify one's inclinations—it is in these very years at Passy that Franklin, in response to James's and Vaughan's letters, wrote those self-conscious pages of the second part of the *Autobiography*. Just as he wrote the lines, he played them. As Carl Van Doren has written, "the French were looking for a hero who should combine the reason and wit of Voltaire with the primitive virtues celebrated by Rousseau. . . . [Franklin] denied them nothing." This is the period of the simple Quaker dress, the fur cap and the spectacles. France went wild in its adulation and Franklin knew why. "Think how this must appear," he wrote a friend, "among the powdered heads of Paris."

But he was also moving with equal ease in that world, the world of the powdered heads of Paris, one of the most cosmopolitan, most preciously civilized societies in history. Although he was no Quaker, Franklin was willing to allow the French to think so. They called him *le bon Quackeur.* The irony was unintentional, a matter of translation. But at the same time that he was filling the role of the simple backwoods democrat, the innocent abroad, he was also playing cavalier in the brilliant salon of Madame Helvétius, the widow of the French philosopher. Madame Helvétius is supposed to have been so beautiful that Fontenelle, the great popularizer of Newton, who lived to be one hundred years old, was said to have paid her the most famous compliment of the age: "Ah, madame, if I were only eighty again!" Madame Helvétius was sixty when Franklin knew her and the classic anecdote of their acquaintance is that Madame Helvétius is said to have reproached him for not coming to see her, for putting off his long anticipated visit. Franklin replied, "Madame, I am waiting until the nights are longer." There was also Madame Brillon, not a widow, who once wrote to Franklin, "People have the audacity to criticize my pleasant habit of sitting on your knee, and yours of always asking me for what I always refuse."

Some, discovering this side of Franklin, have written him off simply as a rather lively old lecher. Abigail Adams, good New England lady that she was, was thoroughly shocked. She set Madame Helvétius down as a "very bad woman." But Franklin, despite his public style, was not so provincial. He appealed to Madame Brillon that he had spent so many days with her that surely she could spend one night with him. She mockingly called him a sophist. He then appealed to her charity and argued that it was in the design of Providence that she grant him his wish. If somehow a son of the Puritans, Franklin had grown far

beyond the reach of their sermonizing. Thomas Hooker had thought, "It's a grievous thing to the loose person, he cannot have his pleasures but he must have his guilt and gall with them." But Franklin wrote Madame Brillon, "Reflect how many of our duties [Providence] has ordained naturally to be pleasures; and that it has had the goodness besides, to give the name of sin to several of them so that we might enjoy them the more."

All this is delightful enough, and for more one need only turn to Carl Van Doren's biography from which I have taken these anecdotes, but what it points to is as important as it is entertaining. It points to Franklin's great capacity to respond to the situation in which he found himself and to play the expected role, to prepare a face to meet the faces that he met. He could, in turn, be the homespun, rustic philosopher or the mocking cavalier, the witty sophist. He knew what was expected of him.

The discovery should not surprise any reader of the *Autobiography.* Throughout it, Franklin insists always on the distinction between appearance and reality, between what he is and what he seems to be.

> In order to secure my credit and character as a tradesman, I took care not only to be in *reality* industrious and frugal, but to avoid all *appearances* of the contrary. I dressed plain and was seen at no places of idle diversion. I never went out a fishing or shooting; a book, indeed, sometimes debauched me from my work, but that was seldom, snug, and gave no scandal; and to show that I was not above my business, I sometimes brought home the paper I purchased at the stores, thro' the streets on a wheelbarrow. Thus being esteemed an industrious, thriving young man, and paying duly for what I bought, the merchants who imported stationery solicited my custom; others proposed supplying me with books, and I went on swimmingly.

Now, with this famous passage, one must be careful. However industrious and frugal Franklin may in fact have been, he knew that for the business of social success virtue counts for nothing without its public dress. In Franklin's world there has to be someone in the woods to hear the tree fall. Private virtue might bring one to stand before the King of kings, but if one wants to sit down and sup with the kings of this world, then one must help them see one's merit. There are always in this world, as Franklin pointed out, "a number of rich merchants, nobility, states, and princes who have need of honest instruments for the management of their affairs, and such being so rare [I] have endeavoured to convince young persons, that no qualities are so likely to make a poor man's fortune as those of probity and integrity."

Yet if one wants to secure one's credit in the world by means of one's character, then the character must be of a piece. There can be no false gesture; the part must be played well. When Franklin drew up his list of virtues they contained, he tells us, only twelve. But a Quaker friend "kindly" informed him that he was generally thought proud and overbearing and rather insolent; he proved it by examples. So Franklin added humility to his list; but, having risen in the world and content with the degree of celebrity he had achieved, he could not bring himself to be humble. "I cannot boast of much success in acquiring the *reality* of this virtue, but I had a good deal with regard to the *appearance* of it."

He repeats, at this point, what he had already written in the first part of his story. He forswears all "positive assertion." He drops from his vocabulary such words as "certainly" and "undoubtedly" and adopts a tentative manner. He remembers how he learned to speak softly, to put forward his opinions, not dogmatically, but by saying, "'I imagine' a thing to be so or so, or 'It so appears to me at present.'" As he had put it to his son earlier, he discovered the Socratic method, "was charmed with it, adopted it, dropped my abrupt contradiction and positive argumentation, and put on the humble enquirer." For good reason, "this habit . . . has been of great advantage to me."

What saves all this in the *Autobiography* from being merely repellent is Franklin's self-awareness, his good humor in telling us about the part

he is playing, the public clothes he is putting on to hide what his public will not openly buy. "In reality," he writes, drawing again the distinction from appearance, "there is perhaps no one of our natural passions so hard to subdue as *pride;* disguise it, struggle with it, beat it down, stifle it, mortify it as much as one pleases, it is still alive and will every now and then peep out and show itself. You will see it perhaps often in this history. For even if I could conceive that I had completely overcome it, I should probably be proud of my humility." Here, despite the difference in tone, Franklin speaks like that other and contrasting son of the Puritans, Jonathan Edwards, on the nature of true virtue. Man, if he could achieve virtue, would inevitably be proud of the achievement and so, at the moment of success, fall back into sin.

The difference is, of course, in the tone. The insight is the same but Franklin's skeptical and untroubled self-acceptance is far removed from Edwards' troubled and searching self-doubt. Franklin enjoys the game. Mocking himself, he quietly lures us, in his Yankee deadpan manner, with the very bait he has just described. After having told us that he early learned to "put on the humble enquirer" and to affect a self-depreciating pose, he quotes in his support the line from Alexander Pope, "To speak, though sure, with seeming diffidence." Pope, Franklin immediately goes on to say, "might have joined with this line that which he has coupled with another, I think less properly, 'For want of modesty is want of sense.'"

> If you ask why *less properly,* I must repeat the lines,
>
> *Immodest words admit of* no defence,
> For *want of modesty is want of sense.*
>
> Now is not the "want of sense" (where a man is so unfortunate as to want it) some apology for his "want of modesty"? and would not the lines stand more justly thus?
>
> *Immodest words admit* but *this defense*
> That want of modesty is want of sense.
>
> This, however, I should submit to better judgements.

Having been so bold as to correct a couplet of the literary giant of the age, Franklin quietly retreats and defers to the judgment of those better able to say than he. Having just described the humble part he has decided to play, he immediately acts it out. If we get the point, we chuckle with him; if we miss the point, that only proves its worth.

But one of the functions of laughter is to dispel uneasiness and in Franklin's case the joke is not enough. Out uneasiness comes back when we stop to remember that he is, as his friends asked him to, writing his story as an efficacious advertisement. We must always ask whether Franklin's disarming candor in recounting how things went on so swimmingly may not be yet another role, still another part he is playing. Actually, even with Yale's sumptuous edition of Franklin's papers, we know little about Franklin's personal life in the early years, except through his own account. The little we do know suggests that his way to wealth and success was not the smooth and open path he would have us believe. This leads us, then, if we cannot answer finally the question who Franklin was, to a different question. What does it mean to say that a character so changeable, so elusive, somehow represents American culture? What is there in Franklin's style that makes him, as we say, characteristic?

At the outset in colonial America, with men like John Winthrop, there was always the assumption that one would be called to one's appropriate station in life and labor in it for one's own good and the good of society. Magistrates would be magistrates and printers would be printers. But in the world in which Franklin moved, the magistrates, like Governor Keith of Pennsylvania who sends Franklin off on a wild-goose chase to England, prove to be frauds while the plain, leather-aproned set went quietly about the work of making society possible at all, creating the institutions—the militia, the fire companies, the libraries, the hospitals, the public utilities—that made society habitable. The notion that underlay an orderly, hierarchical society failed to make sense of such a world. It proved impossible to keep people in their place.

One need only consider in retrospect how swiftly Franklin moved upward through the various levels of society to see the openness, the fluidity of his world. Simply because he is a young man with some books, Governor Burnet of New York asks to see him. While in New Jersey on a job printing money he meets and makes friends with all the leaders of that provincial society. In England, at the coffeehouses, he chats with Mandeville and meets the great Dr. Henry Pemberton who was seeing the third edition of Newton's *Principia* through the press. As Franklin said, diligent in his calling, he raised himself by some degree.

The Protestant doctrine of calling, of industriousness in the world, contained dynamite for the orderly, hierarchical, social structure it was originally meant to support. The unintended consequence showed itself within two generations. Those who were abstemious, frugal and hardworking made a success in the world. They rose. And society, rather than the static and closed order in which, in Winthrop's words, "some must be rich some poor, some high and eminent in power and dignitie; others meane and in subieccion," turned out to be dynamic, fluid and open.

If there is much of our national character implicit in Franklin's career, it is because, early in our history, he represents a response to the rapid social change that has remained about the only constant in American society. He was the self-made man, the jack-of-all-trades. He taught thirteen rules to sure success and purveyed do-it-yourself kits for those who, like himself, constituted a "rising" people. Franklin stands most clearly as an exemplary American because his life's story is a witness to the uncertainties about social status that have characterized our society, a society caught up in the constant process of change. The question, "Who was Benjamin Franklin?" is a critical question to ask of Franklin because it is the question to which Franklin himself is constantly seeking an answer. In a society in which there are no outward, easily discernible marks of social status, the question always is, as we put it in the title of reference works that are supposed to provide the answer, "Who's Who?"

Along with the uncertainties generated by rapid social mobility, there is another aspect to the difficulty we have in placing Franklin, an aspect that is more complex and harder to state, but just as important and equally characteristic. It takes us back again to the Puritans. In Puritan religious thought there was originally a dynamic equipoise between two opposite thrusts, the tension between an inward, mystical, personal experience of God's grace and the demands for an outward, sober, socially responsible ethic, the tension between faith and works, between the essence of religion and its outward show. Tremendous energy went into sustaining these polarities in the early years but, as the original piety waned, itself undermined by the worldly success that benefited from the doctrine of calling, the syntheses split in two and resulted in the eighteenth century in Jonathan Edwards and Benjamin Franklin, similar in so many ways, yet so radically unlike.

Franklin, making his own world as he makes his way through it, pragmatically rejects the old conundrum whether man does good works because he is saved, or is saved because he does good works. "Vicious actions are not hurtful because they are forbidden, but forbidden because they are hurtful," he decides, and then in an added phrase calmly throws out the God-centered universe of his forebears, "the nature of man alone considered."

Content with his success, blandly sure it must be in the design of Providence that printers hobnob with kings, Franklin simply passes by the problem of the relation between reality and appearance. In this world, appearance is sufficient. Humanely skeptical that the essence can ever be caught, Franklin decided to leave the question to be answered in the next world, if there proved to be one. For this world, a "tolerable character" was enough and he "valued it properly." The result was a common sense of utilitarianism which sometimes verges toward sheer crassness. But it worked. For this world, what others think of you is what is important. If Franklin, viewed from the perspective of Max Weber and students of the Protestant ethic, can seem to be the representative, *par excellence*, of the character who internalizes the imperatives of his society and steers his own course unaided through the world, from a slightly different perspective he also turns out to be the other-directed character David Riesman has described, constantly attuned to the expectations of those around him, responding swiftly to the changing situations that demand he play different roles.

We admire, I think, the lusty good sense of the man who triumphs in the world that he accepts, yet at the same time we are uneasy with the man who wears so many masks that we are never sure who is there behind them. Yet it is this, this very difficulty of deciding whether we admire Franklin or suspect him, that makes his character an archetype for our national experience. There are great advantages to be had in belonging to a culture without clearly defined classes, without an establishment, but there is, along with the advantages, a certain strain, a necessary uneasiness. In an open and pluralistic society we have difficulty "placing" people, as we say. Think how often in our kind of society when we meet someone for the first time how our second or third question is apt to be, "What do you do?" Never, "Who are you?" The social role is enough, but in our more reflective moments we realize not so, and in our most reflective moments we realize it will never do for our own selves. We may be able to, but we do not want to go through life as a doctor, lawyer, or Indian chief. We want to be ourselves, as we say. And at the beginning of our national experience, Benjamin Franklin not only puts the question that still troubles us in our kind of society, "Who's Who?" He also raises the question that lies at the heart of the trouble: "Who am I?"

PART TWO

A REVOLUTIONARY PEOPLE

The history of the American Revolution is no longer thought of simply as a story of patriotic ardor overcoming British corruption in the crucible of war. As historians have investigated the meaning of the Revolution to ordinary men and women, to Native Americans, and to African Americans (both bound and free), they have discovered a world of complexity and dispute in which people's allegiance to the patriot cause depended as much on their place in society as on abstract political or constitutional principles.

The Revolutionary War itself was a complex affair. As the essays by Alfred F. Young and James Kirby Martin reveal, ordinary artisans, farmers, laborers, and mariners had their own reasons for supporting the American cause. Like many other artisans, George Robert Twelves Hewes was attracted to the patriot cause because he found in it a way to reject the deference he had been forced to give his "superiors" during the colonial era and because it allowed him to claim an independent political voice for the first time in his life. The men who joined Washington's Continental Army, on the other hand, composed a "Most Undisciplined, Profligate Crew" of poor men from eastern North America's farms and cities. These men from the lower ranks of society risked their lives less from patriotism, Martin claims, than from the promise of the wartime pay and land bounties that might permit them to join the ranks of independent landowners after the Revolution.

The Treaty of Paris, signed in 1783, ended the Revolutionary War and established the United States as an independent nation. At the same time, it posed many new questions to the American people. Drew McCoy's essay "Two Visions of the Constitution" discusses two of the most momentous of these questions: What sort of policy would the national government establish? And what sort of society would its policies promote? In the contrasting visions of Benjamin Franklin and Alexander Hamilton, McCoy argues, lay the future model for American social and political development.

The Federalist domination of national politics during the 1790s marked the temporary triumph of Hamilton's conservative vision of limited popular involvement in political affairs. But Federalist policies did not long remain unchallenged. An opposition movement—whose leaders eventually adopted the label Democratic-Republicans—rose in 1793 to challenge the Federalists and by the end of the decade gained enough popular support to threaten Federalist control of national, state, and local governments. In "Matthew Lyon's Trial for Sedition," Aleine Austin tells the story of a rising Vermont Democratic-Republican leader who ran afoul of Federalist attempts to suppress dissent through the creation of a national sedition law.

The Revolution had a profound impact on those outside the political realm as well. The wartime rhetoric that counterposed American liberty to British slavery brought many Americans to reconsider the institution of slavery in the new nation. Especially in the northern states, where slavery was less important economically, but in the Virginia assembly as well, state legislatures debated the question of abolition, and by the end of the eighteenth century the northern states had sent slavery on the road to extinction. In "Absalom Jones," Gary B. Nash discusses the difficult birth of the nation's most important free black community in Philadelphia. Focusing on Jones, an ex-slave who purchased his own freedom and went on to found the first independent African-American church in America, Nash points to the vital importance of religion in the struggle to form free black communities.

Religion played an equally important role in Native American resistance to white expansion into the trans-Appalachian West. No sooner had the Revolutionary War ended than land-hungry settlers surged over the Appalachians, claiming land in Kentucky, Tennessee, and the Northwest Territory by right of conquest. Faced with internal political divisions, wavering British support, and general white hostility, Native American leaders searched for new ways to deal with the imminent threat to their ancestral homelands. Some, like the Cherokee, chose the path of assimilation, hoping that by adopting white ways, they would be accepted into mainstream American society. Others, like the Shawnee leaders Tecumseh and Tenskwatawa—discussed in R. David Edmunds's essay—chose the path of pan-Indian alliance and armed resistance, arguing that whites would never permit Indian assimilation into the white republic.

The forces of agrarian change that drove tens of thousands of eastern farmers to seek better fortunes in the West are the subject of Robert A. Gross's essay "Culture and Cultivation." The growing penetration of national and international markets into rural Concord, Massachusetts, transformed the lives of its residents, Gross argues, forcing them to balance their family- and community-oriented lives against the impersonal forces of the marketplace. In Concord, as in the rest of the United States, the Revolution set in motion social, economic, and political forces that would transform everyday life in the early nineteenth century.

8

GEORGE ROBERT TWELVES HEWES: A BOSTON SHOEMAKER AND THE AMERICAN REVOLUTION

ALFRED F. YOUNG

By the mid-eighteenth century, questions of political and social authority occupied the minds of Americans of all ranks. While the prosperous governing elites debated the nature of British parliamentary authority in the colonies, those of more humble station challenged existing social arrangements. In rural communities in which land scarcity meant that fathers could no longer offer the promise of propertied independence to their children, sons and daughters began to question the patriarchal control of their fathers and conceived children to force marriage on their own terms. In towns and cities, middling- and laboring-class people joined in questioning the customary authority that the rural gentry and urban merchants exercised. In the mobilization against Britain, these people of lower status demanded a voice in their own affairs that threatened the system of patronage and deference that had dominated social relations for generations.

In Boston, as Alfred F. Young shows, popular questioning of elite control grew in force as the Revolution approached. By following the career of George Robert Twelves Hewes, a humble shoemaker whose experiences were typical of ordinary artisans in America's pre-Revolutionary cities, Young reveals the breakdown of the system of deference that dominated much of the political and social history of colonial America. As the imperial bonds that bound British America to the mother country began to loosen following the Seven Years' War, social relations within the colonies began to change as well. Whereas in 1763 someone such as Hewes felt intimidated and socially inferior when dealing with wealthy and politically influential men such as John Hancock, 15 years later men of Hewes's rank routinely declared themselves equal to all men, regardless of wealth or social position. The rise of this popular egalitarianism was a prominent feature of the Revolutionary era, as ordinary farmers and artisans placed their lives and livelihoods at risk for the patriot cause. By the end of the eighteenth century, these wartime sacrifices brought ordinary men such as Hewes to make unprecedented demands for social equality and popular political participation in the affairs of the new republic.

Seeing the American Revolution through the eyes of a poor shoemaker rather than from the perspective of founding fathers such as Washington, Jefferson, and John Adams has a twofold advantage. First, it enables us to see the role of ordinary people as history makers; second, it shows that a social upheaval such as the American Revolution can involve many agendas—not always shared by the various participants.

"George Robert Twelves Hewes." **William and Mary Quarterly,** *38:4, 561–623.*
Copyright © 1981 by Alfred F. Young. Reprinted by permission.

Late in 1762 or early in 1763, George Robert Twelves Hewes, a Boston shoemaker in the last year or so of his apprenticeship, repaired a shoe for John Hancock and delivered it to him at his uncle Thomas Hancock's store in Dock Square. Hancock was pleased and invited the young man to "come and see him on New Year's day, and bid him a happy New Year," according to the custom of the day, a ritual of noblesse oblige on the part of the gentry. We know of the episode through Benjamin Bussey Thatcher, who interviewed Hewes and wrote it up for his *Memoir* of Hewes in 1835. On New Year's Day, as Thatcher tells the story, after some urging by his master,

> George washed his face, and put his best jacket on, and proceeded straightaway to the Hancock House (as it is still called). His heart was in his mouth, but assuming a cheerful courage, he knocked at the front door, and took his hat off. The servant came:
>
> "Is 'Squire Hancock at home, Sir?" enquired Hewes, making a bow.
>
> He was introduced directly to the *kitchen,* and requested to seat himself, while report should be made above stairs. The man came down directly, with a new varnish of civility suddenly spread over his face. He ushered him into the 'Squire's sitting-room, and left him to make his obeisance. Hancock remembered him, and addressed him kindly. George was anxious to get through, and he commenced a desperate speech—"as pretty a one," he says, "as he any way knew how,"—intended to announce the purpose of his visit, and to accomplish it, in the same breath.
>
> "Very well, my lad," said the 'Squire—"now take a chair, my lad."
>
> He sat down, scared all the while (as he now confesses) "almost to death," while Hancock put his hand into his breeches-pocket and pulled out a crown-piece, which he placed softly in his hand, thanking him at the same time for his punctual attendance, and his compliments. He then invited his young friend to drink his health—called for wine—poured it out for him—and ticked glasses with him,—a feat in which Hewes, though he had never seen it performed before, having acquitted himself with a creditable dexterity, hastened to make his bow again, and secure his retreat, though not till the 'Squire had extorted a sort of

half promise from him to come the next New-Year's—which, for a rarity, he never discharged.

The episode is a demonstration of what the eighteenth century called deference.

Another episode catches the point at which Hewes had arrived a decade and a half later. In 1778 or 1779, after one stint in the war on board a privateer and another in the militia, he was ready to ship out again, from Boston. As Thatcher tells the story: "Here he enlisted, or engaged to enlist, on board the Hancock, a twenty-gun ship, but not liking the manners of the Lieutenant very well, who ordered him one day in the streets to take his hat off to him—which he refused to do for any man,—he went aboard the 'Defence,' Captain Smedley, of Fairfield Connecticut." This, with a vengeance, is the casting off of deference.

What had happened in the intervening years? What had turned the young shoemaker tongue-tied in the face of his betters into the defiant person who would not take his hat off for any man? And why should stories like this have stayed in his memory sixty and seventy years later?

George Robert Twelves Hewes was born in Boston in 1742 and died in Richfield Springs, New York, in 1840. He participated in several of the principal political events of the American Revolution in Boston, among them the Massacre and the Tea Party, and during the war he served as a privateersman and militiaman. A shoemaker all his life, and intermittently or concurrently a fisherman, sailor, and farmer, he remained a poor man. He never made it, not before the war in Boston, not at sea, not after the war in Wrentham and Attleborough, Massachusetts, not in Otsego County, New York. He was a nobody who briefly became a somebody in the Revolution and, for a moment near the end of his life, a hero.

Hewes was one of the "humble classes" that made the success of the Revolution possible. How typical he was we can only suggest at this point in our limited knowledge of the "humble classes." Probably he was as representative a member of the "lower trades" of the cities and as much a rank-and-file participant in the political events and the war as historians have found. The two biographies, which come close to being oral histories (and give us clues to track down Hewes in other ways), provide an unusually rich cumulative record, over a very long period of time, of his thoughts, attitudes, and values. Consequently, we can answer, with varying degrees of satisfaction, a number of questions about one man of the "humble classes." About the "lower trades": why did a boy enter a craft with such bleak prospects as shoemaking? what was the life of an apprentice? what did it mean to be a shoemaker and a poor man in Boston? About the Revolution: what moved such a rank-and-file person to action? what action did he take? may we speak of his "ideology"? does the evidence of his loss of deference permit us to speak of change in his consciousness? About the war: how did a poor man, an older man, a man with a family exercise his patriotism? what choices did he make? About the results of the Revolution: how did the war affect him? to what extent did he achieve his life goals? why did he go west? what did it mean to be an aged veteran of the revolution? What, in sum, after more than half a century had passed, was the meaning of the Revolution to someone still in the "humble classes"?

Where one ended up in life depended very much on where one started out. George was born under the sign of the Bulls Head and Horns on Water Street near the docks in the South End. His father—also named George—was a tallow chandler and erstwhile tanner. Hewes drew the connections between his class origins and his life chances as he began his narrative for Hawkes:

My father, said he, was born in Wrentham in the state of Massachusetts, about twenty-eight miles from Boston. My grandfather having made no provision for his support, and being unable to give him an education, apprenticed him at Boston to learn a mechanical trade. . . .

In my childhood, my advantages for education were very limited, much more so than children enjoy at the present time in my native state. My whole education which my opportunities permitted me to acquire, consisted only of a moderate

knowledge of reading and writing; my father's circumstances being confined to such humble means as he was enabled to acquire by his mechanical employment, I was kept running of errands, and exposed of course to all the mischiefs to which children are liable in populous cities.

Hewes's family on his father's side was "no better off than what is called in New England *moderate,* and probably not as good." The American progenitor of the line seems to have come from Wales and was in Salisbury, near Newburyport, in 1677, doing what we do not know. Solomon Hewes, George Robert's grandfather, was born in Portsmouth, New Hampshire, in 1674, became a joiner, and moved with collateral members of his family to Wrentham, originally part of Dedham, near Rhode Island. There he became a landholder; most of his brothers were farmers; two became doctors, one of whom prospered in nearby Providence. His son—our George's father—was born in 1701. On the side of his mother, Abigail Seaver, Hewes's family was a shade different. They had lived for four generations in Roxbury, a small farming town immediately south of Boston across the neck. Abigail's ancestors seem to have been farmers, but one was a minister. Her father, Shubael, was a country cordwainer who owned a house, barn, and two acres. She was born in 1711 and married in 1728.

George Robert Twelves Hewes, born August 25, 1742, was the sixth of nine children, the fourth of seven sons. Five of the nine survived childhood—his three older brothers, Samuel, Shubael, and Solomon, and a younger brother, Daniel. He was named George after his father, Robert after a paternal uncle, and the unlikely Twelves, he thought, for his mother's great uncle, "whose Christian name was Twelve, for whom she appeared to have great admiration. Why he was called by that singular name I never knew." More likely, his mother was honoring her own mother, also Abigail, whose maiden name was Twelves.

The family heritage to George, it might be argued, was more genetic than economic. He inherited a chance to live long: the men in the Seaver line were all long-lived. And he inherited his size. He was unusually short—five feet, one inch. "I have never acquired the ordinary weight or size of other men," Hewes told Hawkes, who wrote that "his whole person is of a slight and slender texture." In old age he was known as "the little old man." Anatomy is not destiny, but Hewes's short size and long name helped shape his personality. It was a big name for a small boy to carry. He was the butt of endless teasing jibes—George Robert what?—that Thatcher turned into anecdotes the humor of which may have masked the pain Hewes may have felt.

"Moderate" as it was, Hewes had a sense of family. Wrentham, town of his grandfather and uncles, was a place he would be sent as a boy, a place of refuge in the war, and after the war his home. He would receive an inheritance three times in his life, each one a reminder of the importance or potential importance of relatives. And he was quite aware of any relative of status, like Dr. Joseph Warren, a distant kinsman on his mother's side.

His father's life in Boston had been an endless, futile struggle to succeed as a tanner. Capital was the problem. In 1729 he bought a one-third ownership in a tannery for £600 in bills of credit. Two years later, he sold half of his third to his brother Robert, who became a working partner. The two brothers turned to a rich merchant, Nathaniel Cunningham, who put up £3500 in return for half the profits. The investment was huge: pits, a yard, workshops, hides, bark, two horses, four slaves, journeymen. For a time the tannery flourished. Then there was the disastrous falling out with Cunningham: furious fights, a raid on the yards, debtor's jail twice for George, suits and countersuits that dragged on in the courts for years. The Hewes brothers saw themselves as "very laborious" artisans who "managed their trade with good skill," only to be ruined by a wealthy, arrogant merchant. To Cunningham, they were incompetent and defaulters. Several years before George Robert was born, his father had fallen back to "butchering, tallow chandlering, hog killing, soap, boiling &c."

The family was not impoverished. George had a memory as a little boy of boarding a ship with his mother to buy a small slave girl "at the rate of two dollars a pound." And there was enough money to pay the fees for his early schooling. But beginning in 1748, when he was six, there was a series of family tragedies. In 1748 an infant brother, Joseph, died, followed later in the year by his sister Abigail, age thirteen, and brother Ebenezer, age two. In 1749 his father died suddenly of a stroke, leaving the family nothing, it would seem, his estate tangled in debt and litigation. George's mother would have joined the more than one thousand widows in Boston, most of whom were on poor relief. Sometime before 1755 she died. In 1756 Grandfather Seaver died, leaving less than £15 to be divided among George and his four surviving brothers. Thus in 1756, at the age of fourteen, when boys were customarily put out to apprenticeship, George was an orphan, the ward of his uncle Robert, as was his brother Daniel, age twelve, each with a legacy of £2 17s. 4d. Uncle Robert, though warmly recollected by Hewes, could not do much to help him: a gluemaker, he was struggling to set up his own manufactory. Nor could George's three older brothers, whom he also remembered fondly. In 1756 they were all in the "lower" trades. Samuel age twenty-six, and Solomon, twenty-two, were fishermen; Shubael, twenty-four, was a butcher.

The reason why George was put to shoemaking becomes clearer: no one in the family had the indenture fee to enable him to enter one of the more lucrative "higher" trades. Josiah Franklin, also a tallow chandler, could not make his son Benjamin a cutler because he lacked the fee. But in shoemaking the prospects were so poor that some masters would pay to get an apprentice. In addition, George was too small to enter trades that demanded brawn; he could hardly have become a ropewalk worker, a housewright, or a shipwright. Ebenezer McIntosh, the Boston shoemaker who led the annual Pope's Day festivities and the Stamp Act demonstrations, was a small man. The trade was a sort of dumping ground for poor boys who could not handle heavy work. Boston Overseers of the Poor acted on this assumption in 1770; so did recruiting officers for the American navy forty years later. The same was true in Europe. Getting into a good trade required "connections"; the family connections were in the leather trades, through Uncle Robert, the gluemaker, or brother Shubael, the butcher. Finally, there was a family tradition. Grandfather Shubael had been a cordwainer, and on his death in 1756 there might even have been a prospect of acquiring his tools and lasts. In any case, the capital that would be needed to set up shop of one's own was relatively small. And so the boy became a shoemaker—because he had very little choice.

Josiah Franklin had known how important it was to place a boy in a trade that was to his liking. Otherwise there was the threat that Benjamin made explicit: he would run away to sea. Hawkes saw the same thrust in Hewes's life: shoemaking "was never an occupation of his choice," he "being inclined to more active pursuits." George was the wrong boy to put in a sedentary trade that was not to his liking. He was what the Bostonians called "saucy"; he was always in Dutch. The memories of his childhood and youth that Thatcher elicited were almost all of defying authority—his mother, his teachers at dame school, his schoolmaster, his aunt, his shoemaker master, a farmer, a doctor.

Hewes spoke of his mother only as a figure who inflicted punishment for disobedience. The earliest incident he remembered could have happened only to a poor family living near the waterfront. When George was about six, Abigail Hewes sent him off to the nearby shipyards with a basket to gather chips for the fire. At the water's edge George put the basket aside, straddled some floating planks to watch the fish, fell in, and sank to the bottom. He was saved only when some ship carpenters saw the basket without the boy, "found him motionless on the bottom, hooked him out with a boat hook, and rolled him on a tar barrel until signs of life were discovered." His mother nursed him back to health. Then she flogged him.

The lesson did not take, nor did others in school with Miss Tinkum, wife of the town crier. He ran away. She put him in a dark closet. He dug his way out. The next day she put him in again. This time he discovered a jar of quince marmalade and devoured it. A new dame school with "mother McLeod" followed. Then school with "our famous Master Holyoke," which Hewes remembered as "little more than a series of escapes made or attempted from the reign of the birch."

Abigail Hewes must have been desperate to control George. She sent him back after one truancy with a note requesting Holyoke to give him a good whipping. Uncle Robert took pity and sent a substitute note. Abigail threatened, "If you run away again I shall go to school with you myself." When George was about ten, she took the final step: she sent him to Wrentham to live with one of his paternal uncles. Here, George recalled, "he spent several years of his boyhood . . . in the monotonous routine of his Uncle's farm." The only incident he recounted was of defying his aunt. His five-year-old cousin hit him in the face with a stick "without any provocation." George cursed the boy out, for which his aunt whipped him, and when she refused to do the same with her son, George undertook to "chastise" him himself. "I caught my cousin at the barn" and applied the rod. The aunt locked him up but his uncle let him go, responsive to his plea for "equal justice."

Thus when George entered his apprenticeship, if he was not quite the young whig his biographers made him out to be, he was not a youth who would suffer arbitrary authority easily. His master, Downing, had an irascible side and was willing to use a cowhide. Hewes lived in Downing's attic with a fellow apprentice, John Gilbert. All the incidents Hewes recalled from this period had two motifs: petty defiance and a quest for food. There was an escapade on a Saturday night when the two apprentices made off for Gilbert's house and bought a loaf of bread, a pound of butter, and some coffee. They returned after curfew to encounter an enraged Downing, whom they foiled by setting pans and tubs for him to trip over when he came to the door. There was an excursion to Roxbury on Training Day, the traditional apprentices' holiday in Boston, with fellow apprentices and his younger brother. Caught stealing apples, they were taken before the farmer, who was also justice of the peace and who laughed uproariously at Hewes's name and let him go. There was an incident with a doctor who inoculated Hewes and a fellow worker for smallpox and warned them to abstain from food. Sick, fearful of death, Hewes and his friend consumed a dish of venison in melted butter and a mug of flip—and lived to tell the tale.

These memories of youthful defiance and youthful hunger lingered on for seventy years: a loaf of bread and a pound of butter, a parcel of apples, a dish of venison. This shoemaker's apprentice could hardly have been well fed or treated with affection.

The proof is that Hewes tried to end his apprenticeship by the only way he saw possible: escape to the military. "After finding that my depressed condition would probably render it impracticable for me to acquire that education requisite for civil employments," he told Hawkes, "I had resolved to engage in the military service of my country, should an opportunity present." Late in the 1750s, possibly in 1760, as the fourth and last of England's great colonial wars with France ground on and his majesty's army recruiters beat their drums through Boston's streets, Hewes and Gilbert tried to enlist. Gilbert was accepted, but Hewes was not. Recruiting captains were under orders to "enlist no Roman-Catholic, nor any under five feet two inches high without their shoes." "I could not pass muster," Hewes told Hawkes, "because I was not tall enough." As Thatcher embroiders Hawkes's story, Hewes then "went to the shoe shop of several of his acquaintances and heightened his heels by several taps[;] then stuffing his stocking with paper and rags," he returned. The examining captain saw through the trick and rejected him again. Frustrated, humiliated, vowing he would never return to Downing, he took an even more desperate step: he went down to the wharf

and tried to enlist on a British ship of war. "His brothers, however, soon heard of it and interfered," and, in Thatcher's words, "he was compelled to abandon that plan." Bostonians like Solomon and Samuel Hewes, who made their living on the waterfront, did not need long memories to remember the city's massive resistance to the impressment sweeps of 1747 and to know that the British navy would be, not escape, but another prison.

About this time, shoemaker Downing failed after fire swept his shop (possibly the great fire of 1760). This would have freed Hewes of his indenture, but he was not qualified to be a shoemaker until he had completed apprenticeship. As Hewes told it, he therefore apprenticed himself "for the remainder of his minority," that is, until he turned twenty-one, to Harry Rhoades, who paid him $40. In 1835 he could tell Thatcher how much time he then had left to serve, down to the month and day. Of the rest of his "time" he had no bad memories.

Apprenticeship had a lighter side. Hewes's anecdotes give tantalizing glimpses into an embryonic apprentice culture in Boston to which other sources attest—glimpses of pranks played on masters, of revelry after curfew, of Training Day, when the militia displayed its maneuvers and there was drink, food, and "frolicking" on the Common. One may speculate that George also took part in the annual Pope's Day festival, November 5, when apprentices, servants, artisans in the lower trades, and young people of all classes took over the town, parading effigies of Pope, Devil, and Pretender, exacting tribute from the better sort, and engaging in a battle royal between North End and South End Pope's Day "companies."

Hewes's stories of his youth hint at his winning a place for himself as the small schoolboy who got the better of his elders, the apprentice who defied his master, perhaps even a leader among his peers. There are also hints of the adult personality. Hewes was punished often, but if childhood punishment inured some to pain, it made Hewes reluctant to inflict pain on others. He developed a generous streak that led him to reach out to others in trouble. When Downing, a broken man, was on the verge of leaving for Nova Scotia to start anew, Hewes went down to his ship and gave him half of the $40 fee Rhoades had paid him. Downing broke into tears. The story smacks of the Good Samaritan, of the Methodist of the 1830s counting his good deeds; and yet the memory was so vivid, wrote Thatcher, that "his features light up even now with a gleam of rejoicing pride." Hewes spoke later of the "tender sympathies of my nature." He did not want to be, but he was, a fit candidate for the "gentle craft" he was about to enter.

In Boston from 1763, when he entered his majority, until 1775, when he went off to war, Hewes never made a go of it as a shoemaker. He remembered these years more fondly than he had lived them. As Hawkes took down his story, shifting from the third to the first person:

> Hewes said he cheerfully submitted to the course of life to which his destinies directed.
>
> He built him a shop and pursued the private avocation of his trade for a considerable length of time, until on the application of his brother he was induced to go with him on two fishing voyages to the banks of New Foundland, which occupied his time for two years.
>
> After the conclusion of the French war . . . he continued at Boston, except the two years absence with his brother.
>
> During that period, said Hewes, when I was at the age of twenty-six, I married the daughter of Benjamin Sumner, of Boston. At the time of our intermarriage, the age of my wife was seventeen. We lived together very happily seventy years. She died at the age of eighty-seven.
>
> At the time when British troops were first stationed at Boston, we had several children, the exact number I do not recollect. By our industry and mutual efforts we were improving our condition.

He had his own shop—this much is clear, but the rest is surmise. There were at that time in Boston about sixty to seventy shoemakers, most of whom seem to have catered to the local market. If Hewes was typical, he would have made shoes to order, "bespoke" work; this would have made him a cordwainer. And he would have repaired shoes: this would have made him a cobbler. Who were his customers? No business records survive. A shoemaker probably drew his customers from his immediate neighborhood. Located as he was near the waterfront and ropewalks, Hewes might well have had customers of the "meaner" sort. In a ward inhabited by the "middling" sort he may also have drawn on them. When the British troops occupied Boston, he did some work for them. Nothing suggests that he catered to the "carriage trade."

Was his business "improving" or "growing better"? Probably it was never very good and grew worse. From his own words we know that he took off two years on fishing voyages with his brothers. He did not mention that during this period he lived for a short time in Roxbury. His prospects were thus not good enough to keep him in Boston. His marriage is another clue to his low fortune. Sally (or Sarah) Sumner's father was a sexton so poor that his wife and daughters had to take in washing. The couple was married by the Reverend Samuel Stillman of the First Baptist Church, which suggests that this was the church that Benjamin Sumner served. Though Stillman was respected, First Baptist was not "one of the principal churches in town," as Thatcher guessed, but one of the poorest and smallest, with a congregation heavy with laboring people, sailors, and blacks. Marriage, one of the few potential sources of capital for an aspiring tradesman, as Benjamin Franklin made clear in his autobiography, did not lift Hewes up.

Hewes stayed poor. The Boston tax records of 1771, the only ones that have survived for these years, show him living as a lodger in the house of Christopher Ranks, a watchmaker, in the old North End. He was not taxed for any property. In 1773 he and his family, which now included three children, were apparently living with his uncle Robert in the South End; at some time during these years before the war they also lived with a brother. After almost a decade on his own, Hewes could not afford his own place. In January 1774 he inadvertently summed up his condition and reputation in the course of a violent street encounter. Damned as "a rascal" and "a vagabond" who had no right to "speak to a gentlemen in the street," Hewes retorted that he was neither "and though a poor man, in a good credit in town" as his well-to-do antagonist.

Between 1768 and 1775, the shoemaker became a citizen—an active participant in the events that led to the Revolution, an angry, assertive man who won recognition as a patriot. What explains the transformation? We have enough evidence to take stock of Hewes's role in three major events of the decade: the Massacre (1770), the Tea Party (1773), and the tarring and feathering of John Malcolm (1774).

On the night of the Massacre, March 5, Hewes was in the thick of the action. What he tells us about what brought him to King Street, what brought others there, and what he did during and after this tumultuous event gives us the perspective of a man in the street. The presence of British troops in Boston beginning in the summer of 1768—four thousand soldiers in a town of fewer than sixteen thousand inhabitants—touched Hewes personally. Anecdotes about soldiers flowed from him. He had seen them march off the transports at the Long Wharf; he had seen them every day occupying civilian buildings on Griffin's Wharf near his shop. He knew how irritating it was to be challenged by British sentries after curfew (his solution was to offer a swig of rum from the bottle he carried).

More important, he was personally cheated by a soldier. Sergeant Mark Burk ordered shoes allegedly for Captain Thomas Preston, picked them up, but never paid for them. Hewes complained to Preston, who made good and suggested he bring a complaint. A military hearing ensued, at which Hewes testified. The soldier, to Hewes's horror, was sentenced to three hundred fifty lashes. He "remarked to the court that if he had thought the fellow was to be punished so severely for such an offense, bad as he was, he would have said nothing about it." And he saw others victimized by soldiers. He witnessed an incident in which a soldier sneaked up behind a

woman, felled her with his fist, and "stripped her of her bonnet, cardinal muff and tippet." He followed the man to his barracks, identified him (Hewes remembered him as Private Kilroy, who would appear later at the Massacre), and got him to give up the stolen goods, but decided this time not to press charges. Hewes was also keenly aware of grievances felt by the laboring men and youths who formed the bulk of the crowd—and the principal victims—at the Massacre. From extant accounts, three causes can be pieced together.

First in time, and vividly recalled by Hewes, was the murder of eleven-year-old Christopher Seider on February 23, ten days before the Massacre. Seider was one of a large crowd of schoolboys and apprentices picketing the shop of Theophilus Lilly, a merchant violating the anti-import resolutions. Ebenezer Richardson, a paid customs informer, shot into the throng and killed Seider. Richardson would have been tarred and feathered, or worse, had not whig leaders intervened to hustle him off to jail. At Seider's funeral, only a week before the Massacre, five hundred boys marched two by two behind the coffin, followed by two thousand or more adults, "the largest [funeral] perhaps ever known in America," Thomas Hutchinson thought.

Second, Hewes emphasized the bitter fight two days before the Massacre between soldiers and workers at Gray's ropewalk down the block from Hewes's shop. Off-duty soldiers were allowed to moonlight, taking work from civilians. On Friday, March 3, when one of them asked for work at Gray's, a battle ensued between a few score soldiers and ropewalk workers joined by others in the maritime trades. The soldiers were beaten and sought revenge. Consequently, in Thatcher's words, "quite a number of soldiers, in a word, were determined to have a row on the night of the 5th."

Third, the precipitating events on the night of the Massacre, by Hewes's account, were an attempt by a barber's apprentice to collect an overdue bill from a British officer, the sentry's abuse of the boy, and the subsequent harassment of the sentry by a small band of boys that led to the calling of the guard commanded by Captain Preston. Thatcher found this hard to swallow—"a dun from a greasy barber's boy is rather an extraordinary explanation of the origin, or one of the occasions, of the massacre of the 5th of March"—but at the trial the lawyers did not. They battled over defining "boys" and over the age, size, and degree of aggressiveness of the numerous apprentices on the scene.

Hewes viewed the civilians as essentially defensive. On the evening of the Massacre he appeared early on the scene in King Street, attracted by the clamor over the apprentice. "I was soon on the ground among them," he said, as if it were only natural that he should have turned out in defense of fellow townsmen against what was assumed to be the danger of aggressive action by soldiers. He was not part of a conspiracy; neither was he there out of curiosity. He was unarmed, carrying neither club nor stave as some others did. He saw snow, ice, and "missiles" thrown at the soldiers. When the main guard rushed out in support of the sentry, Private Kilroy dealt Hewes a blow on his shoulder with his gun. Preston ordered the townspeople to disperse. Hewes believed they had a legal basis to refuse: "they were in the king's highway, and had as good a right to be there" as Preston.

The five men killed were all workingmen. Hewes claimed to know four: Samuel Gray, a ropewalk worker; Samuel Maverick, age seventeen, an apprentice to an ivory turner; Patrick Carr, an apprentice to a leather breeches worker; and James Caldwell, second mate on a ship—all but Christopher Attucks. Caldwell, "who was shot in the back was standing by the side of Hewes, and the latter caught him in his arms as he fell," helped carry him to Dr. Thomas Young in Prison Lane, then ran to Caldwell's ship captain on Cold Lane.

More than horror was burned into Hewes's memory. He remembered the political confrontation that followed the slaughter, when thousands of angry townspeople faced hundreds of British troops massed with ready rifles. "The

people," Hewes recounted, "then immediately choose a committee to report to the governor the result of Captain Preston's conduct, and to demand of him satisfaction." Actually the "people" did not choose a committee "immediately." In the dark hours after the Massacre a self-appointed group of patriot leaders met with officials and forced Hutchinson to commit Preston and the soldiers to jail. Hewes was remembering the town meeting the next day, so huge that it had to adjourn from Fanueil Hall, the traditional meeting place that held only twelve hundred, to Old South Church, which had room for five to six thousand. This meeting approved a committee to wait on officials and then adjourned, but met again the same day, received and voted down an offer to remove one regiment, then accepted another to remove two. This was one of the meetings at which property bars were let down.

What Hewes did not recount, but what he had promptly put down in a deposition the next day, was how militant he was after the Massacre. At 1:00 A.M., like many other enraged Bostonians, he went home to arm himself. On his way back to the Town House with a cane he had a defiant exchange with Sergeant Chambers of the 29th Regiment and eight or nine soldiers, "all with very large clubs or cutlasses." A soldier, Dobson, "ask'd him how he far'd; he told him very badly to see his townsmen shot in such a manner, and asked him if he did not think it was a dreadful thing." Dobson swore "it was a fine thing" and "you shall see more of it." Chambers "seized and forced" the cane from Hewes, "saying I had no right to carry it. I told him I had as good a right to carry a cane as they had to carry clubs."

The Massacre had stirred Hewes to political action. He was one of ninety-nine Bostonians who gave depositions for the prosecution that were published by the town in a pamphlet. Undoubtedly, he marched in the great funeral procession for the victims that brought the city to a standstill. He attended the tempestuous trial of Ebenezer Richardson, Seider's slayer, which was linked politically with the Massacre. ("He remembers to this moment even the precise words of the Judge's sentence," wrote Thatcher.) He seems to have attended the trial of the soldiers or Preston or both.

It was in this context that he remembered something for which there is no corroborating evidence, namely, testifying at Preston's trial on a crucial point. He told Hawkes:

> When Preston, their captain, was tried, I was called as one of the witnesses, on the part of the government, and testified, that I believed it was the same man, Captain Preston, that ordered his soldiers to make ready, who also ordered them to fire. Mr. John Adams, former president of the United States, was advocate for the prisoners, and denied the fact, that Captain Preston gave orders to his men to fire; and on his cross examination of me asked whether my position was such, that I could see the captain's lips in motion when the order to fire was given; to which I answered, that I could not.

Perhaps so: Hewes's account is particular and precise, and there are many lacunae in the record of the trial (we have no verbatim transcript) that modern editors have assiduously assembled. Perhaps not: Hewes may have "remembered" his brother Shubael on the stand at the trial of the soldiers (although Shubael was a defense witness) or his uncle Robert testifying at Richardson's trial. Or he may have given pretrial testimony but was not called to the stand.

In one sense, it does not matter. What he was remembering was that he had become involved. He turned out because of a sense of kinship with "his townsmen" in danger; he stood his ground in defense of his "rights"; he was among the "people" who delegated a committee to act on their behalf; he took part in the legal process by giving a deposition, by attending the trials, and as he remembered it, by testifying. In sum, he had become a citizen, a political man.

Four years later, at the Tea Party on the night of December 16, 1773, the citizen "volunteered" and became the kind of leader for whom most historians have never found a place. The Tea Party, unlike the Massacre, was organized by the radical whig leaders of Boston. They mapped the strategy, organized the public meetings, appointed the companies to guard the tea ships at Griffin's Wharf (among them Daniel Hewes, George's brother), and planned the official boarding parties. As in 1770, they converted the town meetings into meetings of "the whole body of the people," one of which Hutchinson found "consisted principally of the Lower ranks of the People & even Journeymen. Tradesmen were brought in to increase the number & the Rabble were not excluded yet there were divers Gentlemen of Good Fortunes among them."

The boarding parties showed this same combination of "ranks." Hawkes wrote:

> On my inquiring of Hewes if he knew who first proposed the project of destroying the tea, to prevent its being landed, he replied that he did not; neither did he know who or what number were to volunteer their services for that purpose. But from the significant allusion of some persons in whom I had confidence, together with the knowledge I had of the spirit of those times, I had no doubt but that a sufficient number of associates would accompany me in that enterprise.

The recollection of Joshua Wyeth, a journeyman blacksmith, verified Hewes's story in explicit detail: "It was proposed that young men, not much known in town and not liable to be easily recognized should lead in the business." Wyeth believed that "most of the persons selected for the occasion were apprentices and journeyman, as was the case with myself, living with tory masters." Wyeth "had but a few hours warning of what was intended to be done." Those in the officially designated parties, about thirty men better known, appeared in well-prepared Indian disguises. As nobodies, the volunteers—anywhere from fifty to one hundred men—could get away with hastily improvised disguises. Hewes said he got himself up as an Indian and daubed his "face and hands with coal dust in the shop of blacksmith." In the streets "I fell in with many who were dressed, equipped and painted as I was, and who fell in with me and marched in order to the place of our destination."

At Griffin's Wharf the volunteers were orderly, self-disciplined, and ready to accept leadership.

When we arrived at the wharf, there were three of our number who assumed an authority to direct our operations, to which we readily submitted. They divided us into three parties, for the purpose of boarding the three ships which contained the tea at the same time. The name of him who commanded the division to which I was assigned was Leonard Pitt [Lendell Pitts]. The names of the other commanders I never knew. We were immediately ordered by the respective commanders to board all the ships at the same time, which we promptly obeyed.

But for Hewes there was something new: he was singled out of the rank and file and made an officer in the field.

The commander of the division to which I belonged, as soon as we were on board the ship, appointed me boatswain, and ordered me to go to the captain and demand of him the keys to the hatches and a dozen candles. I made the demand accordingly, and the captain promptly replied, and delivered the articles; but requested me at the same time to do no damage to the ship or rigging. We then were ordered by our commander to open the hatches, and take out all the chests of tea and throw them overboard, and we immediately proceeded to execute his orders; first cutting and splitting the chests with our tomahawks, so as thoroughly to expose them to the effects of the water. In about three hours from the time we went on board, we had thus broken and thrown overboard every tea chest to be found in the ship; while those in the other ships were disposing of the tea in the same way, at the same time. We were surrounded by British armed ships, but no attempt was made to resist us. We then quietly retired to our several places of residence, without having any conversation with each other, or taking any measure to discover who were our associates.

As the Tea Party ended, Hewes was stirred to further action on his own initiative, just as he had been in the hours after the Massacre. While the crews were throwing the tea overboard, a few other men tried to smuggle off some of the tea

scattered on the decks. "One Captain O'Connor whom I well knew," said Hewes, "came on board for that purpose, and when he supposed he was not noticed, filled his pockets, and also the lining of his coat. But I had detected him, and gave information to the captain of what he was doing. We were ordered to take him into custody, and just as he was stepping from the vessel, I seized him by the skirt of his coat, and in attempting to pull him back, I tore it off." They scuffled. O'Connor recognized him and "threatened to 'complain to the Governor.' 'You had better make your will first,' quoth Hewes, doubling his fist expressively," and O'Connor escaped, running the gauntlet of the crowd on the wharf. "The next day we nailed the skirt of his coat, which I had pulled off, to the whipping post in Charlestown, the place of his residence, with a label upon it," to shame O'Connor by "popular indignation."

A month later, at the third event for which we have full evidence, Hewes won public recognition for an act of courage that almost cost his life and precipitated the most publicized tarring and feathering of the Revolution. The incident that set it off would have been trivial at any other time. On Tuesday, January 25, 1774, at about two in the afternoon, the shoemaker was making his way back to his shop after his dinner. According to the very full account in the *Massachusetts Gazette*,

Mr. George-Robert-Twelves-Hewes was coming along Fore-Street, near Captain Ridgway's, and found the redoubted John Malcolm, standing over a small boy, who was pushing a little sled before him, cursing, damning, threatening and shaking a very large cane with a very heavy ferril on it over his head. The boy at that time was perfectly quiet, notwithstanding which Malcolm continued his threats of striking him, which Mr. Hewes conceiving if he struck him with that weapon he must have killed him out-right, came up to him, and said to him, Mr. Malcolm I hope you are not going to strike this boy with that stick.

Malcolm had already acquired an odious reputation with patriots of the lower sort. A

Bostonian, he had been a sea captain, an army officer, and recently an employee of the customs service. He was so strong a supporter of royal authority that he had traveled to North Carolina to fight the Regulators and boasted of having a horse shot out from under him. He had a fiery temper. As a customs informer he was known to have turned in a vessel to punish sailors for petty smuggling, a custom of the sea. In November 1773, near Portsmouth, New Hampshire, a crowd of thirty sailors had "genteely tarr'd and feather'd" him, as the *Boston Gazette* put it: they did the job over his clothes. Back in Boston he made "frequent complaints" to Hutchinson of "being hooted at in the streets" for this by "tradesmen"; and the lieutenant governor cautioned him, "being a passionate man," not to reply in kind.

The exchange between Malcolm and Hewes resonated with class as well as political differences:

Malcolm returned, you are an impertinent rascal, it is none of your business. Mr. Hewes then asked him, what had the child done to him. Malcolm damned him and asked him if he was going to take his part? Mr. Hewes answered no further than this, that he thought it was a shame for him to strike the child with such a club that, if he intended to strike him. Malcolm on that damned Mr. Hewes, called him a vagabond, and said he would let him know he should not speak to a gentleman in the street. Mr. Hewes returned to that, he was neither a rascal nor vagabond, and though a poor man was in as good credit in town as he was. Malcolm called him a liar, and said he was not, nor ever would be. Mr. Hewes retorted, be that as it will, I never was tarred nor feathered any how. On this Malcolm struck him, and wounded him deeply on the forehead, so that Mr. Hewes for some time lost his senses. Capt. Godfrey, then present, interposed, and after some altercation, Malcolm went home.

Hewes was rushed to Joseph Warren, the patriot doctor, his distant relative. Malcolm's cane had almost penetrated his skull. Thatcher found "the indentation as plainly perceptible as it was sixty years ago." So did Hawkes. Warren

dressed the wound, and Hewes was able to make his way to a magistrate to swear out a warrant for Malcolm's arrest "which he carried to a constable named Justice Hale." Malcolm, meanwhile, had retreated to his house, where he responded in white heat to taunts about the half-way tarring and feathering in Portsmouth with "damn you let me see the man that dare do it better."

In the evening a crowd took Malcolm from his house and dragged him on a sled into King Street "amidst the huzzas of thousands." At this point "several gentlemen endeavored to divert the populace from their intention." The ensuing dialogue laid bare the clash of conceptions of justice between the sailors and laboring people heading the action and Sons of Liberty leaders. The "gentlemen" argued that Malcolm was "open to the laws of the land which would undoubtedly award a reasonable satisfaction to the parties he had abused," that is, the child and Hewes. The answer was political. Malcolm "had been an old impudent and mischievious [*sic*] offender—he had joined in the murders at North Carolina—he had seized vessels on account of sailors having a bottle or two of gin on board—he had in other words behaved in the most capricious, insulting and daringly abusive manner." He could not be trusted to justice. "When they were told the law would have its course with him, they asked what course had the law taken with Preston or his soldiers, with Capt. Wilson or Richardson? And for their parts they had seen so much partiality to the soldiers and customhouse officers by the present Judges, that while things remained as they were, they would, on all such occasions, take satisfaction their own way, and let them take it off."

The references were to Captain Preston who had been tried and found innocent of the Massacre, the soldiers who had been let off with token punishment, Captain John Wilson, who had been indicted for inciting slaves to murder their masters but never tried, and Ebenezer Richardson, who had been tried and found guilty of killing Seider, sentenced, and then pardoned by the crown.

The crowd won and proceeded to a ritualized tarring and feathering, the purpose of which was to punish Malcolm, force a recantation, and ostracize him.

With these and such like arguments, together with a gentle crouding of persons not of their way of thinking out of the ring they proceeded to elevate Mr. Malcolm from his sled into a cart, and stripping him to buff and breeches, gave him a modern jacket [a coat of tar and feathers] and hied him away to liberty-tree, where they proposed to him to renounce his present commission, and swear that he would never hold another inconsistent with the liberties of his country; but this he obstinately refusing, they then carried him to the gallows, passed a rope round his neck, and threw the other end over the beam as if they intended to hang him: But this manoeuvre he set at defiance. They then basted him for some time with a rope's end, and threatened to cut his ears off, and on this he complied, and then they brought him home.

Hewes had precipitated an electrifying event. It was part of the upsurge of spontaneous action in the wake of the Tea Party that prompted the whig leaders to promote a "Committee for Tarring and Feathering" as an instrument of crowd control. The "Committee" made its appearance in broadsides signed by "Captain Joyce, Jun.," a sobriquet meant to invoke the bold cornet who had captured King Charles in 1647. The event was reported in the English newspapers, popularized in three or four satirical prints, and dramatized still further when Malcolm went to England, where he campaigned for a pension and ran for Parliament (without success) against John Wilkes, the leading champion of America. The event confirmed the British ministry in its punitive effort to bring rebellious Boston to heel.

The denouement of the affair was an incident several weeks later. "Malcolm recovered from his wounds and went about as usual. 'How do you do, Mr. Malcolm?' said Hewes, very civilly, the next time he met him. 'Your humble servant, Mr. George Robert Twelves Hewes,' quoth he,—touching his hat genteely as he passed by. 'Thank ye,' thought Hewes, 'and I am glad you have

learned *better manners at last.'*" Hewes's mood was one of triumph. Malcolm had been taught a lesson. The issue was respect for Hewes, a patriot, a poor man, an honest citizen, a decent man standing up for a child against an unspeakably arrogant "gentleman" who was an enemy of his country.

Hewes's role in these three events fits few of the categories that historians have applied to the participation of ordinary men in the Revolution. He was not a member of any organized committee, caucus, or club. He did not attend the expensive public dinners of the Sons of Liberty. He was capable of acting on his own volition without being summoned by any leaders (as in the Massacre). He could volunteer and assume leadership (as in the Tea Party). He was at home on the streets in crowds but he could also reject a crowd (as in the tarring and feathering of Malcolm). He was at home in the other places where ordinary Bostonians turned out to express their convictions: at funeral processions, at meetings of the "whole body of people," in courtrooms at public trials. He recoiled from violence to persons if not to property. The man who could remember the whippings of his own boyhood did not want to be the source of pain to others, whether Sergeant Burk, who tried to cheat him over a pair of shoes, or John Malcolm, who almost killed him. It is in keeping with his character that he should have come to the aid of a little boy facing a beating.

Hewes was moved to act by personal experiences that he shared with large numbers of other plebeian Bostonians. He seems to have been politicized, not by the Stamp Act, but by the coming of the troops after 1768, and then by things that happened to him, that he saw, or that happened to people he knew. Once aroused, he took action with others of his own rank and condition—the laboring classes who formed the bulk of the actors at the Massacre, the Tea Party, and the Malcolm affair—and with other members of his family: his uncle Robert, "known for a staunch Liberty Boy," and his brother Daniel, a guard at the tea ship. Shubael, alone among his brothers, became a tory. These shared experiences were interpreted and focused more likely by the spoken than the written word and as much by his peers at taverns and crowd actions as by leaders in huge public meetings.

As he became active politically he may have had a growing awareness of his worth as a shoemaker. McIntosh was clearly the man of the year in 1765; indeed, whigs were no less fearful than loyalists that "the Captain General of the Liberty Tree" might become the Masaniello of Boston. After a shoemaker made the boot to hang in the Liberty Tree as an effigy of Lord Bute, "Jack Cobler" served notice that "whenever the Public Good requires my services, I shall be ready to distinguish myself." In 1772 "Crispin" began an anti-loyalist diatribe by saying, "I am a shoemaker, a citizen, a free man and a freeholder." The editor added a postscript justifying "Crispin's performance" and explaining that "it should be known what common people, even *coblers* think and feel under the present administration." In city after city, "cobblers" were singled out for derision by conservatives for leaving their lasts to engage in the body politic. Hewes could not have been unaware of all this; he was part of it.

He may also have responded to the rising demand among artisans for support of American manufacturers, whether or not it brought him immediate benefit. He most certainly subscribed to the secularized Puritan ethic—self-denial, industry, frugality—that made artisans take to the nonimportation agreement with its crusade against foreign luxury and its vision of American manufactures. And he could easily have identified with the appeal of the Massachusetts Provincial Congress of 1774 that equated the political need "to encourage agriculture, manufacturers and economy so as to render this state as independent of every other state as the nature of our country will admit" with the "happiness of particular families" in being "independent."

But what ideas did Hewes articulate? He spoke of what he did but very little of what he thought. In the brief statement he offered Hawkes about why he went off to war in 1776, he expressed a commitment to general principles as they had been brought home to him by his expe-

riences. "I was continually reflecting upon the unwarrantable sufferings inflicted on the citizens of Boston by the usurpation and tyranny of Great Britain, and my mind was excited with an unextinguishable desire to aid in chastising them." When Hawkes expressed a doubt "as to the correctness of his conduct in absenting himself from his family," Hewes "emphatically reiterated" the same phrases, adding to a "desire to aid in chastising them" the phrase "and securing our independence." This was clearly not an afterthought; it probably reflected the way many others moved toward the goal of Independence, not as a matter of original intent, but as a step made necessary when all other resorts failed. Ideology thus did not set George Hewes apart from Samuel Adams or John Hancock. The difference lies in what the Revolution did to him as a person. His experiences transformed him, giving him a sense of citizenship and personal worth. Adams and Hancock began with both; Hewes had to arrive there, and in arriving he cast off the constraints of deference.

The two incidents with which we introduced Hewes's life measure the distance he had come: from the young man tongue-tied in the presence of John Hancock to the man who would not take his hat off to the officer of the ship named *Hancock*. Did he cast off his deference to Hancock? Hewes's affirmation of his worth as a human being was a form of class consciousness. Implicit in the idea, "I am as good as any man regardless of rank or wealth," was the idea that any poor man might be as good as any rich man. This did not mean that all rich men were bad. On the contrary, in Boston, more than any other major colonial seaport, a majority of the merchants were part of the patriot coalition; "divers Gentelmen of Good Fortunes," as Hutchinson put it, were with the "Rabble." This blunted class consciousness. Boston's mechanics, unlike New York's or Philadelphia's, did not develop mechanic committees or a mechanic consciousness before the Revolution. Yet in Boston the rich were forced to defer to the people in order to obtain or retain their support. Indeed, the entire public career of Hancock from 1765 on—distributing largesse, buying uniforms for Pope's Day marchers, building ships to employ artisans—can be understood as an exercise of this kind of deference, proving his civic virtue and patriotism.

This gives meaning to Hewes's tale of working beside Hancock at the Tea Party—"a curios reminiscence," Thatcher called it, "but we believe it a mistake."

> Mr. Hewes, however, positively affirms, as of his own observation, that *Samuel Adams and John Hancock were both actively engaged in the process of destruction.* Of the latter he speaks more particularly, being entirely confident that he was himself at one time engaged with him in the demolition of the same chest of tea. He recognized him not only by his *ruffles* making their appearance in the heat of the work, from under the disguise which pretty thoroughly covered him,—and by his figure, and gait;—but by his features, which neither his paint nor his loosened club of hair behind wholly concealed from a close view;—and by his voice also, for he exchanged with him an Indian *grunt,* and the expression *"me know you,"* which was a good deal used on that occasion for a countersign.

Thatcher was justifiably skeptical; it is very unlikely that Hancock was there. Participants swore themselves to secrecy; their identity was one of the best-kept secrets of the Revolution. In fact, in 1835 Thatcher published in an appendix the first list of those "more or less actively engaged" in the Tea Party as furnished by "an aged Bostonian," clearly not Hewes. Hancock was not named. More important, it was not part of the patriot plan for well-known leaders to be present. When the all-day meeting that sanctioned the action adjourned, the leaders, including Hancock, stayed behind conspicuously in Old South. Still, there can be little question that Hewes was convinced at the time that Hancock was on the ship: some gentlemen were indeed present; it was reasonable to assume that Hancock, who had been so conspicuous on the tea issue, was there; Hewes knew what Hancock looked like; he was too insistent about details for his testimony to be dismissed as made up. And

the way he recorded it in his mind at the time was the way he stored it in his memory.

Hewes in effect had brought Hancock down to his own level. The poor shoemaker had not toppled the wealthy merchant; he was no "leveller." But the rich and powerful—the men in "ruffles"—had become, in his own revealing word, his "associates." John Hancock and George Hewes breaking open the same chest at the Tea Party remained for Hewes a symbol of a moment of equality. To the shoemaker, one suspects, this above all was what the Revolutionary events of Boston meant, as did the war that followed.

Hewes's decisions from 1775 to 1783—his choice of services and the timing and sequence of his military activities—suggest a pattern of patriotism mingled with a hope to strike it rich and a pressing need to provide for his family.

After the outbreak of hostilities at Lexington and Concord in April 1775, Boston became a garrison town; patriot civilians streamed out—perhaps ten thousand of them—Tory refugees moved in, and the number of British troops grew to 13,500 by July. Hewes sent his wife and children to Wrentham—his father's native town—where they would be safe with relatives. Hs brother Daniel did the same; Solomon went elsewhere; Shubael alone stayed with the British, as butcher-general to General Gage. George himself remained—"imprisoned," as he remembered it—prevented like other able-bodied men from leaving the city. He made a living as a fisherman; the British allowed him to pass in and out of the harbor in exchange for the pick of the day's catch. He was in Boston nine weeks, was harassed by soldiers on the street, witnessed the Battle of Bunker Hill from a neck of land far out in the bay (he "saw [Joseph Warren] fall"), and saw the corpses of British soldiers "chucked" into an open pit at one end of the Common. One morning he bade good-bye to Shubael, hid his shoemaker's tools under the deck of a small boat borrowed from a tory, and, after a narrow scrape with British guards, made good an escape with two friends to nearby Lynn. The Committee of Safety took him to Cambridge, where General Washington plied him with questions about conditions in Boston—an interview we shall return to. Then he made his way south to Wrentham.

Hewes's record of service thereafter can be reconstructed with reasonable accuracy by matching what he claimed in his pension application in 1832 and told his biographers against information from official records and other contemporary sources. After some months, very likely in the fall of 1776, he enlisted on a privateer at Providence on a voyage north that lasted about three months. He returned to Wrentham and a year later, in the fall of 1777, served in the militia from one to three months. In February 1779 he made a second privateering voyage, this time out of Boston, an eventful seven-and-a-half-month trip to the South and the West Indies. In 1780 he very likely was in the militia again at the same time of year. That was his final tour of duty: in the closing years of the war, to avoid the Massachusetts draft, he hired a substitute. All these enlistments were out of Attleborough, the town immediately south of Wrentham. All were as a private; he did not rise in the ranks.

Several things stand out in this record. Hewes did not go at once, not until he provided for his family. He remembered that he did not make his first enlistment until "about two years after the battle of Bunker Hill," although actually it was closer to a year or fifteen months. He served often, twice at sea, at least four and possibly five times in the militia, but not at all in the Continental army, which would have meant longer periods away from home. For almost all of these stints he volunteered; once he was drafted; once he sent a substitute; he drew these distinctions carefully.

This record, put alongside what we know about other Massachusetts men in the war, places Hewes a good cut above the average. He served at least nine months in the militia and ten-and-a-half months at sea—about twenty months in all. In Concord, most men "were credited with under a half a year's time"; in Peterborough, New Hampshire, only a third did "extensive service" of over a year. Hewes served less than the thirty-three months of the average man in the Continental army. He was not one of the men whom John Shy has called the "hard core" of Revolutionary fighters, like the shoemaker "Long Bill" Scott of Peterborough. But neither was he one of the sunshine patriots Robert Gross found in Concord who came out for no more than a few militia stints early in the war. He served over the length of the fighting. Like others who put in this much time, he was poor; even in Concord after 1778, soldiers in the militia as well as the army "were men with little or nothing to lose." Hewes was in his mid-thirties; he and Sarah had four children by 1776, six by 1781. He spent most of the years of war at home providing for them, doing what, he did not say, but possibly making shoes for the army like other country cordwainers. His patriotism was thus tempered by the need for survival.

Going to war was a wrenching experience. When Hewes told his wife he intended to "take a privateering cruise," she "was greatly afflicted at the prospect of our separation, and my absence from a numerous family of children, who needed a father's parental care." Taught from boyhood to repress his emotions ("I cannot cry," Thatcher reported him saying when punishment loomed), Hewes cut the pain of parting by a ruse.

> On the day which I had appointed to take my departure, I came into the room where my wife was, and inquired if all was ready? She pointed in silence to my knapsack. I observed, that I would put it on and walk with it a few rods, to see if it was rightly fitted to carry with ease. I went out, to return no more until the end of my cruise. The manly fortitude which becomes the soldier, could not overcome the tender sympathies of my nature. I had not courage to encounter the trial of taking a formal leave. When I had arrived at a solitary place on my way, I sat down for a few moments, and sought to allay the keenness of my grief by giving vent to a profusion of tears.

Why was privateering Hewes's first choice? Privateering, as Jesse Lemisch has put it, was legalized piracy with a share of the booty for each pirate. Under a state of Continental letter of marque, a privately owned ship was authorized to take enemy vessels as prizes. The government received a share, as did the owners and crew, prorated by rank. During the seven years of war, the United States commissioned 2,000 privateers, 626 in Massachusetts alone, which itself issued 1,524 commissions. In 1776, when Hewes made his decision, Abigail Adams spoke of "the rage for privateering" in Boston, and James Warren told Samuel Adams that "a whole country" was "privateering mad."

War for Hewes meant opportunity: a chance to escape from a humdrum occupation never to his liking; to be at thirty-five what had been denied at sixteen—a fighting man; above all, a chance to accumulate the capital that could mean a house, a new shop, apprentices and journeymen, perhaps a start in something altogether new. He was following a path trod by tens of thousands of poor New Englanders ever since the wars against the French in the 1740s and 1750s. As an economic flyer, however, privateering ultimately proved disastrous for Hewes.

His first voyage went well. He sailed on the *Diamond* out of Providence, attracted possibly by an advertisement that promised fortune and adventure. They captured three vessels, the last of which Hewes brought back to Providence as a member of the prize crew. He said nothing about his share; by inference he got enough to whet his appetite but not enough to boast about. He also nearly drowned off Newfoundland when a line he and two shipmates were standing on broke.

His second voyage was shattering. He went on the Connecticut ship of war *Defence*, commanded by Captain Samuel Smedley and sailing from Boston with the *Oliver Cromwell*. The *Defence* and *Cromwell* captured two richly laden vessels and later, after a layover in Charleston, South Carolina, two British privateers; on the way home, the *Defence* stopped a ship and relieved the tory passengers of their money. The prize money from the two privateers alone was $80,000. But Hewes got nothing. His share was supposed to be $250, "but some pretext was always offered for withholding my share from me; so that I have never received one cent of it." When he asked for his wages, Captain Smedley "told me he was about fitting out an expedition to

the West Indies, and could not, without great inconvenience, spare the money then; but said he would call on his way to Providence . . . and would pay me; but I never saw him afterwards. Neither have I, at any such time since, received a farthing, either of my share of prize money or wages."

There was an adventurous side to privateering. His stories stress the thrill of the chase, the intrepid maneuvering of his ship in battle, the excitement of a boarding party. They also deal with the prosaic. He remembered manning the pumps on the leaking *Defence* "for eight days and eight nights to keep us from sinking." He remembered before battle that "we sat up all night . . . we made bandages, scraped lint, so that we might be prepared to dress wounds as we expected to have a hard time of it." The man of tender sympathies did not become a bloodthirsty buccaneer.

Most important of all was the memory that at sea he had participated in making decisions and that the captains had shown deference to their crews. On his first voyage, the initial agreement was for a cruise of seven weeks. "When that term had expired," said Hewes, "and we had seen no enemy during the time, we were discouraged, and threatened to mutiny, unless he would return." Captain Stacey asked for one more week, after which he promised to sail home if they saw nothing, "to which we assented." On the second voyage, when the *Defence* sighted enemy ships and Captain Smedley "asked us if we were willing to give chase to them, we assented, we were all ready to go and risk our lives with him." In Charleston, their tour of duty legally over, Smedley proposed a five-day extension when the British privateers were sighted. "Our Captain put it to a vote, and it was found we were unanimously agreed to make the cruise." One hesitates to call this process democratic: even the captain of a pirate ship could not function without the support of his crew. What Hewes remembered was that the captains deferred to him and his mates, not the other way around.

This is the motif of his encounter with George Washington in 1775. When Hewes and his fellow escapees from Boston were taken to Washington's headquarters at Craigie House in Cambridge, the Reverend Peter Thatcher recognized him as the nephew of the "staunch Liberty Man" Robert Hewes. Washington invited Hewes into his parlor—"with him, alone. There he told him his story, every word of it, from the beginning to end, and answered all his questions besides." Washington, in Hewes's words, "didn't *laugh,* to be sure, but *looked amazing good-natured* you may depend." Washington then treated him and his companions to punch and invited them and Thatcher to a meal. All this is entirely possible. Washington was considering an invasion of Boston; he would have welcomed intelligence from a street-wise man just out of the town, and as a Virginia planter he knew the importance of the gesture of hospitality. Hewes also claimed that "Madam Washington waited upon them at table all dinner-time," but this is improbable, and Thatcher the biographer erred in stating that she was "known to have been with her husband at the date of the adventure."

In military duty on land there was no recognition of this sort from his betters, though he was in the militia, by reputation the most democratic branch of service. Even his adventures were humdrum. The "general destination" of his units, he told Hawkes, was "to guard the coasts." He saw action at the Battle of Newport Island in August 1778 under General John Sullivan. He remembered "an engagement" at Cobblehill, "in which we beat them with a considerable slaughter of their men." He remembered rowing through the darkness in silence in an attack on a British fort that had to be aborted when one of the rowers talked. He remembered the grim retreat from Newport Island, crossing the waters at Howland's Ferry. On duty at West Point in 1781 he went out on forays against the "cowboys," lawless bands pillaging Westchester County. In all this activity he claimed no moment of glory; there was a lot of marching; a lot of sentry duty; much drudgery. If he mended shoes for soldiers, as did other shoemakers in the ranks, he did not speak of it. And military service did not kindle in him an ambition to rise, as it did in a number of other shoemakers who became officers.

After all this service it hurt to be subjected to an inevitable draft. As Hewes explained to Hawkes with considerable accuracy, Massachusetts required all men of military age to serve "or to form themselves into classes of nine men, and each class to hire an able bodied man, on such terms as they could, and pay him for his services, while they were to receive their pay of the state." Attleborough instituted such a procedure early in 1781. Why did Hewes refuse to go? He was frank with Hawkes: the "extreme exigencies" of his family and the "pressure of his circumstances" forced him to "withdraw his services from the army." The decision was painful, and it was costly. Hewes's substitute "demanded . . . specie while we received nothing of the government but paper money, of very little value, and continually depreciating."

Thatcher was right: his service was "poorly rewarded." Hewes was one of "the mass of people, at large; such as little property to fight for, or to lose, on one hand, and could reasonably expect to gain still less, either in the way of emolument or distinction on the other." Instead, the inequities of civilian life were repeated on an even crasser scale. The rich could easily afford a substitute; the men who had already fought paid through the nose for one. The ship's officers got their share of the prize; the poor sailor got neither prize money nor wages.

But the war meant more than this to Hewes. It left a memory of rights asserted (by a threat of mutiny) and rights respected by captains who put decisions to a vote of the crew, and of the crew giving assent. It was a memory, above all, of respect from his betters: from General Washington at Cambridge, from captains Stacey and Smedley at sea, as from John Hancock in Boston. For a moment, it had been a world that marched to the tune of the old English nursery rhyme supposedly played at Cornwallis's surrender, "The World Turned Upside Down." Then "in a trice" Hewes's world came right side up—but little, if any, better than before.

9

A "MOST UNDISCIPLINED, PROFLIGATE CREW": PROTEST AND DEFIANCE IN THE CONTINENTAL RANKS, 1776–1783

JAMES KIRBY MARTIN

During the first year of the Revolutionary War, the patriot cause enjoyed widespread enthusiasm and support. Expecting a short war with relatively little loss of life and damage to property, American men of all ranks joined local militia units in 1775–1776 to defend their homes and families from British "corruption" and from the red-coated army that had been sent to put down the colonial "rebellion." But as it became clear that this would be a long and costly struggle, men of middling and upper rank began to purchase substitutes or pay nominal fines for nonservice and withdrew to private life. After 1777, the bulk of military service fell to the lower ranks of American society—to poor farmers, laborers, indentured servants, slaves, and free men of color.

In this essay, James Kirby Martin recounts the struggles of these "dispensable" men as they battled not only the British army and epidemic disease but also a lack of support from the Continental Congress and the populace. Martin suggests that these men—poorly equipped and ill-fed, their pay always months in arrears—persevered less from patriotic commitment than from the Congress's promises of freedom to bondsmen and free western land to those who enlisted for the duration of the war. More than any other consideration, the prospects of escaping from the bottom of eighteenth-century society and of achieving freedom and a modest foothold on the social ladder kept Washington's army in the field during the long years of the war.

Martin's account attempts to sort out the motivations and political consciousness of ordinary people. In the heroic version of the American Revolution, men were motivated by "the Spirit of '76"—a love of liberty and a hatred of arbitrary authority. In this more sober account, ordinary people looked to their own interests and chances for advancement. In reading this essay, keep in mind the possibility that both considerations played a role in popular allegiance to the revolutionary cause.

"A 'Most Undisciplined, Profligate Crew': Protest and Defiance in the Continental Ranks, 1776–1783" from Arms and Independence: The Military Character of the American Revolution, eds. Ronald Hoffman and Peter J. Albert (Charlottesville: Virginia, 1984), pp. 119–140. Reprinted by permission of the University Press of Virginia.

A sequence of events inconceivable to Americans raised on patriotic myths about the Revolution occurred in New Jersey during the spring of 1779. For months the officers of the Jersey brigade had been complaining loudly about everything from lack of decent food and clothing to pay arrearages and late payments in rapidly depreciating currency. They had petitioned their assembly earlier, but nothing had happened. They petitioned again in mid-April 1779, acting on the belief that the legislature should "be informed that our pay is now only *minimal*, not *real*, that four months' pay of a private will not procure his wretched wife and children a single bushel of wheat." Using "the most plain and unambiguous terms," they stressed that "unless a speedy and ample remedy be provided, the total dissolution of your troops is inevitable." The Jersey assembly responded to this plea in its usual fashion—it forwarded the petition to the Continental Congress without comment. After all, the officers, although from New Jersey, were a part of the Continental military establishment.

The assembly's behavior only further angered the officers, and some of them decided to demonstrate their resolve. On May 6 the brigade received orders to join John Sullivan's expedition against the Six Nations. That same day, officers in the First Regiment sent forth yet another petition. They again admonished the assembly about pay and supply issues. While they stated that they would prepare the regiment for the upcoming campaign, they themselves would resign as a group unless the legislators addressed their demands. Complaints had now turned into something more than gentlemanly protest. Protest was on the verge of becoming nothing less than open defiance of civil authority, and the Jersey officers were deadly serious. They had resorted to their threatened resignations to insure that the assembly would give serious attention to their demands—for a change.

When George Washington learned about the situation, he was appalled. "Nothing, which has happened in the course of the war, . . . has given me so much pain," the commander in chief stated anxiously. It upset him that the officers seem-

ingly had lost sight of the "principles" that governed the cause. What would happen, he asked rhetorically, "if their example should be followed and become general?" The result would be the "ruin" and "disgrace" of the rebel cause, all because these officers had *reasoned wrong about the means of obtaining a good end."*

So developed a little known but highly revealing confrontation. Washington told Congress that he would have acted very aggressively toward the recalcitrant officers, except that "the causes of discontent are too great and too general and the ties that bind the officers to the service too feeble" to force the issue. What he did promise was that he would not countenance any aid that came "in [such] a manner extorted." On the other hand, the officers had been asking the assembly for relief since January 1778, but to no avail. They, too, were not about to be moved.

The New Jersey legislature was the political institution with the ability to break the deadlock. Some of the legislators preferred disbanding the brigade. The majority argued that other officers and common soldiers might follow the First Regiment's lead and warned that the war effort could hardly succeed without a Continental military establishment. The moment was now ripe for compromise. The assemblymen agreed to provide the officers with whatever immediate relief could be mustered in return for the latter calling back their petitions. That way civil authorities would not be succumbing to intimidation by representatives of the military establishment, and the principle of subordination of military to civil authority would remain inviolate. The assembly thus provided an immediate payment of £200 to each officer and $40 to each soldier. Accepting the compromise settlement as better than nothing, the brigade moved out of its Jersey encampment on May 11 and marched toward Sullivan's bivouac at Easton, Pennsylvania. Seemingly, all now had returned to normal.

The confrontation between the New Jersey officers and the state assembly serves to illuminate some key points about protest and defiance in the Continental ranks during the years

1776–83. Most important here, it underscores the mounting anger felt by Washington's regulars as a result of their perceived (and no doubt very real) lack of material and psychological support from the society that had spawned the Continental army. It is common knowledge that Washington's regulars suffered from serious supply and pay shortages throughout the war. Increasingly, historians are coming to realize that officers and common soldiers alike received very little moral support from the general populace. As yet, however, scholars have not taken a systematic look at one product of this paradigm of neglect, specifically, protest and defiance. The purpose of this essay is to present preliminary findings that will facilitate that task.

Given that there was a noticeable relationship between lack of material and psychological support from the civilian sector and mounting protest and defiance in the ranks, it is also important to make clear that patterns of protest were very complex. A second purpose of this essay is to outline those basic patterns and to indicate why protest and defiance did not result in serious internal upheaval between army and society in the midst of the War for American Independence. To begin this assessment, we must bring Washington's Continentals to the center of the historical arena.

During the past twenty years, historians have learned that there were at least two Continental armies. The army of 1775–76 might be characterized as a republican constabulary, consisting of citizens who had respectable amounts of property and who were defending hearth and home. They came out for what they believed would be a rather short contest in which their assumed virtue and moral commitment would easily carry the day over seasoned British regulars not necessarily wedded to anything of greater concern than filling their own pocketbooks as mercenaries.

The first army had a militialike appearance. Even though phrases of commitment were high sounding, there was not much discipline or rigorous training. These early soldiers had responded to appeals from leaders who warned about "our

wives and children, with everything that is dear to us, [being] subjected to the merciless rage of uncontrolled despotism." They were convinced that they were "engaged . . . in the cause of virtue, of liberty, of *God.*" Unfortunately, the crushing blows endured in the massive British offensive of 1776 against New York undercut such high-sounding phrases about self-sacrifice. The message at the end of 1775 had been "Persevere, ye guardians of liberty." They did not.

The second Continental establishment took form out of the remains of the first. Even before Washington executed his magnificent turnabout at Trenton and Princeton, he had called for a "respectable army," one built on long-term enlistments, thorough training, and high standards of discipline. The army's command, as well as many delegates in Congress, now wanted soldiers who could stand up against the enemy with more than notions of exalted virtue and moral superiority to upgird them. They called for able-bodied men who could and would endure for the long-term fight in a contest that all leaders now knew could not be sustained by feelings of moral superiority and righteousness alone.

To assist in overcoming manpower shortages, Congress and the states enhanced financial promises made to potential enlistees. Besides guarantees about decent food and clothing, recruiters handed out bounty moneys and promises of free land at war's end (normally only for long-term service). Despite these financial incentives, there was no great rush to the Continental banner. For the remainder of the war, the army's command, Congress, and the states struggled to maintain minimal numbers of Continental soldiers in the ranks.

In fact, all began to search diligently for new recruits. Instead of relying on propertied freeholders and tradesmen of the ideal citizen-soldier type, they broadened the definition of what constituted an "able-bodied and effective" recruit. For example, New Jersey in early 1777 started granting exemptions to all those who hired substitutes for long-term Continental service—and to masters who would enroll indentured servants and slaves. The following year Maryland permitted the virtual impressment of vagrants for nine months of regular service. Massachusetts set another kind of precedent in 1777 by declaring blacks (both slave and free) eligible for the state draft. Shortly thereafter, Rhode Islanders set about the business of raising two black battalions. Ultimately, Maryland and Virginia permitted slaves to substitute for whites. The lower South, however, refused to do so, even in the face of a successful British invasion later in the war.

The vast majority of Continentals who fought with Washington after 1776 were representative of the very poorest and most repressed persons in Revolutionary society. A number of recent studies have verified that a large proportion of the Continentals in the second establishment represented ne'er-do-wells, drifters, unemployed laborers, captured British soldiers and Hessians, indentured servants, and slaves. Some of these new regulars were in such desperate economic straits that states had to pass laws prohibiting creditors from pulling them from the ranks and having them thrown in jail for petty debts. (Obviously, this was not a problem with the unfree.)

The most important point to be derived from this dramatic shift in the social composition of the Continental army is that few of these new common soldiers had enjoyed anything close to economic prosperity or full political (or legal) liberty before the war. As a group, they had something to gain from service. If they could survive the rigors of camp life, the killing diseases that so often ravaged the armies of their times, and the carnage of skirmishes and full-scale battles, they could look forward to a better life for themselves at the end of the war. Not only were they to have decent food and clothing and regular pay until the British had been irrevocably beaten, they had also been promised free land (and personal freedom in the cases of indentured servants, black slaves, and criminals). Recruiters thus conveyed a message of personal upward mobility through service. In exchange for personal sacrifice in the short run, there was the prospect of something far better in the long run, paralleling and epito-

mizing the collective rebel quest for a freer political life in the New World.

To debate whether these new Continentals were motivated to enlist because of crass materialism or benevolent patriotism is to sidetrack the issue. A combination of factors was no doubt at work in the mind of each recruit or conscript. Far more important, especially if we are to comprehend the ramifications of protest and defiance among soldiers and officers, we must understand that respectably established citizens after 1775 and 1776 preferred to let others perform the dirty work of regular, long-term service on their behalf, essentially on a contractual basis. Their legislators gave bounties and *promised* many other incentives. Increasingly, as the war lengthened, the civilian population and its leaders did a less effective job in keeping their part of the agreement. One significant outcome of this obvious civilian ingratitude, if not utter disregard for contractual promises, was protest and defiance coming from Washington's beleaguered soldiers and officers.

That relations between Washington's post-1776 army and Revolutionary society deteriorated dramatically hardly comes as a surprise to those historians who have investigated surviving records. Widespread anger among the rank and file became most demonstrable in 1779 and 1780, at the very nadir of the war effort. Pvt. Joseph Plumb Martin captured the feelings of his comrades when he reflected back on support for the army in 1780. He wrote: "We therefore still kept upon our parade in groups, venting our spleen at our country and government, then at our officers, and then at ourselves for our imbecility in staying there and starving in detail for an ungrateful people who did not care what became of us, so they could enjoy themselves while we were keeping a cruel enemy from them." Gen. John Paterson, who spoke out in March 1780, summarized feelings among many officers when he said, "It really gives me great pain to think of our public affairs; where is the public spirit of the year 1775? Where are those flaming *patriots* who were ready to sacrifice their lives, their fortunes, their all, for the public?" Such thoughts were not dissimilar from those of "A Jersey Soldier" who poured his sentiments into an editorial during May 1779 in support of those regimental officers who were trying to exact some form of financial justice from their state legislature. The army, he pointed out, had put up with "a load . . . grown almost intolerable." "It must be truly mortifying to the virtuous soldier to observe many, at this day, displaying their cash, and sauntering in idleness and luxury," he went on, including "the gentry . . . [who] are among the foremost to despise our poverty and laugh at our distress." He certainly approved the actions of his comrades because he resented "the cruel and ungrateful disposition of the people in general, in withholding from the army even the praise and glory justly due to their merit and services," just as he resented society's failure to live up to its contract with the soldiers. These statements, which are only a representative sampling, indicate that the army had come to believe that Revolutionary civilians had taken advantage of them—and had broken their part of the contract for military services.

There were real dangers hidden behind these words. With each passing month beginning in 1777, Washington's regulars, especially that small cadre that was signing on for the long-term fight, became more professional in military demeanor. Among other things, including their enhanced potential effectiveness in combat, this meant that soldiers felt the enveloping (and reassuring) bonds of "unit cohesion." The immediate thoughts of individual soldiers, whether recruited, dragooned, or pressed into service, became attached to their respective primary units in the army, such as the particular companies or regiments in which they served. The phenomenon was nothing more than a developing comradeship in arms. Any threat or insult thus became an assault on the group, especially if that threat or insult were directed at all members of the group. The bonding effect of unit cohesion suggests that collective protest and defiance would become more of a danger to a generally unsupportive society with each passing month, unless civilians

who had made grand promises started to meet their contractual obligations more effectively.

Indeed, the most readily observable pattern in Continental army protest and defiance was that it took on more and more of a collective (and menacing) character through time. At the outset, especially beginning in 1776, most protest had an individual character. Frequently it was the raw recruit, quite often anxious for martial glory but quickly disillusioned with the realities of military service once in camp, who struck back against undesirable circumstances. Protest could come through such diverse expressions as swearing, excessive drinking, assaulting officers, deserting, or bounty jumping. One source of such behavior was the dehumanizing, even brutal nature of camp life. Another had to do with broken promises about pay, food, and clothing. A third was a dawning sense that too many civilians held the soldiery in disregard, if not utter contempt.

It must be remembered that middle- and upper-class civilians considered Washington's new regulars to be representative of the "vulgar herd" in a society that still clung to deferential values. The assumption was that the most fit in terms of wealth and community social standing were to lead while the least fit were to follow, even when that meant becoming little more than human cannon fodder. Perhaps James Warren of Massachusetts summarized the social perceptions of "respectable" citizens as well as any of the "better sort" when he described Washington's troops in 1776 as "the most undisciplined, profligate Crew that were ever collected" to fight a war.

While civilians often ridiculed the new regulars as riffraff, troublemakers, or mere hirelings (while conveniently ignoring the precept that military service was an assumed obligation of all citizens in a liberty-loving commonwealth), individual soldiers did not hold back in protesting their circumstances. In many cases, they had already acknowledged the personal reality of downtrodden status before entering the ranks. Acceptance of these circumstances and the conditions of camp life did not mean, however, that these new soldiers would be passive. Thus it may be an error to dismiss heavy swearing around civilians or repeated drunkenness in camp as nothing more than manifestations of "time-honored military vices," to borrow the words of one recent student of the war period.

At least in some instances, individual soldiers could have been making statements about their sense of personal entrapment. Furthermore, protest through such methods as drunkenness (this was a drinking society but not one that condoned inebriety) was a defensive weapon. One of Washington's generals, for instance, bitterly complained in 1777 that too many soldiers consistently made it "a practice of getting drunk . . . once a Day and thereby render themselves unfit for duty." To render themselves unfit for duty was to give what they had received—broken promises. Defiance that came in the form of "barrel fever" for some soldiers thus translated into statements about how society looked upon and treated them.

Only over time did individual acts of protest take on a more collective character. That transition may be better comprehended by considering the phenomenon of desertion. While it is true that a great many soldiers did not think of desertion as a specific form of protest, they fled the ranks with greater frequency when food and clothing were in very short supply or nonexistent, as at Valley Forge. However, primary unit cohesion worked to militate against unusually high desertion levels. Sustained involvement with a company or regiment reduced the likelihood of desertion. Hence as soldiers came to know, trust, and depend upon one another, and as they gained confidence in comrades and felt personally vital to the long-term welfare of their primary group, they were much less likely to lodge a statement of individual protest through such individualized forms as desertion.

So it appears to have been with Washington's new regulars. Thad W. Tate discovered that, in the regiments of New York, Maryland, and North Carolina, about 50 percent of all desertions occurred within six months of enlistments. Mark Edward Lender, in studying New Jersey's Continentals, also found that the rate of desertion dropped off dramatically for those soldiers who lasted through just a few months of service. The first few days and weeks in the ranks were those in which these poor and desperate new regulars asked themselves whether vague promises of a better lot in life for everyone, including themselves, in a postwar republican polity was worth the sacrifice now being demanded. Many enlistees and conscripts concluded that it was not, and they fled. Since they had little proof that they could trust the civilian population and its leaders, they chose to express their defiance through desertion. Unit cohesion, in turn, helped sustain those who read the equation differently, and it eased the pain of enduring a long war in return for the remote prospect of greater personal freedom, opportunity, and prosperity.

Then there were those individuals who neither deserted nor became hard-core regulars. By and large, this group defied civil and military authority through the practice of bounty jumping. The procedure, which Washington once referred to as "a kind of business" among some soldiers, was straightforward. It involved enlisting, getting a bounty, and deserting, then repeating the same process with another recruiting agent in another location. Some of the most resourceful bounty jumpers got away with this maneuver seven, eight, or even nine times, if not more. Most jumpers appear to have been very poor young men without family roots. The most careful of them went through the war unscathed. Bounties thus provided a form of economic aggrandizement (and survival) in a society that generally treated its struggling classes with studied neglect. To accept a bounty payment, perhaps even to serve for a short period, and then to run off, was a strongly worded statement of personal defiance.

Bounty jumping was invariably the act of protesting individuals; looting and plundering (like desertion) combined individual with collective protest. Certainly there were numerous occasions when hungry soldiers looted by themselves. Just as often, groups of starving men "borrowed" goods from civilians. Even before the second establishment took form, looting had become a serious problem. Indeed, it probably abetted unit cohesion. One sergeant, for example, described how he and his comrades, searching desperately for food, "liberated" some geese belonging to a local farmer in 1776 and devoured them "Hearty in the Cause of Liberty of taking what Came to their Hand." Next "a sheep and two fat turkeys" approached this band of hungry soldiers, but "not being able to give the countersign," they were taken prisoner, "tried by fire and executed" for sustenance "by the whole Division of the freebooters."

When army looting of civilian property continued its unabated course in 1777, General Washington threatened severe penalties. He emphasized that the army's "business" was "to give protection, and support, to the poor, distressed Inhabitants; not to multiply and increase their calamities." These pleas had little impact. Incident after incident kept the commander in chief and his staff buried in a landslide of civilian complaints. Threats of courts martial, actual trials, and severe punishments did not deter angry, starving, protesting soldiers. In 1780 and 1781 Washington was still issuing pleas and threats, but to little avail. Not even occasional hangings contained an increasingly defiant and cohesive soldiery that wondered who the truly poor and distressed inhabitants were—themselves or civilians ostensibly prospering because of the army's travail. To strike back at hoarding, unsupportive citizens, as they had come to perceive the populace whom they were defending, seemed only logical, especially when emboldened by the camaraderie of closely knit fellow soldiers.

Above all else, two patterns stand out with respect to common soldier protest. First, as the war effort lengthened, defiance became more of a collective phenomenon. Second, such protest had a controlled quality. While there was unremitting resentment toward civilians who were invariably perceived as insensitive and unsupportive, protest rarely metamorphosed into wanton violence and mindless destruction. Soldiers may have looted and pillaged, they may have grabbed up bounties, and they may have deserted. But they rarely maimed, raped, or murdered civilians. Pvt. Joseph Plumb Martin

attempted to explain why. Even though "the monster Hunger, . . . attended us," he wrote, and the new regulars "had borne as long as human nature could endure, and to bear longer we considered folly," he insisted that his comrades had become, in the end, "truly patriotic." They were persons who "loved their country, and they had already suffered everything short of death in its cause." The question by 1779 and 1780 was whether these hardened, cohesive veterans would be willing to endure even more privation.

In reflecting positively on the loyalty of his comrades, Martin was commenting on a near mutiny of the Connecticut Line in 1780. Indeed, the specter of collective defiance in the form of line mutinies had come close to reality with the near insubordination of the New Jersey officers in 1779. They had not demonstrated in the field, but they had made it clear that conditions in the army were all but intolerable—and that civil society, when desperate to maintain a regular force in arms, could be persuaded to concede on basic demands. Washington had used the phrase "extorted"; he had also pointed out that, "notwithstanding the expedient adopted for a saving appearances," this confrontation "cannot fail to operate as a bad precedent." The commander in chief was certainly right about the setting of precedents.

Among long-term veterans, anger was beginning to overwhelm discipline. There had been small-scale mutinies before, such as the rising of newly recruited Continentals at Halifax, North Carolina, in February 1776. In 1779 Rhode Island and Connecticut regiments threatened mutinies, but nothing came of these incidents. Then in 1780 another near uprising of the Connecticut Line occurred. Invariably, the issues had the same familiar ring: lack of adequate civilian support as demonstrated by rotten food, inadequate clothing, and worthless pay (when pay was available). On occasion, too, the heavy hand of company- and field-grade officers played its part. The near mutiny of the Connecticut Line in 1780 had been avoided by a fortuitous shipment of cattle and by promises from trusted officers of better treatment. In the end, the Connecticut Line calmed itself down, according to Martin, because the soldiery was "unwilling to desert the cause of our country, when in distress." Nevertheless, he explained that "we knew her cause involved our own, but what signified our perishing in the act of saving her, when that very act would inevitably destroy us, and she must finally perish with us."

By the end of 1780, there were some veterans who would have disputed Martin's reasoning. They had all but given up, let come what might for the glorious cause. On January 1, 1781, the Pennsylvania Line proved that point. Suffering through yet another harsh winter near Morristown, New Jersey, the Pennsylvanians mutinied. Some one thousand determined comrades in arms (about 15 percent of the manpower available to Washington) ostensibly wanted nothing more to do with fighting the war. On a prearranged signal, the Pennsylvanians paraded under arms, seized their artillery, and marched south toward Princeton, their ultimate target being Philadelphia. These veterans had had their fill of broken promises, of the unfulfilled contract. They maintained that they had signed on for three years, not for the duration. If they were to stay in the ranks, then they wanted the same benefits (additional bounty payments, more free land, and some pay in specie) that newer enlistees had obtained.

Formal military discipline collapsed as the officers trying to contain the mutineers were brushed aside. The soldiers killed one and wounded two other officers, yet their popular commander, Anthony Wayne, trailed along, attempting to appeal to their sense of patriotism. Speaking through a committee of sergeants, the soldiers assured Wayne and the other officers that they were still loyal to the cause, and they proved it by handing over two spies that Sir Henry Clinton had sent out from New York to monitor the situation. Moreover, the mutineers, despite their anger and bitterness, behaved themselves along their route and did not unnecessarily intimidate civilians who got in their way.

Later checking demonstrated that many of the mutineers were duration enlistees, yet that was a moot point. When the soldiers reached Trenton, representatives of Congress and the Pennsylvania government negotiated with them and agreed to discharge any veteran claiming three years in rank. Also, they offered back pay and new clothing along with immunity from prosecution for having defied their officers in leaving their posts. Once formally discharged, the bulk of the mutineers reenlisted for a new bounty. By late January 1781 the Pennsylvania Line was once more a functioning part of the Continental army.

These mutineers won because Washington was in desperate need of manpower and because they had resorted to collective defiance, not because their society wanted to address what had been grievances based on the contract for service. Unlike their officers, who had just won a major victory in driving for half-pay pensions, they were not in a position to lobby before Congress. Hence they employed one of the most threatening weapons in their arsenal, collective protest against civil authority, but only after less extreme measures had failed to satisfy their claims for financial justice. They were certainly not planning to overthrow any government or to foment an internal social revolution against better-placed members of their society. They had staked their hopes on a better life in the postwar period and had already risked their lives many times for the proposed republican polity. All told, the extreme nature of this mutiny demonstrated, paradoxically, both that Washington's long-term Continentals were the most loyal and dedicated republican citizens in the new nation, and that they were dangerously close to repudiating a dream that far too often had been a personal nightmare because of the realities of societal support and of service in the Continental army.

More worrisome in January 1781 than the matter of appropriate appreciation of the soldiers' actions was whether this mutiny, and its stillborn predecessors, would trigger further turbulence in the ranks. Also camped near Morristown during the winter of 1780–81 were veteran soldiers of the New Jersey Line. Their officers were aware that the Jersey regulars sympathized with the Pennsylvanians and had been in constant communication with them. Then, on January 20, 1781, the New Jersey Line, having witnessed the success of its comrades, also mutinied. The soldiers had each recently received $5 in specie as a token toward long overdue pay, but they were bothered by the better bounties and terms of enlistment offered newer recruits. Their leaders urged them on by shouting: "Let us go to Congress who have money and rum enough but won't give it to us!"

Within a few days, the Jersey Line had won acceptable concessions and was back under control. Washington, however, had decided that enough was enough. "Unless this dangerous spirit can be suppressed by force," he wrote to Congress, "there is an end to all subordination in the Army, and indeed to the Army itself." To back up his strong words, the commander ordered Gen. Robert Howe and about five hundred New England troops near West Point to march to the Jersey camp at Pompton to make sure that the mutineers were back in line and summarily to execute the most notorious leaders. Howe did as instructed. He reached Pompton on January 27, three days after grievances had been redressed. Deploying his men around the campsite just before dawn, Howe caught the Jersey soldiers off guard. He ordered them to fall in without arms, then singled out three ringleaders and ordered their summary execution, to be shot to death by nine of their comrades. A Jersey officer intervened in one case, but the other two were put to death by firing squad.

It was a brutal ending for men who had dreamed of a better future despite all of society's violations of the contract. Perhaps because of the calculated coldheartedness of Washington's orders, or perhaps because the war picture began to brighten in 1781, there were no major uprisings among Washington's regulars after the mutiny of the New Jersey Line. Then again, the soldiery may have been too worn down physically and mentally to continue their protest and defi-

ance in the name of financial justice, humane treatment, and psychological support. They may have passed beyond the point of despair to that of quiet acceptance of whatever came their way, whether just or unjust.

An important question that must be raised in conclusion has to do with political perceptions and fears: given real concerns in Revolutionary society that a regular army could obtain too much power, could corrupt the political system, and could threaten the civilian sector with some form of tyranny, such as a military dictatorship, why did officers and soldiers never unite effectively and put maximum pressure on the frail Revolutionary political structure by protesting in unison? They could have easily played on fears of a coup. But about the closest such union was the Jersey officers' defiance of 1779. Thus, while common soldiers got drunk, deserted, looted, or mutinied, officers pursued their own (and largely separate) avenues of protest. This is curious, especially since the officers too worried about the personal financial cost of service; they too came to resent civilian indifference, ineptitude, and greed; and they too were dismayed over society's inability to treat them with respect. They feared that their virtuous behavior and self-sacrifice would go unappreciated if not completely unrecognized and unrewarded. Having so much in common with their brethren in the rank and file, then, it is worth considering why the officers almost never aligned with them. For if they had, the alliance might have been powerful enough to have fomented something truly menacing to the vitals of Revolutionary society.

The officer corps developed its own forms of protest, and the pattern paralleled that of the common soldiers. The movement was from a dominant expression of individual defiance (resignations in 1776 and 1777) to collective protest (the drive for half-pay pensions which began in earnest during the fall of 1777 and climaxed with the Newburgh Conspiracy, 1782–83). Like common soldiers, the officers had collectivized their protest. In that sense, unit cohesion among comrades had come into play, but such cohesion never broke through the vertical hierarchy of military rank.

Part of the reason lay in the social gulf separating the two groups. As befit the deferential nature of their times as well as their concern for maintaining sharp distinctions in rank as a key to a disciplined fighting force, officers, many of whom were drawn from the "better sort" in society, expected nothing less than steady, if not blind obedience to their will from the rank and file. In their commitment to pursuing the goals of the Revolution, the officers were anything but social levelers. Indeed, many of them feared that the Revolution might get out of hand and lead to actual internal social upheaval, particularly if the "vulgar herd" gained too much influence and authority, whether in or out of the army. They hesitated to turn their troops against society because these same soldiers could always turn against them as well and, through brute force, undermine all assumed claims to economic and social preeminence in Revolutionary America.

Washington's veteran officers, even though they complained and protested with vehemence, also willingly accepted their responsibilities as the army's leadership cadre. The officers administered harsh discipline to deserters, looters, bounty jumpers, and mutineers whenever it seemed necessary—and sometimes when it was not. They generally supported Washington's desire to set the legal limit for lashes at 500 strokes, and many of them often sanctioned whippings of more than 100 lashes, despite the Articles of War of 1776. For example, officers took with relish to Washington's general orders at Morristown in 1780 to inflict 100 to 500 lashes on duly tried plunderers and to administer up to 50 lashes on the spot, even before formal hearings, when soldiers were caught breaking military laws.

Many officers thus used their authority with impunity and rarely expressed sympathy for the plight of common soldiers in the ranks. They were much more concerned with societal stability and the protection of property, as well as with military decorum and hierarchy, all of which pre-

cluded the officer corps from working in harmony with the soldiery when protesting common grievances against the civilian sector.

Washington's officers, in reality, were caught between the rank and file, for which they had little sympathy, and the larger society, which had little sympathy for them. They pursued their half-pay pension demands, resorting to such defiant acts as threatening to resign en masse during the late summer of 1780. Later they became even more extreme as some toyed with the idea of a full mutiny, if not the possibility of a coup, during the Newburgh crisis. In the end, they failed in their short-term quest for pensions or commutation, as the soldiery fell short in its drive for minimal levels of respectable support. Perhaps those quests would have been more successful had officers and regulars been able to unite in a common bond transcending social class and military rank. If they had, the story of the Revolution might have been quite different. Recalling the common well of bitterness, the ending might well have had more of a Napoleonic cast to it.

That it did not is more than a mere testament to class, hierarchy, and rank. It is also a statement about the evolving feelings among both hardcore officers and regulars, regardless of the multifold reasons that brought them to the service in the first place, that they were fighting for something worthwhile, something of consequence for their particular lives. If they protested, they still maintained residual faith in their personal dreams. They also came to comprehend that, for all of the pain and suffering that was their lot, they could make a lasting contribution. Henry Knox stated the proposition aptly in 1783 when he noted that there was "a favorite toast in the army," that of "'A hoop to the barrel,' or 'Cement to the Union.'" That is the way that these protesting, defying, long-term Continentals should be remembered, not as a "most undisciplined, profligate Crew," but as individuals who, for all of their defiance, made the necessary personal sacrifice to insure that the Revolution and its ideals would succeed when so many about them in their society did not.

10

TWO VISIONS OF THE CONSTITUTION

DREW MCCOY

The men who met in 1787 to consider how best to reform the national government were of a variety of minds. Northerners and southerners, from cities and the country-side, these men represented the diverging interests that marked early America. Yet whatever their differences, these men shared a common concern: as leaders of the world's newest republic, how could they prevent the inevitable slide into decline and despotism that marked the history of all previous republics? To these men, schooled in the classical doctrine that republics required a virtuous people who could put self-interest aside, the competing interests of class, region, and party were sure signs of decay and impending doom. How, then, could they act to prevent these social divisions from developing in America?

As Drew McCoy demonstrates, the men of 1787 offered two answers. Following Benjamin Franklin, many saw the large expanses of land in the West as a safety valve, a way of offering every American man a plot of land that would guarantee his family's independence. With every American a small holder of property, there would be no large accumulations of wealth to challenge the virtuous government of the republic, and every citizen would have a stake—and thus an interest—in society.

A different and more modern view was offered by Alexander Hamilton, who thought the entire Whig conception of government, upon which so much of contemporary thought rested, misconceived. Instead, Hamilton envisioned America as a great commercial and industrial empire on the model of Great Britain. For him, the creation of classes and competing interests was both inevitable and ultimately desirable. Much like modern-day conservatives, Hamilton saw capitalists as the creators of national wealth and sought to link the state with these men of wealth, augmenting their power and influence in society and ensuring American economic development. In this way, Hamilton hoped to move America away from the agrarian republic of Franklin and Jefferson and make it into a modern industrial state. As McCoy shows, it was ultimately these two notions of national development that competed at the constitutional convention of 1787.

From The Elusive Republic: Political Economy in Jeffersonian America *by Drew McCoy. Published for the Institute of Early American History and Culture, Williamsburg, Virginia. Copyright © 1980 The University of North Carolina Press. Used by permission of the author and publisher.*

While speaking in January 1811 in defense of the constitutionality of the Bank of the United States, a Virginia congressman rhetorically asked his colleagues if the authors of the Constitution had not wisely anticipated the irrepressible consequences of social developments in America:

> Is it in the least probable that the men selected for their wisdom, perfectly acquainted with the progress of man in every age; who foresaw the changes which the state of society must undergo in this country from the increase of population, commerce, and the arts, could act so absurdly, as to prescribe a certain set of means to carry on the operations of a Government intended not only for the present but for future generations?

No doubt the framers would have been pleased with this assessment of their prescience. By the summer of 1787 most of them were acutely aware that America was maturing rapidly and that the future promised the development of an even more complex and sophisticated society. Not all of them found it easy to confront the implications of this promise, but very few refused to accept its inevitability. Even those who had not lost faith in Franklin's original vision of a youthful republic recognized more clearly than ever that they could hope only to forestall for as long as possible the unavoidable ramifications of social development.

"Civilization and corruption have generally been found," noted one of the more pessimistic American observers in 1785, "to advance with equal steps." Ultimately, the United States would become as corrupt as the most advanced areas of Europe; yet it was undoubtedly within the power of its citizens to place this "sad catastrophe at a distance." Perhaps more than any other prominent American of the 1780s, James Madison thought precisely in these terms. Like most supporters of the new Constitution, this astute young Virginian believed that a reorganization of American government was the necessary prerequisite to the establishment of a republican political economy. Madison later discovered, however, that not all of his Federalist colleagues shared his particular conception of a republican America;

some of them, he was appalled to learn, even thought in terms of deliberately promoting what he thought necessary to forestall. Different men were developing quite different solutions to the persistent problem of adapting the traditional republican impulse to modern commercial America. Although the ideological flux of the 1780s created the basis for the Federalist consensus of 1787, it also assured future controversy about the precise meaning of American republicanism and the role of the new federal government in securing it.

Madison's initial post-war vision of a republican America was quite similar in its general outline to Franklin's, for above all Madison thought in terms of developing across space rather than through time. Westward expansion was central to Madison's outlook, but equally important were his commitments to the principles of commercial liberalism and to the promise of a new, more open international commercial order. The dynamics of the Virginian's vision were straightforward. If Americans could continue to resort to virgin lands while opening adequate foreign markets for their produce, the United States would remain a nation of industrious farmers who marketed their surpluses abroad and purchased the "finer" manufactures they desired in return. Household industry would be relied upon to supply the coarser manufactures that were necessary to prevent a dangerously unfavorable balance of trade. Like Adam Smith, Madison believed this brand of social "development" proper because it comported with natural law. America could remain young and virtuous, while offering both a haven for the landless poor of Europe and a bountiful market for the advanced manufacturers that a fully peopled Europe was forced to produce. Indeed, Madison's commitment to westward expansion and "free trade" put him in the mainstream of republican thought at the end of the war.

Like most Americans, however, Madison always realized that the viability of landed expansion in America was contingent on the ability of new settlers to get their surpluses to market. If frontier farmers had no way of marketing what they produced, there was little incentive to emigrate to the West at all. A nonexistent or inaccessible market would turn those who did settle the frontier into lethargic subsistence farmers instead of industrious republicans. This perception of the importance of commerce to the settlement of the frontier had always carried serious implications for the character of American society. If the men and women who emigrated to the West were not properly tied to a commercial nexus, various commentators had long suggested, they would degenerate into a socially and politically dangerous form of savagery. Expressions of this concern often accompanied appeals for the construction of "internal improvements"—roads and canals—that would rescue the fringes of American settlement from this danger by integrating them into a commercial economy. As early as 1770, for example, Pennsylvanians anxious to promote a canal in their state had typically cited the "complicated and numerous" mischiefs that arose from the isolation of their western settlements. "It is from hence," one writer asserted, "that many of the distant back inhabitants are become uncivilized, and a little better than barbarians.—They are lazy, licentious, and lawless—and, instead of being useful members of society, are become seditious, and dangerous to the community." Once these settlers were drawn into the civilizing orbit of commerce, however, a dramatic transformation in their character would occur: "The uncivilized will, by a communication with the civilized, lose their ignorance and barbarism. They will learn industry from the industrious, virtue from the virtuous, loyalty from the loyal; and thereby become useful members of society, and good subjects." Most important, they would be molded into productive citizens: "Render it practicable for them to gain by their industry, and they will be industrious, and, by their industry, add to the surplus of our foreign exportation." This matter of civilizing the West had seemed particularly pressing before the Revolution to eastern Pennsylvanians who were disturbed by the chronic political turmoil on their frontier, but the

content and wide-ranging implications of their concern were of continuing relevance to all American republicans who worried about the character of their landed expansion.

As America looked westward in the 1780s, control of the Mississippi River to its mouth became an essential goal of national policy, for this river was the necessary avenue to foreign markets for those who were settling the immediate frontier. This concern drew the United States into an inevitable confrontation with the Spanish, who in early 1784 formally denied Americans the right to navigate the Mississippi and to deposit their goods at New Orleans. The problem of gaining uncontested American control of the Mississippi River arose from the disputes over the boundary settlements of the peace treaties that ended the Revolution and would not be fully resolved until the Louisiana Purchase of 1803. During the initial decade of independence, control of the Mississippi posed an especially disturbing dilemma for Madison and other American republicans.

Madison was both outraged and perplexed by the unexpected display of Spanish arrogance, and he insisted that it was not in the interests of either Spain or the United States to deny Americans use of the Mississippi. Writing to Jefferson in the summer of 1784, Madison argued that American settlement of the back-country, which only a free use of the Mississippi could promote, would benefit all European nations who traded with the United States by delaying the establishment of competitive American manufactures for many years and by increasing the consumption of foreign manufactures. If Americans were kept profitably occupied in agriculture, in other words, there would be no "supernumerary hands" to produce manufactures who might compete with foreign producers for the American market. In a passage that reflected many of the traditional assumptions of eighteenth-century political economy, Madison sketched two possible scenarios for American development:

The vacant land of the U.S. lying on the waters of the Mississippi is perhaps equal in extent to the land actually settled. If no check be given to emigrations from the latter to the former, they will probably keep pace at least with the increase of people, till the population of both become nearly equal. For 20 or 25 years we shall consequently have few internal manufactures in proportion to our numbers as at present, and at the end of that period our imported manufactures will be doubled. . . . Reverse the case and suppose the use of the Miss. denied to us, and the consequence is that many of our supernumerary hands who in the former case would [be] husbandmen on the waters of the Missipi will on this other supposition be manufacturers on this [side] of the Atlantic: and even those who may not be discouraged from seating the vacant lands will be obliged by the want of vent for the produce of the soil and of the means of purchasing foreign manufactures, to manufacture in a great measure for themselves.

The thrust of Madison's analysis was clear; in order to remain predominantly agricultural, America needed to combine landed and commercial expansion. If, on the contrary, Americans were denied access to export markets for their produce, a fundamental reorientation of their political economy in the direction of increased manufacturing was inevitable.

The diplomatic crisis in the West neatly fused the issues of western expansion and foreign trade, but Madison's concern with the latter issue extended far beyond the question of the Mississippi River. By the mid-1780s the commercial crisis afflicting the United States was wreaking havoc in virtually all areas of the country. This commercial problem, according to Madison, spawned the political and moral chaos that threatened the republican character of America. "Most of our political evils," he wrote in March 1786, "may be traced up to our commercial ones, as most of our moral may to our political." Like most Americans, Madison was particularly concerned with the restrictions Britain placed on American trade with its West Indian islands. Many Americans argued that the interest of every state was involved with this trade and, in a broader sense, that American commerce as a whole was dependent on it, since without a pros-

perous intercourse with these islands the balance of American trade with Great Britain would inevitably be unfavorable. "Access to the West Indies," as Jefferson put it in 1785, "is indispensably necessary to us." Several ways existed to improve the unfavorable balance of American trade, including the exercise of self-restraint on the part of those citizens who overindulged in their consumption of foreign luxuries. The key for Madison, however, was to liberate American trade from the shackles of British mercantilism. Above all, the United States had to break down the barriers that confined its commerce to "artificial" channels and denied it full access to "natural" markets like those in the West Indies.

By 1786 many Americans had decided that a policy of commercial retaliation against restrictions on their trade was mandatory. Few of them, however, could match Madison's faith in the efficacy of such a policy. His confidence in the ability of the United States to coerce Britain and other foreign countries into lowering barriers to American commerce was predicated on several key assumptions, the primary belief being that young, virile society had natural advantages in its intercourse with older, fully peopled, more complex societies. Due to its highly advanced, luxury-ridden condition, for instance, Britain depended on foreign demand to employ its surplus inhabitants. "It is universally agreed," wrote one American of England, "that no country is more dependent on foreign demand, for the superfluous produce of art and industry;—and that the luxury and extravagance of her inhabitants, have already advanced to the ultimate point of abuse, and cannot be so increased, as to augment the home consumption, in proportion to the decrease that will take place on a diminution of foreign trade." The prosperity of the British economy was thus contingent on access to the rich American market. Should the United States ever restrict this market for British manufacturers in retaliation for restraints on its export trade, the "manufacturing poor" in England would be thrown out of work and perhaps even starve. Such were the pitfalls, Franklin and Madison would have reminded the British, of a mercantilist political economy geared to the exportation of finer manufactures and luxuries.

By 1786 Madison thought it obvious that the implementation of an effective commercial policy, as well as the resolution of the crisis in the West, required a national government stronger than the Continental Congress. In a broader sense, this reorganization of the American political system was necessary to create the basis for a republican political economy. Madison feared, as did many other members of the American elite, that the disorder and unrest of the 1780s signified the decay of industry, diligence, frugality, and other republican character traits among the American people. The task at hand was to form a national political economy capable of permitting and encouraging Americans to engage industriously in virtue-sustaining occupations. To Madison this task entailed the creation of a central political authority able to reverse the dangerous trends of the decade and to stave off, for as long as possible, the advance of America into a more complicated and dangerous stage of social development. Because social conditions in the United States encouraged such reflection, Madison entered the constitutional convention in the spring of 1787 having already given much serious thought to the problems of poverty and unemployment in advanced, densely populated societies.

Of particular interest in this regard is an exchange of letters between Madison and Jefferson in late 1785 and early 1786. Writing from France, Jefferson pondered the plight of the laboring and idle poor of Europe. He blamed their wretchedness on an unequal division of property and entrenched feudal privilege, then further observed that "whenever there is in any country, uncultivated lands and unemployed poor, it is clear that the laws of property have been so far extended as to violate natural right." The earth had been given as a common stock for all men to labor and live on, and "if, for the encouragement of industry we allow it to be appropriated, we must take care that other

employment be furnished to those excluded from the appropriation." Jefferson extended this analysis of the situation in France to his native land. Although it was "too soon yet in our country to say that every man who cannot find employment but who can find uncultivated land, shall be at liberty to cultivate it, paying a moderate rent," it was "not too soon to provide by every possible means that as few as possible shall be without a little portion of land." Indeed, Jefferson's sobering contact with the landless poor in Europe made him all the more anxious to prevent the development of a similar class in America.

Madison agreed that Jefferson's reflection formed "a valuable lesson to the Legislators of every Country, and particularly of a new one." However, in assessing the causes of the comparative comfort of the people in the United States, at least for the present, he asserted that more was involved than the absence of entrenched feudal privileges. "Our limited population," Madison argued, "has probably as large a share in producing this effect as the political advantages which distinguish us." "A certain degree of misery," he stated, as a general rule "seems inseparable from a high degree of populousness." This rule had profoundly disturbing implications for Madison, because it meant that even if a nation's land was equitably distributed and its laws thoroughly liberal and republican, a large population in itself might still create dangerous social problems. "No problem in political economy has appeared to me more puzzling," he wrote,

> than that which relates to the most proper distribution of the inhabitants of a Country fully peopled. Let the lands be shared among them ever so wisely, and let them be supplied with labourers ever so plentifully; as there must be a great surplus of subsistence, there will also remain a great surplus of inhabitants, a greater by far than will be employed in cloathing both themselves and those who feed them, and in administering to both, every other necessary and even comfort of life. What is to be done with this surplus? Hitherto we have seen them distributed into manufacturers of superfluities, idle proprietors of productive funds,

domestics, soldiers, merchants, mariners, and a few other less numerous classes. All these classes not withstanding have been found insufficient to absorb the redundant members of a populous society.

Madison thus wrestled with the familiar problem of securing viable and sufficient sources of employment for the landless human surplus characteristic of then highly developed, old countries of Europe. He was struck, furthermore, by a depressing irony. Referring to the "manufacturers of superfluities, idle proprietors of productive funds, domestics, soldiers, merchants, mariners," and the like, he observed that "a reduction of most of those classes enters into the very reform which appears so necessary and desirable." The equal, more republican division of landed property that Jefferson espoused, he explained, would inevitably lead to "a greater simplicity of manners, consequently a less consumption of manufactured superfluities, and a less proportion of idle proprietors and domestics," while a "juster government" would also occasion "less need of soldiers either for defence against dangers from without, or disturbances from within." Republican reforms thus eventually compounded rather than ameliorated the problem, since they closed off the customary avenues of escape for an idle, surplus population. For this reason, Madison implied, the dilemma in a "fully-peopled" republic would ironically be even worse than in a corrupt, luxury-ridden society.

As always, Madison had one eye on the American future. During the constitutional convention, Charles Pinckney of South Carolina chastised his countrymen for considering themselves "the inhabitants of an old instead of a new country," and Madison's response to this charge is revealing. Pinckney made the traditional argument for America's youthfulness by pointing to the West: "In a new Country, possessing immense tracts of uncultivated lands, where every temptation is offered to emigration and where industry must be rewarded with competency, there will be few poor, and few dependent." Indeed, Pinckney concluded, "that vast extent of unpeopled territory which opens to the

frugal and industrious a sure road to competency and independence will effectually prevent for a considerable time the increase of the poor or discontented, and be the means of preserving that equality of condition which so eminently distinguishes us."

Madison was not convinced by Pinckney's analysis of American society. "In all civilized Countries," he observed, "the people fall into different classes havg. a real or supposed difference of interests." In addition to creditors and debtors, farmers, merchants, and manufacturers, there "will be particularly the distinction of rich and poor." Madison agreed with Pinckney that America had neither the hereditary distinctions of rank nor the horrendous extremes of wealth and poverty that characterized Europe, but he quickly added that "we cannot however be regarded even at this time, as one homogenous mass, in which every thing that affects a part will affect in the same manner the whole." Indeed, America was already a fairly complex, stratified society. "The man who is possessed of wealth, who lolls on his sofa or rolls in his carriage," Madison was reported to have argued, "cannot judge of the wants or feelings of the day laborer." And when Madison looked at the inevitable ramifications of continued population growth in America, he became even more pessimistic. "In framing a system which we wish to last for ages, we shd. not lose sight of the changes which ages will produce. An increase of population will of necessity increase the proportion of those who will labour under all the hardships of life, and secretly sigh for a more equal distribution of its blessings." When in time such men would outnumber "those who are placed above the feelings of indigence," there would be a serious danger of social upheaval and of radical attacks on property. Referring to the Shays uprising in Massachusetts, Madison remarked that although "no agrarian attempts have yet been made in this Country, . . . symptoms of a leveling spirit . . . have sufficiently appeared in a certain quarters to give notice of the future danger."

Madison returned to this general theme again and again during the course of the convention.

"In future times," he predicted of the United States, "a great majority of the people will not only be without landed, but any other sort of property." As the population of America increased, its political economy would inevitably become more complex. Although the relative proportion between the commercial and manufacturing classes and the agricultural was yet small, Madison contended that it would daily increase. "We see in the populous Countries in Europe now," he declared, "what we shall be hereafter." And in the Virginia ratifying convention of 1788, Madison hinted strongly that the day when "population becomes so great as to compel us to recur to manufactures" lay not very far in the future: "At the expiration of twenty-five years hence, I conceive that in every part of the United States, there will be as great a population as there is now in the settled parts. We see already, that in the most populous parts of the Union, and where there is but a medium, manufactures are beginning to be established."

The profound impact of the economic and social dislocations of the 1780s on Madison's vision of America is perhaps best revealed in his correspondence with John Brown in 1788 concerning a constitution for the prospective state of Kentucky. Madison argued strongly that property be made a qualification for suffrage, and that there be a dual suffrage for the upper and lower houses of the legislature in order to protect both "the right of persons" and "the rights of property." His reasoning here was that both the indigent and the rich, who invariably formed classes in any civilized society, had each to be given its proper share in government. Madison reminded Brown that although the specific need to protect property rights had not been given much attention at the commencement of the Revolution, subsequent experience had demonstrated the naiveté of the assumption that the United States was a peculiarly undifferentiated society in which "the rights of property" and "the rights of persons" were synonymous.

In the existing state of American population and American property[,] the two classes of rights were so little discriminated [at the commencement of the Revolution] that a provision for the rights of persons was supposed to include of itself those of property, and it was natural to infer from the tendency of republican laws, that these different interests would be more and more identified. Experience and investigation have however produced more correct ideas on this subject. It is now observed that in all populous countries, the smaller part only can be interested in preserving the rights of property. It must be foreseen that America, and Kentucky itself will by degrees arrive at this state of Society; that in some parts of the Union a very great advance is already made towards it.

Prudence thus demanded that the Kentucky constitution, as well as the United States Constitution, allow for the changes that the future would inevitably bring.

While Madison always worried about the political implications of these future developments, he never really resolved his underlying dilemma: once the inevitable pressure of population increase had created large numbers of propertyless indigents in America, what would sustain the republican character of the United States? At the core of republicanism was an intense concern with the autonomy or "independence" of the individual, and particularly with the material or economic basis for that autonomy. Since the abject dependence of the landless or laboring poor rendered them vulnerable to bribery, corruption, and factious dissension, a society with large numbers of these dependents was hardly suited to the republican form. Although Madison evinced a fatalistic acceptance of the future as he envisioned it, always urging that the new Constitution be so drawn that it could accommodate these social changes, he seemed unable to escape the traditional fear that all republics, including the one in America, were necessarily short-lived. It was wise to anticipate and provide for future changes; it was even wiser to forestall their development for as long as possible. Madison's republic was in a race against time.

The new Constitution promised to create a government equal to the task of forestalling, if not preventing, these adverse developments. A stronger national government with the power to raise revenue and regulate commerce would ideally be capable of resolving the foreign policy problems that threatened to prematurely age the country. Such a government could pave the way for westward expansion by dealing forcefully with threatening foreign powers like Spain, but even more important, it could fulfill the commercial promise of the Revolution by forcing the dismantling of the restrictive mercantilist systems that obstructed the marketing of American agricultural surpluses. As Oliver Ellsworth of Connecticut argued in defense of the Constitution, American farmers suffered because American merchants were "shut out from nine-tenths of the ports in the world" and forced to sell at low prices in the "few foreign ports" that were open to them. Addressing the farmers of America, he asserted that "you are oppressed for the want of power which can protect commerce, encourage business, and create a ready demand for the productions of your farms." Thomas Jefferson, writing in early 1789, agreed that the American system should be to "pursue agriculture, and open all the foreign markets possible to our produce."

Continued westward expansion would ease the impact of a rapidly increasing population in the United States, and the opening of foreign markets for American produce would further ensure that Americans not be forced into occupations detrimental to the republican character of their society. It could be hoped, then, that Madison's human "surplus" in America might continue to produce "necessaries" required by foreigners for as long as possible rather than be forced by adverse circumstances like those of the 1780s to become manufacturers of superfluities, idle proprietors of productive funds, soldiers, or the like. In short, the exportation of American agricultural surpluses appeared to offer a tentative republican solution to the "problem in political economy" that had so puzzled the young Virginian. America needed open markets as well as open space to make republicanism work. Perhaps a government strong enough to encourage the proper form of westward expansion and

to force free trade could answer the dilemma of population growth in an agricultural and republican nation—at least for the foreseeable future.

One of Madison's closest allies in the struggle to ratify the Constitution was a brilliant lawyer from New York, Alexander Hamilton, who several years earlier in *The Continentalist* had warned his countrymen against their obsession with classical republicanism. In many respects Hamilton was an anomaly; perhaps more than any of his countrymen, he had succeeded in discarding the traditional republican heritage that had so heavily influenced the Revolutionary mind. He was particularly receptive in this regard to the writings of David Hume as they applied both to political economy and to constitutional thought. Indeed, it seems clear that Hamilton's introduction to many of Hume's works during the course of the Revolution had greatly influenced the development of his social and political outlook. He came to accept the commercialization of society as not only inevitable but fundamentally salutary as well, and he never doubted that the real disposition of human nature was toward luxury and away from classical virtue. Such a condition, he concluded, made traditional or classical republicanism hopelessly irrelevant to the American experience. Any talk either of Spartan equality and virtuous agrarianism, or of fear of commercial corruption, was nothing more than sententious cant that evaded the necessary realities of life in modern commercial society. In this connection, his reaction to Pinckney's speech in the constitutional convention was even more incisive than Madison's. "It was certainly true," Hamilton remarked, "that nothing like an equality would exist as long as liberty existed, and that it would unavoidably result from that very liberty itself." The "difference of property" in America was already great, and "commerce and industry" would inevitably increase it still further.

Hamilton's commitment to constitutional revision long predated the convention of 1787. He subscribed to the formula for reform that Robert Morris and other nationalists had established at the end of the war, a formula that integrated constitutional change with the funding of the Revolutionary debt and a vigorous program of economic expansion tied to the consolidation and mobilization of mercantile capital. Hamilton envisioned America not as a virtuous agrarian republic, but as a powerful, economically advanced modern state much like Great Britain—a state that would stand squarely on the worldly foundations of "corruption" that Bernard Mandeville had spoken of in *The Fable of the Bees.* Thus Hamilton's vision of the future was not clouded by the traditional republican fears that continued to plague Madison and much of agrarian America. He simply accepted social inequality, propertyless dependence, and virtually unbridled avarice as the necessary and inevitable concomitants of a powerful and prosperous modern society. In one sense, Madison was still caught between the conflicting claims of classical republicanism and modern commercial society, struggling to define and implement a viable synthesis that was relevant to the American experience. Hamilton had stepped confidently and unequivocally into modernity.

On a very general but significant level, therefore, Hamilton supported the new Constitution for reasons quite different from Madison's. He did not intend to use the new government as a means of promoting the conditions that would stabilize America at a predominantly agricultural state of development; he wanted instead to use that new government to push the United States as rapidly as possible into a higher stage of development, for he interpreted this change as progress, not decay. Unlike Madison, in other words, Hamilton had an unabashedly positive sense of development through time. As his famous economic reports of the next decade revealed, he looked forward to the establishment of advanced, highly capitalized manufacturers in the United States and did everything he could within the constraints of his fiscal system to promote them. An anonymous pamphleteer caught the spirit of Hamilton's vision in 1789 when, after praising England as "the most opulent and powerful nation in Europe," he urged the new national government to give every possible encouragement to large-scale manufactures, the hallmark of British greatness. To men of this stripe, England offered a positive rather than a negative model for American development. Both Madison and Hamilton had abandoned the idea of perpetual youth for the republic; both accepted the inevitability of social complexity and the futility of the purely classical vision. Nevertheless, they brought very different attitudes and expectations to bear on their incipient careers as national political leaders.

The new American government thus began its operations in April 1789 in an ideological environment that can best be described as confused and transitional. The dislocations of the 1780s had raised complex questions and problems about the nature of American society and its republican potential. Caught between ancient and modern ways of thinking, most Americans came to realize that there could be no simple formula for a republican America. Perhaps no better evidence of the recognition of this new complexity can be found than in two premiums offered by the *American Museum* in 1789. The first was for "the best essay on the proper policy to be pursued in America, with respect to manufactures—and on the extent to which they may be carried, so as to avoid, on the one hand, the poverty attendant on an injurious balance of trade—and, on the other, the vices—the misery—and the obstruction of population, arising from assembling multitudes of workmen together in large cities or towns." The second premium was for "the best essay on the influence of luxury upon morals—and the most proper mode, consistent with republican freedom, to restrain the pomp and extravagance of ambitious or vain individuals."

These premiums reflected an ideological universe in flux. No single individual, however, could possibly have done more to draw and harden the lines of ideological combat among Americans than Alexander Hamilton who, as the first secretary of the Treasury, quickly seized the policymaking initiative in the new federal government.

11

MATTHEW LYON'S TRIAL FOR SEDITION

ALEINE AUSTIN

By 1790, anti-Federalism was moribund as a political movement and most Americans, Federalists and anti-Federalists alike, accepted the Constitution of 1787 as the foundation of national government. But the Federalist victory did not end factional strife. As the Federalists began to put their policies of economic development into practice and the national leadership began to drift toward a more authoritarian concept of government, an opposition movement grew to counter the Federalist monopoly of local, state, and national offices.

One crucial aspect of the struggle to build such an opposition movement in the new nation was the battle for citizens' minds, and a growing volume of criticism of Federalist policies, politicians, and principles punctuated the final decade of the eighteenth century. At issue was the nature of politics in the new republic. The Federalists, who sought stability through a return to the deferential politics of the colonial era, believed that the wealthy, educated, and leisured classes were best fit to rule. For them, the Revolution had unleashed an excess of democracy, and they believed that popular rule would soon bring anarchy and the eventual collapse of the Republic. Their Democratic-Republican opponents, on the other hand, favored a republic of small property holders and viewed Federalism as nothing less than an attempt to reestablish aristocratic rule in America. For them, elite rule meant the creation of a quasi-monarchical government and a return to the corruption of British and European politics.

Such a fundamental debate led Federalists and opposition leaders to attack each other with a ferocity seldom seen in American politics. But by the end of the 1790s, Democratic-Republican strength had grown rapidly, and the Federalists faced the prospect of political defeat. In 1798, in a last-ditch effort to retain power, the Federalist Congress attempted to cripple the opposition movement and silence its critics by passing the Sedition Act, which made conspiracy to oppose "any measure or measures of the government" and the publication of "false, scandalous and malicious writings" that might bring the government or its officials into disrepute crimes punishable by fine and imprisonment. A direct assault on the free speech and free assembly clauses of the First Amendment, the Sedition Act took effect in 1798, and Federalists rushed to imprison newspaper editors, politicians, and even ordinary citizens who publicly criticized the government. In this essay, Aleine Austin recounts the sedition trial of one of the Federalists' most outspoken critics, Vermont Congressman Matthew Lyon. The Federalists tried and convicted Lyon, but they could not silence him. In fact, they made him a martyr, ensured his election to Congress, and gave added weight to the national Democratic-Republican cause.

The Sedition Act of 1798, passed during the threat of war with France, was the first important challenge to the freedoms guaranteed in the Bill of Rights. Many others would follow, usually during periods of war. This raises the important question of how a democracy preserves its basic liberties under the stress of wartime pressures for quelling dissent and promoting patriotism.

From Matthew Lyon, "New Man" of the Democratic Revolution *by Aleine Austin (University Park: The Pennsylvania State University Press, 1981), pp. 108–118. Copyright © 1981 The Pennsylvania State University. Reprinted by permission of the publisher.*

The tensions engendered in the election campaign of 1798 reached their climax in a courtroom in western Vermont. There Congressman Matthew Lyon was the first to stand trial under the Sedition Act.

Long before his return to Vermont in July, Lyon had begun to campaign for reelection from Congress. As early as January, a prominent Massachusetts Federalist reported to Congressman Theodore Sedgwick, "In Vermont there is the devil to pay—Lyon's letters, covering Bache's papers, have wrought a wonderful stock of Jacobinical principles—The poison is increasing and spreading even over the mountain—To judge of the present disposition Lyon will most assuredly be reelected and Governor Tichnor dropped." The letter went on to urge more vigorous action by Vermont Federalists in Congress, who should "condescend to write influential characters and explain the measures of Government." To expedite this urgent matter, the author volunteered to carry up any letter Nathaniel Chipman might wish to write.

Several months later a scathing letter attacking Lyon as a corrupt Jacobin appeared in *Spooner's Vermont Journal* (May 28, 1798). The author, whose biting style bore Nathaniel Chipman's characteristic stamp, concluded his diatribe with the charge that Lyon was criminally guilty of acting in opposition to the Executive.

In a white heat, Lyon replied to Chipman's accusations in a letter to the editor, dated June 20. One of the passages contained the following acerbic remarks concerning his attitude toward the President:

> As to the Executive, when I shall see the efforts of that power bent on the promotion of the comfort, the happiness, and accommodation of the people, that Executive shall have my zealous and uniform support. But when I see every consideration of the public welfare swallowed up in a continual grasp for power, in an unbounded thirst for ridiculous pomp, foolish adulation, or selfish avarice; when I shall behold men of real merit daily turned out of office for no other cause but independence of sentiment; when I shall see men of firmness, merit, years, abilities, and experience,

> discarded on their application for office, for fear they possess that independence; and men of meanness preferred for the ease with which they take up and advocate opinions, the consequence of which they know but little of; when I shall see the sacred name of religion employed as a State engine to make mankind hate and persecute one another, I shall not be their humble advocate.

This passage was soon to become Count One in Lyon's indictment under the Sedition Act. Ironically, Lyon concluded this letter with his warning that Congress was considering a Sedition Bill and that he intended to ignore it because it prevented "due investigation" and exposure of the truth to the electorate.

Upon his return to Vermont, Lyon lived up to these words by ignoring the threat of the Sedition Act, and exposing "the truth" to his constituents. One of the major emphases of his campaign was to clarify the Republicans' position concerning France. After the XYZ disclosures, many of Lyon's former supporters were swept up in the general frenzy over the alleged threat of a French invasion. Lyon commented that the "noise" about the XYZ Papers "had answered the purposes of the aristocrats over the mountain completely to exasperate the unthinking people against every republican" (Lyon to Mason).

Avoidance of war was Lyon's keynote; reawakening the former feelings of attachment to France's Republicanism and opposition to British monarchism were among his main objects. While he was in Congress, he heard a letter read that ideally suited his purposes. It was written by the popular American poet Joel Barlow, the bard of the American and French Revolutions, who was then in France on both private and public business. The letter, addressed to Barlow's brother-in-law, Abraham Baldwin, a Republican congressman from Georgia, was a denunciation of President Adams's message to congress advocating preparedness for war with France. The letter struck Lyon as an informative "statement of the causes of the differences between this country and France" (*SA*, Dec. 15, 1798); he obtained permission to copy it on the proviso that he not publish it. The key paragraph of the letter, which later was to constitute Counts Two and Three of Lyon's indictment under the Sedition Act, read as follows:

> The misunderstanding between the two Governments has become extremely alarming, confidence is completely destroyed, mistrusts, jealousy, and a disposition to a wrong attribution of motives, are so apparent as to require the utmost caution in every word and action that are to come before your Executive—I mean if your object is to avoid hostilities. Had this truth been understood with you before the recall of Monroe, before the coming and second coming of Pinckney; had it guided the pens that wrote the bullying Speech of your President, and stupid answer of your Senate, at the opening of Congress in November last, I should probably have had no occasion to address you this letter. But when we found him borrowing the language of Edmund Burke, and telling the world that, although he should succeed in treating with the French, there was no dependence to be placed on any of their engagements; that their religion and morality were at an end; that they had turned pirates and plunderers; and it would be necessary to be perpetually armed against them, though they are at peace; We wondered that the answer of both Houses had not been an order to send him to a madhouse. Instead of this, the Senate have echoed the Speech with more servility than ever George III experienced from either House of Parliament.

Lyon read his copy of the Barlow letter to listeners in town after town as he campaigned throughout western Vermont. A glimpse into the tension surrounding Lyon's campaign can be gleaned from the trial testimony of two young Federalists who claimed that Lyon's reading of the Barlow letter had caused a tumult at Middletown. Lyon accused them "of following me on purpose to cause a disturbance" (Lyon to Mason). Apparently the incendiary issues of the day were argued in the town squares, and partisan feelings flared high.

In this atmosphere Lyon carried on his crusade for Republicanism, knowing full well its potential dangers. Expecting the worst from his enemies, it probably came as no surprise to him when a friend appeared at his home on October 5 to warn him that steps were being taken to indict him for violating the Sedition Act. When the bill was before Congress, Lyon had told his colleague Senator Stevens T. Mason "that it was doubtlessly intended for the members of Congress, and very likely would be brought to bear on me the very first" (Lyon to Mason).

His Vermont friend urged Lyon "to be out of the way of being taken" because the jurymen had been selected from towns unfriendly to Lyon. Twelve out of the fourteen selected had opposed Lyon in the last election, he warned, and there were "several zealous partisans for Presidential infallibility among them." Lyon thought better of this advice, and assured the deputy marshal "he need bring no posse . . . there should be no resistance." The following night the marshal appeared with the warrant for his arrest. Lyon appeared at the Rutland Court House at 9:00 the following morning. There he was called to the bar to hear the indictment of the Grand Jury (Lyon to Mason).

Describing Lyon as "a malicious and seditious person, and of a depraved mind and a wicked and diabolical disposition," it charged him with violating the Sedition Act on three counts: (1) writing and procuring publication of the letter in *Spooner's Vermont Journal;* (2) the publication of Barlow's letter on September 1; and (3) the assisting, aiding, and abetting of the publication of Barlow's letter.

The indictment cited in full the passages quoted earlier in this chapter, charging that each contained "scandalous and seditious writing, or libel," and that Lyon "did with force and violence, wickedly, knowingly, and maliciously write, print, utter and publish" them. He did so with "intent and design to excite against the said Government and President the hatred of the good people of the United States, and to stir up sedition in the United States" by "deceitfully, wickedly and maliciously contriving . . . with intent and design to defame the said Government of the United States."

The key words of the indictment, as far as the applicability of the Sedition Act is concerned, are "intent and design." Did Lyon, in uttering or writing the passages cited, *intend* to defame the President and government and stir up sedition? This issue was the nub of the trial.

Lyon emphatically pleaded not guilty to the charges of the indictment, but informed the court he was without counsel to defend his plea. The court offered to postpone the trial until the May session of the court in Windsor, but Lyon declined, feeling that in eastern Vermont the jury was bound to be completely hostile to him (Lyon to Mason). He therefore posted bonds of $1,000 for his appearance in court the following Monday. The two men who acted as surety for Lyon during the trial were Stephen Williams and Elias Buell, former president of the Rutland Democratic Society. Each put up $1,000 bail to assure the defendant's appearance before the court from day to day. Their presence is one of the few indications in the trial record that anyone befriended Lyon during this time of crisis.

Over the weekend Lyon sent a messenger to Bennington to obtain the legal services of two prominent Republican lawyers, Messrs. Fay and Robinson. The messenger, delayed by the storms of the weekend, had not arrived when the court opened on Monday. When he finally did appear, he bore the tidings that neither lawyer could serve as counsel. Mr. Fay's wife was very ill, and Mr. Robinson was preparing to attend the session of the state legislature.

As a last resort, Lyon selected as his counsel his old rival, Israel Smith. Now a judge, Smith also was running against Lyon in the present election; but he was a Republican, and Lyon's friends prevailed upon him to assist Lyon (Lyon to Mason). According to *The Spectator*'s account of the trial, Smith "declined being particularly assigned as counsel, but at Mr. Lyon's desire he sat by him during the trial and advised." Later in the campaign, Lyon accused Smith of opportunism in Congress and desertion of Republicanism (*SA*, Nov. 1, 1798). This leads to speculation on how cooperative the courtroom

relationship between the two longstanding rivals really was. In any case, Lyon acted as his own attorney throughout the trial, cross-examining witnesses and pleading his own defense.

The trial opened on Monday, October 9. On the bench were the presiding judges: Associate Justice of the Supreme Court William Paterson, and District Judge Samuel Hitchcock, Lyon's principal opponent in the runoff election for congressman in 1796. The prosecuting attorney was Federal District Attorney Charles Marsh, who derived his "old school ideal of paternalistic government" from his training at Tapping Reeve's Litchfield Law School.

Marsh's Litchfield background is not without significance. There was a curious link between the Litchfield environment and the Federalists whose animus toward Lyon was most pronounced. Nathaniel Chipman, for example, was also raised and trained for the law in Litchfield County. In Vermont, Charles Marsh was his close friend and political associate, leading one writer to suggest the possibility that Chipman instigated Marsh to bring Lyon to trial under the Sedition Act. Congressman John Allen also illustrates the Litchfield connection. This graduate of the Litchfield Law School was actually present in the courtroom throughout Lyon's trial. Allen's derisive opposition to Lyon in Congress, his strong advocacy of the Sedition Act, combined with his presence at the trial, suggests the possibility that he too may have played a role in securing Lyon's indictment. As a member of the Litchfield Junto, Allen had close connections with a number of prominent personages who harbored a deep hatred of Lyon and deplored all that this former Litchfield indentured servant symbolized. Frederick Wolcott, brother-in-law of Roger Griswold and a leading figure in this junto, later that year involved himself in the concerted campaign against Lyon by incarcerating the Reverend Dr. John C. Ogden, who had petitioned the President to pardon the Vermont congressman.

The question of the composition of the jury was the first matter to come before the court. In an open letter to his congressional ally Stevens T. Mason, Lyon maintained that the marshal, Jabez Fitch, had intentionally summoned the jurors "from towns that were particularly distinguished by their enmity to me," and that the jury was composed predominantly of "men who had been accustomed to speak ill of me." However, "of the fourteen jurymen before me I thought I saw one or two persons who knew me and would never consent to say that I was guilty of an intention of stirring up sedition." His plan was to "object off the inveterate part of the jury." When he challenged two of the jurors, Judge Paterson inquired, "For what reason?" Lyon replied that he thought he had a right to challenge a number of jurors without giving a reason. Astonishingly, the judge informed him that he had no such right and that he would have no such right in a similar case in the state court, commenting that Lyon did not know the laws of his own state. At the time, Lyon accepted the judge's ruling and comment, but while in jail he looked up the state laws and discovered that in state cases punishing individuals for defaming any court of justice or magistrate judge, the defendant could preemptively challenge six of the jurors without cause and any additional ones by showing good cause. Inferring that this was the state practice to which Judge Paterson referred, Lyon lamented, "Thus it may be seen how I have been dealt with about a jury" (Lyon to Mason).

Disadvantaged by his lack of professional legal representation, Lyon succeeded in eliminating only one juror, "who was shown to have been the author of an article in a newspaper, inveighing politically and personally against the defendant." Judge Paterson ruled: "The cause shown is sufficient, as a difference of this nature is a disqualification."

District Attorney Marsh also challenged a juror, a Mr. Board. Marsh "produced one of the Deputy Sheriffs who had summoned the jury, who testified that he heard the juror say he thought Mr. Lyon would not, or should not, be condemned." The judge disqualified him. Commented Lyon, "Thus was the only man

sworn away that knew me enough to judge of my intentions" (Lyon to Mason).

As soon as the jury was sworn, Lyon interposed a plea challenging the jurisdiction of the court on the grounds that the Sedition Act was unconstitutional. Judge Paterson overruled the plea, but said Lyon could make use of the argument in another stage of the trial.

District Attorney Marsh opened the case by presenting Lyon's letter that had been published July 31 in *Spooner's Vermont Journal.* The letter was dated June 20, and bore the Philadelphia postmark July 7. Both these dates preceded the passage of the Sedition Act on July 14. The District Attorney interrogated two witnesses in an effort to prove that the letter did not reach the newspaper in Windsor until after July 14. Lyon reported, "The printer's boy thought it did not arrive until the 20th, and Mr. Buck saw the setting from it about the 23rd or later; I acknowledged the letter" (Lyon to Mason).

The technical problem facing the district attorney was to prove Lyon guilty of having violated the Sedition Act on the basis of the "libelous" contents of a letter that had been written before the Sedition Act was passed.

The purpose of the District Attorney's questions was to prove that the letter was published after the Sedition Act and that Lyon was responsible for procuring its publication. The Republicans subsequently insisted that this ex post facto application of the Sedition Act to Lyon's letter was a violation of Article 1 of the Constitution. As a member of the Constitutional Convention, Judge Paterson was particularly sensitive to this accusation, which he attempted to refute in an extensive correspondence with Congressman Joseph H. Nicholson. Acknowledging that "nothing can be more evident to a legal mind than that an indictment cannot be sustained under a statute for an offense perpetrated before the statute was made," he nevertheless insisted that the jury acted within the law. He gave as grounds for this assertion the fact that Lyon's letter was published on July 31, seventeen days after the Sedition Act was enacted, maintaining "that he, who procures another to publish a libel, becomes the publisher himself."

In reply, Nicholson cogently argued, "I presume the only manner in which it is pretended that he procured the Printer to publish it, was by his letter dated in June in Philadelphia; at which time his Right to publish was not impaired—If then at that time he had a Right to print or publish, he certainly had a Right to Request another to print or publish, for the Right to do it himself would not exist without the Right to request another to do it likewise." In conclusion, Nicholson queried:

> What kind of presumption is that, which makes Mr. Lyon acquainted with a Law that had no existence at the time of his Request, punished him for knowingly and willingly violating its Provisions when it is impossible from the nature of things that he could be acquainted with them or that they could be known to anyone?

Had Nicholson thus defended Lyon at the trial itself, it is doubtful that he would have dissuaded Justice Paterson from circumventing the ex post facto protections of the Constitution. According to Lyon's later account of the trial, "the party judge," after acknowledging that Lyon had written the letter before passage of the Sedition Act, admonished the jury to note that he was a member of Congress who knew the Sedition Act was about to be passed and probably hurried his letter to evade the law.

When District Attorney Marsh turned to the Barlow letter, he extensively developed the government's case. The witnesses he called upon testified they had heard Lyon read the letter often during his political campaign and that its effect upon a gathering in Middletown was to promote revolution and provoke disorder. Lyon countered by attempting to prove, in his cross-examination, that it was the boisterous heckling of these very witnesses that provoked the disturbance (Lyon to Mason). As far as the publication of the letter was concerned, a printer testified that Lyon's wife brought him a copy to publish; but, upon Lyon's cross-examination, he acknowl-

edged that Lyon "had endeavored to prevent it from being printed." Years later, in a speech to Congress, Lyon clarified this seemingly contradictory testimony. "The fact was," he explained, "that my wife was persuaded by a gentleman who is now a member of this House that the Republican cause and my election (which was pending) would be injured if the letter was not published." Consequently she gave the letter to the printer in Lyon's absence; but when he learned of its publication, he immediately "suppressed the remainder of the edition," because of his promise to Abraham Baldwin. As far as Justice Paterson was concerned, whether or not Lyon secured the printing of the Barlow letter, he in all events was guilty of its publication, for "reading a libel . . . to a number of people . . . amounts to a publication."

In his summation, Marsh dwelt at length upon the libelous nature of the passages in the indictment. He called the jury's special attention to the intent of Lyon's words, charging that Lyon's libels were expressly intended to do the things the Sedition Act prohibited: defame the President and government, excite the hatred of the American people, and stir up sedition.

After the prosecution rested its case, Judge Paterson rose to give his charge to the jury. Lyon interrupted to ask why he should not address the jury, since his counsel had declined on the grounds that he had not had time to prepare his case. Receiving permission, Lyon addressed the jury for over two and a half hours. Unfortunately, what he said is only briefly recorded. According to Wharton's record of the trial:

> The defendent stated his defense to consist in three points:
> first, that the court had no jurisdiction of the offence, the act of Congress being unconstitutional and void, if not so generally, at least as to writings composed before its passage; second, that the publication was innocent; and third, that the contents were true. . . . The defendent addressed the jury at great length, insisting on the unconstitutionality of the law, and the insufficiency of the evidence to show anything more than legitimate opposition.

Of primary interest is the question: Upon what grounds did Lyon argue the unconstitutionality of the Sedition Act? It has been noted previously that in his magazine Lyon took the general Republican position that the seditious libel laws were the exclusive province of state legislation. Apparently he used this as one of his arguments during his address to the jury, for in Justice Paterson's notes on the trial, we find this counterargument: "Govt. must defend itself—must not appeal to another state or tribunal . . . the offense is agt. the United States."

Equally significant is an earlier entry in Judge Paterson's notes, marked "free discussion." This notation is the only one the Justice chose to underline, and indicates that Lyon strongly challenged the constitutionality of the Sedition Act on the grounds that it violated the First Amendment's protection of freedom of speech. This impression is corroborated by the following notes that Justice Paterson also made on Lyon's summation: "Thought there was a majority in Congress not well disposed to the liberties of the country. Did not vote for the bill and saying so is seditious. . . . Such an arbitrary act. Consider his situation as a representative."

Piecing together the fragmentary material from Justice Paterson's notes and Francis Wharton's record of the trial, one is led to the conclusion that Lyon based his defense primarily on his concept of "legitimate opposition," which in essence meant freedom to criticize and oppose policies of the government. He wrote a clear statement of this position in *The Scourge of Aristocracy* just before his indictment; it is not unlikely that he repeated many of these ideas in his address to the jury:

> I do not understand what people can mean by opposition to Government, applied to the Representatives of the People, in that capacity. We have been accustomed to suppose that Representatives are sent to vote, and support by their arguments their own opinions, and that of their constituents, and to act for the interest of their country. It is quite a new kind of jargon to call a Representative of the People an Opposer of the Government, because he does not, as a Legislator, advocate and acquiesce in every proposition that comes before the Executive. I have no particular interest of my own in crossing the view of the Executive. When a proposition comes from that quarter, which I think, if gained, will be injurious to my constituents and the Constitution, I am bound by oath, as well as by every consideration of duty to oppose it; if outvoted it is my duty to acquiesce—I do so; but measures which I opposed from duty, as injurious to the liberty and interest of this country in Congress, you cannot expect me to advocate at home. (*SA*, Oct. 1, 1798)

Following this line of argument, Lyon attempted to disprove what he called the prosecution's charge of "evil intentions" (Lyon to Mason). According to the *Spectator,* Mr. Lyon proceeded to read several parts of the publications complained of, and to make several observations. When Lyon says he addressed the jury on the "innocence of the passage in my letter, and the innocence of the manner in which I read the letter," his line of argument becomes more clear (Lyon to Mason). He probably read sections of the passages in question to show that the intent of the material was innocent; that is, the intent was not to defame or stir up sedition against the Executive and the Government, but to oppose legitimately policies with which he was in disagreement.

Since the Sedition Act allowed the truth of statement to be presented as a defense, Lyon attempted to prove the validity of his statements concerning President Adams. This section of his summation lent the one humorous note to his trial. In a completely unorthodox move, he called upon Justice Paterson to testify. Was it not true, Lyon asked the Justice, that he had frequently dined with the President and observed his "ridiculous pomp and parade"? Judge Paterson in turn replied that he had dined with the President on rare occasions, but had observed only "plainness and simplicity." Lyon pressed the point further. Was it not true, he asked, that the Judge had seen more pomp and servants at the President's than at the tavern in Rutland? To this the Justice made no reply.

Ludicrous as this cross-examination may have been, it illustrates the weakness of the Sedition Act's provision that statements which could be proven true would not be punishable under the Act. Whether President Adams surrounded his office with "pomp and parade" or "plainness and simplicity" was a matter of opinion dependent upon the vantage point of the observer. Neither opinion could be proven true or false. What was true for Matthew Lyon, the self-made frontiersman, differed markedly from the truth as seen by William Paterson, the eminent Supreme Court Justice.

In his charge to the jury, Judge Paterson spelled out clearly the issues upon which the jurors were to decide Lyon's guilt or innocence: "You have nothing whatever to do with the constitutionality or unconstitutionality of the sedition law. . . . The only question you are to determine is . . . Did Mr. Lyon publish the writing given in the indictment? Did he do so seditiously? On the first point the evidence is undisputed, and in fact, he himself concedes the fact of publication as to a large portion of libellous matter."

According to Lyon, Judge Paterson also implied the Barlow letter was a forgery, saying, "Let men of letters read that letter and compare it with Barlow's writings, and they would pronounce it none of his" (Lyon to Mason).

The essential emphasis of the charge was on the question of intent; here too Judge Paterson made his position clear:

> As to the second point you will have to consider whether language such as that here complained of could have been uttered with any other intent than that of making odious or contemptible the President and government, and bringing them both into disrepute. If you find such is the case, the offence is made out, and you must render a verdict of guilty. Nor should the political rank of the defendent, his past services, or the dependant position of his family, deter you from this duty.

At the end of his charge, he added: "In order to render a verdict of guilty, you must be satisfied beyond all reasonable doubt that the hypothesis of innocence is unsustainable."

The jury deliberated an hour. It returned with a verdict of guilty. The judge gave Lyon the opportunity to show cause why judgment should not be pronounced. Lyon declined to comment. He was then told to describe his ability or inability to pay a fine. Lyon explained that his property had been valued around $20,000 several years ago, but since then he had been forced to sell a great share of it, and what remained would barely bring in $200 in the present circumstances of scarcity of cash and reduced values of land (Lyon to Mason).

Before passing sentence, Judge Paterson first addressed Lyon on the gravity of his crime:

> Matthew Lyon, as a member of the federal legislature, you must be well acquainted with the mischiefs which flow from an unlicensed abuse of government, and of the motives which led to the passage of the act under which this indictment is framed. No one, also, can be better acquainted than yourself with the existence and nature of the act. Your position, so far from making the case one which might slip with a nominal fine through the hands of the court, would make impunity conspicuous should such a fine be imposed. What, however, has tended to mitigate the sentence which would otherwise have been imposed is, what I am sorry to hear of, the reduced condition of your estate.

He then delivered the sentence: "The judgement of the court is, that you stand imprisoned four months, pay the costs of prosecution, and a fine of one thousand dollars, and stand committed until this sentence be complied with."

The sentence came as a thunderbolt to the defendant. "No one expected imprisonment," he asserted (Lyon to Mason). Accustomed as he was to political acrimony, particularly during election campaigns, he was unprepared for outright political persecution.

The situation whereby a Congressman could be imprisoned for criticizing the policies of the government focused sharply the question of opposing political parties. The impact of the Sedition Act was to deny the legitimacy of party politics. According to the Federalists' view of the political process sanctioned by the Constitution, once the elected government decided upon a policy, the populace was obliged to support it. There was no room in Federalist thought for opposition to the government. At the least, such opposition was factious. At the most, an organized opposition party that appealed to the populace to change government policy was seditious.

Matthew Lyon and the other victims of the Sedition Act, who were mainly editors of Republican newspapers, forced the country to face the issues of free speech and legitimate party opposition, and eventually to forge a broader concept of the democratic process.

12

ABSALOM JONES: FREE BLACK LEADER

GARY B. NASH

The American Revolution wrought profound changes in the lives of the nation's African-American peoples. In the North, the new state governments passed gradual emancipation laws that set slavery on the road to extinction for the thousands of blacks held in bondage above the Mason-Dixon line. In the South, where the continuation of slavery was ensured by the rapid expansion of cotton production after the 1790s, masters found their bondspeople increasingly emboldened by the rhetoric of the Revolution and by the successful desertion of thousands of slaves to the British ranks during the war. While much has been written about post-Revolutionary slavery, until recently historians have paid relatively little attention to the free blacks who resided in the North. Yet scholarship has revealed that the end of slavery in the northern states prompted one of the most dramatic migrations in American history. Fleeing from rural isolation and the legacy of bondage, newly freed blacks flocked to northern cities in search of jobs, communities, and family life.

Of all the northern cities, Philadelphia exerted the greatest magnetic attraction for free blacks. At the center of Philadelphia's free black community stood the religiously oriented Free African Society and the African Church. More than any other institution, independent black churches symbolized and reinforced the African-American quest for racial parity following the Revolution. In this essay, Gary B. Nash tells the story of Absalom Jones, an ex-slave who became one of the leaders of Philadelphia's free black community. By setting Jones's life in the context of the city's developing black religious institutions, Nash reveals the difficulties and prejudice faced by free blacks as well as their steadfast desire to become free and equal citizens of the new republic.

"I, Absalom Jones, was born [a slave] in Sussex [Delaware] on the 6th of November, 1746." So he wrote nearly half a century later when he was a free man, a leader of the free black community in Philadelphia, and the first licensed black minister in the United States. Though hardly noticed in traditional history books, nor even in the recent wave of writing on Afro-American history, the story of Absalom Jones encapsulates much of the experience of the first generation of freed slaves in America. Moreover, his accomplishments, especially his role in establishing the first separate black church in America, entitle him to a place among the "men of mark"—the early black leaders who laid the foundations of modern Afro-American life by fashioning social and religious institutions that carried forward the black quest for freedom and equality after the American Revolution.

His master, Benjamin Wynkoop, took him from the fields, Absalom remembered, when "I was small . . . to wait and attend on him in the house." Removed from the world of field labor, he developed a desire for learning. With pennies given to him from time to time, he recalled, "I soon bought myself a primer and begged to be taught by any body that I found able and willing to give me the least instruction. Soon after this, I was able to purchase a spelling book . . . and a Testament." Literacy could only have increased the distance between him and those of his age who did not live in the big house; and hence Absalom—who had only this slave name— became introspective, or "singular," as he termed it. Then, in 1762, at age 16, his master sold his mother, five brothers, and a sister after deciding to move north to Philadelphia, the Quaker capital of Pennsylvania.

The breaking up of his family, though doubtless traumatic, proved to be a turning point in his life. While bereft of his kin, he was taken to the earliest center of abolitionism in America and to the city where humanitarian reformers had created an atmosphere conducive to education and family formation among slaves.

Thus, while he had to work his master's shop from dawn to dark, Absalom soon prevailed upon Wynkoop to allow him to attend a night school for blacks.

In 1770 Absalom married the slave of his master's neighbor, taking vows in the Anglican church where the Wynkoop family worshipped. Soon after this, encouraged by the abolitionist sentiment that Quakers and others had spread through Philadelphia, he put the tool of literacy to work. Drawing up an appeal for his wife's release, he carried it, with his wife's father at his side, to "some of the principal Friends [Quakers] of this city," asking for their support. "From some we borrowed, and from others we received donations," he recounted. Thereafter, Absalom "made it my business to work until twelve or one o'clock at night, to assist my wife in obtaining a livelihood," and to pay the money that was borrowed to purchase her freedom. It took years to repay the debt. But by 1778, while the American Revolution was occurring, Absalom had apparently discharged his obligations because he was then pleading with his master to allow him to purchase his own freedom. Wynkoop would not consent to this until October 1, 1784—six years after the first of what Absalom remembered as a series of humble requests.

It was probably in 1784, upon gaining his release, that Absalom authenticated his freedom to the world around him by taking the surname Jones. It was a common English name but nonetheless one that *he* had chosen and one that could not be mistaken for the Dutch name of his master whom he had served until the age of 38. But he acted as if he bore his master no grudges. Forbearing and even tempered, he continued to work in Wynkoop's shop. Years later, in an obituary for Jones, it was said that his master "always gave him the character of having been a faithful and exemplary servant, remarkable for many good qualities; especially for his being not only of a peaceable demeanour, but for being possessed of the talent for inducing a disposition to it in others."

Two years after gaining his freedom in Philadelphia, Absalom Jones met another recently freed slave from Delaware named Richard Allen. Allen was much Jones's junior in years but much his senior in his commitment to leading out of physical bondage fellow Africans still enslaved and out of psychological bondage those who had been recently freed. While still a slave, Allen had been converted to Methodism by itinerant preachers during the revolutionary years in Kent County, Delaware. After gaining his freedom in 1780 he spent six years interspersing work as a sawyer and wagon driver with months of riding the Methodist circuits from South Carolina to New York. He learned to preach with great effect to black and white audiences and traveled with some of the leading Methodist sojourners. By the time he arrived in Philadelphia in 1786, full of Methodist zeal and convinced that God had appointed him to special tasks, Allen seems to have completed the crucial psychological middle passage by which those who gained freedom in a legal sense procured as well the emotional autonomy that came only when they overcame servility to whites and dependence upon them.

Invited to preach in the white Methodist church in Philadelphia, Allen soon "raised a Society . . . of forty-two members." Among them was Absalom Jones, who had abandoned Christ Church where his former master worshipped in favor of St. George's Methodist Church. Like taking a surname, this was a step in the forging of a new self-identity, a part of the difficult throwing off of dependency that was indispensable in learning how to live as a fully free person.

Within months of Allen's arrival in Philadelphia Absalom Jones and several other recently freed slaves joined the Methodist preacher to discuss forming an independent black religious society. Religion and education had been the mainsprings of freedom and achievement for all these men. So it was natural that when they looked around them to find the majority of former slaves illiterate and unchurched, they "often communed together upon this painful and important subject" and determined "to form some kind of religious society." Shortly thereafter, Allen proposed this "to the most respectable people of color in this city," only to be "met with opposition." Leading white

Methodists objected even more strenuously, using "very degrading and insulting language to try to prevent us from going on." Nevertheless, out of these deliberations came the Free African Society of Philadelphia, which Jones and Allen founded in April 1787. Though mutual aid was its purported goal, the Society was quasi-religious in character and, beyond that, was an organization for building black strength and pride through collective and independent action. Before we can examine how the Free African Society midwived the birth of the first black churches in North America we must form a mental picture of the world these former bondspersons found themselves in and explore their understanding of the possible strategies that they might adopt in hammering out a postslavery existence that went beyond mere legal release from thralldom.

Black Philadelphians, like former slaves in other parts of America, had to rethink their relationship to white society in the early days of the Republic. Were they Africans in America who might now return to their homelands? Were they Afro-Americans whose future was bound up in creating a new existence on soil where they had toiled most of their lives but whose cultural heritage was African? Or were they simply Americans with dark skin, who in seeking places as free men and women had to assimilate as quickly as possible to the cultural norms and social institutions of white society?

Outwardly, Philadelphia represented a haven from persecution and a arena of opportunity for manumitted blacks. It was the center of Quaker abolitionism, the location of the national government that had issued ringing phrases about freedom and equality for all, and the capital of the state that in 1780 had passed the first abolition act in America. It was also a bustling maritime center that held out the promise of employment for migrating Afro-Americans. For all these reasons Philadelphia became a magnet for those released from bondage during the 1780s, and this drawing power also owed something to the considerable sympathy among some of its white inhabitants for freed blacks setting out on the road to freedom. Hence, from a city with about

450 slaves and an equal number of free blacks at the end of the American Revolution Philadelphia grew to contain 2,100 blacks, all but 273 of them free, in 1790, and more than 6,500 blacks, of whom only 55 remained in bondage, in 1800.

In its internal workings, however, Philadelphia was far from ideal for former slaves. The illiterate and often unskilled men and women who trekked there after the Revolution had to compete for jobs with lower-class Irish and German immigrants and did not always find work. Though not disenfranchised by law, free blacks were prohibited by white social pressure from voting. Also, virtually every institution and social mechanism in the city—religious or secular, economic and social—engaged in discriminatory practices which flowed like a natural force from the pervasive belief in black inferiority. The common assumption was that blacks were either innately handicapped or had been irreparably degraded by the experience of slavery.

For black wayfarers who found their way to Philadelphia after the Revolution overcoming patterns of behavior peculiar to slavery became a crucial matter. By its nature, slavery assumed the superiority of the white master class, and even the most benevolent master occupied a power relationship vis-á-vis his slaves that daily reminded blacks of their lowly position and condition. Probably few American slaves believed they were inferior human beings, but slavery required them to act so, and daily behavior became so patterned that dependency and servility developed as a way of life among many of them. Newly freed, they had to face the dominant culture, which was far from ready to treat them as equals and continued to demand deferential comportment from them. We can infer from the fact that almost all the early black institutions in the North used the adjective "African" in their titles—the Free African Society, the African School, the African Church of Philadelphia—that these ex-slaves identified positively with their ancestral homelands and did not subscribe to the common white characterizations of Africa as a dismal, cultureless environment. Nonetheless, white racism impinged on their lives at every turn and, although

not of the virulent form it would assume early in the nineteenth century, it tended to keep cowed the poorest and weakest members of the emerging black communities.

Recognizing the hidebound nature of white attitudes and the psychic scars inflicted by slavery, a few former slaves in the North attempted to solve the problem simply by opting out of American society and returning to Africa. But the small colonization movement of the 1780s that was centered in New England made virtually no impact on black Philadelphians, who overwhelmingly cast their lot with America. Nonetheless, the will to plan rationally, to strive for an independent and dignified existence, and to work for the future of their children depended upon throwing off the incubus of slavery, an institution which had perpetuated itself by exacting a terrible price for black attempts at independent or self-reliant behavior. Some freedmen in Philadelphia believed that in this work of emotional self-reconstruction their future lay not in trying to pry open the doors of white institutions but in building autonomous black organizations where the people emerging from the house of bondage could gather strength, develop their own leaders, and socialize and worship in their own ways.

In the post-Revolutionary era free blacks also had to confront the role that benevolence played in perpetuating feelings of servility and in shaping black–white relations. "There can be no greater disparity of power," writes David Brion Davis, "than that between a man convinced of his own disinterested service and another man who is defined as a helpless object." Thus, white benevolence perpetuated black dependence, often stood in the way of mutual respect, and impeded the growth of positive self-images among freedmen and freedwomen, who could not feel truly free so long as they had to rely on white help in creating a new life for themselves.

Only a few years out of bondage in the 1780s, Philadelphia's free blacks thus lived in a highly fluid situation full of dangers and full of opportunities. Their lowly position and circumscribed means made it imperative to accept the support of benevolent whites who offered education, sometimes jobs, and almost always moral guidance. Likewise, they could hardly hope to obtain the release of their racial brethren still in bondage without white leadership and support. Yet many of them understood that while short-term circumstances required white patronage, the long-term goal must be to stand independent of white largesse.

It is within this ideological context that we can see the Free African Society of Philadelphia as much more than a black mutual aid society. Beginning as an organization in which free blacks were taking the first halting steps toward developing their own leaders and solving their own problems, it became a society which founded churches, assumed a supervisory role over the moral life of the black community, and worked to create a visionary black consciousness out of the disparate human material that had found its way to Philadelphia in this period. But this took time.

While the Free African Society got underway, Richard Allen's preaching and Absalom Jones's quiet aid to those he found in need increased the black congregants at St. George's. Philadelphia's blacks, both slave and free, had married, baptized their children, and attended religious services at most of the city's churches since before the Revolution and had particularly flocked to the Anglican churches, which encouraged them with religious and secular instruction. Now they began transferring their allegiance to the Methodist church, an offshoot of the Anglican church which had declared itself independent only in 1784. This transfer of allegiance is not difficult to understand, for the new Methodist ministers "made no pretensions to literary qualifications," as the first black historian of the African Church of Philadelphia wrote in the 1850s, "and being despised and persecuted as religious enthusiasts, their sympathies naturally turned towards the lowly, who like themselves, were of small estimate in the sight of worldly greatness." Also commending Methodism to former slaves were the well-known antislavery views of founder John Wesley and the Methodist discipline and

polity formulated in 1784, which attacked slave trading and slaveholding and barred persons engaged in these practices from holding church offices.

Meanwhile, Jones and Allen enlarged the activities of the Free African Society. In early 1790 the Society attempted to lease the Stranger's Burial ground in order to turn it into a black cemetery under black control. In the next month the Society instituted "a regular mode of procedure with respect to . . . marriages" and began keeping a book of marriage records. Having assumed quasi-ecclesiastical functions, the Society took the final step in September 1790 when a special committee led by Jones recommended the initiation of formal religious services.

All of these enlarged functions bore a decidedly Quakerly stamp, reflecting the strong influence of the Society of Friends on many of the leading members. More particularly, this influence came through the work of Anthony Benezet, the wizened, saintly little Huguenot immigrant who dedicated so much of his life to the Negro's cause. Benezet wrote half a dozen pamphlets against slavery and the slave trade between 1759 and 1784, founded a school for blacks in 1770, and tirelessly devoted himself to it for the rest of his life. In 1780 he personally lobbied with every member of the Pennsylvania legislature to pass a gradual abolition act. When Benezet died in 1784, slaves and free blacks alike turned out en masse to follow his funeral procession to the graveyard and testify to his work on their behalf.

While Quaker support was indispensable to the African Society at first, it also caused difficulties and eventually a deep rift in the black ranks. Quaker humanitarianism was never of the sort that was based on a deep sense of the "likeness among all persons." Quakers held themselves apart from other people, white and black, and in fact the Society of Friends was the only religious group in Philadelphia that refused to accept blacks as members in the 1780s. Theirs was more a policy "of stewardship than a true humanitarianism," and their efforts on behalf of blacks "partook more of condescension than humanitarianism."

The Quakerly leanings of many Free African Society members caused Richard Allen great pain. He made no objections when the African Society adopted Quaker-like visiting committees in early 1788 to call on black families or when they instituted the disownment practices of Quakers in September of that year, to disenroll wayward members. But two months later, when the Society adopted the Friendly practice of beginning meetings with fifteen minutes of silence, Allen led the withdrawal of "a large number" of dissenters whose adherence to Methodism had accustomed them to "an unconstrained outburst of their feelings in religious worship." Allen came no more to meetings of the African Society but privately began convening some of its members in an attempt to stop the drift of the organization toward the practices of the Quakers.

Jones and others made repeated efforts to bring Allen back into the bosom of the group and censured him "for attempting to sow division among us." When their efforts failed, they followed the Quaker procedure of declaring that "he has disunited himself from membership with us." This was in June 1789. Nineteen months later, following four months of deliberations, they began holding formal religious meetings in the Quaker African Schoolhouse.

After Allen's disownment from the Free African Society, the leadership role fell primarily to Absalom Jones. It was the mild-mannered and conciliatory Jones who made the crucial connections in the white community that launched plans for building a black church. The ties with the Society of Friends were wearing thin by the summer of 1791 because many Quakers objected to the Sunday psalm singing by blacks in the Quaker schoolhouse. But Jones had been forging new patronage lines to one of Philadelphia's most influential citizens—the powerful, opinionated doctor, Benjamin Rush. Over the next four years it was Rush who became the Anthony Benezet of

the 1790s so far as Philadelphia's free blacks were concerned.

As a young physician before the American Revolution, Rush had written a passionate antislavery pamphlet. But this ardor for the cause had cooled during the war, and he had played no role in the work of the Pennsylvania Abolition Society when it was reestablished in 1784. Then, in a poignant example of trans-Atlantic abolitionist influence, Rush threw himself into the fray in 1787 after reading Thomas Clarkson's recently published *Essay on the Slavery and Commerce of the Human Species,* which in turn had been inspired by Clarkson's reading of Anthony Benzet's *Historical Account of Guinea,* one reading of which convinced him to devote his life to abolitionism. So thoroughly was Rush converted to the free blacks' cause that he immediately joined the Pennsylvania Abolition Society, freed his slave, William Gruber, and shortly thereafter wrote to a friend that "I love even the name of Africa, and never see a Negro slave or freeman without emotions which I seldom feel in the same degree towards my unfortunate fellow creatures of a fairer complexion."

During the summer of 1791 plans went forward for promoting the black church, although white opposition among those who had claimed to be friends of the free blacks surfaced quickly. Working with Absalom Jones, and perhaps with Richard Allen, who had reconciled his differences with members of the African Society, Rush drew up a plan of church government and articles of faith. A white merchant, Robert Ralston, joined Rush in composing subscription papers to be carried about the city to solicit building funds. Aware that many Philadelphians regarded him as impetuous and idiosyncratic, Rush tried to stay in the background, convinced that "the work will prosper the better for my keeping myself out of sight." Rush was hardly capable of self-effacement, however, and word of his role in the plans circulated through the city. Within days of composing the plan of government Rush found himself accosted in the street by William White, rector of Christ Church and recently appointed bishop of the Episcopal Church in Pennsylvania. White "expressed his disapprobation to the proposed African church" because "it originated in pride." Leading Quakers also conveyed their displeasure to Absalom Jones, and the Methodists threatened disownment of any black Methodist who participated in the undertaking. Paternalistic Philadelphians discovered that helping their black brothers gave greater satisfaction than seeing them help themselves.

Such criticism from Anglicans, Quakers, and Methodists, many of whom had been active in the Abolition Society, drove home the lesson that benevolent whites regarded freedmen as deeply inferior and could not abide independent action—pride, Bishop White called it—that challenged that characterization. An early historian of black Methodism, reflecting in 1867 on the final separation of Richard Allen from the white Methodist church, dwelt on precisely this point. "The giant crime committed by the Founders of the African Methodist Episcopal Church, " wrote Benjamin Tanner, "was that they dared to organize a Church of men, men to think for themselves, men to talk for themselves, men to act for themselves: A Church of men who support from their own substance, however scanty, the ministration of the Word which they receive; men who spurn to have their churches built for them, and their pastors supported from the coffers of some charitable organization; men who prefer to live by the sweat of their own brow and be free."

No chance yet existed in 1791 for Philadelphia's free blacks to gain the full meaning of freedom through completely independent action. Half of them still lived in the households of whites as domestic servants and hired hands; many had to indenture out their children through the good offices of the Abolition Society; and, as a group, they still were obliged to rely heavily on benevolent white Philadelphians for organizing schools and, in the present case, the African Church. Hence, Absalom Jones and the other black leaders worked closely with Benjamin Rush, Robert Ralston, and other whites in the summer of 1791 to raise subscriptions for their own place of worship. The work went on "swim-

mingly," Rush reported in August. An "Address of the Representatives of the African Church," an appeal for building funds, was carried to prominent men in the city. This succeeded in garnering some modest contributions, including donations from George Washington and Thomas Jefferson. Attempting to appeal as widely as possible to both blacks and whites, Jones and the other leaders adopted articles of association and a plan of church government "so general as to embrace all, and yet so orthodox in cardinal points as to offend none." But the flow of money soon stopped, perhaps because of the opposition to the church expressed by leading white churchmen. So Jones and Allen decided to broaden their appeal. Believing "that if we put our trust in the Lord, he would stand by us," Allen recounted, they took to the streets in March 1792. "We went out with our subscription paper," recalled Allen, "and met with great success," collecting $360 on the first day.

But thereafter the going got harder and some of the early optimism began to fade. The early subscriptions proved sufficient to buy two adjacent lots on Fifth Street, only a block from the Statehouse, for $450. But most blacks had little to contribute from their meager resources, and most whites seem to have snapped their pocketbooks shut at the thought of a black church. Whereas they had initially responded to the idea of an "African" church as a piece of arrogance on the part of a people so recently released from slavery, they now began calculating the effect on their own churches. "The old and established [religious] societies," wrote Rush, "look shy at them, each having lost some of its members by the new association." Still, Rush did not waver in his conviction that "the poor blacks will succeed in forming themselves into a distinct independent church."

Despite these early difficulties, the resolve of black Philadelphians to form a separate church grew mightily in the fall of 1792 after one of the most dramatic confrontations in early American church history. A number of black leaders were still attending services at St. George's Methodist Church, where the congregation had outgrown the seating capacity. When the white elders decided to expand their house of worship, black Methodists contributed money and labor to the effort. But on the first Sunday after the renovations were completed the elders informed the black worshipers who filed into the church that they must sit in a segregated section of the new gallery rather than along the walls, as had been their custom before. Richard Allen later recounted:

> We expected to take the seats over the ones we formerly occupied below, not knowing any better. We took those seats; meeting had begun, and they were nearly done singing, and just as we got to the seats, the Elder said, "Let us pray." We had not been long upon our knees before I heard considerable scuffling and loud talking. I raised my head up and saw one of the trustees, H——M——, having hold of the Rev. Absalom Jones, pulling him up off his knees, and saying "You must get up, you must not kneel here." Mr. Jones replied, "Wait until prayer is over, and I will get up, and trouble you no more." With that he beckoned to one of the trustees, Mr. L—— S——, to come to his assistance. He came and went over to William White to pull him up. By this time prayer was over, and we all went out of the church in a body, and they were no more plagued by us in the church.

The St. George's incident confirmed what many blacks had already suspected—that there would be no truly biracial Christian community in the white churches of the city. If they were to worship with dignity, it must be in churches of their own. The first black historian of the black church movement described this striving for dignity in the black exodus from St. George's that followed the discriminatory treatment. It was an "age of general and searching inquiry," wrote William Douglass, "into the equity of old and established customs," a time when "a moral earthquake had awakened the slumber of ages" and caused "these humble men, just emerged from the house of bondage . . . to rise above those servile feelings which all their antecedents were calculated to cherish and to assume, as they did, an attitude of becoming men conscious of

invaded rights . . ." They were determined, wrote Allen, "to worship God under our own vine and fig tree" and "were filled with fresh vigor to get a house erected to worship God in."

Despite such renewed commitment Jones, Allen, and the other black leaders reluctantly concluded by late 1792 that they could not raise sufficient money to build their African church on the lots they had purchased. To their rescue came the unlikeliest of figures—the Welsh immigrant John Nicholson, who had blazed meteorically onto the Philadelphia scene after the war as state comptroller and high flying speculator in western lands and revolutionary loan certificates. Barely accepted in polite Philadelphia circles, not attached to any church, and uninvolved in the work of the Abolition Society, Nicholson provided what none of the Philadelphia elite would offer—a large loan of $1,000 with which to begin construction. "Humanity, charity, and patriotism never united their claims in a petition with more force than in the present instance," wrote Rush to Nicholson in a letter hand carried by William Gray and Absalom Jones. "You *will* not—you *cannot* refuse their request." Five days later Jones and Gray wrote Nicholson suggesting a 10-year mortgage with "Lawful interest to be paid Quarterly" and pressed their request "for the sake of Religion & Christianity and as this is the first Institution of the kind. . . ."

It took another two months to execute the mortgage and another to draw up building contracts. Finally, in March 1793, as reports of black rebellion in the French West Indies filtered into Philadelphia, the city's free blacks and some of their white benefactors gathered to see earth turned for the church. Richard Allen remembered the day vividly a quarter of a century later. "As I was the first proposer of the African Church, I put the first spade into the ground to dig the cellar for the same. This was the first African Church or meeting house to be erected in the United States of America."

Before the two-story building on Fifth Street could be completed its humble founders had to endure additional difficulties. Like most visionaries, Jones and his cohorts had planned expansively, designing a church capacious enough to seat 800. The cost estimates for the building ran to $3,560. Even with the $1,000 loan from Nicholson, more money had to be raised. Ironically, black revolt in the Caribbean undermined this attempt. With hundreds of French planters fleeing the black rebellion in Saint Domingue and streaming into Philadelphia with French-speaking slaves at their sides, many white city dwellers reneged on their pledges to the African Church in order to help the destitute white slaveholders taking refuge in their city. Philadelphia's free blacks learned that even the most sympathetic whites placed the distress of white slaveowners ahead of the aspirations of those who had been slaves.

John Nicholson again came to the rescue, loaning another $1,000 in mid-August. Ten days later the black leaders staged a roof-raising banquet in an open field on the edge of the city. About 100 whites, most of them construction artisans, sat down at long tables "under the shade of several large trees" and consumed a bounteous dinner complete with excellent liqueurs and melons for dessert. They were served by a company of free blacks. Then, in a display of racial reciprocity, the whites arose, about fifty blacks took their places, and were waited on at a second sitting of the banquet by "six of the most respectable of the white company." Benjamin Rush toasted "Peace on earth and goodwill to men" and "May African churches everywhere soon succeed to African bondage." Describing to his wife the outpouring of emotion on that hot afternoon, he wrote: "Never did I witness such a scene of innocent—nay more—such virtuous and philanthropic joy. After dinner all the blacks converged on Nicholson and clasped the hand of the city's entrepreneur who had loaned $2,000 for the building of the church. One old man "addressed him in the following striking language: 'May you live long, sir, and when you die, may you not die eternally.'" Rush concluded: "To me it will be a day to be remembered with pleasure as long as I live."

But even as glasses were raised in toast on that August afternoon ill fortune struck again, and this time it delayed the completion of the church for nearly a year. It came in the form of the worst epidemic of yellow fever in the history of North America. The first victims succumbed late in July 1793, but another month passed before the fever reached epidemic proportions. By late August twenty Philadelphians were dying every day of the putrid fever, shopkeepers were closing their doors, and all who could afford it were commandeering horses, wagons, and carriages to carry their families out of the city. Hardest hit were the laboring poor. Living in crowded alleys and courts, where the fever spread fastest, they were too poor to flee, too poor even to pay a doctor.

By early September the social fabric of the city was falling to pieces. The work of tending the sick and burying the dead proved beyond the capacity of the doctors and city authorities because most nurses, carters, and gravediggers, fearing for their own lives, refused to go near the sick, dying, and dead. Husbands fled wives of many years in throes of death, parents abandoned sick children, masters thrust servants into the streets. Mathew Carey, the main chronicler of the catastrophe, wrote that "less concern was felt for the loss of a parent, a husband, a wife or an only child that, on other occasions, would have been caused by the death of a servant, or even a favorite lap-dog." Hundreds perished for lack of treatment, "without a human being to hand them a drink of water, to administer medicines, or to perform any charitable office for them." By mid-September the poor were starving and the dead were lying everywhere in the streets, while thousands of middle- and upper-class Philadelphians fled to the country.

Into this calamitous breach stepped Philadelphia's free blacks. Benjamin Rush, who played generalissimo of the relief forces, implored Absalom Jones and Richard Allen in early September to lead their people forward as nurses, gravediggers, and drivers of the death carts. Assuring the black leaders that the malignant fever "passes by persons of your color," he suggested that this God-bestowed exemption from the disease laid blacks "under an obligation to offer your services to attend the sick."

The Free African Society met on September 5 to consider Rush's request. Much of what had transpired in the last six years might have inclined them to spurn the requests for aid—the humiliating incident at St. George's, the opposition to establishing a church of their own, and the readiness of even those who had signed their subscription lists to beg off in order to aid slave-owning French planters who arrived with their chattel property in tow and then attempted to evade the state law which required the manumission of any slave brought into the state within six months. But much had also transpired that argued for contributing themselves to the white community's desperate plight—the encouragement they had received in planning their church, the dedicated work of the Abolition Society, and the personal solicitation of Rush, their closet advisor. Indeed, their explanation of how they decided to come forward suggests that they saw this as a God-sent opportunity to prove their courage and worth, to show they could drive anger and bitterness from their hearts, to dissolve white racism by demonstrating that in virtue and civic mindedness they were not inferior, but in fact superior, to those who regarded former slaves as a degraded, hopelessly backward people. The "god who knows the hearts of all men, and the propensity of a slave to hate his oppressor," wrote Jones and Allen "hath strictly forbidden it in his chosen people." They would succor those who despised and opposed them because "the meek and humble Jesus, the great pattern of humanity, and every other virtue that can adorn and dignify men hath commanded to love our enemies, to do good to them that hate and despitefully use us."

On September 6, 1793, Jones and Allen offered their services to the mayor, who immediately placed notices in the newspapers notifying citizens that they could apply to Jones or Allen for aid. "The African Society, intended for the relief of destitute Negroes," writes the best authority on the epidemic, "suddenly assumed the most onerous, the most disgusting burdens of demoralized whites." They nursed the sick, carried away the dead, dug graves, and transported the afflicted to an emergency lazaretto set up outside the city. Jones, Allen, and William Gray, under instructions from Rush, acted as auxiliary doctors, bleeding patients and administering purges. By September 7, wrote Rush, Jones and Gray "furnish nurses to most of my patients." Before the epidemic ran its course they had bled more than 800 persons, making notes on each case for Rush as they worked through the day. Then at night they drove the death carts to the cemeteries.

Within two weeks, Rush's claims that Negroes were immune to the infectious fever transmitted by the *Aedes aegypti* mosquito had proven a ghastly error. Seventy Philadelphians were dying each day and now blacks were numerous among them. "The Negroes are everywhere submitting to the disorder," Rush wrote disconsolately on September 26, "and Richard Allen who has led their van is very ill." In the first weeks of October the mortality raged through the half-abandoned city like a brushfire. On October 11 alone 119 died. Still convinced "that it was our duty to do all the good we could to our suffering fellow mortals," Allen, Jones, and the other blacks carried out their gruesome tasks. By the end of the month nearly 12,000 whites, along with most of the national government, had fled the city, and nearly 4,000 persons, including about 300 blacks, had succumbed to the fever. Not until early November did the epidemic pass.

Work on the African Church, suspended for nearly three months during the yellow fever crisis, resumed in December 1793. By the end of the year workmen had covered in the building and completed the exterior work. It took further fundraising and another six months to complete the interior work. In soliciting support in the white community the black leaders may have expected to draw on the credit they had accumulated through their heroic efforts during the terrible days of autumn. But even this altruism had to be defended, for Mathew Carey, the Irish immigrant publisher in the city, publicly vilified the free blacks for opportunistically charging exorbitant fees to nurse the sick and remove the dead.

Carey's pamphlet, *A Short Account of the Malignant Fever,* was itself a lesson in deriving profit from mass misery. Selling briskly, it went through four editions between November 14 and December 20. Carey provided a narrative account of the holocaust, lists of the dead, and a discussion of the origins of the epidemic. But the saviors of the city in Carey's account were the rising immigrant merchant Stephen Girard and other whites who organized an emergency hospital just outside the city, where they selflessly tended the sick and dying. For the black Philadelphians who drove the death carts, buried the dead, and nursed the sick in the back streets and alleys of the city Carey had mostly words of denigration.

Carey's *Short Account* drew a shocked response from Jones and Allen. The black leaders did not deny that some persons "in low circumstances," both white and black, charged extravagant prices to nurse the infected. They argued that this was to be expected, "especially under the loathsomeness of many of the sick, when nature shuddered at the thoughts of the infection, and the task was aggravated by lunacy, and being left much alone" with the sick. But Philadelphians should balance such stories, they argued, alongside those of the many blacks who asked no recompense at all and were content to take whatever the patient thought proper to give. One old black woman, when asked her fee, answered, "A dinner, master, on a cold winter's day." Ceasar Cranchell, a founding member of the African Society, swore he would not "sell his life for money, even though he should die," which he did in the process of tending sick whites. Jones, Allen, Gray, and most other blacks had remained in the city throughout the biological terror, while nearly 20,000 whites, including Carey, had fled in fear of their lives. Widely assured that blacks were immune from the disease, they had learned otherwise, so that before cold weather ended the scourge nearly one-tenth of the black population died, nearly as great a morality rate as among whites. "Was not this in a great degree the effects of the services of the

unjustly vilified black people?" asked Jones and Allen.

As the workmen completed the African Church in the spring of 1794, Philadelphia's blacks gathered to make a momentous decision about denominational affiliation. Absalom Jones and Allen still favored uniting with the Methodists, even though the white elder stationed in the city remained opposed to a separate black church and "would neither be for us nor have anything to do with us." But the "large majority" favored uniting with the Anglicans (now called Episcopalians), which is understandable in light of the fact that so many of them, both as slaves and free persons, had married, worshiped, and christened their children in the city's three Anglican churches. Steadfast in his conviction that "there was no religious sect or denomination that would suit the capacity of the colored people as well as the Methodist," Allen quietly withdrew again. Nor could he accept the invitation of the majority to be their minister. "I informed them," he wrote later, "that I could not be anything but a Methodist, as I was born and awakened under them, and I could go no further with them, for I was a Methodist, and would leave them in peace and love."

With Allen declining to lead them, the deacons and elders turned to Absalom Jones. He lacked Allen's exhortatory gifts, but his balance, tenacity, education, and dignified leadership all commended him. In July steps were taken to formalize the decision to unite with Episcopal Church. The black Philadelphians pragmatically agreed to "commit all the ecclesiastical affairs of our church to the government of the Protestant Episcopal Church of North America," while at the same time securing internal control of their church through a constitution that gave them and their successors "the power of choosing our minister and assistant minister," provided that members were to be admitted only by the minister and churchwardens, and specified that the officers of the church—the vestrymen and deacons—were to be chosen by ballot from among members of at least twelve months standing.

Finally, only "men of color, who are Africans, or the descendants of the African race," could elect or be elected into any church office except that of minister and assistant minister. With the help of Benjamin Rush, they had contrived a formula for maintaining black control of the church, while allowing for the absence of trained blacks to fill the ministry.

On July 17, 1794, the African Church of Philadelphia opened its doors for worship. The published account of the dedication ceremony indicates that much of the white ministerial opposition had melted. "The venerable Clergy of almost every denomination, and a number of other very respectable citizens were present," it was noted. Samuel Magaw, rector of St. Paul's Church, gave the sermon from the text "Ethiopia shall soon stretch out her hands unto God." The discourse was from Isaiah: "The people that walked in darkness have seen a great light"—the same epigram that was etched in marble above the church doors.

Magaw's sermon provided a window into the attitudes of Philadelphia's benevolent white leadership at this time. Reconciled to the idea of a black church, they still remained convinced of the free blacks' inferiority and consequently focused on the overriding importance of moral management and social control. Showing his ignorance of the mainsprings of action in the black community, Magaw stressed the need for gratitude and deference on the part of the blacks who crowded the church. They or their fathers, he preached, had come from the heathenish lands of Senegal, Gambia, Benin, Angola, and Congo, and that burden of birth had been increased by the dismal effects of slavery, which "sinks the mind, no less than the body . . . destroys all principle; corrupts the feelings; prevents man from either discerning, or choosing aright in anything." Having been brought from "a land of Pagan darkness, to a land of Gospel light" by white Christian goodness, these former slaves must now maintain their gratitude to those who freed them and donated or loaned money to build the church. They must pray—but not take

action—for their brethren still in bondage.

The emphasis in Magaw's sermon was on black passivity and moderation in all things. He warned the black congregation to suppress pride, which he claimed was on the rise among them. Rather they should cultivate "an obliging, friendly, meek conversation." Their church, he counseled them in a perfect display of white paternalism, owed its existence to the benevolent action of whites. That it had been born in strife and had risen only when free blacks defied the passive roles assigned them escaped his notice. But if we set alongside Magaw's dedication sermon the "Causes and Motives" for establishing the African Church, written by Absalom Jones just a month later, we can better comprehend the dialectical struggle that free blacks were engaged in. It is this document, which also announced the decision to name the church St. Thomas's African Episcopal Church of Philadelphia, in honor of the apostle, that indicates the quest for a black ideology and for strategies that would promote strength, security, and meaning in the lives of the first generation of ex-slaves in America. They had been encouraged, Jones wrote, "to arise out of the dust and shake ourselves, and throw off that servile fear, that the habit of oppression and bondage trained us up in." This statement can be taken as almost directly evidence of the influence of Anthony Benezet, under whom Jones and many of the other blacks active in the African Society had been schooled. The Quaker teacher had frontally challenged the deeply rooted doctrine of black inferiority, urged his pupils to regard themselves as "citizens of the world," argued doggedly as early as 1762 that the African environment had produced notable cultures and must not be considered as a place of jungle barbarism, and thus taught his black students that it was the environment of slavery, not innate condition, that turned Africans in America into degraded and defective human beings.

Inspired by Benezet's theories of human brotherhood and the environmentalist argument that it was slavery that had incapacitated Africans in America, Absalom Jones, Richard Allen, and others received further encouragement to strike out on their own from Benjamin Rush and others. An equally important factor in the shedding of the debilitating fear "that the habit of oppression and bondage trained us up in" was the day-to-day accomplishments of Philadelphia's blacks during the decade that followed the Revolution. Through their ability to establish families and residences, by their demonstrated capacity to sustain themselves as free laborers and artisans, and in their success at conducting themselves morally, soberly, and civilly they had proved to themselves the groundless character of the prevalent white view that former slaves were permanently corrupted and unassimilable people.

The reports of the Pennsylvania Abolition Society, which conducted house-to-house surveys of black families in the mid-1780s, and the observation of other Philadelphians bear out the successful transition to freedom that blacks made in the city after the war. In 1785 Benjamin Rush reported that "the slaves who have been emancipated among us are in general more industrious and orderly than the lowest class of white people." Two years later the Abolition Society reiterated this observation. In 1790 the first federal census takers found only three blacks among the 273 inmates of the almshouse and five black prisoners among the 191 felons in the Walnut Street Prison, indicating a much lower incidence of poverty and criminality among a people only a few years out of bondage than among the free white population. Five years later, after conducting a census of black households, the Abolition Society noted that more than one-fourth of the free blacks owned houses, most "live comfortably," and their behavior, "in point of morality, is equal to those whites who are similarly situated as to employment and means for improvement."

This is not to argue that the transition from slavery to freedom was easy. Philadelphia was full of struggling black migrants in the 1790s—poor and often unskilled sojourners who arrived by water and land from every direction. Hundreds of them could not establish independent black households at first, many had to bind out their children, and most lived in pinched and precarious circumstances. But their general ability to fashion a respectable life for themselves must have given credence to the arguments of Benezet and others. Hence, it was a fusion of ideas inculcated by white tutors and ideas derived from daily experience that galvanized black leaders and convinced them of the need—and of their capacity—to establish a separate church.

In drawing up their "Articles of Association" with the Protestant Episcopal Church, Absalom Jones and his cohorts indicated their understanding that, while they had made progress, the road ahead was strewn with barriers that could be surmounted only with the support of white patrons. The Articles announced, in a direct reference to the charges of Bishop White about black "pride," that they wished "to avoid all appearance of evil, by self-conceitedness, or an intent to promote or establish any new human device among us," and hence they had decided to "resign and conform ourselves" to the Episcopal Church of North America. Nonetheless, this was to be a black church, as their constitution spelled out.

In September 1794, one month after the constitution for their church had been accepted by the Convention of the Episcopal Church in Pennsylvania, the trustees and "representatives of the congregation" moved to solidify the racial character of their church by requesting Bishop White to qualify Absalom Jones "to act as our minister." Many years later it was recorded that Jones's "devotion to the sick and dying" during the yellow fever epidemic of 1793 had brought him wide recognition in the black community. "Administering to the bodily as well as spiritual wants of many poor sufferers, and soothing the last moments of many departing souls among his people, he became greatly endeared to the colored race." The Episcopal Convention took nearly a year before approving Jones as the minister of St. Thomas's, and it did so only after arranging a *quid pro quo* whereby they waived the Greek and Latin requirement for the ministry in exchange for the stipulation that the African church forego the right to send a representative to the yearly convention where denominational policy was set.

As St. Thomas's African Episcopal Church was being completed and its affiliation with the white Episcopal church formalized, Richard Allen pursued his vision of black Methodism. Successful as a carter, master chimney sweep, and trader, he used his own money to purchase a lot at Sixth and Lombard streets and to purchase a blacksmith's shop, which he hauled to the site and renovated as a house of worship. Seventeen days before the dedication of St. Thomas's Bishop Francis Asbury officiated at the first service and Reverend John Dickens, the white Methodist elder in Philadelphia, prayed "that it might be a 'Bethel' to the gathering of thousands of souls." This marked the birth of "Mother Bethel," the first congregation of what would became 22 years later the independent African Methodist Episcopal Church, the largest black Christian movement in the United States.

The separate black churches led by Absalom Jones and Richard Allen became the first major expression of racial pride and a major instrument for furthering the social and economic liberation of recently freed slaves. Bishop White had been correct, though in ways he knew not, when he reacted in anger in 1791 to word that the free blacks were planning a church of their own by charging that their plan "originated in pride."

The pride was really a growing feeling of strength and a conviction that black identity, black self-sufficiency, black self-determination, and the black search for freedom and equality in the early years of the republic could best be nurtured through the black church.

Absalom Jones spent nearly a quarter of a century ministering to his flock at St. Thomas's before he died in 1818 at the age of 72. In this role he was far more than a religious leader, for the black church was the center of social, educational, and political life as well. As W. E. B. Du Bois observed, it "is the world in which the Negro moves and acts." Jones's church launched a school for young black children in the late 1790s. It organized several mutual assistance and moral reform societies. Its members stood prominently among petitioners to the state and national legislatures who over the years called for ending the slave trade, abolishing slavery, and repealing discriminatory laws. Both a place of refuge in a hostile white world and a site from which to attack discrimination and exploitation, the church built by the humble slave from Delaware stood at the center of the black struggle for dignity, freedom, and social justice in the new American nation.

13

TECUMSEH, THE SHAWNEE PROPHET, AND AMERICAN HISTORY

R. DAVID EDMUNDS

The close of the Revolutionary War meant many things to the American people. To some it conferred a guarantee of freedom, to others a return to the peacefulness of everyday life, and to yet others an opportunity to establish a life of independence beyond the Appalachian Mountains. But for Native Americans, the defeat of the British meant the removal of the last defense against expanding American settlements full of farmers hungry for their land. Even before the war ended in 1783, settlers poured onto Indian land in the middle South and the Ohio River valley. There they met tribes that, cut off from a reliable supply of arms and trade goods, had difficulty preventing these incursions on their ancestral land. Moreover, in the eyes of the advancing Americans, who had gained vast military experience during the Revolution, Indians were enemies, having sided with the British during the Revolution in hope of receiving royal protection for their lands.

As tribes were pushed west, small pockets of resistance began to develop. Settler outposts were raided, outlying settlements attacked, farmers and livestock killed. But these remained isolated incidents and offered little prospect for sustained resistance to white incursions. It was against this background that two extraordinary Indian leaders emerged. Tenskwatawa and Tecumseh, Shawnee brothers, learned of the rapacity of American land hunger at an early age and from the dishonor of displacement dreamed of an Indian nation as strong and vigorous as the 13 colonies that had just won their independence. In different ways they both worked for the revitalization of Native American culture and the securing of an independent nation for all Native Americans. Their quest is the subject of this essay by R. David Edmunds, who offers a different view of the better-known Tecumseh than is generally found in history books.

"Tecumseh, the Shawnee Prophet, and American History: A Reassessment."
Western Historical Quarterly, 14 (1983), pp. 261–276. Reprinted by
permission of Western Historical Quarterly.

High upon a granite pedestal overlooking "the Yard" at the United States Naval Academy at Annapolis stands a bronze statue of an Indian warrior. Midshipmen passing in and out of Bancroft Hall traditionally salute the statue before taking examinations in the hope that the renowned warrior's medicine will assist them during their tests. Most midshipmen, if asked whom the statue represents, will reply that it is a replica of Tecumseh, the famous war chief of the Shawnees. In reality, however, the statue was never intended to be Tecumseh. It represents Tamened, a chief among the Delawares.

The midshipmen's incorrect identification of the bronze figure is not surprising, for Americans have long regarded Tecumseh as one of their foremost Indian heroes. He is one of the few militant Indian leaders who was almost universally praised by his white contemporaries. During the War of 1812 both British and American officers spoke highly of the Shawnee, and since his death his image has grown accordingly. Eulogized by historians, Tecumseh has achieved an almost legendary status. His biographers have presented an Indian of superhuman qualities; and Alvin M. Josephy, in his volume *The Patriot Chiefs,* entitles his chapter on the Shawnee as "Tecumseh: The Greatest Indian."

If the white observers and historians have been laudatory in their description of Tecumseh, they have been universal in their condemnation of his brother, Tenskwatawa, the Shawneee Prophet. Both British and American leaders denounced the holy man as a "pretender" and a "coward," and historians have enlarged upon such qualities to present an image of a charlatan who manipulated the tribesmen for his own purposes. While Tecumseh's political and military movement is pictured as logical and praiseworthy, the Prophet represents the darker side of Indian life. A religious fanatic, Tenskwatawa is presented as riding his brother's coattails to a position of minor prominence.

Unquestionably, the Shawnee brothers emerged to positions of leadership during a period of great stress for Native Americans. Although the Treaty of Greenville supposedly had drawn a line between Indian and American lands in Ohio, the treaty was ignored. Frontier settlement continued to advance north from the Ohio Valley, threatening the remaining Indian land base in the region. Meanwhile, white hunters repeatedly trespassed onto Indian lands to hunt game needed by the tribesmen, and by the first decade of the nineteenth century game was becoming scarce. The fur trade declined in a similar manner, and after 1800 many warriors were hard pressed to provide for their families. Not surprisingly, the Indians retaliated by stealing settlers' livestock, and the resulting clashes produced casualties on both sides. Obviously, both Indians and whites suffered, but losses were much larger among the natives. Governor William Henry Harrison of Indiana admitted that "a great many of the Inhabitants of the Fronteers [*sic*] consider the murdering of the Indians in the highest degree meritorious," while Governor Arthur St. Clair of the Northwest Territory reported that "the number of those unhappy people [the Indians] who have been killed since the peace at Greenville . . . is great enough to give serious alarm for the consequences."

Much of the Indian–white conflict was triggered by alcohol. Frustrated over their declining political and economic status, beleaguered tribesmen drowned their sorrows in frontier whiskey. Although illegal, alcohol was in plentiful supply, and brawls resulting from the Bacchanalia spread social chaos throughout the Indian villages. Once-proud warriors quarreled among themselves or abused their kinsmen, while others retreated into drunken stupors. Some Shawnees, weakened by their dissipation, fell victims to influenza, smallpox, and other diseases. Others sat passively in their lodges, bewildered by the changes swirling around them. Meanwhile, the clans—traditional kinship systems designed to regulate and provide cohesiveness among the separate Shawnee villages—were unable to cope with the multitude of problems besetting the tribe.

Overwhelmed by the chaos within their villages, the Shawnees pondered the causes. Although many tribesmen realized that the majority of their problems emanated from out-side sources such as loss of lands, economic deterioration, injustice, and alcohol, others suspected darker elements and probed inward, examining the fabric of tribal society. Predictably, traditional Shawnees concluded that much of their trouble resulted from witchcraft, for the fear of witches and their evil power permeated Shawnee culture, and neighboring tribes believed the Shawnees to have a particular affinity for sorcery and the supernatural.

The basis for such fear lay deep in tribal tradition. The Shawnees believed that in the dim past, when they first crossed the Great Water in search of their homeland, they had been opposed by a huge water serpent who represented the evil powers in the universe. Although their warriors had killed the serpent, witches had saved part of its body, which still held a potent and malevolent power. Contained in medicine bundles, this evil had been passed down through the ages and was used by witches to spread disorder throughout the tribe.

The balance between order and chaos formed a focal point for Shawnee cosmology. The Shawnees believed they were a people chosen by the great power in the universe—"the Master of Life"—to occupy the center of the earth and bring harmony to the world. For their assistance, the Master of Life provided the Shawnees with a sacred bundle possessing powerful medicine that could be used for good. He also gave the tribe a series of laws regulating their personal conduct. If the Shawnees cherished the bundle, and used its medicine properly, and if they followed the sacred laws, they would prosper and their world would be orderly. But if witches gained the ascendancy, or if the Shawnees relinquished the ways of their fathers, their lives would be full of turmoil. In the years following the Treaty of Greenville, many traditional Shawnees believed that the witches had gained the upper hand.

Not surprisingly, many associated the Americans with these forces of evil. The Shawnees believed that the sea was the home of the Great Serpent—the embodiment of disorder.

Their forefathers had always warned that pale-skinned invaders might emerge from the water to disrupt the harmony of the Shawnee homeland. Since the Americans had first appeared on the eastern seashore, many tribesmen were certain the invaders were the children of the Serpent, intent upon the Indians' downfall. In 1803 Shawnees at Fort Wayne informed Indian agents that their ancestors had stood on the eastern seashore, watching as a strange ship came over the horizon.

> At first they took it to be a great bird, but they soon found it to be a monstrous canoe filled with the very people who had got the knowledge which belonged to the Shawnees. After these white people had landed, they were not content with having the knowledge which belonged to the Shawnees, but they usurped their lands also.—But these things will soon end. The Master of Life is about to restore to the Shawnees their knowledge and their rights and he will trample the Long Knives under his feet.

And even Black Hoof, a government chief committed to the American cause, admitted, "The white people has spoiled us. They have been our ruin."

Yet the same chaos that threatened the tribesmen also produced a man who promised them deliverance. Known as a Lalawethika ("The Noisemaker" or "Loud Mouth"), the man had been born in 1775 on the Mad River in eastern Ohio. Prior to Lalawethika's birth, his father had been killed by the Americans and his mother had abandoned him when he was only four years old. Raised by a sister, his childhood had been overshadowed by two older brothers, Chiksika and Tecumseh. Lalawethika never excelled as a hunter or a warrior, and during his adolescence he became an alcoholic. Following the Treaty of Greenville he lived in a small village headed by Tecumseh, where he unsuccessfully aspired to the status of shaman. But in April 1805 this alcoholic ne'er-do-well experienced a vision that changed his life and propelled him to the forefront of Indian leadership.

While lighting his pipe from the fire in his lodge, Lalawethika collapsed, falling into a coma so deep his wife and neighbors believed him to be dead. As his wife began her mourning song he astonished his family by first stirring, then regaining consciousness. Visibly shaken, he informed the gathered onlookers that indeed he had died and had visited heaven, where the Master of Life had shown him both an Indian paradise and a hell where eternal fires lay in wait for sinful tribesmen. Alcoholics like himself suffered the most, for molten lead was poured down their throats until flames shot out their nostrils. Amidst much trembling, Lalawethika vowed to renounce his former ways and never again drink the white man's whiskey. No longer would he be known as Lalawethika. Henceforward he would be called Tenskwatawa—"The Open Door"—a name symbolizing his new role as a holy man destined to lead his people down the narrow road to paradise.

In the following months Tenskwatawa experienced other visions and enlarged upon his doctrine of Indian deliverance. Much of his teachings addressed the decline of traditional moral values among the Shawnees and other tribes. Tenskwatawa claimed he "was particularly appointed to that office by the Great Spirit" and that his "sole object was to reclaim the Indians from bad habits and to cause them to live in peace with all mankind." While he continued to denounce whiskey as "poison and accursed," he also condemned the violence that permeated tribal society. He urged warriors to treat each other as brothers, to stop their quarreling, and to refrain from striking their wives and children. Husbands and wives should remain faithful to each other, and marriages should be monogamous. Shawnee warriors currently married to more than one woman "might keep them," but such marriages displeased the Master of Life.

Convinced that his forefathers had enjoyed a happier existence, the new Shawnee Prophet attempted to revitalize some facets of traditional tribal culture. Indeed, much of Tenskwatawa's teaching was nativistic in both tone and content.

He asked his followers to return to the communal life of the past and to renounce all desire to accumulate property as individuals. Those tribesmen who hoarded their possessions were doomed, but others who shared with their kinsmen, "when they die are happy; and when they arrive in the land of the dead, will find their wigwams furnished with everything they had on earth." He also instructed them to use only the food, implements, and dress of their fathers. Pork, beef, and mutton were unclean, and the tribesmen were instructed to eat only the game they killed in the forests. Neither were the Indians to eat bread, but only corn, beans, and other crops raised by their ancestors. Stone or wood implements should replace metal tools, and although guns could be used for self-defense, the warriors were to hunt with bows and arrows. With the exception of weapons, all items of American manufacture were to be discarded. In a similar manner, the Indians were to dress in skin or leather clothing and were ordered to shave their heads, leaving only the scalp lock of their forefathers. False gods should be forgotten, but the tribesmen should pray to the Master of Life, asking that he return fish to the streams and game to the forest. To assist his disciples, Tenskwatawa provided them with sacred "prayer sticks." The sticks were inscribed with pictographs illustrating certain spirits who would help the tribesmen in their supplications. If the Shawnees were faithful and their hearts pure, the Master of Life would restore order, the earth would be fruitful, and they would prosper.

While Tenskwatawa attempted to revitalize some part of the Shawnee culture, he condemned others. He warned that many of the traditional dances and ceremonies no longer had any meaning and offered new ones in their place. He also instructed his followers to throw away their personal medicine bundles, which he claimed had been powerful in the past, but no longer possessed the potency needed to protect the Shawnees from the new dangers that threatened them. Tenskwatawa alone spoke for the Master of Life, and only those tribesmen who subscribed to the new faith would ever know happiness. But his disciples would be rewarded above all men, for they alone would eventually "find your children or your friends that have long been dead restored to life."

If the Prophet condemned some of the old religious practices, he was particularly suspicious of those tribesmen who held religious beliefs differing from his own. At best those shamans or medicine men who opposed his doctrine were misguided fools. At worst they were witches, in league with the Great Serpent to spread disorder among the tribes. And the Prophet did not limit his accusations to religious leaders. For the holy man, religion and politics were the same. He had been chosen by the Master of Life to end the chaos in the Shawnee world. All those who opposed him also opposed the Master of Life. Therefore, he was particularly suspicious of tribesmen who were becoming acculturated or who had been converted to Christianity. Such men also were suspect of witchcraft. Unless they repented, they too should be destroyed.

Tenskwatawa's distrust of those Indians who adhered to American values reflected his general condemnation of the Long Knives. He informed his followers that the Master of Life had made the British, French, and Spanish, but the Americans were the children of the Great Serpent. In his visions Tenskwatawa had seen the Americans take the form of a great crab that crawled from the sea, and the Master of Life had told him, "They grew from the scum of the great water when it was troubled by the Evil Spirit. And the froth was driven into the woods by a strong east wind. They are numerous, but I hate them. They are unjust. They have taken away your lands, which were not made for them." Only if the Indians rejected the Americans would order ever be restored to the Shawnee world. The Prophet instructed his people to cease all contact with the Long Knives. If they met an American in the forest, they might speak to him from a distance, but they should avoid touching him or shaking his hand. They were also forbidden to trade Indian foods to their white neighbors, for these provisions were the special gifts of

the Master of Life, to be used by his children, not the spawn of the Serpent. Tenskwatawa instructed his disciples to cut their ties with frontier merchants, and "because they [the Americans] have cheated you," the Indians were to pay "no more than half their credits." Moreover, Indian women married to American men should return to their tribes, and the children of such unions were to be left with their fathers.

The new faith soon spread to other tribes, who like the Shawnees were unable to adjust to the great changes sweeping around them. By the autumn of 1805 warriors from the Delawares and Wyandots were traveling to Greenville, Ohio, where the Prophet had established a new village. There Tenskwatawa converted the visitors, then sent them back to proselytize their home villages. The Delawares proved particularly susceptible to the new religion, and during the late winter of 1806 they accused about one dozen of their tribesmen of witchcraft. In March 1806 the Prophet journeyed to the Delaware villages, where he examined the captives, exonerating some, but condemning others. The Delawares eventually burned four of their kinsmen before the witch-hunt terminated. Predictably, all those burned were converted Christians whose acculturation made them more suspicious.

The witch-hunt among the Delawares frightened Moravian missionaries associated with the tribe and brought a storm of protest from government officials. During the spring of 1806 Harrison wrote to the Delawares denouncing the Prophet and asking, "If he is really a prophet, ask him to cause the sun to stand still—the moon to alter its course—the rivers to cease to flow—or the dead to rise from their graves. If he does these things, you may believe that he has been sent from God."

Ironically, Harrison's challenge played into Tenskwatawa's hands. In the spring of 1806 several astronomers had traveled through Indiana and Illinois locating observation stations to study an eclipse of the sun scheduled to occur on June 16. Although Harrison either ignored or forgot about the event, the Prophet remembered.

Among the Shawnees such an eclipse was known as a "Black Sun," an event surrounded with dread and portending future warfare. Accepting Harrison's challge, in early June Tenskwatawa surprised even his closest followers by promising to darken the sun. On June 16, while his disciples and skeptics both assembled in his village, the Prophet remained secluded in his lodge throughout most of the morning, but as the noon sun faded into an eerie twilight he stepped forth exclaiming, "Did I not speak the truth? See the sun is dark!" He then assured his audience that he would restore the sun's former radiance, and as the eclipse ended even those tribesmen who still remembered him as Lalawethika, the drunken loudmouth, now were convinced of his medicine.

Following the eclipse, the Prophet's influence spread rapidly. During the summer of 1806 Kickapoos from the Wabash visited his village, were converted, and by the following summer their towns in eastern and central Illinois had become seedbeds for the new religion. Early in 1807 large numbers of Potawatomis and Ottawas from the Lake Michigan region traveled to Greenville and then carried the new faith back to the western Great Lakes. One of the Ottawas, Le Magouis, or "the Trout," became a special envoy for Tenskwatawa and journeyed into upper Michigan where he taught the Prophet's doctrines to the Chippewas. The results were phenomenal. At Chequamegon Bay hundreds of Chippewas gathered opposite Madeline Island to "dance the dances and sing the songs" of the new deliverance. Subscribing to the Prophet's instructions, they threw their medicine bags into Lake Superior and made plans to visit the holy man in Ohio. In the following months so many tribesmen were en route to the Prophet's village that white traders found most of the Chippewa towns along the southern shores of Lake Michigan deserted. The Menominees, Sacs, and Winnebagos also were swept up in the religious frenzy, and during the summer of 1807 they trekked to Greenville in large numbers.

Unable to comprehend the religious nature of the movement, American officials at first believed that Tenskwatawa was only a figurehead controlled by more traditional chiefs among the Shawnees. During 1807 several groups of American agents arrived at the Prophet's village to investigate the character of the new movement. After meeting with Tenskwatawa, most of the envoys agreed that the holy man was the dominant Indian leader in the village. Moreover, the Prophet was able to persuade them that his religion posed no threat to the government. But Harrison and other officials refused to admit that the movement was an indigenous uprising, resulting from desperate conditions among the Indians. Instead, they charged that the Prophet was actually a British agent, intent upon raising the tribes against the United States.

Yet the British were as mystified about Tenskwatawa as were the Americans. During the summer of 1807 British agents were active among the Indians of Michigan and Wisconsin, but they remained suspicious of the Prophet. Although they invited the Shawnee to visit them in Canada, he refused. In response, William Clause, Deputy Superintendent of Indian Affairs for Upper Canada, warned other Indians to avoid him, speculating that the holy man might be working for the French.

The large numbers of Indians who journeyed to Tenskwatawa's village enhanced his prestige, but they also alarmed white settlers in Ohio. Moreover, the influx of tribesmen exhausted Tenskwatawa's food supply, and he was hard pressed to feed his followers. In November 1807 the Potawatomis suggested that he withdraw from Greenville and establish a new village on the Tippecanoe River in Indiana. The new site would be much less exposed to white influence and was located in a region where game was more plentiful. Therefore, in April 1808 the Prophet and his followers abandoned Ohio and moved to Prophetstown.

The withdrawal to Indiana temporarily removed Tenskwatawa from white scrutiny, but his logistical problems continued. Since Prophetstown was located further west, it was more accessible to potential converts, and during 1808 and 1809 Indians flocked to the new village in numbers surpassing those who had visited him at Greenville. Although the villagers planted fields of corn and scoured the surrounding countryside for game, they could not feed the multitude. To obtain additional food, the Prophet brazenly turned to the Americans. In June 1808 he sent a delegation of warriors to Harrison assuring the governor of his peaceful intentions and asking for provisions. The Indians were so persuasive that Harrison sent food to Prophetstown and invited Tenskwatawa to meet with him in Vincennes. Two months later, in August 1808, the Prophet and his retinue arrived at Vincennes and spent two weeks conferring with Harrison. The governor was astonished at "the considerable talent of art and address" with which Tenskwatawa mesmerized his followers. Moreover, the holy man's pleas of friendship toward the United States were so convincing that Harrison provided him with additional stores of food and gunpowder and reported to his superiors that his earlier assessments of the Shawnee were in error, for "the influence which the Prophet has acquired will prove advantageous rather than otherwise to the United States."

Tenskwatawa was also able to hoodwink John Johnston, the Indian agent at Fort Wayne. In May 1809 he met with Johnston, and although the agent previously had expressed misgivings about the Prophet's motives, Tenskwatawa assured him of his friendship. The Shawnee spent four days, denying "in the most solemn manner, having any view inimical to [the Americans'] peace and welfare." Indeed, when the conference ended, Johnston, like Harrison, exonerated the holy man from all charges and reported, "I have taken much pains and have not been able to find that there existed any grounds for the alarm."

But the facade of friendship was too fragile to last. Although the Prophet feigned goodwill toward the government, he could not control his followers, many of whom were no less devious in their relations with the United States. As Indian depredations spread along the Wabash Valley, Harrison became convinced of the Shawnee's duplicity. During the summer of 1809

Tenskwatawa again visited with the governor in Vincennes, but this time Harrison was less hospitable. Tenskwatawa's protestations of friendship had little impact, and Harrison informed the War Department that his suspicions of the Prophet "have been strengthened rather than diminished in every interview I have had with him since his arrival." Moreover, by the summer of 1809 Harrison was making preparations for the Treaty of Fort Wayne, and he assumed that such a transaction would terminate any pretense of amity between the government and the holy man.

Harrison was correct. The Treaty of Fort Wayne, signed in September 1809, ceded over three million acres in Indiana and Illinois to the United States. Negotiated by friendly chiefs among the Miamis, Delawares, and Potawatomis, the treaty was adamantly opposed by Tenskwatawa. In response, he redoubled his efforts to win new disciples. Messengers were sent to the Ottawas and Potawatomis, and many Wyandots who earlier had shunned the new faith now were converted to the Prophet's teachings. Once again Harrison received reports that the Indians were burning witches, and friendly chiefs among the Miamis and Piankashaws complained that warriors long faithful to the government now were flocking to Prophetstown.

Concerned over the new upsurge in the Prophet's influence, Harrison sent informers to the Tippecanoe and invited Tenskwatawa to again meet with him in Vincennes, but the holy man refused. He also ignored an invitation by the governor to travel to Washington and meet with the president. Instead, he informed Harrison that the recent treaty was illegal and threatened to kill all those chiefs who had signed it. He also vowed that the lands would never be settled by white men and warned Harrison to keep American settlement south of the mouth of the Vermillion River.

The Treaty of Fort Wayne ended any pretense of cooperation between Tenskwatawa and the government. By 1810 the lines were drawn. Tenskwatawa and his movement were unequivocally opposed to American expansion, and in the years following the treaty the anti-American sentiment was both transformed and intensified.

Tecumseh's role in the formation of this movement was entirely a secondary one. He subscribed to the new faith and lived with the Prophet at Greenville, where he assisted his brother in meeting the delegations of both Indian and white visitors. Tecumseh sometimes spoke in council upon such occasions, but no more so than Blue Jacket, Roundhead, or other Indians prominent in the village. In 1807 he accompanied a group of tribesmen who met with Governor Thomas Kirker of Ohio, but in this instance he spoke in defense of his brother, convincing the governor that the Prophet and his movement were no threat to peace. Although primary materials from this period are full of references to the Prophet, almost none mention Tecumseh. Most accounts of Tecumseh's activities during these years are from the "reminiscences" of American observers recorded decades later.

Indeed, Tecumseh did not challenge the Prophet's position of leadership until 1810, two years after the move to Prophetstown and five years after the religious movement's beginnings. During 1808 Indians continued to flock to Prophetstown to see the holy man, not his brother; and in that year it was the Prophet, not Tecumseh, who met with Harrison at Vincennes. In the summer of 1808 Tecumseh did visit Malden seeking supplies for the Indians at Prophetstown, but he made no claims to leadership; and British accounts of the visit, which are quite specific in listing other Indians' names, refer to him only as "the Prophet's brother," not as Tecumseh, a chief among the Shawnees.

The springboard to Tecumseh's emergence was the Treaty of Fort Wayne. From Tecumseh's perspective it was obvious that the religious emphasis of his brother could no longer protect the remaining Indian land base. During the summer of 1809 he visited a few Indian villages in Illinois, but after the treaty Tecumseh took a new initiative and began to travel widely, emphasizing a political and military solution to the Indians'

problems. The tribesmen should still adhere to the new religion, but they should abandon their old chiefs who remained friendly to the Americans. Instead, all warriors should politically unite under Tecumseh, for in his own words, "I am the head of them all. . . . I am alone the acknowledged chief of all the Indians."

Therefore, for two years—in 1810 and 1811—Tecumseh traveled extensively among the Indians of the West. During these years he met twice with Harrison, who reported to his superiors that Tecumseh now had emerged as "really the efficient man—the Moses of the family." In this period Tecumseh slowly eclipsed the Prophet's position of leadership, but ironically as the character of the Indian movement changed, its appeal to the tribesmen declined. In 1810 and 1811 parties of warriors recruited by Tecumseh temporarily joined the village at Prophetstown, but their numbers never approached the multitude of Indians who earlier had flocked to the Prophet. And although the Prophet no longer dominated the movement, he continued to exercise considerable influence. For example, his ability to convince his followers that they could easily obtain a victory over the Americans contributed to their ill-fated attack upon Harrison's forces at the Battle of Tippecanoe in 1811. Obviously, after the battle the Prophet's influence was broken, and Tecumseh remained the dominant leader of the battered movement. But Tecumseh's preeminence was of short duration, for he was killed less than two years later, on October 5, 1813, at the Battle of the Thames.

It is evident, therefore, that the Prophet, not Tecumseh, was the most important figure in the emergence of the Indian movement prior to the War of 1812. Tecumseh used the widespread religious base earlier established by his brother as the foundation for his unsuccessful attempt to unite the tribes politically and militarily. Although the Prophet has been pictured as either a charlatan or a religious fanatic whose teachings seem quite bizarre, such an appraisal reflects an ethnocentric bias. He certainly seemed logical to the Indians, and for several years he exercised a widespread influence throughout the Old Northwest. In retrospect, such a phenomenon is not surprising. In times of oppression native American peoples have often turned to a religious deliverance. The Shawnee Prophet fits into a historical pattern exemplified by the Delaware Prophet, Handsome Lake, Wovoka and the Ghost Dance, and many others. Indeed, Tecumseh's emphasis upon political and military unification was much less typical than the Prophet's messianic nativism.

Why then has Tecumseh emerged as "the Greatest Indian"? The answer is obvious. If white Americans could design an "ideal Indian," they would have designed Tecumseh. His concepts of political and military unification under a centralized leadership appealed to whites because it was what *they* would have done. His solution had much less appeal to native Americans who had little tradition of either centralized leadership or of pan-Indian confederacies in response to American expansion. White Americans also praised Tecumseh's intervention in behalf of prisoners, but such intervention reflected European concepts of warfare more than those practiced by native Americans. Much of traditional Indian warfare was based upon vendetta, and prisoners expected the worst. Indeed, captured warriors took pride in their ability to withstand torture and laugh in the faces of their captors.

White Americans have championed Tecumseh because he, more than any other Indian, exemplifies the American or European concept of the "noble savage": brave, honest, a true "prince of the forest"—natural man at his best. Since his death, his American and British contemporaries and later historians have continued to embellish his memory with qualities and exploits that have added to his image. Many of the attributes and incidents were apocryphal (for example, his reputed love affair with the white woman, Rebecca Galloway, or the assertion that his skin was of a lighter hue than other Indians), but they only strengthened what Americans wanted to believe and have been incorporated into his biographies. Even his death added to the romantic appeal of the man. He fell, fighting to the last, in the Battle of the Thames—the red Armageddon. And his body was not among the dead on the field, but buried mysteriously by his followers in the forest. In contrast, the poor Prophet survived the war, was exiled in Canada, returned to the United States, was removed to the West, and in 1836 died an inglorious death in Kansas.

This reassessment does not mean that Tecumseh was not a remarkable man. Indeed, he was a brave and farsighted leader who sacrificed his life for his people. But the real Tecumseh stands on his own merits. He does not need the romantic embellishments of ethnocentric historians. Tragically, the Tecumseh who has emerged from the pages of history is, in many respects, a "white man's Indian."

14

CULTURE AND CULTIVATION: AGRICULTURE AND SOCIETY IN THOREAU'S CONCORD

ROBERT A. GROSS

For the first 300 years of its history, the United States was predominantly a land of farmers. As late as 1800, more than nine out of ten people lived in agrarian settings, most of them members of small, independent farming families. Regulated by the yearly cycle of the seasons and the daily rhythms of the field and barnyard, life on these farms changed little between the seventeenth and early nineteenth centuries. Life in these pastoral communities centered around land and family, and even such apparently economic transactions as the purchase of land and the borrowing of money were family affairs undertaken in the spirit of neighborliness. But as regional and international commerce expanded after the Revolution and new markets in the trans-Appalachian South and West fostered the beginnings of industrialization, farmers found themselves dealing with a rapidly changing world in which contracts and money were valued more than neighborliness and community.

In this essay, Robert A. Gross explores the transformation of northern agriculture between the Revolution and the Civil War by focusing on the well-known town of Concord, Massachusetts. As markets expanded in post-Revolutionary America, they placed an ever-increasing number of new products within the reach of farmers and rural artisans, who had previously produced by themselves most of the goods their families needed. It was this intense contact with a growing market in manufactured goods and agricultural products that transformed social and economic relationships in Concord. But, as Gross reminds us, this rural transformation was a slow and uneven process that took generations—not years—to complete. Despite the growing importance of market relationships, many of the family and community values of Revolutionary Concord continued to direct everyday life there as late as the Civil War.

Gross's account of Concord entering a new age reminds us of one of the historian's greatest concerns: tracing both change and continuity. Concord changed—sometimes dramatically—in the early nineteenth century, but as Gross also shows, much in rural life remained untouched by the new system of agrarian capitalism.

"Culture and Cultivation: Agriculture and Society in Thoreau's Concord." Journal of American History, *69, pp. 42–61. Copyright © 1982 by the Organization of American Historians. Reprinted by permission of the* Journal of American History.

The town of Concord, Massachusetts, is usually thought of as the home of minutemen and transcendentalists—the place where "the embattled farmers" launched America's war for political independence on April 19, 1775, and where Ralph Waldo Emerson and Henry David Thoreau, more than a half-century later, waged their own struggles for intellectual independence, both for themselves as writers and for American culture as a whole. But in the late nineteenth century, Concord acquired a distinction it never possessed in the years when it was a seedbed of revolutionary scholars and soldiers. It became a leading center of agricultural improvement. Thanks to the coming of the railroad in 1844, Concord farmers played milkmen to the metropolis and branched out into market gardening and fruit raising as well. Concord was nursery to a popular new variety of grape, developed by a retired mechanic-turned-horticulturist named Ephraim Bull. And to crown its reputation, the town called the cultural capital of antebellum America by Stanley Elkins became the asparagus capital of the Gilded Age. Concord was, in short, a full participant in yet another revolution: the agricultural revolution that transformed the countryside of New England in the middle decades of the nineteenth century.

The progress of that agricultural revolution forms my central theme. The minutemen of 1775 inhabited a radically different world from that of their grandchildren and great-grandchildren on the eve of the Civil War. We know the general outlines of how things changed—that farmers gradually abandoned producing their own food, clothing, and tools and turned to supplying specialized, urban markets for a living. In the process, they rationalized their methods and altered the ways they thought about their work. Theirs was a new world in which modern science was wedded to agricultural capitalism. But the process by which that world came into being is little known. Historians have given their attention chiefly to more dramatic events—to the rise of cities and factories, to the story of Boston and Lowell. No less important was the revolution in the countryside. Without it, the creation of an urban-industrial society would have been impossible.

Together, the city and the country underwent a great transformation. The years from around 1800 to 1860 comprise what Emerson called an "age of Revolution"—a time "when the old and the new stand side by side and admit of being compared; when the energies of all men are searched by fear and by hope; when the historic glories of the old can be compensated by the rich possibilities of the new era." What could be a better time to be alive, Emerson asked. That is essentially the inquiry I am undertaking—an inquiry into what it was like to make and to experience the great transition to modern agricultural capitalism in Concord.

This investigation represents an early effort to gather together the evidence of agricultural change in Concord and to suggest its implications for the lives of farming people in the middle decades of the nineteenth century. The principal sources have been town valuations and assessment lists and the United States agricultural census of 1850. These enumerations of land, livestock, and crops, among other goods, cover more than a century of Concord history, from the mid-eighteenth century to the eve of the Civil War. They allow us to view the agricultural changes of the antebellum era in long perspective—to date the beginning of fundamental breaks in the old way of life, to observe the parallel decay of the old and the rise of the new, and to pinpoint just when the adoption of new practices decisively accelerated and culminated in the triumph of a new agricultural regime. For the agricultural revolution did not come suddenly in an irresistible wave of change. The process was a slow and uneven one, proceeding by fits and starts and sometimes encountering setbacks along the way. Some things never really changed at all, and not until the end of the period, with the coming of the railroad, had a new world truly been born.

All of this, of course, can be said only with the historian's benefit of hindsight. To the participants in the process, who did not know the outcomes, the transition must have been at times a deeply unsettling experience. It challenged old habits and practices, demanded new responses while promising only uncertain rewards, and swept up those who wanted only to be left alone, comfortably carrying on their fathers' ways. Even those farmers and entrepreneurs who successfully rode the tide must have had their doubts. Those who resisted or just plain failed said little about their fate, succumbing to what Thoreau saw as lives of "quiet desperation." In the effort to reconstruct the experience of the transition, Thoreau's observations bear close reading. Thoreau was the most powerful and articulate critic of agricultural capitalism that America produced in the decades before the Civil War.

Had a visitor come to Concord around 1800 and lived through the 1850s, he would certainly have been unprepared for the ways things changed. At the opening of a new century, the agricultural economy was very much tied to the past. In the size of their farms, in the crops and livestock they raised, in the ways they used the land, farmers still carried on as their fathers had.

For one thing, the number of farms was the same in 1800 as it had been in 1750 and 1771: about 200. And the average size of a farm was no bigger in 1800 than it had been before: around sixty acres. These were unchanging facts of life in eighteenth-century Concord; nothing—not even revolution, war, and depression—would alter them in the slightest.

This fundamental stability in the number and size of farms was no accident, no haphazard outcome of social evolution. It was a deliberate creation, a rational adaptation to the conditions of farming and family life in the preindustrial, household economy. This arrangement of farms on the landscape arose in response to a basic dilemma Concord began to encounter as early as the 1720s: there were too many young people in town and not enough land for them all—not enough, at least, for them to support families in the usual way. Markets did not exist to sustain comfortable livings on very small farms. Nor would the farming methods of the day have enabled the yeomen of Concord to produce substantial surpluses had the demand for them suddenly appeared. As a result, so long as families

continued to be fruitful and multiply as successfully as they did and so long as death continued to stalk New Englanders less relentlessly than it did people in the Old World, the people of Concord would have to face up to the inevitable outcome. There was a fundamental imbalance between numbers and resources. Something would have to give.

As it turned out, what gave was the aspiration of colonial patriarchs to settle all their sons close-by on family lands. As early as the 1720s, it was becoming clear that some estates in Concord could not be split up "without Spoiling the Whole." Instead, increasingly, one son—often, but not invariably, the eldest—would inherit the homestead intact. The other children would have to go into trade, take portions and dowries in cash, or, in what was commonly the case, move away and settle on frontier lands. In effect, a continuing exodus of young people to new lands underwrote the stability of Concord's farms. Emigration was the key to the future, to insuring that old patterns would go on unchanged. That mechanism worked so successfully that the colonial framework of farming in Concord—some 200 farms of about sixty acres on the average—survived intact not just until 1800 but until the eve of the Civil War. No matter how much things changed, young people growing up on farms in nineteenth-century Concord had in common with their eighteenth-century forebears the expectation that most would move away and make new lives in another town.

For those who stayed behind on the homesteads around 1800, farming went on in traditional ways. In the household economy of Concord the needs of the family and the labor it supplied largely determined what was produced and in what amounts. This does not mean that farms were self-sufficient. Farmers normally strove to obtain a surplus of goods to exchange with neighbors and to enter into the stream of trade. Given the limited markets and the constraints on production in the eighteenth century, surpluses were necessarily small. Most farmers lacked the incentive or the capacity to participate extensively in trade.

Indeed, most farmers even lacked the ability to be fully self-sufficient. Historians have been led astray by the image of the independent yeoman, wholly dependent on his own resources, that eighteenth-century writers like J. Hector St. John Crèvecoeur have handed down to us. What we would think of as the basic necessities of colonial husbandry—plows, oxen, pastures, sheep—were absent on a great many farms. A third of Concord's farmers did not own oxen, and if they were like the farmers in the towns of Groton, Marlborough, and Dedham, whose inventories have been examined by Winifred Rothenberg at Brandeis University, half of them did not possess a plow and three-quarters (72 percent) had no harrow (this was the case down to 1840). Nor were farmers in Concord any more self-sufficient in the production of textiles. Almost half had no sheep in 1771, and in 1750 some 56 percent raised no flax at all.

What did people do, then, for basic necessities? They borrowed from neighbors or kin, exchanged goods or labor with others, or resorted to the store. Perhaps most often, they made do with what they had. This was a world of scarcity in which expectations were modest and always circumscribed. People had to accept the fact that labor and capital were required to supply all one's necessities "from within." It was the rich—the large landholders and the men who combined farming with a profitable trade—who could aspire to independence. It was they who produced most of the flax in Concord in 1750, planting about one-fourth to one-half an acre on the average, which is what the books say the ordinary farmer usually had. And it was they who could provide a wise variety of their own foods. The wealthy were able to take care of these needs precisely because they were engaged in trade, thereby acquiring the resources to hire labor and diversify livestock and crops. Market participation and self-sufficiency were not at opposite ends of a spectrum. Rather, market dependence without facilitated independence within. So when we read about the self-sufficient farmer, we should be skeptical: he was the exceptional man, uniquely favored by fortune. The edi-

tor of *Old Farmer's Almanack,* Robert Bailey Thomas, spoke for a good many readers when he remarked that "there is a great satisfaction derived from living as much as possible upon the produce of one's own farm." But it was a satisfaction that only a few farmers ever enjoyed. Although independence was the general ambition, interdependence was the inescapable fact of life.

The world of trade, then, offered a way out of the pervasive dependency of farmers on one another—out of the constant borrowing back and forth, the necessity of exchanging work, the endless keeping of accounts to ascertain one's standing in the community-wide network of credits and debts. And trade in agricultural surpluses played an important role in colonial Concord, shaping the principal uses to which people put their lands. In 1774, not long after he fled the fury of revolution for sanctuary in England, Massachusetts Gov. Thomas Hutchinson was received by George III. One might think that the king would have examined Hutchinson closely about the political situation in the colony. But no; George III was famous not only for losing an empire but also for promoting the cause of agriculture, and he wanted to know about farming in Massachusetts. "To what produce is your climate best adapted?" asked the king. "To grazing, Sir," Hutchinson replied. "Your Majesty has not a finer Colony for grass in all your dominions: and nothing is more profitable in America than pasture, because labour is very dear."

Hutchinson may have misjudged the political temper of the countryside, but he knew the lay of the land. Throughout the second half of the eighteenth century, farmers in Concord and elsewhere in eastern Massachusetts kept most of their improved land in grass. In Ipswich, over 90 percent of the improved land in 1771 was in meadows and pasture; in Concord that year, 80 percent. In a sense, farmers were doing what came naturally; as Hutchinson said, the soil was well suited to raising grass. But it was the pull of urban markets that prompted farmers to emphasize their mowing and grazing lands. Concord was beef country in the late colonial era. The agricultural economy was based on cereals—mainly rye and corn—for home consumption and beef for market.

This was an extensive agricultural regime, where farmers saved on labor by exploiting land. The trouble was that by the eve of the Revolution, the land was losing its capacity to support livestock. Between 1749 and 1771, cattle holdings increased by a fifth, but to feed them farmers had to expand their pasturage by 84 percent, even though sheep raising was declining sharply. Concord was starting to experience a serious agricultural decline. Indeed, so poor was the town's farming reputation that it blighted the marriage prospects of a young cabinet maker and farmer named Joseph Hosmer. It is said that when he asked for the hand of a wealthy farmer's daughter in Marlborough, Massachusetts, in 1759, he was rejected out of hand. "Concord plains are sandy," complained the father. "Concord soil is poor; you have miserable farms there, and no fruit. There is little hope that you will ever do better than your father, for you have both farm and shop to attend to, *and two trades spoil one.* Lucy shall marry her cousin John; he owns the best farm in Marlboro', and you must marry a Concord girl, who cannot tell good land from poor." Joseph Hosmer ultimately won the girl, but he had to pasture his cattle outside of Concord—in Rutland and Princeton, Massachusetts.

By 1801, though still very much bound to the past, Concord was beginning to feel the stirrings of agricultural change. Markets were opening up everywhere for farmers, thanks to the extraordinary prosperity the United States enjoyed during the era of the Napoleonic wars. The port cities—merchants to the world in the 1790s and early 1800s—boomed, and so, in turn, did their hinterland. Concord farmers began to raise substantial surpluses of rye, wood, and hay for the market. They met the needs not only of Boston and Charlestown but also of the rapidly growing nonfarming population at home. Between 1771 and 1801, the share of Concord's population engaged in crafts and trade doubled, from 15 percent to 33 percent.

The agricultural economy remained essentially what it had been: an economy based on cereals, grasses, and cattle. It would stay that way up through 1840. That year 86 percent of the improved land lay in meadows and pasture. But within that framework, farmers steadily devoted more and more of their energies to producing for market. They raised three principal commodities for sale: oats, hay, and wood. The production of oats was clearly geared to city markets; it far outstripped the growth in the numbers of horses in Concord, and it clearly paralleled the periods of most rapid increase for Boston and Lowell. Expanded hay production came as a result of the increasing conversion of pastures and unimproved land to what were called "English and upland meadows," land plowed and seeded with clover, timothy, and herd's-grass. Adoption of English hay was the major agricultural improvement of the era, and Concord farmers took it up with zeal. They cultivated meadowlands for cash, while relying on the natural river meadows of the Concord and Assabet rivers to feed their own livestock. As a result, the average farmer doubled his production of English hay from 4 to 8 tons between 1801 and 1840, while his output of fresh meadow hay barely increased from about 8 to 8.5 tons. For the most part, the land converted to English hay was made available by the clearing of vast woodlands for market.

At the same time as farmers were concentrating on these staples, they also sought out new crops. They experimented with teasels, broomcorn, and silk, none of which worked. They added potatoes for both family use and sale. A few wealthy farmers engaged in commercial wool growing on a large scale, raising flocks of one thousand or so sheep before the entire business collapsed in the 1830s from cheap western competition. Far more typical were the small-scale efforts of men like "Uncle Ben" Hosmer—Joseph's younger brother—to assemble surpluses for sale.

The story is told that in the 1790s, Ben Hosmer began taking butter, eggs, and other goods to Cambridge market. He lacked a wagon, as did most farmers in those days; so he had to sling baskets full of butter and eggs across the "old mare's" back and ride her into town. One day Ben Hosmer, who was notoriously impulsive, suddenly decided to pack up the horse and go to market. He was feeling "grand poorly" he declared, and was almost out of "black-strap." Besides, there was no West India rum in the house to serve if Parson Ripley stopped by. "It was a hot dog-day morning in August," we are told, and by the time Ben Hosmer got going, he was in quite a hurry. He pushed the old mare over the hills to Lexington so fiercely—his cane was four feet long and an inch in diameter—that she was sweating "profusely" by the time they stopped for rest at a brook in East Lexington. He intended only for her to take a cool drink, but once that mare felt the refreshing waters of the brook, she would have nothing less than a bath. With the panniers full of butter and eggs still on, the mare rolled over and over in the brook.

"To say that Uncle Ben was surprised and astonished," it is said, "would be to draw it very mild; nay, he was dumb founded. He had a tremendous voice, and at once opened up the bottom scale." By the time people had rushed to his aid, he was in greater lather than the horse; it was all he could do to sputter curses at her. "Don't you know any better than to lie down in the brook with Dinah's butter and eggs on your condemned back?" The horse had no answer. Soon Ben Hosmer was pounding the poor animal severely. A crowd gathered round, and when he had finally worked off his rage, one latecomer asked him politely if the mare really had lain down in the brook with the butter and eggs. "Don't you see the yolks running all down the ole mare's belly, and the butter is fit for nothing more than grease!"

Ben Hosmer's adventures may seem comical now—they probably did then—but they illustrate the difficulties and risks of carrying foods like butter and eggs to market in the early days of the new republic. By 1840 wagons and roads had so improved that a good deal of butter was being made and sold in Concord. But it was not until the coming of the railroad that large-scale production of milk, eggs, fruits, and garden vegeta-bles became truly profitable in Concord. Before then, small farmers like Ben Hosmer had to concentrate on bulky goods—oats, hay, and wood—supplemented by whatever other surpluses they could get. And note that it was Dinah Hosmer, not Ben, who put up the butter and eggs.

In these circumstances, it is not surprising that farmers continued the effort to supply their own necessities, even as they sought new products for market. To be sure, they were quick to abandon raising their own cloth when cheap textiles started streaming out of the new mills. But a great many farmers never had been able to furnish their own linen or wool. When it came to food-stuffs, they still did as much as they could for themselves. Rye steadily declined in relative importance from 1800 to 1840, but even in 1840 three-quarters of the farmers in town still raised enough for their bread. The same holds true for fodder crops. English hay went to market; the fresh meadows fed livestock at home.

This combination of production for both markets and home use meant, in practice, that farmers were adding greatly to the burdens of their work. One crop was not substituted for another. Farmers simply exploited themselves more intensively than ever. Once they had spread their labor over the land, plowing shallowly, manuring thinly, and cultivating infrequently, with the result that yields were low. That was acceptable when farmers chiefly raised grain crops for family use and the profits came from grazing livestock. But now farmers depended for a living on far more intensive work: chopping wood, reclaiming land for English hay, digging potatoes, making butter, and occasionally even nursing mulberry bushes.

Farmers not only labored more intensively than ever. They did so in a radically new setting. By the mid-1820s, the evidence strongly suggests that hired labor had come to supplant family labor on the farm. Between 1801 and 1826 the ranks of landless men in Concord expanded from around 150 to 250, even as opportunities in crafts and trade stagnated and the number of farms remained unchanged. Those laborers must have been doing something for a living. Since farmers' sons were continuing the exodus out of Concord—but at an earlier age and to lands farther and farther from home—it is likely the laborers were taking their place. The hired hand had become a commonplace figure on the farm as early as 1815. Thomas's "Farmer's Calendar" for May of that year assumed that farmers had already "hired a man for a few months, to help along with your work," and it offered this advice: "If you have a good faithful one, then set store by him and treat him well, and, mind me now, don't you fret.—*Steady, boys, steady,* is the song for a farmer—If you get yourself into a habit of continually fretting, as some do, then it is ten to one if your can get good men to work for you. But some prefer a dull, lazy lubber, because he is cheap! but these *cheap* fellows I never want on my farm."

Thomas's comments suggest that a calculating, even suspicious spirit dominated the relations between farmers and their help. Where once farm boys had labored for their fathers out of duty, love, and an expectation that they would inherit land of their own someday, now it was money—and money alone—that kept help working on the farm. The social relations of production were imbued with the ethos of agricultural capitalism.

The same rationalizing, economizing impulse transformed the work customs of the community. As late as 1840, many farmers still lacked basic resources to do their work, even as they added to the demands on themselves. Nonetheless, they gave up cooperative practices like the huskings and apple bees of old. These were now condemned as uneconomical and wasteful "frolics," given over to heavy drinking and coarse entertainment. When one writer in the *Concord Gazette* of 1825 wistfully lamented the disappearance of bundling, country dances, and "the joyous huskings" of the past, he was roundly denounced by another for peddling immorality in the press. Neighborly sharing and cooperation probably diminished in another way as well. Agricultural reformers urged farmers to be as sparing as possible in "changing works." Again the *Old Farmer's Almanack* tells the changing

sentiment. "There are some," Thomas complained in 1821, "who cannot bear to work alone. If they have a yard of cabbages to hoe, they must call in a neighbour to change work. Now this is very pleasant, but it tends to lounging and idleness and neglect of business; for we cannot always have our neighbours at work with us." Concord farmers likely took such advice; in *Walden,* Thoreau assumes that the farmer characteristically works alone and is starved for company by the time he comes back from the fields. An era had come to an end: farmers now relied on the claims of cash rather than the chain of community to do their work.

Edward Jarvis, a prominent nineteenth-century medical reformer who grew up in Concord, celebrated this development as a positive force in social life. "The people of Concord are none the less kind, sympathetic and generous than their fathers, but they are stronger in body and in beast. They are more self-sustaining, and it is better that each should do his own work, with his own hands or by such aid as he can compensate in the ordinary way. . . . The world's work is now as well and completely done as ever and people both individually and socially are as happy and more prosperous, and are loving, generous and ready to aid in distress, poverty, and sickness, wherever these shall present themselves, in any family or neighborhood."

Jarvis wrote in 1878, at the end of the long transition, and he summarized as progress what small farmers at the time may have experienced as a very mixed blessing. Huskings may have wasted corn; changing works may have been a bother; and the exchange of goods and labor among farmers could sometimes end up in hard feelings and lawsuits on both sides. Still, the farmer who lacked money to hire all the help he needed had no alternative but to depend on his neighbors or exploit himself to the hilt.

It is possible, of course, that improvements in farm tools let people do more work in less time. There were certainly people in Concord who were alert to the latest innovations. One of them was the first to use a cast-iron plow at the annual plowing match in Brighton, sponsored by the

Massachusetts Society for Promoting Agriculture. Moreover, about a third of Concord's farmers in the mid-nineteenth century belonged to the Middlesex Agricultural Society. But from the absence of plows and harrows from inventories as late as 1840 and from the fact that 40 percent of Concord farmers still had no oxen even then, it appears that labor-saving inventions did not have widespread impact until after the coming of the railroad.

We may gain some clues, too, from the agricultural reform literature of the day. It is full of complaints that boys no longer want to follow their fathers on the farm. Even more to the point, the central theme of that literature—the overwhelming burden of the many pieces on crop rotations, saving manure, raising turnips, and storing tools, among other subjects—is the absolute necessity for system in farm work. The trouble with farming, complained one observer after another, is that men do everything "by halves"—"half fencing, half tilling, and half manuring"—and without any forethought or plan. They labor hard, far harder than they ought, but "to no kind of good purpose."

"Their work hurries them on," a New Hampshire writer observed, "and they have not time to make the necessary retrenchments and improvements: but continue (to use the common expression) 'slashing on, heels over head,' without consideration—zeal without improvement; thus they make perfect slaves of themselves, and never reform, pass through the world without enjoying the sweets of living—they follow their fathers' paths and swerve not."

Even before the railroad era, then, Concord farmers had entered the world of modern capitalism, with its characteristic institutions of money and markets. Producing for market had not, however, wholly displaced traditional activities on the farm; men still tried to furnish their food from within. This attempt to combine new demands with old ones added significantly to the burden of farm work; it amounted to a speed-up: more output in less time.

The intensification of farm work accelerated even more sharply after the railroad linked Concord more tightly and speedily to Boston market. The goods that the city demanded were those that required long hours of unremitting toil. Dairying was probably to become the most important. Between 1800 and 1840, as farmers turned to making butter for sale, the average herd of cows on a farm rose slightly from 4 1/2 to 5. The next decade saw that figure increase again to 6. More dramatically, the proportion of men owning ten cows or more doubled from 11 to 22 percent. It was in the 1840s, too, that farmers began on a large scale to reclaim the many acres of boggy meadow in town for English hay. This was immensely costly and labor-intensive work. Those who could afford it hired Irish laborers to do the job; increasingly, cheap foreign labor displaced native help. Finally, the demand for wood boomed in these years; so vigorously did farmers respond to the market that by 1850 they had reduced the forests of Concord to a mere tenth of the town. Some people were already alarmed at the prospect of timber running out. In short, the steady chopping of the ax; the bustle of men spading up meadows, hauling gravel, and raking hay; the clanging of milk pails—these were the dominant sounds on Concord's farms in the 1840s. These sounds reverberate through *Walden*, and all of them finally were orchestrated to the movements of that locomotive whose piercing whistle as it swept into town announced the triumph of a new order of things.

It was, of course, precisely that new system of agricultural capitalism that Thoreau assailed so incisively, so unrelentingly. We tend to forget that Thoreau addressed *Walden* first of all to his neighbors, in the faint hope of waking them up, and he invariably drew his evidence of the false "economy" of his time from the life immediately around him. It was the farmers of Concord who plowed their manhood into the soil and pushed barns and lands before them as they crept down the road of life. It was they who were the slave-masters of themselves. Behind these strictures lay a deeper critique of what small farmers were doing to themselves as they tried to keep up with the market. Thoreau's attack was remarkably comprehensive. It emphasized:

1. the extending division of labor in society. People were becoming tools of their tools, individuals reduced to functions.

2. the intensification of work, which meant a tight constriction of individual autonomy. People rationalized their work and harnessed their lives to the clock. There was little in the way of true leisure.

3. the commercialization of life and dominance of commodities over men. Things were in the saddle and rode mankind. People spent their lives accumulating goods they would never enjoy.

4. the inequality of the results: the vast disparity in living standards between different levels of society. Luxuries, Thoreau thought, were built on exploitation of the many by the few.

5. most important of all, a decay of the spirit. Farmers treated nature not as a medium of spiritual growth but merely as a commodity, as a means for turning crops and livestock into money. And that narrow materialism extended into all their lives. The farmers and merchants would spend for barns and lands and imposing town halls. But they stinted the lyceum and did too little for the libraries and schools. There was no true culture in Concord.

Yet Thoreau's critique was flawed by his idealization of the preindustrial order. In his travels through Concord he talked to old-timers about what life used to be like and came away romanticizing their picture of independence and self-sufficiency on the farm—a world that hardly ever was. The real world of eighteenth-century farming demanded interdependence and mutual cooperation among households that would never have suited one who marched to a different drummer. Thoreau was too much a part of his own time ever to approve of the more leisurely ways of the eighteenth century. He may have looked suspiciously idle to his neighbors as he wandered off into the woods, but the prescription he offered in *Walden* was close in spirit to the advice of agricultural reformers. People, he said, needed to systematize, to rationalize their lives so that they might cultivate their higher selves in the very process of getting a living. But in giving this counsel and holding up his own experience at Walden Pond, Thoreau inverted the values of the agricultural writers, subjecting them to his highly individualistic, transcendental purposes. By paring back their material needs, providing as much—one might say, as little—as possible for themselves, and keeping their purchases to a minimum, people would be liberated from the grip of economic necessity and into lives of true leisure.

That solution, of course, required enormous self-discipline, parents nearby, and a bachelor's solitary existence. Even then, Thoreau wearied of growing beans and preferred a hunter-gatherer's life. In the end, the critique proved far more powerful than the alternative. There was little the small farmer could do to survive but move to cheaper lands farther west or adapt as best he could to the market, specializing ever more in profitable crops, buying ever more of his necessities at the store, intensifying ever more his exploitation of himself and/or his laborers. Perhaps only those with access to substantial capital or with unenviable capacities for restricting their own wants would come to enjoy the new world of agricultural capitalism. A great many more farming families would be lost in the transition. Theirs was an experience unvarnished with the trappings of a successful middle-class culture. Recovering that experience is the key to understanding what was lost as well as gained in America's "age of Revolution."

PART THREE

AN EXPANDING PEOPLE

In the 40 years leading to the Civil War, the United States grew in many dramatic ways. The population more than doubled between 1820 and 1860 and—equally important—the mixture of peoples who made up the country's population became more diverse. Mexicans and new groups of Native Americans were annexed by the expanding nation, while Germans, Irish, and Chinese immigrants flocked to its coastal cities and inland farms. The nation grew physically as well. Of the 23 states that made up the union in 1820, only Louisiana lay west of the Mississippi River; by the beginning of the Civil War, the nation counted 11 new states, all but three of them in the trans-Mississippi West. In 1860, the United States stretched from the Atlantic to the Pacific.

Not only did the nation's economy grow during the antebellum years, but the Northeast developed into an early industrial center. In the northern states, what had been a region of independent farmers, artisans, and shopkeepers became increasingly a region of employers and their dependent employees. In the southern states, the international demand for cotton rejuvenated the system of plantation slavery that led the two regions along increasingly divergent courses.

The human side of northern economic transformation is analyzed in essays by Bruce Laurie and Christine Stansell. Looking at the dynamic culture of Philadelphia artisans at a time when their craft system was under unrelenting assault by sweatshops and competition from cheaper and less-skilled immigrant labor, Laurie shows that the craftsmen's boast that they did "Nothing on Compulsion" was more ironic than real. In New York City, on the other hand, the concerns of poor women—especially those who were heads of households—involved more than maintaining their families. By the middle of the nineteenth century, these women also had to deal with middle- and upper-class reformers who used charity as a form of social engineering, granting aid to those whom they judged "respectable" and denying it to those who clung to the culture of the streets. As Stansell argues, the conflict over the "uses of the streets" was as much a struggle over the proper role of women in the new industrial order as a confrontation between women of different social classes.

The migration to and settlement of the trans-Mississippi West has long been the subject of historical romance, with stories of heroic pioneers, malevolent Indians, and traditional roles for women and men. In "A Maid of All Traids," Julie Roy Jeffrey turns the sharp light of historical investigation onto this western myth. Analyzing the lives of western women during the early years of settlement, she tells a very different story of isolation, constant labor, and endangered femininity.

As the northern states industrialized and pioneers settled the western states, the South experienced an economic renaissance based not on industry but on a new staple crop: cotton. In "Gouge and Bite, Pull Hair and Scratch," Elliott J. Gorn analyzes the culture of ordinary white male southerners. Violence was endemic in a society that relied on physical coercion to maintain discipline among its slave labor force, and, as abolitionists often claimed, the ubiquitousness of violence distorted white society as well as black.

While most slaves labored in agriculture, some slaves and most free blacks lived and worked in cities and, occasionally, in southern factories. In every setting, however, African Americans created their own communities that drew their power and strength from family ties and local churches. John T. O'Brien investigates the operation of one such community in Richmond, Virginia, the center of antebellum tobacco production and the site of the South's largest iron and steel foundry.

The Civil War has long occupied a privileged place in American history. The spectacle of American fighting American, of family pitted against family, has fired the imagination of generations of Americans, beginning as soon as the war ended. Historians, too, have felt the urgency of conflict and the importance of the issues involved, but their professional concerns turn more to explaining the causes and impact of the war. In "Advocate of the Dream," Stephen B. Oates takes us inside the mind of the sixteenth president as he grappled with the weightiest issues of our nation's history. Oates concludes that Lincoln was, in every respect, a man of abiding principle. Although often cloaked in romance, the actual battles of the Civil War were anything but romantic. In "Heroes and Cowards," Bell I. Wiley recounts the frightening experience of combat as seen through the eyes of ordinary Confederate soldiers. As he reveals, there was little romance in the everyday struggles of Civil War soldiers to remain healthy, warm, fed, and alive.

15

"NOTHING ON COMPULSION": THE LIFE STYLES OF PHILADELPHIA ARTISANS, 1820–1850

BRUCE LAURIE

The growth of factories in the first half of the nineteenth century was the most visible aspect of American industrialization. The creation of large three- and four-story buildings housing hundreds of operatives who worked to the rhythm of steam- or water-driven machinery presented a striking contrast to the predominantly rural scale and pace of American life.

But while the factory system has long been the hallmark of America's transformation from an agrarian to an industrial nation, the most important industrial changes took place not in the factory but in the small artisan shops that dominated the American economy. As late as 1850 Philadelphia, one of America's industrial centers, counted fewer than a third of its work force employed in shops with more than 20 workers.

In these shops skilled craftsmen, who had learned their trades through long years of apprenticeship and journeyman training, controlled the daily output, product quality, and the rhythm of work itself following long-established craft rules and customs. Beginning early in the nineteenth century, however, growing numbers of merchants and master craftsmen began to view the slow pace of craft production as a hindrance in their quest to supply large quantities of cheap manufactured goods to the rapidly expanding West and South. Breaking craft skills into simple, easily learned tasks and hiring unskilled workers to perform them, these early manufacturers undercut the craft system and placed all aspects of production under their control.

The demise of the craft system meant more than changes in work regimes, however; it announced the end of an ancient culture and way of life as well. In this study of Philadelphia artisans at the cusp of industrialization, Bruce Laurie explores the variety of life styles exhibited by craftsmen and the challenges they faced in attempting to maintain their own unique way of life.

***

"'Nothing on Compulsion': The Life Styles of Philadelphia Artisans, 1820–1850."
Labor History, 15 (1974), pp. 337–366. Reprinted by permission of B. P. Ink.

Labor historians are only beginning to appreciate the cultural dimensions of working-class life. Progress has been slow principally because students of working people find it difficult to transcend the legacy left by John R. Commons and his associates. Commons and company were institutional economists who focused on the position of wage earners in the marketplace and the adjustments they made to new modes of distribution and production. Workers, to them, were members of trade unions who did little else than defend their immediate and long-range interests by striking or by voting for third parties when the opportunity presented itself. They ignored working-class attitudes toward the market itself, or toward work for that matter, and consequently left the impression that workers are mono-dimensional men obsessed with economic matters of one sort or another and condemned to a life of incessant toil. This essay attempts to go beyond the narrow constraints of institutional history in order to explore preindustrial working-class culture and to examine how and why that culture changed between 1820 and 1850 in the city of Philadelphia.

Philadelphians saw their world dramatically altered by wholesale changes in transportation between 1820 and 1850. Private promoters and the state legislature invested heavily in transportation, developing in the process a network of canals and railroads which linked Philadelphia with New York and Baltimore, the coal region of northeastern Pennsylvania, and interior towns and cities in the west. Seagoing transportation developed and boomed as Philadelphians, following their more innovative rivals in New York, introduced packets in the coastal and transatlantic trade in the 1820s. More reliable than regular traders or transients, packets made scheduled runs and merchants quickly took advantage of them. By 1827 they carried more than half of the city's coastal trade, delivering agricultural products and manufactured goods to southern and Caribbean ports in return for cotton, hides, and other vital raw materials.

Improvements in transportation paved the way for mass production by reducing shipping costs and penetrating new markets. Manufacturers of textiles, shoes, clothing, and other commodities gained access to the rich markets in Pennsylvania's back country as well as in the Ohio Valley and also strengthened traditional ties with the South. The textile industry, in turn, spurred the city's small but innovative machine tool industry, which was the envy of many foreign observers. By the Civil War, Philadelphia was surpassed only by New York as a manufacturing center.

Rapid population increases and ethnic diversification went hand in hand with economic change. The population of Philadelphia County tripled between 1820 and 1850, increasing from about 136,000 to just over 408,000. The factors which contributed to such impressive growth are not yet known, but it is probable that natural increase and in-migration from nearby farm areas gave way to immigration from western Europe. Ireland and Germany sent the bulk of the immigrants, and the greatest inflows probably occurred in the late 1820s–early 1830s and the mid 1840s. By 1850, the first year for which we have accurate data on nationality, the Irish comprised 27 percent of the population and the Germans accounted for 11.4 percent.

Immigrants and native-born Americans clustered in select tiers of Philadelphia's highly diversified occupational hierarchy by 1850 but also overlapped at certain points. The Irish, who arrived in America without benefit of skills, concentrated at the bottom, performing the most menial tasks. Over 42 percent of them toiled as day laborers, carters, teamsters, and the like. An equal proportion reported skilled trades at mid-century, but they were chiefly confined to the most "dishonorable" trades. Many of them had manned hand looms in Ireland and England and dominated this easily learned trade in Philadelphia. Others moved into trades which were undergoing segmentation of labor and dilution of skill, such as tailoring and shoemaking. By 1850 they comprised nearly 25 percent of the city's tailors and shoemakers. Germans practiced skilled trades in the Old World and readily assumed the role of craftsmen in America.

Slightly more than two-thirds of them plied skilled trades in Philadelphia by 1850. They had a special affinity for woodworking, tailoring, and shoemaking, which together accounted for nearly 20 percent of their number. Native-born Americans could be found in the most prestigious occupations. About a third of them worked at non-manual jobs, while only 10 percent, the smallest proportion of all groups, were unskilled laborers. They supplied a smaller proportion of their number to the crafts (57 percent) than did the Germans, but dominated the most honorable trades, such as printing, the building trades, and the metal trades.

Most working people resided in the county's industrial suburbs, which formed a semi-circular ring around the old port city. They clustered according to occupation, ethnicity, or both, and lived in close proximity to their place of employment. Indeed, dwelling and shop were one for hand loom weavers as well as for many tailors and shoemakers who worked at home under the putting-out system. For the great majority of the labor force, the shop was not the mill or factory which we commonly associate with the "take-off stage" of economic growth. The average shop size in 1850 hovered around ten workers; the median was slightly less than four. Most of these workers, moreover, did not operate power-driven machinery. Three-quarters of them were handicraftsmen employed by bosses whose sole source of power was the journeyman himself.

Even without the aid of mechanization this emerging capitalist order bore down heavily on the wage earner. Merchant capitalists captured mass markets by contracting with buyers in distant markets and with producers in Philadelphia. Most of these producers were small employers who increased productivity by closely supervising teams of highly specialized workers and by slashing piece rates at every opportunity. Master shoemakers cut the rates on first-rate boots from $2.75 to $1.12 a pair, and reduced the scale on "cheap work" 30 percent in the late 1820s and early 1830s, which compelled journeymen to turn out "triple the quantity . . . to obtain a liv-

ing. . . ." Some employers compounded this insult by demanding better craftsmanship without additional compensation, which moved one journeyman to protest that the "improvement in the finish of every article produced by the Mechanic, requiring thereby more time in its production, and the improvement bringing with it no extra remuneration, was in fact a reduction of . . . wages. . . ." Carpet weavers lodged a similar protest in 1836, staging a strike when offered an advance in rates to weave a new design. The new pattern required "extra work," and the "extra labor required reduced the quantity each could turn out," which cancelled the advance.

The response of these wage earners to such exploitation in the 1830s has been well charted. It is now common knowledge that between 1834 and 1839 all manner of wage earner—skilled and unskilled, native-born and foreign-born—formed trade unions and joined together under the aegis of the General Trades' Union of the City and County of Philadelphia in protest against low wages and excessive toil. The Trades' Union reached its membership peak in 1836 when it represented over fifty unions and 10,000 workers, but it is best remembered for the general strike of the previous summer. In early June carpenters and shoemakers affiliated with the Trades' Union dropped their tools and joined day laborers on strike for a ten-hour day. Bearing signs with the slogan "6 to 6," they paraded through Philadelphia, attracting supporters along the way. Within a week the cause spread to every conceivable trade, including factory hands, and thereby produced the first general strike in our history. Such unprecedented solidarity convinced most employers and the city council to concede.

For most workers, however, the general strike proved to be a Pyrrhic victory. The devastating depression of 1837 depleted the ranks of many trade unions and destroyed others, leaving workers defenseless against employers determined to restore the long work day. Mill owners imposed longer hours when prosperity resumed, and those who did not do so accomplished the same result by cutting piece rates. One of their victims complained in 1849 that "almost every pursuit of labor, has within ten or fifteen years . . . been shorn of from one-third to one-half of its former gains; or where the rates remain nominally the same, instability of employment . . . has produced the same effect; though in a majority of cases, an actual reduction of rates is the active cause." Numerous artisans pointed out the obvious consequence of plummeting piece rates, namely a longer workday to compensate for their loss and more intensive pace of work.

Yet these same wage earners complained about unemployment as bitterly as they complained about overwork. They repeatedly lamented the days, weeks, and even months spent jobless or in search of work, though historians have been more attentive when they protested against excessive toil, perhaps because such protests normally precede or accompany dramatic events which make for exciting reading. This oversight is unfortunate, since it has encouraged a narrow view of working-class experience.

A number of factors contributed to sporadic employment, one of which was the nature of the transportation system. The very system which made mass production and its consequences possible also contributed to slack times. The "Transportation Revolution" may have penetrated new markets, but it did not reduce irregularities and discontinuities in supply and demand. Delays, spoilage, and loss of goods plagued Pennsylvania's canals. The Main Line, which connected Philadelphia with Pittsburgh by a series of canals, railroads, and a motorized inclined plane, angered merchants and manufacturers because of high costs and delays caused by bottlenecks at transshipment points as well as by excessive lockage on waterways. Some of them grew so frustrated that they preferred to use the Erie Canal, despite the inconvenience of shipping through New York City. Others gave up on the Main Line and moved to New York to take even greater advantage of the Erie.

Railroads conquered the weather but little else. Lines that employed steam engines were so beset by breakdowns that they kept teams of horses in reserve. Service improved with advances in steam engines, but many problems remained. Faulty track, poor scheduling, and plain carelessness caused repeated wrecks and derailments, giving antebellum railroads a "nightmarish quality." Connections between different lines were lacking because competitors refused to adopt a standard gauge. The Pennsylvania and Ohio lines had seven distinct gauges, which inspired contemporaries to dub their rivalry the "war of gauges."

Coastal packets offered the most dependable mode of shipment, but they had their own drawbacks. They made scheduled sailings only during the "season," which stretched from early fall to late spring. Shippers cut back in summer, transferring some craft to the transatlantic run and sending others northward or southward only when guaranteed adequate cargo. Coastal packets therefore resembled ordinary traders in the warm months when they were governed by profits rather than schedules. Merchants and manufacturers sometimes waited months for an arrival.

The capriciousness of these transportation facilities may well have aggravated the nagging problem of erratic deliveries of goods. Such unpredictable deliveries inevitably made work itself unpredictable and helped shape the work habits of artisans. Wage earners could expect fairly steady employment when markets were good and raw materials available, but faced frequent layoffs when raw materials failed to arrive on time, if at all. This was the assessment of an Englishman who spent part of a tour of America toiling in a hatter's shop. He reported that journeymen anticipated being laid off when they exhausted the supply of fur and leather. Rather than spread the work by slowing down, however, the more experienced hands made hats as quickly as possible in order to garner enough money to tide them through the impending layoff. In slack times hatters and other journeymen either left the city to search for work elsewhere or took whatever employment they could find. Many shoemakers and tailors found temporary employment in repair work of day labor; some hand-loom weavers were so accustomed to shifting into casual labor during periodic downturns that they considered themselves weavers/laborers.

Winter months were unusually trying. Frozen waterways curtailed trade and brought on the slack season, throwing journeymen out of work for long periods and forcing them to seek relief from Philadelphia philanthropists who distributed soup, bread, and fuel. Seasonal fluctuations in trade also determined wage rates. Journeymen, aware that the warm months normally ushered in brisk business, negotiated differential wage scales, demanding higher rates in spring and summer. Carpenters, for example, earned about 10 percent more per day in spring and summer than in fall and winter. Hand-loom weavers negotiated contracts twice yearly—in early spring and late fall—and exacted higher rates in the warm season.

The shape of Philadelphia's industrial plant also determined the quantity and quality of employment. The dominant form of business organization, the small shop, was extremely fragile. Owners operated on hopelessly thin profit margins and were so anxious to reduce fixed costs that they slashed employment rolls at the "slightest hint" of a downturn in trade. They kept the best workers, leaving slower, less experienced hands to forage for work or wait until business improved.

Incessant toil, in a word, was not the bane of Philadelphia's antebellum artisan. What really gnawed at him was the combination of plummeting wage rates and the fitful pace of work, the syncopated rhythm of the economy with its alternating periods of feverish activity broken by slack spells. In slow months, the dull season, or periods with "broken days," he was on his own, without work or the ability to meet day-to-day costs of running the household. Such times could be extremely demoralizing and may be a factor in the frequency of working-class suicides reported in local newspapers. In the case of shoemaker William Reed there is no question about the cause. January 2, 1845, marked his sixth week without work: "The prospective appeared gloomy, and starvation apparently surrounding

him, caused him to seek repose in death" by slitting his throat with his shoemaker's knife.

Fluctuations in trade were not the only determinants of employment. Popular attitudes toward work also figured prominently in the equation, for many artisans who lived in the transitional period between the preindustrial and industrial age adhered to values, customs, and traditions that went against the grain of early industrial discipline. Prizing leisure as well as work, they engaged in a wide spectrum of leisure-time activities, ranging from competitive sport to lounging on street corners. Many of them also belonged to volunteer organizations, which successfully competed with their places of employment for their attention and devotion.

Traditions die hard, and perhaps none died harder than drinking habits. Advances in science and medicine, early industrial change, and, as we shall see, the advent of revivalism, eroded customary drinking habits among some sectors of the medical profession, the clergy, and the emerging industrial elite. But the old commercial classes and most artisans still clung tenaciously to older ways. They valued alcohol for its own sake and used it as a stimulant or as medicine to combat fatigue, to cool the body in summer or warm it in winter, and to treat common illness.

Numerous contemporaries report that artisans were not particular about where they imbibed. Presbyterian minister Sylvester Graham found them drinking in workshops as well as at home in the early 1830s and, he lamented, they especially enjoyed a drink in the late afternoon when "treating" time arrived and journeymen took turns sipping from a jug. Graham's observations are supported by Benjamin T. Sewell, a tanner and vice president of the Trades' Union in 1834 and 1836 who became a Methodist minister in the 1850s. Looking back on his days as a journeyman, Sewell recalled that young apprentices learned to drink while they learned a trade. Journeymen arrived at work with flasks and appointed an apprentice to make periodic trips to the local pub in order to have them filled, "for which service" he "robs the mail . . . takes a drink before he gets back. . . ." This training ground turned many young wage earners into hardened drinkers, inclined to go on an occasional binge. Such workers, said another observer, toil "soberly and industriously for a season, and then, by way of relaxation, indulge in a carouse, often of some day's continuance. The saturnalia and its effects being terminated, they again return to their former occupations and habits of very moderate drinking."

Employers winced at such behavior, but one ought not assume that all of them were martinets who enforced regulations against drink. Owners of textile mills could afford to do so because they relied upon a semi-skilled labor force which could be replaced with relative ease. The concentration required by operators of power-driven machinery, moreover, caused some to relinquish drink without much prompting from employers. The millhands of Manayunk, for example, boasted in 1835 that they formed a temperance society "without the aid or countenance of the influential or talented members of the community," for experience taught them that drinking was a liability which tended to "confuse the brain, cloud the mind, and warp the judgment, thereby rendering the person who indulges in them [textile mills] totally unfit to superintend the movements of complicated machinery." Smaller employers, on the other hand, were more tolerant of workers who drank. Reverend Thomas P. Hunt went so far as to claim that masters also enjoyed an occasional dram or two. He knew a young man who was fired on account of "idleness and neglect of business but not for drinking; for they all [including the employer] drank themselves." We should allow for some exaggeration on Hunt's part, but there is truth in his assessment. Many, if not most, small employers were former journeymen themselves steeped in preindustrial culture, and those who did custom work anticipated fluctuations in trade and therefore tolerated irregular work habits. These employers "expected" journeymen to shun the shop on holidays—official as well as self-proclaimed—and they endured drinking, as long as their journeymen worked "tolerably regularly" and managed to avoid getting "absolutely drunk."

Most artisans did their drinking in pubs, and pubs probably assumed greater importance in their lives after some employers began to prohibit drinking in the shop. Working-class pubs had a style all their own. Signs with piquant inscriptions hung above entranceways and stood in bold contrast to the sedate placards which graced the vestibules of middle-class establishments. "The Four Alls," a public house in Moyamensing, owed its namesake to the following apothegm.

1. *King*—I govern all.
2. *General*—I fight for all.
3. *Minister*—I pray for all.
4. *Laborer*—I pay for all.

Immigrant taverns sometimes advertised popular political causes. An Irish tavern in Kensington, for example, sported a placard with a bust of Daniel O'Connell and the slogan:

Hereditary bondsmen! who would be free,
Themselves must strike the blow.

These tavern offered a wide variety of entertainment, illicit and otherwise. Cockfighting, a popular spectator sport in colonial times but eschewed by people of social standing thereafter, prospered in the working-class pubs of antebellum Philadelphia. Cockfights drew either handfuls of fans or large crowds, depending upon the size of the facility. One of the larger and more popular cockpits could be found in William Cook's pub in Moyamensing. Cook constructed an amphitheater around the pit, which comfortably seated 75 enthusiasts. He also concealed it in the tavern loft, since cockfighting invited betting, which was illegal.

Working-class gamblers not excited by cockfights could try their hand at games in the gambling halls or the taverns. Policy houses, which operated lotteries, dotted Philadelphia and concentrated in the suburbs. Furtively located on side streets and in back alleys, they lured workers who wagered from "3¢ to 50¢ with the sanguine hope of having this money returned fourfold. . . ." Taverns sponsored games that probably resembled "menagerie," in which participants sat around a circular board divided into pie-shaped units, each of which bore the picture of an animal. Each player placed a coin on his choice and waited breathlessly while a pinwheel whirled and designated the winner upon coming to a stop.

Despite these attractions most workers, we may believe, visited pubs for the sake of camaraderie. At the end of the workday homebound artisans made detours to their favorite taverns, where they exchanged stories or discussed politics over drams or mugs of a variety of malt liquor. Outworkers broke the boredom of toiling alone by visiting the local pub during the day, and shopworkers probably went there to celebrate the completion of a task or an order. Most observers agree that tavern traffic increased dramatically on Sunday night and in winter when trade slowed.

Circuses and road shows also captured the fancy of workingmen. Heavily publicized in newspapers and in broadsides posted on fences, such entertainments rarely respected the industrial time clock. Occurring on weekdays as well as on weekends, they dazzled throngs of onlookers with bizarre acts and feats. One of the most prestigious companies that thrilled Philadelphians was the internationally acclaimed team of Messrs. LaConta and Gonzalo and Master Minich of exotic Spain. LaConta captured the limelight in the Pennsylvania Museum when he danced the popular "fisherman's hornpipe on the tightrope, and performed the much more difficult exercise of saltation on the same rope with a living boy tied to each foot." Less elaborate but equally exciting fare took place in the streets when daredevils or athletes visited Philadelphia. Sizable crowds gathered to watch balloonists ascend or to witness competition staged by tramping athletes. Long-distance runner William Jackson, affectionately known as the "American Deer," attracted a crowd upon challenging all bettors that he could run eleven miles in less than an hour. The outcome of this race against time is unknown, but those who gathered at the finish line had quite a time "gambling, fighting, drinking, etc."

Though fascinated by these events, artisans especially enjoyed pastimes in which they could participate. They simply loved shooting matches and hunting small game, according to an observer who bemoaned that "every fair day" yielded a "temptation to forsake the shop for the field." The most avid hunters, he contended, were artisans who toiled indoors, for they found a jaunt in the fields especially relaxing. Artisans who resided in the same neighborhood sometimes set aside time for exercise by declaring holidays and staging competitive games; hand-loom weavers, for instance, often did so. In August 1828, those living near Third and Beaver streets laid down their shuttles and passed the day—a classic "Blue Monday"—footracing and merrymaking.

Sport, merrymaking, and drinking were also staples at ethnic gatherings. English, German, and Irish immigrants honored Old World customs and traditions, celebrated weddings and holidays, or gathered simply in order to socialize regardless of the time of day or day of the week. Germans, for instance, set aside Monday as their "principal day for pleasure," and festivities could spill into the middle of the week. Würtemburgers once journeyed to Philadelphia's rural suburbs for a *Volksfest* which stretched from Sunday to Tuesday, ample time for them to consume untold kegs of beer, participate in games, and dance at weddings. The Irish were also known to set aside Monday for outings in the suburbs. Their national games, the Donneybrook Fair, traditionally attracted hundreds of enthusiasts and no self-respecting Irish Protestant missed the annual July 12 parade commemorating the glorious victory on the banks of the Boyne in 1690. On July 12, 1831, Orangemen marched through Philadelphia and taunted angry Catholic bystanders with offensive songs such as "Kick the Pope" and "Croppies Go Home." Tensions built steadily until the Catholics, unable to restrain themselves any longer, attacked the paraders, touching off a melee which led to many arrests. Witnesses from both sides appeared in court, including journeyman James Mitchell, a perky young artisan who, speaking in behalf of his class, testified that he joined the procession because "all work and no play makes Jack a dull boy. . . ."

An elderly tailor elaborated upon this point. Reclining in a field with a companion, he met James W. Alexander, a Presbyterian minister from nearby Princeton, who sought their reaction to the 1837 depression. Alexander assumed that hard times kept both men from their workplace. "Not at all," snapped the quick-witted old man, "we are only enjoying the *Tailor's Vacation*. *Pressure* is well enough, to be sure," he went on, "as I can testify when the last dollar is about to be pressed out of me; but *Vacation* is capital. It tickles one's fancy with the notion of choice. 'Nothing on compulsion' is my motto."

Membership in voluntary fire companies also interrupted the daily work routines of Philadelphia artisans. Indeed, the city fire department enjoyed its greatest growth between 1826 and 1852, when 68 new companies appeared. The department was nearly equally divided between hose companies, which connected lengths of hose to fire plugs and to pumps, and engine companies, which transported mobile pumps. City law limited engine companies to 50 members and hose companies to 25, but the ordinance was a dead letter. Memberships swelled and sometimes reached 200 or 300 to the company.

Firemen were fierce competitors. Hose companies fought for the fire plugs nearest a blaze, and engine companies did battle for rights to the prime hose locations. Firemen loved racing their gaudy tenders and hose carriages through the city streets and went to extraordinary lengths to preserve their pride, shoving wrenches into the spokes of a rival rig, cutting its tow ropes, or assaulting its towers. Races usually ended in brief scuffles, but competition reached fever pitch in the 1840s when ethnic tensions polarized Philadelphians and artisans formed fire companies along ethnic lines. Irish Catholic, Irish Protestant, and nativist companies emerged and allured gangs of intensely loyal young toughs so that, when rivals crossed paths, riots ensued which caused enormous property damage and some loss of life.

As competition increased, so did the devotion of firemen. An observer knew a volunteer who "work[ed] better after a long sun and race with the P—— and had beaten her, but if his company was waxed, he could'[nt][*sic*] work at all and had to lose a day." The most devoted firemen earned the title of "bunkers." Spending the night in the firehouse, they took turns watching for fires from the house tower in the hope of getting the jump on rivals and arriving first at the scene of a blaze. Some of them even "delighted in a day watch."

These pursuits and activities—drinking and gaming, participating in popular sports and in fire companies—characterized a vibrant, preindustrial style of life. A number of factors underpinned this style, the most significant of which were demographic and material. First, as Herbert Gutman notes, it was repeatedly replenished by waves of immigrants and rural-urban migrants, who came from widely divergent sub-cultures but whose values and behavior collided with the imperatives of early industrial discipline. Second, and perhaps more important, at mid-century many wage earners worked in traditional (as against modern) settings which, together with the boom-bust quality of the economy, supported sporadic work habits. Those who knew this environment best were outworkers—especially hand-loom weavers, shoemakers, and tailors—who toiled at home without direct supervision of employers and custom workers, who fashioned consumer goods to the taste of individuals and who thereby evaded the more vigorous regimen of workers producing for the mass market.

Outworkers and custom workers displayed traditional forms of behavior in that they made no sharp distinction between work and leisure. Blending leisure with work, they punctuated workdays with the activities sketched above. Nor did they respect the specialization of role and function which normally accompanies modernization. Instead they persisted in assuming the dual role of artisans and firemen in the face of strong opposition from urban reformers who wished to relegate firefighting to paid professionals. It is probable, moreover, that the values, activities, and organizations of this style of life filled the basic needs of its adherents by sanctioning and supplying vehicles for recreation, neighborhood cohesion, ethnic identity, and camaraderie.

At the same time, however, there emerged a competing culture with its own organizations and institutions. Unlike preindustrial culture, it made a sharp distinction between work and leisure and regarded preindustrial culture as wasteful, frivolous, and, above all, sinful. Sanctioning a more modern style of life, it originated not among the working class but with the emerging industrial elite and the Presbyterian clergy. This elite was in the process of displacing the old Quaker oligarchy and included manufacturers who represented the most advanced industries, such as locomotive builder Matthias W. Baldwin, as well as merchants and professionals with investments in industry and transportation, such as Thomas Newkirk, a dry goods merchant, banker, and railroad promoter, and the merchant-investor Alexander Henry. Nearly all of them shifted their political loyalty from the Federalists to the Whigs. They filled the first few pews of the fashionable Presbyterian churches of the center city, and some were attentive to evangelical ministers like Albert Barnes. Adapting Protestantism to industrial capitalism, Barnes assaulted the embattled ramparts of orthodoxy (paving the way of the 1837 schism), and preached a brand of Protestantism that bordered on Arminianism. Such ministers did not proselytize for the vindictive, arbitrary God of John Calvin, but a benevolent deity who promised salvation to all who willed it, rewarded worldly success with grace, and exhorted His people to do good in the world. God thus freed man to accumulate wealth without the pangs of guilt that had tortured the orthodox conscience and He inspired them to launch a moral crusade against sin.

These ministers and their lay advocates did not regard sin as doctrinal error but as moral laxity of the sort displayed by Philadelphia's working class. Such behavior threatened the material progress sanctioned by God himself, and those who crusaded against preindustrial behavior did God's work and their own at the same time. The elite pursued its God-given commission with staggering energy, forming and funding a spate of moral reform organizations, beneficial societies, and lobbies designed to proscribe working-class pastimes and to teach working-class children the value of deference and self-discipline.

It is difficult to assess the extent to which reformers succeeded in some of these efforts but it is doubtful that they enjoyed much success prior to the Civil War. While they convinced the state to establish a system of free public schools in 1834, working-class parents did not immediately take advantage of it. They appear to have had more interest in teaching a trade to their children than in schooling them, which may account for low, erratic attendance in antebellum classrooms. The elite found it difficult to regulate working-class pastimes because it did not have authority over the police, the principal agent of social control. Each suburban district raised its own police force prior to 1854 from the very population the elite wished to control, and voluntary policemen were notoriously lax in their day-to-day duties. They exerted authority only in cases of emergency.

Temperance may have been another matter entirely. The elite, and large factory owners in particular, found working-class drinkers quite troublesome and equated them with gremlins whose behavior interrupted operations in mills and factories. The "steady arm of industry," went one bizarre metaphor, "withers" from drink. And so the elite channeled its energies into changing the drinking habits of wage earners.

Philadelphia's temperance movement formally began in 1827 when parishioners in the stylish Second Presbyterian church joined like-minded ministers, physicians, and industrialists and formed the Pennsylvania Society for Discouraging the Use of Ardent Spirits. The Society's name belied its intentions, however, since it soon advocated the extreme position of total abstinence from all intoxicants, as did the Pennsylvania Temperance Society, which succeeded it in 1834. These organizations supported lectures and distributed polemics which linked intemperance to poverty and economic ruin and marshalled the latest medical opinion about drinking on their side. They relied heavily on Presbyterian ministers, some of whom, like evangelists Thomas P. Hunt and C. C. Cuyler, rejected Arminianism but endorsed revivalism and preached temperance in the late 1820s and early 1830s. Their efforts swelled the rolls of Presbyterian churches, filling the pews with thousands of converts, who formed local temperance societies and affiliated with the Pennsylvania Society. By 1834 the Pennsylvania Society boasted a following of 4,300.

Membership lists of these affiliates do not survive, which makes it difficult to assess their class composition. But it appears that the movement did not reach very deeply into the social structure, except perhaps in Southwark and Northern Liberties where aggressive ministers converted some artisans. The typical temperance advocate of the 1830s is best described, however, as a church-going member of the middle and upper-middle classes.

The temperance crusade of the late 1820s and 1830s aroused the suspicion of most wage earners because it was so closely identified with the Presbyterians and advocated total abstinence. Presbyterian domination of the temperance movement did not sit well with most workers whose religious interests ranged from the popular sects to Free Thought and skepticism, and who looked upon the crusade as a subterfuge for Presbyterian influence or for creeping priestcraft. Some workers were offended by the Presbyterians' upper-class pretentiousness; so was Thomas P. Hunt, a Presbyterian minister himself, who accused his colleagues of being "too conservative" and prone to "cast a look of suspicion upon all workingmen." Wage earners, moreover, endorsed temperance, if anything, in the 1830s and equated partisans of total abstinence with "fanatics." Holding this opinion, Benjamin Sewell recalls having had "no objection" to moderate drinking in that decade. "My company all drank, a little," he recalled, "'but nothing to hurt' we used to say." Men like Sewell and his friends were so accustomed to drinking, so convinced of its value, that they could not break the habit—even if so inclined—simply by signing their names to a total abstinence pledge, which the Pennsylvania Temperance Society naively considered "essential to the support and prosperity" of the cause. They needed the encouragement and understanding of peers, but most workers were not yet prepared to lend such support. Sewell, for example, recalls the tragedy of a young friend who signed a total abstinence pledge against the advice of his comrades, who suggested that he simply "cut down." Stigmatized as a teetotaler and chided by his friends, he relapsed into heavy drinking and lost his job. So he left for a suburb in west Philadelphia in order to "hunt work and reform," but was told by an employer acquainted with his drinking problem "we have no work for *you*." Distraught and demoralized, he wandered aimlessly for a few days and then hanged himself.

Between 1837 and 1843, however, a new temperance crusade suddenly developed, which bore little resemblance to the older movement in terms of organizations, constituency, and tactics. It appeared in the form of temperance-beneficial societies which were located in the industrial suburbs. The membership lists of these organizations indicate they were dominated by skilled journeymen and master craftsmen with small numbers of small shopkeepers, clerks, and unskilled workers as well. Their supporters were critical of the older societies, which had "no provision by which all members may be brought together at short intervals" so as to exert their "united influence." Temperance-beneficial societies remedied this glaring shortcoming by holding frequent meetings, sometimes nightly gatherings, not just in churches but in the streets and public squares—or anywhere they could attract a crowd. In anticipation of the Washingtonians, they appealed to hardened drinkers and drunkards, who the older societies had studiously ignored and would become featured speakers at temperance rallies, visible examples of the possibility of self reform. Such tactics yielded striking results. Temperance-beneficial societies mushroomed between 1837 and 1841 when the *Public Ledger* counted 17,000 teetotalers in the country and exulted that, in two months of 1841 alone, 4,300 formerly wayward souls enlisted in the crusade. These organizations did not necessarily turn drinkers into teetotalers overnight. Apostasy continued to plague them, but they did establish a significant foothold among the lower middle class and working class by employing peer-group pressure, eternal vigilance, and the power of example.

To what can we attribute the sudden emergence of this temperance movement? We ought to extend credit to those who pioneered the crusade, since some of their converts emerged in the temperance-beneficial societies. But the movement would not have enjoyed such a mass following without the economic turmoil of the late 1830s and early 1840s. The new movement flourished in the wake of the 1837 panic, the most devastating and prolonged economic downturn in Philadelphia's experience. Press and pulpit concurred in attributing hard times to God's wrath visited upon people fallen from grace and, it is hardly surprising, the depression triggered a new wave of revivals. Revivalists were especially active in the industrial suburbs, where their protracted meetings made thousands of conversions and brought hundreds into the churches. There was unprecedented growth for the Methodists, though it is difficult to determine the precise rate because they suffered defections in 1828 and 1843 which tend to skew the figures before and during the depression. Even with these losses, however, they made impressive gains. Between 1815 and 1836, for example, Methodists enjoyed fairly steady growth, attracting about 240 members per year, while they lost about 140 members yearly between 1844 and 1850. But during the depression years (1837–1843), they more than doubled their previous rate of growth, taking in slightly less than 540 new members a year. This accretion is probably several times greater than it appears because hundreds who experienced conversion attended church but did not become members.

The depression not only swelled the membership of the Methodist Church (and other denominations as well), it also altered the message its ministers conveyed to communicants. Methodists lagged behind the Presbyterian vanguard in adjusting their discipline to the exigencies of industrial capitalism. The General Conference, for instance, did not restore Wesley's ban on buying and selling liquor, repealed in 1791, until 1848. The reasons for this lag are not entirely clear, though we might consider the fact that the Methodist ministry was recruited from the lower classes and less influenced by the industrial elite than were Presbyterian clergymen. Whatever the reason, the Methodists did not wax enthusiastic over the prospect of a prosperous, industrial America until the 1830s. Some of them then hailed the rise of railroads and steam power as evidence of God's blessing and "man's elevation" and began to attack behavioral patterns that impeded such progress, emphasizing instead "habits of industry." Most Philadelphia ministers, however, showed precious little enthusiasm for temperance or total abstinence until the depression, which they interpreted as God's punishment for man's depravity. Hard times strengthened the resolve of some clergymen to tighten morality and converted others to the cause, for when the Philadelphia Conference met in 1841, it suspended a rule permitting the use of alcohol for medicinal purposes, resolved to recommend "total abstinence from all intoxicating liquors as a beverage" to "all our people," and applauded the "triumphs" in the crusade against liquor "during the past year."

These ministers had every reason to be pleased. They played a key role in delivering messages of total abstinence to the working class by joining together with other revivalists as well as laymen to form the temperance beneficial societies. Working people who flocked to these societies in the late 1830s formed their own temperance societies, often along craft lines, in the early 1840s.

The revived temperance crusade turned into the first of a series of events which pitted middle-class and working-class Protestants against the city's growing Catholic minority. Catholics perceived a threat to their culture in the evangelical zeal of the movement and began to disrupt temperance rallies. Their activity aroused the anger of Protestant workingmen chastened by hard times and disposed to look for scapegoats. Catholics were the most convenient targets, and they became even more vulnerable when their leaders protested against Protestant domination of the public schools. They objected to the use of anti-Catholic texts and to the reading of the King James Bible during opening exercises and requested that the school board permit their children to hold separate religious exercises. This emotionally charged issue incited revivalist ministers (who were also involved in the temperance crusade) to form the American Protestant Association in the winter of 1842–43, which interpreted the Catholic request as a veiled threat to "kick" the King James Bible out of the public schools and to undermine American institutions. The convergence of the school controversy and the temperance crusade breathed life in nativist American Republican Associations which had been operating since 1837 without much success. Middle-class temperance advocates led by Lewis Levin, editor of the *Temperance Advocate and Literary Repository,* fused their cause with the nativists, drawing thousands of working-class teetotalers with them. American Republicans scored a landslide victory in the 1844 municipal election which proved to be ephemeral in the center city as voters returned to the Whig fold the following year. But in most formerly Democratic suburbs the American republicans showed more staying power and tallied solid majorities at the polls in the 1840s.

American Republicans did not enlist all working-class temperance advocates. Some of them remained loyal Democrats, but the temperance movement of the depression and American Republicanism shared much the same constituency. American Republicanism, repellent to the Presbyterian and Quaker elite, drew its strength from the native-born Protestant middle class and working class. Such people fancied themselves the solid "middle" of society, bone and sinew of Protestant Republicanism. Their leaders continually stressed the connection between temperance and prosperity. Total abstinence, one of them was convinced, "restores the drunkard to his prosperity, and makes him secure. . . ." Another gave assurance that the cause inspired people to "maintain their *glorious independence,* which has contributed so essentially to their health, happiness, respectability and worldly prosperity." Such claims were clearly those of ambitious people, but American Republicanism was not simply the mother's milk of *parvenus* or of paranoids suffering from fear of domination by immigrants. It was more complex and more subtle than that. It conveyed a strong sense of class identity and what might be called a modern work ethic.

American Republicans cut their teeth on the labor theory of value. This doctrine, which had informed the General Trades' Union and which existed in the popular mind well into the 1890s, held that labor is the source of all wealth. People created wealth by blending their labor with the soil or with raw materials, and those who did so were considered to be "producers," chiefly mechanics, farmers, or anyone who produced commodities by working with his hands. Those who did not—doctors, lawyers, merchants, bankers, landlords, and the like—but who amassed wealth by selling commodities made by producers, by performing services, or by investing capital, were stigmatized as "accumulators." They were drones and parasites, but nonetheless powerful people who exacted special privileges from legislators in the form of bank and corporate charters, land grants, and the like. They were responsible for the enormous maldistribution of wealth and for the misery of the majority.

The analysis of American Republicans allowed for only two classes, and middle-class nativists differed over where employers fit in. A minority, comprised of former journeymen, considered small, traditional masters to be "producers" and, defending them, contrasted these small masters with the ambitious, innovative bosses who squeezed workingmen. One of them contended that a "conscientious man in these times, can scarcely expect to earn more than a *competency.* If more than this is aimed at, man is apt to become the oppressor of his fellows—taking advantage of their necessities and obtaining the fruits of their labor without rendering them a just recompense." On another occasion he admonished, "National prosperity, as it is generally described, (that is, the prosperity of the wealthy classes, or capitalists,) is perfectly reconcilable with a prostrate and miserable condition of the laboring people." Oliver P. Cornman, who rose from journeyman house painter to editor of the principal organ of the American Republican Party, the *Daily Sun*, aped the leaders of the General Trades' Union when, in the late 1840s, he drew a distinction between masters and employers. As a former workingman he was well acquainted with the "soulless men who would grind down the journeyman to the point of starvation and drive his family to the point of desperation." Such men were "'masters' in name (only). . . ." Honorable masters respected the maxim that the journeyman was worthy of his hire and of being paid a just wage.

Most middle-class nativists, however, found fault only with the crudest, most grasping employers such as those who exploited women and children. They normally praised entrepreneurs and endorsed those who accumulated wealth. Commending employers, master printer H. H. K. Elliott exhorted an audience of mechanics to "Look around . . . and . . . discover in your own city, among those who now have high places, great wealth and much respect, very many who started in life as, and who continue to be mechanics." Master craftsmen, after all, were producers whose honest labor had created capital and "capital acquired by labor," claimed a nativist editor, "is a friend of labor . . ."

Middle-class American Republicans in fact had nothing but disdain for detractors of employers. They looked upon the class warfare of the previous decade with some regret and imagined their cause as a bridge between employer and employee. Levin, for example, considered temperance the "most effectual means of closing this fatal chasm in our social system, of knitting up those sympathies again. . . ." And while Levin and his middle-class colleagues recognized working-class poverty, they sought to convince workers that their immiseration had less to do with the advance of industrial capitalism than with the crimes perpetrated by accumulators and immigrants.

These American Republicans pronounced accumulators guilty of cultural and economic crimes, each of which caused poverty in its own way. These accumulators had a style of life which bred intemperance and disrespect for hard work and honest toil. Levin thus traced the "rise and prevalence of intemperance" to the "mushroom aristocracy" who "rioted on the wealth bequeathed to them by their fathers, affected to despise the honest industry by which it had been acquired, and by their upstart and debauched habits set a pernicious example. . . ." The same people who led others to ruin by spreading depravity also controlled the vital purse strings of the economy and exploited masters and journeymen alike. Employers were simply the *agent[s]* of capital," beholden to the iron laws of supply and demand. When capital was plentiful, wages were high and everyone benefitted. But when the money market contracted, masters had to slash wages or lay off workers. The real culprits were monied aristocrats, bankers, and speculators who had the "leisure to combine . . . scheme and make enormous profits, sometimes without investing a cent. . . ." They also had the "power to elevate or depress the market . . . make money plenty [*sic*] or scarce . . . gamble with impunity, and even control, by combination and monopoly, the very circulating medium. While they lounge at ease in their palatial mansions, or roll about in their carriages, in elegant indolence and luxury. . . ."

Catholics, on the other hand, threatened native-born workers from the bottom of society. They depressed the wages of honest workers because they flooded the labor market and because they were accustomed to "liv[ing] on less than the Native" and more than willing to work for pittance. Unchecked immigration promised to "reduce" American workers to the level of Irish peasants. American Republican politicians rarely missed an opportunity to raise this specter, but did not object to the Irish simply because they competed with native-born workers in the labor market.

Middle-class American Republicans harbored an image of a Catholic life style at variance with the new virtues of sobriety, respectability, and self-control. And since they measured Catholics by the same standards they applied to accumulators, they employed common metaphors to describe both groups and held strikingly similar images of them. Both groups loved to drink, and "riotous," wreckless accumulators had counterparts among Catholics who engaged in "disgusting debauchery" and "rioted" in the city streets as every observer of the 1844 riots was aware. At least one nativist conceded that all Catholics were not necessarily lower class. Some were aristocrats, others mobocrats. "If the former class, they are generally the profligate gambler, spendthrift or worse. If the latter, they are either lazy, drunken paupers, or transported felons. . . ." The aristocrats, like their American counterparts, spent their lives in "riotous living"; the others were a "riotous, drunken set. . . ."

Nor did the Irish qualify as producers in the opinion of nativists. "Three-forths of the grocery stores, and nine-tenths of the liquor stores, in this country," one of them declared, "seem to be kept by Irishmen." These stores, he emphasized, "are not *productive* occupations. . . ." Irishmen who did find honorable employment did not linger there very long, because "as soon as they get five or ten dollars 'ahead,' we find them opening grog shops, peddling lemons, or . . . in some other occupation which is little better than idleness, or perhaps a little *worse*." . . . That some Irish did accumulate property did not surprise another nativist. They saved enough money to purchase property by "living in mean, squalid, filth and degradation . . . and harder landlords than these are seldom to be found."

American Republicanism, then, can be viewed as the amalgam of the labor theory of value and the revivalism of the depression years. This merger provided native-born, middle-class Protestants with their own sense of identity, a

means of distinguishing themselves from the mercantile and financial upper class and the foreign-born lower class. And while it is difficult to distinguish the contributions each of these forces made to the American Republican synthesis, it may be said that revivalism imbued Party members with faith in industrial capitalism, intolerance of immigrants, and a moral code which deprecated moral laxity and stressed sobriety, diligence, and respectability. The labor theory of value imparted a peculiar class analysis of society which located exploitation not in the relationship between employer and employee but in the relationship between producers and accumulators. The synthesis of these forces, in turn, offered a multi-causal analysis of the plight of producers. That is, workers were impoverished because they did not work hard enough and because immigrants depressed wages. And all producers—journeymen and masters—were not justly rewarded because of the machinations of accumulators.

At first glance it appears that native-born wage earners accepted this analysis. In 1845, for example, a handful of skilled workers and master mechanics met at the Jefferson Temperance Hall and formed the Order of United American Mechanics (U.A.M.), which quickly established branches throughout the country. Membership was limited to native-born producers—masters and journeymen—who upheld the new respectability by pledging to honor "Honesty, Industry, and Sobriety," and by listening attentively to lectures on how to save money and to accumulate property. Ostensibly a fraternal-beneficial organization, the U.A.M. sponsored a funeral fund and paid benefits to members too ill to work. It also vowed to employ "every honorable means to obtain a 'fair day's wage for a fair day's work'" so that workers could "support themselves and their families in comfort and respectability . . ." and "accumulate a sufficient sum, during many months of toil, to support and sustain them through the mischances and mishaps of a 'rainy day'. . . ." These means included pressure upon employers to hire only native-born Americans. It also included encouraging consumers to patronize American craftsmen and to boycott businesses owned by foreigners in the hope that employers would increase their businesses and then pay better wages. But higher wages alone did not guarantee that journeymen would live a respectable life. So members policed one another's morality to guarantee that they did not engage in dissipation, reporting cases of intemperance and frivolity and visiting those who claimed eligibility for welfare payments—in order to make sure that they did not feign illness. Members found guilty of immoral conduct were either reprimanded or expelled.

Like most nativist organizations, the U.A.M. assumed that employers and employees had common interests, that journeymen did not have interests peculiar to them as a class. But the model nativist worker who joined a temperance society, belonged to the U.A.M., and voted for or held membership in the American Republican party was also likely to be a militant working-class spokesman. Leaders of unions of house carpenters, printers, shoemakers, saddlers, and other trades belonged to both organizations. They firmly believed the labor theory, but unlike their middle-class coreligionists, they endorsed the corollary that the wage earner was entitled to the full product of his labor. Precisely what they meant by this remains somewhat of a mystery. But it clearly implied that wage earners had rights to what *they* produced and were entitled to wages sufficient to support themselves and their families in dignity and respectability. This theory, moreover, armed workers with a principle that distinguished their interests from those of employers.

American Republican wage earners, consequently, found themselves pursuing the illusory goal of aspiring to a respectable life style on subsistence wages. One such American Republican was George F. Turner, a founding member of the United American Mechanics and President of the Association of Journeymen House Carpenters in 1850–51. Like most unions led by nativists, the carpenters refused to organize the foreign-born members of their trade until they

learned that this strategy was counterproductive. But it invited immigrants to undermine the bill of prices which the union had sacrificed so much to establish, and by the late 1840s and early 1850s the carpenters dispatched organizers to Irish districts during "standouts," as their walkouts were called. One of these strikes was particularly bitter and protracted. It began in the fall of 1850, collapsed, and then recommenced the following spring. It elicited numerous letters from strikers to local newspapers, one of which was by Turner. Describing the dilemma of the respectable artisan, he asserted that the "worthy mechanic" was entitled to "a house . . . on a front street, three stories high, bath room, hydrant, good yard, cellar . . . house furniture, bedding, clothing, amusements. . . ." But the cost of these "necessities" left him without sufficient income to feed his family adequately. The only course of action bringing respectability to the journeymen was pursuit of their class interests: "Unite to work fewer hours, and organize and inquire into that system of acquisition and distribution of the products of their own industry. . . ." Carpenters who had failed to obtain the rate advance followed Turner's advice and formed their own producers' cooperative.

Printers behaved in much the same manner. American Republicans who belonged to temperance societies or the U.A.M. occupied nearly every elective office in the printers' union, the Franklin Typographical Society. They steadfastly declined to cooperate with a union of German printers until 1850, when they launched a work stoppage for a series of non-wage demands and a rate advance. Those who failed to convince employers of the justice of their cause also formed a cooperative. Their leader, George W. Heilig, revealed the mentality of the newly evangelized workingman when he explained that man was no longer content simply to "eat and clothe himself," because science and art "have at this day disclosed an *artificial, intellectual, moral, and social life,* which . . . is as essential to maintain as the merely natural; and, as it is more refined and exalted, so also does it require a freer and more liberal nourishment." Printers who worked for

Philadelphia's large book houses did not earn enough money "to meet the demands of this more elevated life, which . . . is the religious as well as the political duty of every American to seek and maintain. The *true light* now lighteth every man that cometh into the world, and *it will be received*. We must, therefore, also be in a condition that will enable us to contribute to the support of churches and other associations that will afford us the opportunity of engaging in such religious exercises and social duties as may tend to bring into genial activity our religious feelings and moral affections."

Not all native-born Protestant workers who enrolled in the American Republican Party and its auxiliary organizations necessarily subscribed to these values. A sizable sector of the Party, which appears to have been comprised of young, unmarried men, embraced nativism simply because they hated Catholics. They adhered to older values and forms of behavior, shunning the church, frequenting pubs, taverns, and gaming houses, joining fire companies, and engaging in the rough-and-tumble life of the streets. On the other hand, some nativist workers endorsed the middle-class version of American Republicanism and became obsequious employees, repelled by trade unionism and radicalism alike. There is no way of knowing the origins of these people, though it is probable that they were recent rural-urban migrants who lacked the laboring traditions of Philadelphia's more experienced workers and, perhaps, most upwardly mobile artisans.

The more vocal working-class partisans of American Republicanism, however, did not fulfill the expectations of their middle-class exponents by acting the part of submissive workers wedded to employers by common economic and cultural interests. Day-to-day experience with entrepreneurs who refused to recognize their rights to what they produced made a compelling case that "wage slavery" was more responsible for poverty than intemperance, a glutted labor market, or the exploitation of accumulators. But while they rejected the American Republican analysis of immiseration, they did not cast off the new morality imparted by it. The irony is that this

morality of sobriety, self-control, and respectability emphasized the grim reality; namely, that workers could not support a respectable style of life on wage labor alone. It is also ironic, as Paul Faler suggests, that this morality fortified workers in their struggle against competitive capitalism by arming them with a sense of self-discipline and commitment to purpose. The final irony may be that in employing the new morality in their own interests, they followed the advice of a middle-class nativist who described the ideal society as one which recognized the maxim: *"Act well thy part—there all the honor lies."*

One can safely equate nativist morality with the "cult of respectability," which British labor historians associate with the Victorian middle class and the "aristocracy of labor." The nature of this morality is not in dispute. Most writers agree that it rejected the spontaneity and moral laxity of preindustrial culture for a morality that valued sobriety, hard work, and respectability. Instead, what appears to be at issue is the means by which wage earners became exponents of it.

Implicitly or explicitly, most American writers argue that the new morality was foisted upon workers by Whig industrialists and Presbyterian clergymen who operated through the government and private organizations. While it is clear that these reformers erected the organizational apparatus with which they could manipulate or control their social inferiors, it is improbable that they experienced much success in the period under discussion. The evidence presented here suggests an alternative explanation.

There is little doubt that early industrialization gave rise to a new form of evangelical Protestantism which emphasized the morality of self-control. Nor is there much doubt that workers engaged in those modern industries which required the most discipline—textile mills for example—endorsed evangelical Protestantism and the new morality in the late 1820s and early 1830s. But these workers were a decided minority both in terms of their work environment and religious convictions. Most artisans worked either in traditional or transitional settings at mid-century, laboring at home or in small shops without power-driven machinery. Those who produced for mass markets were forced to toil more intensively as time wore on, and some of them may have been inspired to adopt the new morality. But trade was also rather erratic. Consequently, the work environment of most artisans encouraged sporadic work habits, not steady application to work. And precious few artisans, or Methodist clergymen, found the new morality appealing prior to the depression of 1837.

The chilling effect of hard times appears to have changed their attitudes dramatically. The depression expedited the conversion of Methodist divines to the new morality and made the lower middle class as well as the upper echelon of the working class receptive to it. Methodists and New School Presbyterians in the industrial suburbs struck a resonant chord among these elements in the social strata when they claimed that the depression was inflicted by a God of wrath, angered over the moral depravity of man. They converted thousands of Philadelphians to the new morality, which gained political salience in the American Republican party and its auxiliary organizations. Nativism, then, was the means by which many artisans registered their commitment to a more modern work ethic, and those who converted them were not the elite and its clergy but their own clergy and that of the lower middle class.

Just as preindustrial culture filled the needs of its adherents, so nativism catered to the needs of its followers. It offered both the lower middle class and the upper level of the working class a coherent and seemingly credible explanation for their plight, which the rigors of hard times and the strain of industrial change had brought. It enabled them to assert their dignity and sense of self-worth. It held out prospect of prosperity and worldly success to those who would shun drink, the gaming room, and moral laxity in favor of sobriety and self-discipline. It promised to eliminate class conflict by uniting employers and employees on cultural issues.

Yet nativism fell short of being this cement for masters and journeymen. Those who were native born were, to be sure, united at the polls and in various nativist organizations, but parted ways over divisive class issues in the workshop. Journeymen mediated nativism through values which proclaimed their right to the full product of their labor. Grafting nativist morality onto this formula, they emerged as militant spokesmen for their class.

16

WOMEN, CHILDREN, AND THE USES OF THE STREETS: CLASS AND GENDER CONFLICT IN NEW YORK CITY, 1850–1860

CHRISTINE STANSELL

The years between 1820 and 1860 witnessed the development of an intensive campaign to redefine the proper place of women in American society. Coming at a time of intense social and cultural change, the impulse to create a distinctively American conception of womanhood and definition of female virtue spread rapidly throughout America. Depicting the home as a domestic haven in an increasingly competitive and commercial world, the "Cult of True Womanhood" attributed to women a vital function in maintaining republican virtue during a threatening period of industrialization and urbanization. This "Cult of True Womanhood" prescribed a series of characteristics for women, as guardians of national virtue, to cultivate. Of these, the most important were religious piety, moral purity, submissiveness to men, and the maintenance of the home as place of comfort and moral education.

While many women embraced the virtues of "true womanhood," a life of domesticity was never a real possibility for poor and working-class women. Forced to work in order to maintain their families and lacking the resources and leisure necessary to maintain a middle-class household, these working women carved out lives regulated by their own distinctive social and cultural values. But, as Christine Stansell reveals in this essay, this working-class women's culture came into increasing conflict with the domestic ideal of middle- and upper-class women reformers in the course of the nineteenth century. Offering moral advice and economic aid to working-class women through a growing network of benevolent organizations, Bible societies, and temperance associations, these middle-class women sought to force working-class women from the public world of the streets and tenements into the private world of domesticity. By granting assistance only to those women who would adopt their notions of respectable living, these reforming women attempted to make the domestic ideal a universal reality in antebellum America.

"Women, Children, and the Uses of the Streets: Class and Gender Conflict in New York City, 1850–1860." Feminist Studies, 8:2, (1982) pp. 309–335. Reprinted by permission of the publisher, Feminist Studies, Inc., c/o Women's Studies Program, University of Maryland, College Park, MD 20742.

On a winter day in 1856, an agent for the Children's Aid Society (CAS) of New York encountered two children out on the street with market baskets. Like hundreds he might have seen, they were desperately poor—thinly dressed and barefoot in the cold—but their cheerful countenances struck the gentleman, and he stopped to inquire into their circumstances. They explained that they were out gathering bits of wood and coal their mother could burn for fuel and agreed to take him home to meet her. In a bare tenement room, bereft of heat, furniture, or any other comforts, he met a "stout, hearty woman" who, even more than her children, testified to the power of hardihood and motherly love in the most miserable circumstances. A widow, she supported her family as best she could by street peddling; their room was bare because she had been forced to sell her clothes, furniture, and bedding to supplement her earnings. As she spoke, she sat on a pallet on the floor and rubbed the hands of the two younger siblings of the pair from the street. "They were tidy, sweet children," noted the agent, "And it was very sad to see their chilled faces and tearful eyes." Here was a scene that would have touched the heart of Dickens, and seemingly many a chillier mid-Victorian soul. Yet in concluding his report, the agent's perceptions took a curiously harsh turn.

> Though for her pure young children too much could hardly be done, in such a woman there is little confidence to be put . . . it is probably, some cursed vice has thus reduced her, and that, if her children be not separated from her, she will drag them down, too.

Such expeditions of charity agents and reformers into the households of the poor were common in New York between 1850 and 1860. So were such harsh and unsupported judgments of working-class mothers, judgments which either implicitly or explicitly converged in the new category of the "dangerous classes." In this decade, philanthropists, municipal authorities, and a second generation of Christian evangelicals, male and female, came to see the presence of poor children in New York's streets as a central element of the problem of urban poverty. They initiated an ambitious campaign to clear the streets, to change the character of the laboring poor by altering their family lives, and, in the process, to eradicate poverty itself. They focused their efforts on transforming two elements of laboring-class family life, the place of children and the role of women.

There was, in fact, nothing new about the presence of poor children in the streets, nor was it new that women of the urban poor should countenance that presence. For centuries, poor people in Europe had freely used urban public areas—streets, squares, courts, and marketplaces—for their leisure and work. For the working poor, street life was bound up not only with economic exigency, but also with childrearing, family morality, sociability, and neighborhood ties. In the nineteenth century, the crowded conditions of the tenements and the poverty of great numbers of metropolitan laboring people made the streets as crucial an arena as ever for their social and economic lives. As one New York social investigator observed, "In the poorer portions of the city, people live much and sell mostly out of doors."

How, then, do we account for this sudden flurry of concern? For reformers like the agent from CAS, street life was antagonistic to ardently held beliefs about childhood, womanhood, and, ultimately, the nature of civilized urban society. The middle class of which the reformers were a part was only emerging, an economically ill-defined group, neither rich nor poor, just beginning in the antebellum years to assert a distinct cultural identity. Central to its self-conception was the ideology of domesticity, a set of sharp ideas and pronounced opinions about the nature of a moral family life. The sources of this ideology were historically complex and involved several decades of struggles by women of this group for social recognition, esteem, and power in the family. Nonetheless, by midcentury, ideas initially developed and promoted by women and their clerical allies had found general acceptance, and an ideology of gender had become firmly embedded in an ideology of class. Both women and men valued the home, an institution which they perceived as sacred, presided over by women, inhabited by children, frequented by men. The home preserved those social virtues endangered by the public world of trade, industry, and politics; a public world which they saw as even more corrupting and dangerous in a great city like New York.

Enclosed, protected, and privatized, the home and the patterns of family life on which it was based thus represented to middle-class women and men a crucial institution of civilization. From this perspective, a particular geography of social life—the engagement of the poor in street life rather than in the enclave of the home—became in itself evidence of parental neglect, family disintegration, and a pervasive urban social pathology. Thus in his condemnation of the impoverished widow, the CAS agent distilled an entire analysis of poverty and a critique of poor families: the presence of her children on the streets was synonymous with a corrupt family life, no matter how disguised it might be. In the crusade of such mid-Victorian reformers to save poor children from their parents and their class lie the roots of a long history of middle-class intervention in working-class families, a history which played a central part in the making of the female American working class.

Many historians have shown the importance of antebellum urban reform to the changing texture of class relations in America, its role in the cultural transformations of urbanization and industrialization. Confronted with overcrowding, unemployment, and poverty on scale theretofore unknown in America, evangelical reformers forged programs to control and mitigate these pressing urban problems, programs which would shape municipal policies for years to come. Yet their responses were not simply practical solutions, the most intelligent possible reactions to difficult circumstances; as the most sensitive historians of reform have argued, they were shaped by the world view, cultural affinities, conceptions

of gender, class prejudices, and imperatives of the reformers themselves. Urban reform was an interaction in which, over time, both philanthropists and their beneficiaries changed. In their experience with the reformers, the laboring poor learned—and were forced—to accommodate themselves to an alien conception of family and city life. Through their work with the poor, the reformers discovered many of the elements from which they would forge their own class and sexual identity, still ill-defined and diffuse in 1850; women, particularly, strengthened their role as dictators of domestic and familial standards for all classes of Americans. The reformers' eventual triumph in New York brought no solutions to the problem of poverty, but it did bring about the evisceration of a way of urban life and the legitimation of their own cultural power as a class.

The conflict over the streets resonated on many levels. Ostensibly the reformers aimed to rescue children from the corruptions and dangers of the city streets; indeed the conscious motives of many, if not all, of these well-meaning altruists went no further. There were many unquestioned assumptions, however, on which their benevolent motives rested, and it is in examining these assumptions that we begin to see the challenge which these middle-class people unwittingly posed to common practices of the poor. In their cultural offensive, reformers sought to impose on the poor conceptions of childhood and motherhood drawn from their own ideas of domesticity. In effect, reformers tried to implement their domestic beliefs through reorganizing social space, through creating a new geography of the city. Women were especially active; while male reformers experimented, through a rural foster home program, with more dramatic means of clearing the streets, middle-class ladies worked to found new working-class homes, modeled on their own, which would establish a viable alternative to the thoroughly nondomesticated streets. Insofar as the women reformers succeeded, their victory contributed to both the dominance of a class and of a specific conception of gender. It was, moreover, a victory which had enduring and contradictory consequences for urban women of all classes. In our contemporary city streets, vacated, for the most part, of domestic life yet dangerous for women and children, we see something of the legacy of their labors.

CHILDREN'S USES OF THE STREETS

Unlike today, the teeming milieu of the New York streets in the mid-nineteenth century was in large part a children's world. A complex web of economic imperatives and social mores accounted for their presence there, a presence which reformers so ardently decried. Public life, with its panoply of choices, its rich and varied texture, its motley society, played as central a role in the upbringing of poor children as did private, domestic life in that of their more affluent peers. While middle-class mothers spent a great deal of time with their children (albeit with the help of servants), women of the laboring classes condoned for their offspring an early independence—within bounds—on the streets. Through peddling, scavenging, and the shadier arts of theft and prostitution, the streets offered children a way to earn their keep, crucial to making ends meet in their households. Street life also provided a home for children without families— the orphaned and abandoned—and an alternative to living at home for the especially independent and those in strained family circumstances.

Such uses of the streets were dictated by exigency, but they were also intertwined with patterns of motherhood, parenthood, and childhood. In contrast to their middle- and upper-class contemporaries, the working poor did not think of childhood as a separate stage of life in which girls and boys were free from adult burdens, nor did poor women consider mothering to be a full-time task of supervision. They expected their children to work from an early age, to "earn their keep" or to "get a living," a view much closer to the early modern conceptions which Philippe Ariès describes in *Centuries of Childhood.* Children were little adults, unable as yet to take up all the duties of their elders, but nonetheless bound to

do as much as they could. To put it another way, the lives of children, like those of adults, were circumscribed by economic and familial obligations. In this context, the poor expressed their care for children differently than did the propertied classes. Raising one's children properly did not mean protecting them from the world of work; on the contrary, it involved teaching them to shoulder those heavy burdens of labor which were the common lot of their class, to be hardworking and dutiful to kin and neighbors. By the same token, laboring children gained an early autonomy from their parents, an autonomy alien to the experience of more privileged children. But there were certainly generational tensions embedded in these practices: although children learned independence within the bounds of family obligation, their self-sufficiency also led them in directions that parents could not always control. When parents sent children out to the streets, they could only partially set the terms of what the young ones learned there.

Streetselling, or huckstering, was one of the most common ways for children to turn the streets to good use. Through the nineteenth century, this ancient form of trade still flourished in New York alongside such new institutions of mass marketing as A.T. Stewart's department store. Hucksters, both adults and children, sold all manner of necessities and delicacies. In the downtown business and shopping district, passers-by could buy treats at every corner: hot sweet potatoes, bake-pears, teacakes, fruit, candy, and hot corn. In residential neighborhoods, hucksters sold household supplies door to door: fruits and vegetables in season, matchsticks, scrub brushes, sponges, strings, and pins. Children assisted adult hucksters, went peddling on their own, and worked in several low-paying trades which were their special province: crossing-sweeping for girls; errandrunning, bootblacking, horseholding, and newspaperselling for boys. There were also the odd trades in which children were particularly adept, those unfamiliar and seemingly gratuitous forms of economic activity which abounded in nineteenth-century metropolises; one small boy whom a social investigator found in 1859 made his living in warm weather by catching butterflies and peddling them to canary owners.

Younger children, too, could earn part of their keep on the streets. Scavenging, the art of gathering useful and salable trash, was the customary chore for those too small to go out streetselling. Not all scavengers were children; there were also adults who engaged in scavenging full-time, ragpickers who made their entire livelihoods from "all the odds and ends of a great city." More generally, however, scavenging was children's work. Six- or seven-year-olds were not too young to set out with friends and siblings to gather fuel for their mothers. Small platoons of these children scoured neighborhood streets, ship and lumber yards, building lots, demolished houses, and the precincts of artisan shops and factories for chips, ashes, wood, and coal to take home or peddle to neighbors. "I saw some girls gathering cinders," noted Virginia Penny, New York's self-styled Mayhew. "They burn them at home, after washing them."

The economy of rubbish was intricate. As children grew more skilled, they learned how to turn up other serviceable cast-offs. "These gatherers of things lost on earth," a journal had called them in 1831. "These makers of something out of nothing." Besides taking trash home or selling it to neighbors, children could peddle it to junk dealers, who in turn vended it to manufacturers and artisans for use in industrial processes. Rags, old rope, metal, nails, bottles, paper, kitchen grease, bones, spoiled vegetables, and bad meat all had their place in this commercial network. The waterfront was especially fruitful territory: there, children foraged for loot which had washed up on the banks, snagged in piers, or spilled out on the docks. Loose cotton shredded off bales on the wharves where the southern packet ships docked, bits of canvas and rags ended up with paper- and shoddy-manufacturers (shoddy, the cheapest of textiles, made its way back to the poor in "shoddy" ready-made clothing). Old rope was shredded and sold as oakum, a fiber used to caulk ships. Whole pieces of hardware—nails, cogs, and screws—could be resold: broken bits

went to iron- and brass-founders and coppersmiths to be melted down; bottles and bits of broken glass, to glassmakers. The medium for these exchanges were the second-hand shops strung along the harbor which carried on a bustling trade with children despite a city ordinance prohibiting their buying from minors. "On going down South Street I met a gang of small Dock Thieves . . . had a bag full of short pieces of old rope and iron," William Bell, police inspector of second-hand shops, reported on a typical day on the beat in 1850. The malefactors were headed for a shop like the one into which he slipped incognito, to witness the mundane but illegal transaction between the proprietor and a six-year-old boy, who sold him a glass bottle for a penny. The waterfront also yielded trash which could be used at home rather than vended: tea, coffee, sugar, and flour spilled from sacks and barrels, and from the wagons which carried cargo to nearby warehouses.

By the 1850s, huckstering and scavenging were the only means by which increasing numbers of children could earn their keep. A decline in boys' positions as artisans' apprentices and girls' positions as domestic servants meant that the streets became the most accessible employer of children. Through the 1840s, many artisan masters entirely rearranged work in their shops to take advantage of a labor market glutted with impoverished adults, and to survive within the increasingly cutthroat exigencies of New York commerce and manufacturing. As a result, apprenticeship in many trades had disappeared by 1850. Where it did survive, the old perquisites, steady work and room and board, were often gone: boys' work, like that of the adults they served, was irregular and intermittent.

There were analogous changes in domestic service. Until the 1840s, girls of the laboring classes had easily found work as servants, but in that decade, older female immigrants, whom employers preferred for their superior strength, crowded them out of those positions. By the early 1850s, domestic service was work for Irish and German teenagers and young women. In other industrial centers, towns like Manchester and Lowell, children moved from older employments into the factories; New York, however, because of high ground rents and the absence of sufficient water power, lacked the large establishments which gave work to the young in other cities. Consequently, children and adolescents, who two generations earlier would have worked in more constrained situations, now flooded the streets.

The growth of the street trades meant that increasing numbers of children worked on their own, away from adult supervision. This situation magnified the opportunities for illicit gain, the centuries-old pilfering and finagling of apprentices and serving-girls. When respectable parents sent their children out to scavenge and peddle, the consequences were not always what they intended: these trades were an avenue to theft and prostitution as well as to an honest living. Child peddlers habituated household entryways, with their hats and umbrellas and odd knick-knacks, and roamed by shops where goods were often still, in the old fashion, displayed outside on the sidewalks. And scavenging was only one step removed from petty theft. The distinction between gathering spilled flour and spilling flour oneself was one which small scavengers did not always observe. Indeed, children skilled in detecting value in random objects strewn about the streets, the seemingly inconsequential, could as easily spot value in other people's property. As the superintendent of the juvenile asylum wrote of one malefactor, "He has very little sense of moral rectitude, and thinks it but little harm to take small articles." A visitor to the city in 1857 was struck by the swarms of children milling around the docks, "scuffling about, wherever there were bags of coffee and hogshead of sugar." Armed with sticks, "they 'hooked' what they could." The targets of pilfering were analogous to those of scavenging: odd objects, unattached to persons. The prey of children convicted of theft and sent to the juvenile house of correction in the 1850s included, for instance, a bar of soap, a copy of the *New York Herald,* lead and wood from demolished houses, and a board "val-

ued at 3¢." Police Chief George Matsell reported that pipes, tin roofing, and brass doorknobs were similarly endangered. Thefts against persons, pickpocketing and mugging, belonged to another province, that of the professional child criminal.

Not all parents were concerned about their children's breaches of the law. Reformers were not always wrong when they charged that by sending children to the streets, laboring-class parents implicitly encouraged them to a life of crime. The unrespectable poor did not care to discriminated between stolen and scavenged goods, and the destitute could not afford to. One small boy picked up by the CAS told his benefactors that his parents had sent him out chip picking with the instructions "you can take it wherever you can find it"—although like many children brought before the charities, this one was embroidering his own innocence and his parents' guilt. But children also took their own chances, without their parents' knowledge. By midcentury, New York was the capital of American crime, and there was a place for children, small and adept as they were, on its margins. Its full-blown economy of contraband, with the junk shops at the center, allowed children to exchange pilfered and stolen goods quickly and easily: anything, from scavenged bottles to nicked top hats could be sold immediately.

As scavenging shaded into theft, so it also edged into another street trade, prostitution. The same art of creating commodities underlay both. In the intricate economy of the streets, old rope, stray coal, rags, and sex all held the promise of cash, a promise apparent to children who from an early age learned to be "makers of something out of nothing." For girls who knew how to turn things with no value into things with exchange value, the prostitute's act of bartering sex into money would have perhaps seemed daunting, but nonetheless comprehensible. These were not professional child prostitutes; rather, they turned to the lively trade in casual prostitution on occasion or at intervals to supplement other earnings. One encounter with a gentleman, easy to come by in the hotel and business district, could bring the equivalent of a month's wages in domestic service, a week's wages seamstressing, or several weeks' earnings huckstering. Such windfalls went to pay a girl's way at home or, more typically, to purchase covertly some luxury—pastries, a bonnet, cheap jewelry, a fancy gown—otherwise out of her reach.

Prostitution was quite public in antebellum New York. It was not yet a statutory offense, and although the police harassed streetwalkers and arrested them for vagrancy, they had little effect on the trade. Consequently, offers from men and inducements from other girls were common on the streets, and often came a girl's way when she was out working. This is the reason a German father tried to prevent his fourteen-year-old daughter from going out scavenging when she lost her place in domestic service. "He said, 'I don't want you to be a rag-picker. You are not a child now—people will look at you—you will come to harm,'" as the girl recounted the tale. The "harm" he feared was the course taken by a teenage habitue of the waterfront in whom Inspector Bell took a special interest in 1851. After she rejected his offer of a place in service, he learned from a junk shop proprietor that, along with scavenging around the docks, she was "in the habit of going aboard the Coal Boats in that vicinity and prostituting herself." Charles Loring Brace, founder of the CAS, claimed that "the life of a swill-gatherer, or coal-picker, or chiffonier [ragpicker] in the streets soon wears off a girl's modesty and prepares her for worse occupation," while Police Chief Matsell accused huckster-girls of soliciting the clerks and employees they met on their rounds of counting houses.

While not all girls in the street trades were as open to advances as Brace and Matsell implied, their habituation to male advances must have contributed to the brazenness with which some of them could engage in sexual bartering. Groups of girls roamed about the city, sometimes on chores and errands, sometimes only with an eye for flirtations, or being "impudent and saucy to men," as the parents of one offender put it. In the early 1830s, John R. McDowall, leader of the militant Magdalene Society, had observed on fashionable Broadway "females of thirteen and fourteen walking the streets without a protector, until some pretended gentleman gives them a nod, and takes their arm and escorts them to houses of assignation." McDowall was sure to exaggerate, but later witnesses lent credence to his description. In 1854, a journalist saw nearly fifty girls soliciting one evening as he walked a mile up Broadway, while diarist George Templeton Strong referred to juvenile prostitution as a permanent feature of the promenade in the early 1850s: "no one can walk the length of Broadway without meeting some hideous troop of ragged girls." But despite the entrepreneurial attitude with which young girls ventured into prostitution, theirs was a grim choice, with hazards which, young as they were, the could not always foresee. Nowhere can we see more clearly the complexities of poor children's lives in the public city. The life of the streets taught them self-reliance and the arts of survival, but this education could also be a bitter one.

The autonomy and independence which the streets fostered through petty crime also extended to living arrangements. Abandoned children, orphans, runaways, and particularly independent boys made the streets their home: sleeping out with companions in household areas, wagons, marketplace stalls, and saloons. In the summer of 1850, the *Tribune* noted that the police regularly scared up thirty or forty boys sleeping along Nassau and Ann streets; they included boys with homes as well as genuine vagabonds. Police Chief Matsell reported that in warm weather, crowds of roving boys, many of them sons of respectable parents, absented themselves from their families for weeks. Such was Thomas W., who came to the attention of the CAS; "sleeps in stable," the case record notes. "Goes home for clean clothes; and sometimes for his meals." Thomas's parents evidently tolerated the arrangement, but this was not always the case. Rebellious children, especially boys, evaded parental demands and discipline by living on the streets full-time. Thus John Lynch left home because of some difficulty with his father: he was sent on his parents' complaint to the juvenile house of correction on a vagrancy charge.

Reformers like Matsell and the members of the CAS tended to see such children as either orphaned or abandoned, symbols of the misery and depravity of the poor. Their perception, incarnated by writers like Horatio Alger in the fictional waifs of sentimental novels, gained wide credibility in nineteenth-century social theory and popular thought. Street children were essentially "friendless and homeless," declared Brace. "No one cares for them, and they care for no one." His judgment, if characteristically harsh, was not without truth. If children without parents had no kin or friendly neighbors to whom to turn, they were left to fend for themselves. Such was the story of the two small children of a deceased stonecutter, himself a widower. After he died, "they wandered around, begging cold victuals, and picking up, in any way they were able, their poor living." William S., fifteen years old, had been orphaned when very young. After a stay on a farm as an indentured boy, he ran away to the city, where he slept on the piers and supported himself by carrying luggage off passenger boats: "William thinks he has seen hard times," the record notes. But the testimony garnered by reformers about the "friendless and homeless" young should also be taken with a grain of salt. The CAS, a major source of these tales, was most sympathetic to children who appeared before the agents as victims of orphanage, desertion, or familial cruelty; accordingly, young applicants for aid sometimes presented themselves in ways which would gain them the most favor from philanthropists. The society acknowledged the problem, although it claimed to have solved it: "runaways frequently come to the office with fictitious stories . . . Sometimes a truant has only one parent, generally the mother, and she is dissipated, or unable to control him. He comes to the office . . . and tells a fictitious story of orphanage and distress." Yet in reality, there were few children so entirely exploited and "friendless" as the CAS believed.

Not surprisingly, orphanage among the poor was a far more complex matter than reformers perceived. As Carol Groneman has shown, poor families did not disintegrate under the most severe difficulties of immigration and urbanization. In the worst New York slums, families managed to keep together and to take in those kin and friends who lacked households of their own. Orphaned children as well as those who were temporarily parentless—whose parents, for instance, had found employment elsewhere—typically found homes with older siblings, grandparents, and aunts. The solidarity of the laboring-class family, however, was not as idyllic as it might seem in retrospect. Interdependence also bred tensions which weighed heavily on children, and in response, the young sometimes chose—or were forced—to strike out on their own. Step-relations, so common in this period, were a particular source of bad feelings. Two brothers whom a charity visitor found sleeping in the streets explained that they had left their mother when she moved in with another man after their father deserted her. If natural parents died, step-parents might be particularly forceful about sending children "on their own hook." "We haven't got no father nor mother," testified a twelve-year-old wanderer of himself and his younger brother. Their father, a shoemaker, had remarried when their mother died; when he died, their stepmother moved away and left them, "and they could not find out anything more about her."

Moreover, the difficulties for all, children and adults, of finding work in these years of endemic underemployment created a kind of half-way orphanage. Parents emigrating from New York could place their boys in apprenticeships which subsequently collapsed and cast the children on their own for a living. The parents of one boy, for example, left him at work in a printing office when they moved to Toronto. Soon after they left, he was thrown out of work; to support himself he lived on the streets and worked as an errand boy, news boy, and bootblack. Similarly, adolescents whose parents had left them in unpleasant or intolerable situations simply struck out on their own. A widow boarded her son with her sister when she went into service; the boy ran away when his aunt "licked him." Thus a variety of circumstances could be concealed in the category of the street "orphan."

All these customs of childhood and work among the laboring poor were reasons for the presence of children, girls and boys, in the public life of the city, a presence which reformers passionately denounced. Children and parents alike had their uses for the streets. For adults, the streets allowed their dependents to contribute to their keep, crucial to making ends meet in the household economy. For girls and boys, street life provided a way to meet deeply ingrained family obligations. This is not to romanticize their lives. If the streets provided a way to meet responsibilities, it was a hard and bitter, even a cruel one. Still, children of the laboring classes lived and labored in a complex geography, which reformers of the poor perceived only as a stark tableau of pathology and vice.

To what degree did their judgments of children redound on women? Although reformers included both sexes in their indictments, women were by implication more involved. First, poverty was especially likely to afflict women. To be the widow, deserted wife, or orphaned daughter of a laboring man, even a prosperous artisan, was to be poor; female self-support was synonymous with indigence. The number of self-supporting women, including those with children, was high in midcentury New York: in the 1855 census report for two neighborhoods, nearly 60 percent of six hundred working women sampled had no adult male in the household. New York's largest charity reported in 1858 that it aided 27 percent more women than men. For women in such straits, children's contributions to the family income were mandatory. As a New York magistrate had written in 1830: "of the children brought before me for pilfering, nine out of ten are those whose fathers are dead, and who live with their mothers." Second, women were more responsible than men for children, both from the perspective of reformers and within the reality of the laboring family. Mothering, as the middle class saw it, was a expression of female identity, rather than a construction derived from present

and past social conditions. Thus the supposedly neglectful ways of laboring mothers reflected badly not only on their character as parents, but also on their very identity as women. When not depicted as timid or victimized, poor women appeared as unsavory characters in the annals of reformers: drunken, abusive, or, in one of the most memorable descriptions, "sickly-looking, deformed by over work . . . weak and sad-faced." Like prostitutes, mothers of street children became a kind of half-sex in the eyes of reformers, outside the bounds of humanity by virtue of their inability or unwillingness to replicate the innate abilities of true womanhood.

REFORMERS AND FAMILY LIFE

In the 1850s, the street activities of the poor, especially those of children, became the focus of a distinct reform politics in New York. The campaign against the streets, one element in a general cultural offensive against the laboring classes which evangelical groups had carried on since the 1830s, was opened in 1849 by Police Chief Matsell's report to the public on juvenile delinquency. In the most hyperbolic rhetoric, he described a "deplorable and growing evil" spreading through the streets. "I allude to the constantly increasing number of vagrants, idle and vicious children of both sexes, who infest our public thoroughfares." Besides alerting New York's already existing charities to the presence of the dangerous classes, Matsell's expose affected a young Yale seminarian, Charles Loring Brace, just returned from a European tour and immersed in his new vocation of city missionary. Matsell's alarmed observations coalesced with what Brace had learned from his own experiences working with boys in the city mission. Moved to act, Brace in 1853 founded the CAS, a charity which concerned itself with all poor children, but especially with street "orphans." Throughout the 1850s, the CAS carried on the work Matsell had begun, documenting and publicizing the plight of street children. In large measure because of its efforts, the "evil" of the streets became a central element in the reform analysis of poverty and a focus of broad concern in New York.

Matsell, Brace, and the New York philanthropists with whom they associated formed—like their peers in other northeastern cities—a closely connected network of secular and moral reformers. By and large, these women and men were not born into New York's elite, as were those of the generation who founded the city's philanthropic movement in the first decades of the century. Rather, they were part of an emerging middle class, typically outsiders to the ruling class, either by birthplace or social status. Although much of the ideology which influenced reformers' dealings with the poor is well known, scholars have generally not explored the extent to which their interactions with the laboring classes were shaped by developing ideas of gentility: ideas, in turn, based upon conceptions of domestic life. Through their attempts to recast working-class life within these conceptions, this still-inchoate class sharpened its own vision of urban culture and its ideology of class relations. Unlike philanthropists in the early nineteenth century, who partook of an older attitude of tolerance to the poor and of the providential inevitability of poverty, mid-Victorians were optimistic that poverty could be abolished by altering the character of their almoners as workers, citizens, and family members. The reformers of the streets were directly concerned with the latter. In their efforts to teach the working poor the virtues of the middle-class home as a means of self-help, they laid the ideological and programmatic groundwork for a sustained intervention in working-class family life.

What explains the sudden alarm about the streets at midcentury? The emergence of street life as a target of organized reform was partly due to the massive immigrations of those years, which created crises of housing, unemployment, and crime. The influx of Irish and German immigrants in the 1840s greatly increased the presence of the poor in public areas. Thousands of those who arrived after 1846 wandered through the streets looking for housing, kin, work, or, at the least, a spot to shelter them from the ele-

ments. A news item from 1850 reported a common occurence.

> Six poor women with their children, were discovered Tuesday night by some police officers, sleeping in the alleyway, in Avenue B, between 10th and 11th streets. When interrogated they said they had been compelled to spend their nights whereever they could obtain any shelter. They were in a starving condition, and without the slightest means of support.

Indeed, severe overcrowding in the tenements meant that more of the poor strayed outside, particularly in hot weather. "The sidewalks, cellar doors, gratings, boxes, barrels, etc. in the densely populated streets were last night literally covered with gasping humanity, driven from their noisome, unventilated dens, in search of air," reported the *Tribune* several weeks later.

The existence of the new police force, organized in 1845, also aggravated the reformers' sense of crisis by broadening their notions of criminal behavior. The presence of these new agents of mediation between the poor and the propertied shed light on a milieu which theretofore had been closed to the genteel. Indeed, the popularization of the idea of the dangerous classes after 1850 was partly due to publicized police reports and to accounts written by journalists who accompanied the police on their rounds. The "vicious" activities of the laboring classes were elaborated in such reports as Matsell's, published in pamphlet form for philanthropic consumption, and novelists' and journalists' exposes like those of Ned Buntline and Charles Dickens's description of Five Points in his *American Notes*.

The police also seem to have enforced prohibitions on street life with their own definitions of juvenile crime. Because conceptions of vagrancy depended on whether the police considered the child's presence in the streets to be legitimate, it is possible that some of the high number of juvenile commitments—about two thousand a year—can be attributed to conflicting notions of the proper sphere of children. Brace was struck by the drama of children, police, and mothers in Corlear's Hook (now the Lower East Side). The streets teemed with

> wild ragged little girls who were flitting about . . . some with baskets and poker gathering rags, some apparently seeking chances of stealing. . . . The police were constantly arresting them as "vagrants," when the mothers would beg them off from the good-natured justices, and promise to train them better in the future.

As for petty larceny, that at least some of the arrests were due to an ambiguity about what constituted private property was testified to by one New York journalist. The city jail, he wrote, was filled, along with other malefactors, "with young boys and girls who have been caught asleep on cellar doors or are suspected of the horrible crime of stealing junk bottles and old iron!" As children's presence in the public realm became inherently criminal, so did the gleaning of its resources. The distinction between things belonging to no one and things belonging to someone blurred in the minds of propertied adults as well as propertyless children.

There were, then, greater numbers of children in the New York streets after 1845, and their activities were publicized as never before. Faced with an unprecedented crisis of poverty in the city, reformers fastened on their presence as a cause rather than a symptom of impoverishment. The reformers' idea that the curse of poor children lay in the childrearing methods of their parents moved toward the center of their analysis of the etiology of poverty, replacing older notions of divine will. In the web of images of blight and disease which not only reflected but also shaped the midcentury understanding of poverty, the tenement house was the "parent of constant disorders, and the nursery of increasing vices," but real parents were the actual agents of crime. In opposition to the ever more articulate and pressing claims of New York's organized working men, this first generation of "experts" on urban poverty averred that familial relations rather than industrial capitalism were responsible for the misery

which any clear-headed New Yorker could see was no transient state of affairs. One of the principal pieces of evidence of "the ungoverned appetites, bad habits, and vices" of laboring-class parents was the fact that they sent their offspring out to the streets to earn their keep.

The importance of domesticity to the reformers' own class identity fostered this shift of attention from individual moral shortcomings to the family structure of a class. For these middle-class city dwellers, the home was not simply a place of residence; it was a focus of social life and a central element of class-consciousness, based on specific conceptions of femininity and childrearing. There, secluded from the stress of public life, women could devote themselves to directing the moral and ethical development of their families. There, protected from the evils of the outside world, the young could live out their childhoods in innocence, freed from the necessity of labor, cultivating their moral and intellectual faculties.

From this vantage point, the laboring classes appeared gravely deficient. When charity visitors, often ladies themselves, entered the households of working people, they saw a domestic sparseness which contradicted their deepest beliefs about what constituted a morally sustaining family life. "[Their] ideas of domestic comfort and standard of morals, are far below our own," wrote the Association for Improving the Condition of the Poor (AICP). The urban poor had intricately interwoven family lives, but they had no *homes*. Middle-class people valued family privacy and intimacy: among the poor, they saw a promiscuous sociability, an "almost fabulous gregariousness." They believed that the moral training of children depended on protecting them within the home; in poor neighborhoods, they saw children encouraged to labor in the streets. The harshness and intolerance with which midcentury reformers viewed the laboring classes can be partly explained by the disparity between these two ways of family life. "Homes—in the better sense—they never know," declared one investigating committee; the children "graduate in every kind of vice known in that curious school which trains them—the public street." The AICP scoffed at even using the word: "Homes . . . if it is not a mockery to give that hallowed name to the dark, filthy hovels where many of them dwell." To these middle-class women and men, the absence of home life was not simply due to the uncongenial physical circumstances of the tenements, nor did it indicate the poor depended upon another way of organizing their family lives. Rather, the homelessness of this "multitude of half-naked, dirty, and leering children" signified an absence of parental love, a neglect of proper childrearing which was entwined in the habits and values of the laboring classes.

THE CHILDREN'S AID SOCIETY

Although Brace shared the alarm and revulsion of reformers like Matsell at the "homelessness" of the poor, he also brought to the situation an optimistic liberalism, based upon his own curious and ambiguous uses of domesticity. In his memoirs of 1872, looking back on two decades of work with the New York laboring classes, Brace took heart from the observation that the absence of family life so deplored by his contemporaries actually operated to stabilize American society. Immigration and continual mobility disrupted the process by which one generation of laboring people taught the next a cultural identity, "that continuity of influence which bad parents and grandparents exert." Brace wrote this passage with the specter of the Paris Commune before him; shaken, like so many of his peers, by the degree of organization and class consciousness among the Parisian poor, he found consolation on native ground in what others condemned. "The mill of American life, which grinds up so many delicate and fragile things, has its uses, when it is turned on the vicious fragments of the lower strata of society."

It was through the famed placing-out system that the CAS turned the "mill of American life" to the uses of urban reform. The placing-out program sent poor city children to foster homes in rural areas where labor was scarce. With the wages-fund theory, a common Anglo-American liberal reform scheme of midcentury which pro-

posed to solve the problem of metropolitan unemployment by dispersing the surplus of labor, the society defended itself against critics' charges that "foster parents" were simply farmers in need of cheap help, and placing-out, a cover for the exploitation of child labor. At first, children went to farms in the nearby countryside, as did those the city bound out from the Almshouse, but in 1854 the society conceived the more ambitious scheme of sending parties of children by railroads to the far Midwest: Illinois, Michigan, and Iowa. By 1860, 5,074 children had been placed-out.

At its most extreme, the CAS only parenthetically recognized the social and legal claims of working-class parenthood. The organization considered the separation of parents and children a positive good, the liberation of innocent, if tarnished, children from the tyranny of unredeemable adults. Here, as in so many aspects of nineteenth-century reform, the legacy of the Enlightenment was ambiguous: the idea of childhood innocence it had bequeathed, socially liberating in many respects, also provided one element of the ideology of middle-class domination. Since the CAS viewed children as innocents to be rescued and parents as corrupters to be displaced, its methods depended in large measure on convincing children themselves to leave New York, with or without parental knowledge or acquiescence. Street children were malleable innocents in the eyes of the charity, but they were also little consenting adults, capable of breaking all ties to their class milieu and families. To be sure, many parents did bring their children to be placed-out, but nonetheless, the society also seems to have worked directly through the children. In 1843, the moral reformer and abolitionist Lydia Maria Child had mused that the greatest misfortune of "the squalid little wretches" she saw in the New York streets was that they were not orphans. The charity visitors of the CAS tackled this problem directly: where orphans were lacking, they manufactured them.

Placing-out was based on the thoroughly middle-class idea of the redeeming influence of the Protestant home in the countryside. There, the morally strengthening effects of labor, mixed with the salutary influences of domesticity and female supervision, could remold the child's character. Thus domestic ideology gave liberals like Brace the theoretical basis for constructing a program to resocialize the poor in which force was unnecessary. Standards of desirable behavior could be internalized by children rather than beaten into them, as had been the eighteenth-century practice. With home influence, not only childrearing but the resocialization of a class could take the form of subliminal persuasion rather than conscious coercion.

Earlier New York reformers had taken a different tack with troublesome children. In 1824, the Society for the Reformation of Juvenile Delinquents had established an asylum, the House of Refuge, to deal with juvenile offenders. As in all the new institutions for deviants, solitary confinement and corporal punishment were used to force the recalcitrant into compliance with the forces of reason. But Brace thought the asylum, so prized by his predecessors, was impractical and ineffectual. Asylums could not possibly hold enough children to remedy the problem of the New York streets in the 1850s; moreover, the crowding together of the children who were incarcerated only reinforced the habits of their class. The foster home, however, with its all-encompassing moral influence, could be a more effective house of refuge. "We have wished to make every kind of religious family, who desired the responsibility, an Asylum or a Reformatory Institution . . . by throwing about the wild, neglected little outcast of the streets, the love and gentleness of home. The home was an asylum, but it was woman's influence rather than an institutional regimen that accomplished its corrections.

This is an overview of the work of the CAS, but on closer examination, there was also a division by sex in the organization, and domesticity played different roles in the girls' and boys' programs. The emigrants to the West seem to have been mostly boys: they seem to have been more allured by emigration than were girls, and parents were less resistant to placing-out sons than

daughters. "Even as a beggar or pilferer, a little girl is of vastly more use to a wretched mother than her son," the society commented. "The wages of a young girl are much more sure to go to the pockets of the family than those of a boy." Brace's own imagination was more caught up with boys than girls; his most inventive efforts were directed at them. Unlike most of his contemporaries, he appreciated the vitality and tenacity of the street boys; his fascination with the Western scheme came partly from the hope that emigration would redirect their toughness and resourcefulness, "their sturdy independence," into hearty frontier individualism. Similarly, the agents overseeing the foster home program were men, as were the staff members of the society's much-touted Newsboys' Lodging-House, a boardinghouse where, for a few pennies, news boys could sleep and eat. The Lodging-House, was, in fact, a kind of early boys' camp, where athletics and physical fitness, lessons in entrepreneurship (one of its salient features was a savings bank), and moral education knit poor boys and gentlemen into a high-spirited but respectable masculine camaraderie.

Women were less visible in the society's literature, their work less well-advertised, since it was separate from Brace's most innovative programs. The women of the CAS were not paid agents like the men, but volunteers who staffed the girls' programs: a Lodging-House and several industrial schools. The work of the women reformers was, moreover, less novel than that of the men. Rather than encouraging girls to break away from their families, the ladies sought the opposite: to create among the urban laboring classes a domestic life of their own. They aimed to mold future wives and mothers of a reformed working class: women who would be imbued with a belief in the importance of domesticity and capable of patterning their homes and family lives on middle-class standards.

Yet it was this strategy of change, rather than Brace's policy of fragmentation, which would eventually dominate attempts to reform working-class children. The ladies envisioned homes which would reorganize the promiscuously sociable lives of the poor under the aegis of a new, "womanly" working-class woman. In the CAS industrial schools and Lodging-House, girls recruited off the streets learned the arts of plain sewing, cooking, and housecleaning, guided by the precept celebrated by champions of women's domestic mission that "nothing was so honorable as industrious *house-work*." These were skills which both prepared them for waged employment in seamstressing and domestic service and outfitted them for homes of their own: as the ladies proudly attested after several years of work, their students entered respectable married life as well as honest employment. "Living in homes reformed through their influence," the married women carried on their female mission, reformers by proxy.

Similarly, the women reformers instituted meetings to convert the mothers of their students to a new relationship to household and children. Classes taught the importance of sobriety, neat appearance, and sanitary housekeeping: the material basis for virtuous motherhood and a proper home. Most important, the ladies stressed the importance of keeping children off the streets and sending them to school. Here, they found their pupils particularly recalcitrant. Mothers persisted in keeping children home to work and cited economic reasons when their benefactresses upbraided them. The CAS women, however, considered the economic rationale a pretense for the exploitation of children and the neglect of their moral character. "The larger ones were needed to 'mind' the baby," lady volunteers sardonically reported, "or go out begging for clothes . . . and the little ones, scarcely bigger than the baskets on their arms, must be sent out for food, or chips, or cinders." The Mother's Meetings tried, however unsuccessfully, to wean away laboring women from such customary practices to what the ladies believed to be a more nurturant and moral mode of family life: men at work, women at home, children inside.

In contrast to the male reformers, the women of the society tried to create an intensified private life within New York itself, to enclose children within tenements and schools rather than to send them away or incarcerate them in asylums. There is a new, optimistic vision of city life implied in their work. With the establishment of the home across class lines, a renewed city could emerge, its streets free for trade and respectable promenades, and emancipated from the inconveniences of pickpockets and thieves, the affronts of prostitutes and hucksters, the myriad offenses of working-class mores and poverty. The "respectable" would control and dominate public space as they had never before. The city would itself become an asylum on a grand scale, an environment which embodied the eighteenth-century virtues of reason and progress, the nineteenth-century virtues of industry and domesticity. And as would befit a city for the middle class, boundaries between public and private life would be clear: the public space of the metropolis would be the precinct of men, the private space of the home, that of women and children.

In the work of the CAS female volunteers lie the roots of the Americanization campaign which, half a century later, reshaped the lives of so many working-class immigrants. The settlement houses of turn-of-the-century New York would expand the mothers' classes and girls' housekeeping lessons into a vast program of nativist assimilation. Female settlement workers would assure immigrant mothers and daughters that the key to decent lives lay in creating American homes within the immigrant ghettoes: homes that were built on a particular middle-class configuration of possessions and housekeeping practices and a particular structure of family relations. And, as in the 1850s, the effort to domesticate the plebeian household would be linked to a campaign to clear the streets of an ubiquitous, aggressive, and assertive working-class culture.

Neither the clearing of the streets nor the making of the working-class home were accomplished at any one point in time. Indeed, these conflicts still break out in Manhattan's poor and working-class neighborhoods. Today, in the Hispanic *barrios* of the Upper West and Lower East sides and in black Harlem, scavenging and street huckstering still flourish. In prosperous quarters as well, where affluent customers are there for the shrewd, the battle continues between police on the one hand, hucksters and prostitutes on the other. Indeed, the struggle over the streets has been so ubiquitous in New York and other cities in the last 150 years that we can see it as a structural element of urban life in industrial capitalist societies. As high unemployment and casualized work have persisted in the great cities, the streets have continued to contain some of the few resources for the poor to make ends meet. At the same time, the social imagination of the poor, intensified by urban life, has worked to increase those resources. All the quick scams—the skills of the con men, street musicians, beggars, prostitutes, peddlers, drug dealers, and pickpockets—are arts of the urban working poor, bred from ethnic and class traditions and the necessities of poverty.

Neither is the conflict today, however, identical to the one which emerged in the 1850s. The struggle over the streets in modern New York takes place in a far different context, one defined by past victories of reformers and municipal authorities. Vagrancy counts against children are now strengthened by compulsory school legislation; child labor laws prohibit most kinds of child huckstering; anti-peddling laws threaten heavy fines for the unwary. Most important, perhaps, the mechanisms for "placing out" wandering children away from "negligent" mothers are all in place (although the wholesale breakdown of social services in New York has made these provisions increasingly ineffectual, creating a new problem in its wake). The street life of the work-

ing poor survives in pockets, but immeasurably weakened, continually under duress.

In more and more New York neighborhoods, the rich and the middle-class can walk untroubled by importunate prostitutes, beggars, and hucksters. The women gossiping on front stoops, the mothers shouting orders from upstairs windows, and the housewife habituees of neighborhood taverns have similarly disappeared, shut away behind heavily locked doors with their children and television sets. New York increasingly becomes a city where a variant of the nineteenth-century bourgeois vision of respectable urban life is realized. "NO LOITERING/PLAYING BALL/SITTING/PLAYING MUSIC ON SIDEWALKS IN FRONT OF BUILDINGS," placards on the great middle-class apartment houses warn potential lingerers. The sidewalks are, indeed, often free of people, except for passers-by and the doormen paid to guard them. But as Jane Jacobs predicted so forcefully two decades ago, streets cleared for the respectable have become free fields for predators. The inhabitants of modern-day New York, particularly women and children, live in a climate of urban violence and fear historically unprecedented save in wartime. In the destruction of the street life of the laboring poor, a critical means of creating urban communities and organizing urban space has disappeared. As the streets are emptied of laboring women and children, as the working-class home has become an ideal, if not a reality, for ever-widening sectors of the population, the city of middle-class hopes becomes ever more bereft of those ways of public life which once mitigated the effects of urban capitalism.

17

"A MAID OF ALL TRAIDS": WOMEN IN THE WEST

JULIE ROY JEFFREY

Between 1840 and the Civil War, tens of thousands of families left the familiar surroundings of their homes, kin, and friends to travel into the trans-Mississippi West. For most, the midwestern prairies, the Rocky Mountains, and the valleys of the Pacific coast held out the promise of a new beginning, a second chance for winning the independence and moderate prosperity that were waning in the industrializing East. Across the country, men, women, and children loaded seed, tools, and a few personal belongings onto the "prairie schooners" that bumped and lurched across the Overland Trail. Their journeys lasted three to six months, and in the process men's and women's traditional roles blurred as the labor of the entire family became the only hedge against failure. Wind, rain, disease, and boredom were the constant companions of these early pioneers as they struggled to reach their destinations.

Every pioneer felt the burden of this transmigration, but perhaps none as fully as the frontier woman. Separated—often for life—from the female friends and relatives that were the center of her social and emotional world, and forced by circumstance to engage in "unwomanly" work along the trail, the pioneer woman could only hope that the family dream of western settlement would bear fruit. In this essay, Julie Roy Jeffrey explores the life of such women once they reached their destinations and set about the task of reconstructing homes and communities. As she reveals, the rigors of migration were only the beginning of women's travail.

"My heart arose in gratitude to God that we were spared to reach this land," Esther Hanna wrote in her journal a few days before ending it in September 1852. "I can scarcely realize that we are so near our contemplated home." For women like Esther Hanna, the journey's conclusion was a joyous event. Misgivings about the frontier evaporated as families began their new lives. For others, however, the period of adjustment to new surroundings was trying. Physical exhaustion from the trip's rigors, a reduced emotional resilience, and meager family resources contributed to a sense of desolation in the days after arrival. Clothes were tattered. The trail was littered with treasured possessions, discarded as animals had weakened, then died. No matter how carefully the trip had been planned, few arrived with much cash, and even the lucky ones found their reserves could not replace what they had thrown away in desperation. "There were no luxuries to be had even if we had ever so much money," one early pioneer recalled. But just as important as the physical and financial condition in which so many emigrants found themselves at the trip's end was the shock of confronting the reality of the frontier. Many women had survived the trip by fantasizing about their future "happy home in a happy land." When they reached their destination, they saw not a home but wilderness. "After the way we had suffered and struggled to get here," a Missouri woman wrote to her mother, "I had all I could do to keep from asking George to turn around and bring me back home." As dreams collapsed, some gave in to feelings. One band of women arriving in Puget Sound in November 1851 spent a long dreary afternoon helping their husbands carry possessions up the beach beyond the reach of the tide. Then, overwhelmed by their situation, one of the husbands later recalled, "the women sat down and cried." It was not long, of course, before some sort of shelter, however rudimentary, was constructed. But a permanent "home" often proved elusive. Journals, letters, and census data suggest several moves during the early years of settlement, as families sought the right claim or the right job.

Women settling the farming frontier, far from the Pacific coast, also found adjustment difficult in the early months and years after their trip. Although they were not so fatigued after a journey ending in Nebraska or western Iowa, their situation initially seemed bleak. Prairies and plains struck many women as depressing. "As long as I live I'll never see such a lonely country," was how one woman described her reaction to the Texas plains, while a Nebraska pioneer reflected, "These unbounded prairies have such an air of desolation—and the stillness is very oppressive." Like settlers of Oregon and Washington, emigrants pushing the frontier west from the Mississippi arrived at their destination with little capital to soften the burdens of homesteading. Like their counterparts in the Far West, emigrants found their dreams of a permanent home illusory.

The early years of settlement on the farming frontier, of course, differed according to time, location, and settlers' backgrounds. The mid-century plains and prairie frontier offered emigrants coming from Europe and the Mississippi Valley not only fertile soil and sufficient rainfall, for example (unlike the arid plains, sweeping from the Dakotas south to Texas, settled later in the century, where the rainfall could not support traditional farming), but also special problems stemming from the region's geography and climate. Although emigrants could use familiar agricultural methods, the weather, with its extremes of temperature and its high winds, could mean low yields, crop failure, and the destruction of valuable livestock. Timber for building and fuel, so abundant in the Far West, was rare on the prairies and plains, and its scarcity compounded problems of settlement. Hunger, poverty, and ruin hovered closer to the pioneers of this frontier than those of the Far West. There, however, though subsistence was assured, poor transportation and inadequate markets meant a continuing shortage of capital, which affected the quality of life.

Although different parts of the frontier challenged settlers in different ways, there were enough common threads to the pioneering experience to make it possible to generalize about pioneer life and women's response to it. During the initial period of settlement, women on all frontiers shared crude living conditions and similar domestic situations. Because of the shortage of capital and labor, early farming efforts were on a small diversified scale and demanded the participation of the entire family, especially women. The first years of settlement, therefore, continued the trail experience by demanding that women depart from cultural and social behavioral norms for the sake of their family's survival. The sense of dislocation some felt initially stemmed from this enforced departure from familiar behavior. The early years of settlement, in fact, would test many facets of the cultural framework which women had brought west with them. The test suggested how firmly women clung to the framework and the meaning which it could provide for their lives even on the frontier.

As one Oregon woman noted, the frontier was "a hard country for woman." It was hard, she knew, because "things . . . are rather in a primitive state." Crude housing was part of this "primitive state," which all women shared no matter where they settled on the farming frontier. A dugout or sod house on the plains, a small shack, cabin, or hole in the Far West served for shelter. Other more exotic alternatives appeared. "During father's trip he had seen two stumps standing a few feet apart," recollected one pioneer later, "and he laughingly told mother she might live in them. . . . She insisted that father clean them out, put on a roof, and we moved in, a family of eight persons." Whatever the arrangements, home was often open to the weather, uncomfortable, crowded, with little privacy. Families lived for months in these dwellings, sometimes for years, as money and time went into other improvements. Early homes challenged domestic ideals and the concept of gentility, and women were sometimes discouraged. "What a contrast to the wheels of time unrolle to our view, compared with our home in Ill. one year since," sighed one.

The preparation of food, an important domestic duty, was arduous without the familiar ingredients and utensils. An Oregon pioneer of the 1840s described setting up housekeeping with her new husband with only one stew kettle (for making coffee, bread, and cooking meat) and three knives. Since the stoves with which many pioneer families had set out over the Oregon Trail had been too heavy to survive the trip, this woman, like so many others, did all her cooking over an open fire. No wonder some pioneers looked back to this initial period with distaste. "I assure you," Maria Cutting wrote, "we had many privations and Hardships to endure and O such makeouts sometimes having to use shorts instead of flour, sometimes sugar sometimes none."

Yet others took great pride in preparing tasty food despite all the obstacles; women's response to difficult living conditions often seemed related to their early attitude to emigration. As one Iowa pioneer explained, "I came here willingly believing it to be for the best and am determined to try with the assistance of Providence to make the best out of it." In any case, they knew they had no options beyond making "the best out of it." There was no returning home. As Margaret Wilson told her mother in a letter written in 1850, "You will wonder how I can bear it, but it is unavoidable, and I have to submit without complaining."

No matter how women reacted to primitive living conditions, few cared for their primitive neighbors. Oregon Trail diaries revealed that many women feared Indians, especially males. On the trail, however, the wagon train offered fainthearted women the protection of numbers; in any case, offensive natives were always left behind as the company moved on. Now settled, however temporarily, women on many parts of the frontier found themselves living in the midst of Indians.

They didn't like it. "I suppose Mother had more trouble there [in Oregon], really, than she had on the road; because we were surrounded by Indians," one daughter explained. Even friendly Indians made women anxious by their way of silently appearing, wanting food or just a look at the white woman and her children. Even though their accounts show them dealing directly and even courageously with Indian visits, women felt vulnerable in these meetings. Many were persuaded that the Indian men were particularly aggressive when their husbands were away. Whether this was true or merely reflected the women's view of themselves as the weaker sex is unclear. Certainly, their actions showed few signs of weakness. Sarah Sutton was typical. When Indians came for food when her men were absent, she dealt with them by jerking "a tent pole and laying it about her with such good effect that she had her squat of Indians going on a double quick in a very short time." At other times, she wielded a pistol rather than the tent pole. Still, the incidents were unpleasant, and unnerving.

Although women sometimes trained Indians as servants, they described them at best as shiftless and curious, at worst as treacherous, savage, and cruel. Only rarely could white women reach across the barriers of race and culture to establish sympathetic contact with Indian women. Most accepted cultural generalizations and were convinced that "the native inhabitants must soon submit to 'manifest destiny.'" Pioneer women were unsympathetic to the clash between cultures and unaware that white behavior often provoked the Indian behavior they disliked so much. In one sense they were right to be suspicious and fearful, since the settlement period was punctuated by Indian violence and hostility. The Indian Wars in Oregon from 1855 to 1858 were only one example that the so-called inferior race could strike out in a deadly fashion against white settlers and their families. But women's negative attitudes increased their sense of vulnerability and isolation. "We had no neighbors nor company save a straggling land hunter, or the native Indians," recalled Susannah Willeford, an Iowa pioneer. "The latter were seldom if ever welcome visitors as far as I was concerned."

Isolation from white women also shaped most women's responses to the earliest period of settlement. Although women had their own domestic circles, they missed female friends. A husband might be no substitute for a close friend or relative of their own sex, as Nellie Wetherbee discov-

ered. "I have been very blue," she wrote in her journal, "for I cannot make a friend like mother out of Henry. . . . It's a bore—and Mother is so different and home is so different. . . . Oh dear dear." The difficulty of finding female friends stemmed, of course, from the scattered pattern of settlement (the Oregon Donation Law, for example, provided each family with 640 acres, thus ensuring isolation) and also from the fact that there were fewer women than men on the frontier in the first years. As Mollie Sanford noted in her diary, "I do try to feel that it is all for the best to be away off here [Nebraska]. I can see and feel that it chafes mother's spirit. . . . If the country would only fill up. . . . We do not see a woman at all. All men, single or bachelors, and one gets tired of them."

But the sexual imbalance was not so great as many popular accounts have suggested. The 1850 male–female ratio for the country as a whole was 106 men to every 100 women, while in rural Oregon that same year, there were approximately 137 men to every 100 women. By 1860, however, the sex ratio in frontier counties approximated that in the East. Various studies of frontier settlements show, then, that the frontier was not overwhelmingly masculine. But given the role female friendship played in women's lives and the difficulties which made it hard for women to meet, the loneliness they felt was understandable.

Real isolation was, however, a short-lived phenomenon, usually lasting only two or three years on most parts of the frontier. Some of the men turning up in the census or in Mollie Sanford's diary were preparing homesteads for their families. The immigration pattern of Whidbey Island, near the coast of Washington, suggests the rapidity of the settlement process. Attracted by its fertile prairie land and pleasant climate, Isaac Ebey, an 1848 pioneer from Missouri, selected the island for his future home. By the time his wife, Rebecca, and their two sons joined him three years later, there were several other families on Whidbey and more coming. In June 1852 Rebecca was writing, "We have plenty of company four families of us here 12 children." Although her guests eventually moved to their own claims on the island, Rebecca's diary catalogues numerous visitors, both new emigrants and old. After Rebecca died in 1853, emigrants to Whidbey included the Ebey cousins, her husband's father, mother, brother, his two sisters, some children, and a single man who eventually married her daughter the next year. Nor was the Ebey clan the only one on the island, for other families as well as some unmarried settlers also migrated to Whidbey during these few years. Loneliness may have been a very real part of the frontier experience for women, but total isolation for an extended length of time usually was not.

If women shared common physical and social conditions on the farming frontier, they also shared a similar family environment. The stereotypical view of the frontier family suggests a familial experience which modern women would find oppressive and burdensome. Most historians have casually asserted that women on the frontier routinely married at fourteen or fifteen and that they then proceeded to bear children with monotonous regularity. Families with ten or twelve children are pictured as the norm. With such heavy maternal responsibilities, to say nothing of the arduous nature of pioneer life itself, pioneer women not only worked harder than women in the East, this interpretation implies, but differed from them culturally. Census data show that throughout the nineteenth century the size of American families was shrinking, not because of reduced mortality rates, but because women bore fewer and fewer children. In 1800 white women who reached menopause bore on the average 7.04 children. Forty years later the figure had fallen to 6.14, reaching 4.24 in 1880. A dramatic difference in family size on the frontier would imply a "frontier" set of values.

Unfortunately, there are not enough studies of the frontier family in the trans-Mississippi West to allow a definitive description of frontier family structure, but the stereotype appears to be misleading. Western women's fertility patterns were not very different from those of other women in the country. One study based on the 1860 census returns ranging from New Hampshire to Kansas, for example, revealed lower fertility rates in frontier townships that those in the more populated areas directly to the east. Young children who were unable to contribute to the frontier family's welfare in those crucial early years were not an asset but a burden.

"Will I be a happy beloved wife, with a good husband, happy home, and small family," Mollie Sanford, a Nebraska pioneer, had mused, "or an abused, deserted one, with eight or nine small children crying for their daily bread?" Scattered studies of different parts of the trans-Mississippi frontier suggest that Mollie Sanford's chances for marital satisfaction in the terms in which she posed them were good. The typical frontier household, though somewhat larger than those in the East, was made up of parents and a few children living together. An analysis of Iowa frontier families showed families with one to four children living at home, while a detailed study of a Texas pioneer area with 896 families turned up only twelve families with ten or more children. The "average" family household in this part of Texas contained four children, but fully *half* of the families had three children or fewer living at home. The 1850 manuscript for Oregon yielded similar results. Since none of these figures take into account children who were grown and on their own or include infant mortality figures, they do not disclose how many children women actually conceived and bore, but the figures suggest that pioneer households in the West were comparable in size with the American experience elsewhere.

Women on the frontier were, then, most often wives and mothers. Their small households suggest they believed in limiting the size of their families. Certainly contraceptive information was available. Newspapers between 1820 and 1873 advertised both contraceptives and abortifacients, while pamphlets, birth-control circulars, popular health books, and books also told women how to control conception. Contraceptive practices were long described in folklore. Although personal testimony concerning the use of birth control on the frontier is rare, a few references show that frontier women knew of and practiced birth control. An Oregon midwife, for example, described an abortion, a method of family limitation which increased during the nineteenth century. "I went to the woman's place several times," she recollected. "She had staged several sham battles. You see, they didn't do what was right, and had tried, too soon, to have the baby and get rid of it. When it was far along, it was a killing job. Hot salt water was what they used, and it sometimes passed. After the woman herself would be about to die as well as the baby, they'd call for help."

If pioneer women were not the fecund breeders of popular history, neither they nor their husbands were the excessively youthful group so often described. Most studies of pioneer families show husbands typically in their thirties or forties, with wives several years younger. Nor did women marry routinely in their early teens. One pioneer woman recalled a proposal when she was thirteen. "I said, *no! Why I'm only a child*. I have never given marriage a thought yet." Studies of age of marriage in Oregon and Texas turn up little evidence of early unions. Information which exists on the frontier family seems to suggest that married women on the farming frontier did not have the burdens of youthful inexperience or swarms of young children added to the difficulties of creating a new life in the wilderness.

These relatively small families, of course, provided the context for women's emotional and work lives during the initial years of settlement, when the interaction with outsiders was limited. Many pioneer women resolved consciously, as did Susannah Willeford, "to devote my time, life and energies to the welfare and interest of my family." This was no small resolve; women's work for and with their families was extraordinary. Since few pioneers arrived with substantial financial or material resources, and since hired help was unavailable, every family was thrown back on itself in the struggle to get started. All cooperated in the work of establishing the farm, but because women often were the only adults besides their husbands, they had to contribute more than a woman's share.

"I am maid of all traids," one woman remarked in her diary in 1853. As had proved true on the trail, necessity blurred the relationship between men's and women's work. The tasks seemed endless. Women did heavy outside "male" chores, helping to dig cellars, to build cabins, "as there was no other man . . . [Father] could get to help him," helped with the plowing and planting, again since "there were neither man nor boy that we could hire in the country." Then there were the conventional female jobs, sewing, "sweeping dusting churning ironing baking bread and pies dishwashing &c." And always there was laundry, an arduous undertaking which many women seem to have particularly disliked. "Dreaded washing day," wrote one, and added, "And as Mr. Taylor is not well he brings me water I finish by noon then scrub in the after noon feeling quite tired." Women cared for vegetable gardens, cows, chickens. As farmers, cooks, seamstresses, and laundresses, their labor contributed to the family's well-being and survival in almost every way.

But women did more than these tasks, since they shared "a strong desire to provide the necessary comforts for our family." In many cases they seem to have become small-scale economic entrepreneurs. One resourceful but not unusual woman, for example, started out by cutting up wagon covers to make shirts to sell to the Indians. Then she moved on to making gloves for soldiers stationed nearby, a task with which her husband helped. "So, before spring, they were turning out very handsome gloves, also buckskin money belts." Later, as emigrants began to come into Oregon, she baked bread, pies, and cookies to sell. Female enterprises changed as opportunities changed, though the sale of butter and eggs seems to have provided a fairly steady source of income for women. These funds were especially important because of the chronic shortage of capital on the frontier. And as one observer pointed out, women often supported their families while their husbands learned how to farm. Occasionally women viewed their earnings as their own, but most often they were not a source of economic independence but rather a means of supplementing the family's income.

"Female hired help was not to be obtained,"

one man pointed out when reflecting on his pioneer years. "I assisted my wife all I could—probably did as much housework as she did." Continuing the pattern emerging on the journey west, men performed some female chores. Letters and journals show them helping with the washing, the cooking, and caring for children. But as on the trip west, men usually assumed these responsibilities only occasionally, when their wives were tired, ill, or in childbirth.

Much of the heavy labor women did initially could also be categorized as helping husbands out in the absence of male assistance. But wives more routinely assumed male responsibilities than their husbands took on female responsibilities. When men left their homesteads, as they did when gold was discovered, or when they went off to fight Indians, do political business, or herd cattle, they were often gone for months at a time. The women who stayed behind were left in charge. "As we live on a farm," wrote one, "whatever is done I have got to attend to and so I have a great deal of out doors work." As she listed her chores, they included caring for hogs, hens, milking the cows, and running the dairy. A hired man worked on the grain. On the plains, men often hired themselves out for cash, leaving their wives to oversee the crops and animals for weeks.

As their economic enterprises, their letters, and journals indicate, women were both practically and emotionally involved in economic matters as they sought to improve the family economic status. Even Kate Blaine, a Methodist minister's wife from the Northeast, wished she could be making some money. "If I were not the preacher's wife I should take in [washing]. . . . It is very profitable," she confessed. Despite the claim of nineteenth-century culture that there was a gap between woman's world, the home, and man's world, the workplace, the two coincided on the frontier. Nor were women "disinterested" in economic matters. As women shared men's work, they adopted men's perspectives.

Home was not the quiet and cozy retreat that nineteenth-century culture envisioned, but a busy center of endless chores and economic ventures. Moreover, women were determined to

defend it. One who recounted how a flood destroyed her family's investment added, "It did seem almost hopeless to start practically from the beginning again, but I was willing to do it." Destitution on the plains in the 1870s produced the same kind of female resolution when women refused to admit economic defeat. A spectacular case of courage and devotion to property was provided by the illiterate widow of a California squatter. When the rightful claimant to the land (who had killed her squatter husband) tried to drive her off the property, gun in hand, the widow seized her own pistols, approached her opponent, and dared him shoot her dead. Her defiance proved too much for him, and the woman retained the land to which she was so devoted.

If the frontier blurred sexual distinctions in the world of work, it also tolerated other departures from the female sphere. Women were occasionally involved in politics. Widow Sims of Arkansas noted, "The papers are full of Politics as this is the year for the Presidential elections . . . of course I take sides as every one does so I espouse the cause of Filmore." At least one woman did more than talk. "During these years," David Staples, an early pioneer on the West Coast recalled, "Mrs. Staples cast as many votes as any man. Voters from Arkansas and Missouri, who could not read would walk around . . . and ask her for whom they should vote. She would take the ballot, and running her pencil across certain names, would say I would not vote for that man. By this means, she very materially altered the complexion of the results." Women occasionally conducted religious services in the absence of preachers. They filed claims, took care of business, and, as one wrote, "I had a gun and could shoot with any of them."

The activities of these self-reliant pioneer women defied a number of nineteenth-century stereotypes about women. But this did not necessarily mean that pioneer women abandoned the larger conception of women's nature or that they ceased to value female culture. Nor did it mean that they attempted to work out a new definition of woman's sphere. Their behavior and their attitude toward their family, their attempts to replicate female culture suggest that their new environment, although it changed what they did, had only a limited impact on their views.

One might expect, for example, that women's economic importance to the family enterprise might result in a reordering of family relations and the reallocation of power within the family. Ideology, of course, characterized the nineteenth-century family as a patriarchy, with men making decisions and women obediently accepting them. Actually, all American women probably had considerably more power than this model implied. As foreign visitors to the United States noted, "Woman is the centre and lawgiver in the home of the New World." Ideology never tells all.

If ideology does not describe reality, the nature of power relations in families of the past is elusive. Power is difficult to measure at any time. Who wins or loses family confrontations obviously reveals something about the allocation of power and can more easily be observed than the ways in which family members may influence or modify decisions. Yet any judgment about who wields power and how much depends on the latter process as well as the former. In dealing with the nineteenth-century frontier family, the normal problems of analysis are compounded by the lack of direct information about the day-to-day decision process. The privacy of family life, symbolized by the notion of home as retreat, worked against recording situations which might reveal power dynamics. As Elizabeth Lord, reminiscing about her pioneer life in Oregon, pointed out, "Of many things connected with our family I do not care to speak in these pages, such as my marriage, the loss of my first child and the birth of my second, which meant much to all of us and was a great event in our lives, and is something that especially belongs to ourselves."

Conclusions about the power structure of frontier families are, thus, drawn from hints rather than from direct evidence. Census data provide a few uncertain clues. They show, for example, that there was no great disparity of age between frontier husbands and wives, which may suggest some limitations of male authority. The small surplus of males on the frontier gave single women some freedom to pick and choose before marriage, which could have affected the nature of the marriage relation. And the falling birth rate may signify female power or a process of mutual decision-making. Certainly we know that when husbands were away in the mines, at the legislature, or on the range, women had real authority in their families.

But what evidence there is suggests that though women were co-partners in the frontier adventure, husbands still made major decisions. Men seem to have determined whether the family would move on to a better piece of land or pursue a business opportunity just as they had decided to bring their family west. Yet, in both cases, men initiated discussions but did not dictate. They consulted their wives, and it may be that female power was really the right of consultation. Both men and women testify to the interaction. Milo Smith, a Colorado pioneer, pointed out, "There is not an enterprise that I have ever gone into that I have not talked the details over with my wife before hand," while another pioneer described a lengthy period of negotiation between herself and her husband, who wanted to take up a new claim. "Finally, after much deliberation on my part, and persuasion on the part of my husband, I consented to taking up a . . . claim," she reported, but only after learning that there would be a colony of thirty settlers from Baltimore nearby.

Women on the frontier did make many minor decisions, although they still deferred to men, negotiated with them, and often worked for their goals indirectly. A revealing account of an Iowa pioneer family shows how many women operated. Although the husband planned to support the family by doing carpenter work, "Mother had different ideas. During his absence she had accumulated nine cows. . . . She was able to support the family nicely. . . . But milking cows did not appeal to father; one week from the time he returned there was only one left." Yet this was not the end of dairying after all, even though a definitive male decision appeared to have been made. The woman did not block her husband, but with an inheritance she again invested in cows. With the proceeds from dairying she bought winter clothing and supplies. The message was clear. Eventually the family acquired hogs to help consume the milk; stock raising ended as the family's main economic activity. Female deference and patience succeeded.

Throughout, women were careful to maintain the idea of male superiority. As Kate Robins explained to her mother in New England, "Abner would not like it if he knew I sent for you to send me things." The implication was that women would work behind men's backs and avoid direct confrontations with male authority. Frontier women were not attempting to upset the traditional male–female relationship; they did not consciously covet male power. Women's letters and journals describing the ways in which they managed when their husbands were away make this point explicitly. "My husband was absent so much of the time," wrote one woman, "engrossed in mining or in politics, that the care of the family and the farm was left entirely to me, and I was physically unequal to this double burden." Since her reminiscences show her to be a woman with great physical energy, one suspects that it was the constant responsibility which she disliked. Women were reluctant to take on the burden of decision-making alone, and when they did, it was with the expectation that they would do so only temporarily.

Mary Ann Sims, a widow at twenty-five, expressed her anguish at having to play a man's role on a more permanent basis. "I have been busy all day casting up accounts and attending to business," she wrote in January 1856. "I had no idie that it was as much trouble to superentend and take care of a family as it is I feel tired sometimes." A few weeks later she added, "Allway beeing accostum to have someone to depende on it is quite new to attend to business transactions and it pesters me no little." Two years later she observed, "I see a woman cannot fill the sphere of a woman and man too." By 1859 her thinking had crystallized. "It has often been a source of regret to me that my daughters were not sons a man can change his station in life but a woman scarcely ever arrives at more exalted station than the one which she is born in if we ecept those whose minds are masculine enough to cope with men, a woman whose mind is supirior and whose feelings has been cast in a more exquisit mould to be compell to associate with *courser* minds who cannot understand is compill to feel loanly." Cultural prescriptions were so strong that the widow found herself physically and emotionally exhausted by male responsibilities. On the other hand, despite many offers of marriage, she remained single for several years. A study of frontier Texas illustrates a similar reluctance on the part of propertied widows to remarry. Perhaps the burden of decision-making lessened as women learned "to live alone and act for [themselves]."

Possibly women's fundamental importance in the early years of settlement set definite limits to female deference. "The women were not unaware" of their role in helping to support the family, one reminiscence noted, "and were quite capable of scoring a point on occasion when masculine attitudes became too bumptious." Though there may have been limits to deference and though women may have felt an underlying tension because of the contrast between the passive female stereotype and their own lives, most tried to observe cultural prescriptions concerning familial behavior. Direct confrontations occurred but appear to have been unusual. The evidence is, of course, weighted toward literate women, the very ones exposed to cultural role definitions. But studies of peasant women who prove to be less independent than educated women suggest that a dramatic reallocation of power within humble pioneer families was unlikely.

An examination of letters, journals, and memoirs which touch upon marriage and courtship also indicate how many women carried conventional ideals west with them. Although it has been suggested that frontier women were drab work partners with few sentimental illusions, many of them held to romantic views appropriate for any true woman. Nineteenth-century society had glorified romantic love as a necessary precondition for marriage. Advice books, novels, and schooling described the rapture which a potential husband could be expected to inspire. The rigors of frontier life modified but did not undercut the value of romance.

In fact, the situation of single women on the frontier encouraged romantic fancy. Scattered studies of pioneer families indicate that single women married not in their early teens but in their late teens and early twenties. The sex ratio on the frontier meant that young women did not have to accept the first available suitor who presented himself but could bide their time and choose among several. Frontier demography made romantic ideas and love and courtship meaningful for a woman could wait for "one of those purely spiritual and intellectual creatures" to appear rather than accepting a humdrum and unworthy admirer.

The selection of a mate was not without a functional aspect, however, which it may have lacked in settled urban areas (but probably not in farm communities). "Young women were really sincere when they sought to excel in the preparation of household articles," one pioneer woman commented. "Their teaching was such that such excellence brought its reward in desirable matrimonial favor and the final fulfillment of woman's mission in life." Both sexes agreed that industriousness and competence were desirable for a marriage. A series of letters from a young Nebraska pioneer to his mother reveals this perspective. "You wanted to know," he wrote, "when I was going to get married. Just as quick as I can get money ahead to get a cow and to get married. I want to before I commence shucking corn if I can to Aunt Jennie's oldest girl. She is a good girl and knows how to work. . . . A fellow cant do much good on a place when he has everything to do both indoors and out both. She says if we marry right away, she is going to do the work in the house and shuck down the row when I am gathering corn, but I will be glad enough to get rid of the housework." After his marriage, he reported with satisfaction, "She makes everything look neat and tidy and is willing to help me all she can."

The realization that marriage represented a working partnership hardly precluded romantic ecstasy, at least on the part of women. Capable as she was of seeing through some of romantic ideology ("How pleasant it would be to have a comfortable little home with one I *love*. I am afraid the anticipation is more pleasant than the participation would be"), Elizabeth Wardall faithfully recorded her raptures in a courtship lasting several years. "O: what a blessed thing is *love*," she wrote, while Harriet Strong told her future husband, "How glad I am *love* is indescribable. I would dislike to think anything that *could be fathomed* could effect you and me as it does."

Nor did marriage necessarily dull tender feelings. Women did not see their husbands merely as work partners, although this aspect of the relationship may well have provided a strong basis for their affection. Susannah Willeford described her husband as "my first and only choice. The man to whom I had first given my heart and confidence. The man with whom I had sacrificed my home and friends, the man with whom I had shed tears and shared his gladness and with whom I had shared many difficulties and by whom I had borne eight children." Her words convey their warm relationship, as do the testimonials of many others about their marriage. Pioneer wives both expected and experienced the feelings which nineteenth-century literature suggested were part of married life. Separation often led women to express these emotions in romantic terms. Roselle Putnam called her husband "the idol of my heart" and remarked, "Never did I know what it was to sufer anciety untill I knew what it was to be separated from [him]," while the long-married Mrs. Stearns spoke of her husband's "dear face." When husbands finally returned, women like Rebecca Ebey captured the emotional tone of their marriages: "And one thing which made [the day] . . . seem more exceedingly delightful, My dear husband arrived safe at home."

Nor was love without a sexual component. Although an argument has been made that nineteenth-century women neither wanted nor enjoyed physical affection, scattered evidence from married and single women on the frontier shows that passion had a place. Since nineteenth-century women were reticent about sex, these references are all the more remarkable. Wrote one woman to her husband in 1867, "Dear Husband you say you think that I could get plenty to hug me well I don't know whether I could or not I don't think I look very hugable now at least to any but your self as there is no-one knows how well I can hug but you." That a chaste hug was perhaps not what she meant is suggested by a letter written a few weeks later when she revealed, "I dreamed of seeing you last night and I thought I had a pair of twins." In a similarly suggestive manner, Kate Blaine told her mother she missed her absent husband as a bedfellow. "Now when I sleep alone the bed is so cold and my feet will not keep warm." A few women were less ambiguous than Kate. Mary Sims lamented she had not met a suitable marriage partner and acknowledged the sexual satisfactions she missed. "I know that there is not a woman . . . that is capable of feeling a more devoted affection than [I] I am naturely impolsive and affectionate and I loved my husban[d] with all intencity that my nature was capable of feeling but I must confess it was more the passionate ideial love of youth," she wrote. Though she implied that passion should disappear with maturity, it was not so for her. Her final diary entries show her struggling to overcome her feelings for a man she described as wild and dissipated.

It is certainly true, as Phoebe Judson pointed out, that "the inconveniences of our environment and the constant drudgery eventually took all the romance and poetry out of our farm life." Phoebe was, of course, talking not of marriage but of her idealized vision of farming life, but her comment raises a valid point. Pioneer women worked hard most of the time, and their difficult life certainly put limits on flights of romantic fancy. But they were more than work drudges and their occasional references to love suggest that the roman-

tic revolution had affected their attitudes and expectations.

The majority of frontier women were wives and mothers during the early years of settlements; primitive conditions and women's workloads complicated motherhood. But the idea that frontier women had no time for the luxury of maternal feelings, considered so central to the conception of motherhood, and even less time to lavish attention on their children, needs some modification. Frontier women obviously worked hard, but this did not mean that they did not take their role of mother seriously or that they were unconscious of a nineteenth-century mother's duty. "How forsably I feel the responsibility of a Mother," sighed one.

Only rarely did frontier women reveal how they felt about pregnancy and birth (which they called a time of sickness). Giving birth was, however, part of a "female ritual" which called for the involvement and support of other women on the frontier as it did in the East. To be alone at such a moment was a dreadful fate to be avoided. "I do not know what they will do when she is *confined* not having any Neighbours," wrote one woman, expressing the common fear of being without female support at such a moment. When it was at all possible, frontier women gathered round during childbirth, with little thought of monetary reward. The ritual had rules. "A woman that was expecting had to take good care that she had plenty fixed for her neighbors when they got there," explained one frontier woman. "There was no telling how long they was in for. There wasn't no paying these friends so you had to treat them good."

If women were reticent before birth, and gave few indications of what their views of motherhood were, not so afterward: "Well, old journal," Almira Beam exclaimed in 1861. "You have been rather silent these few months past: but it could not be helped. You have great cause to be thankful that we ever met. Arthur is asleep in his cradle below, and mother is getting dinner." In their letters east, women indicated their deep emotional concern for their children, recording the smallest details about their babies—their clothes, habits, small achievements. "I would tell you that he is the prettiest baby in the world," wrote Sarah Everett from Kansas, "if I was not intending to send his likeness." Occasionally mothers expressed ambivalent feelings about their female children. Two years earlier Sarah had described another baby as "the newcomer who seems to cause more rejoicing among her distant relatives than those at home—we think of calling [her] Clara Elizabeth. . . . It isn't of much consequence however seeing it's nothing but a girl anyway."

Yet four months later Sarah reported the death of "*sweet little Clara*—She brought a great deal of sunshine into our homely cabin this summer, and when she was carried out of it, it certainly seemed very dark to me." Whatever Sarah's earlier comment meant, Clara's death revealed the way in which her mother saw the maternal relationship as central and emotionally absorbing. A child's death robbed the mother of one "more dear to me than any thing ever had been." The sentimentalism of such testimonials strikes the twentieth century as maudlin, but it was typical in the nineteenth century. Though children's death on the frontier was a fact (twenty of the thirty-five reported deaths in Cass County on the Nebraska frontier in 1860 were children six or younger), the attitude was anything but pragmatic.

The nineteenth century defined the regulation of children and the formation of their characters as a mother's central tasks. Life on the frontier complicated them, as Mollie Sanford suggested. "Mother . . . fears I am losing all the dignity I ever possessed." "I know I am getting demoralized, but I should be more so, to mope around and have no fun." The pressure of other duties and the lure of the wilderness made regulating children difficult. Children remembered running "wild in the woods without any restraints," "carefree all through the woods and . . . hills." Mother, noted Wilda Belknap in her autobiography, seemed to have little time to devote to the children after infancy. But this hardly signified an abnegation of maternal responsibility. Children also remembered punishments and disciplinary measures. In later years pioneer women often pointed to their children as symbols of their life-work, testifying to the importance they attributed to their work as mothers.

When they could, then, pioneer mothers molded and educated their children. Rebecca Ebey, a pioneer from Virginia, taught her children lessons, but not just in reading and writing. "We . . . spend our time in training the young minds of our children in the principles of Christ and creating within them a thirst for moral knowledge," she explained. If knowledge of Christian principles was one goal, the inculcation of the habits of steady industry was another. Women expressed disapproval of idleness and indolence in children and sought to encourage them to be useful. On the frontier mothers expected their children to work, so much so that one recollection of a pioneer childhood stated the obvious, "You will gather from what I have related that work and plenty of it was the lot of pioneer children."

Tasks were not assigned solely on the basis of sex. Girls recalled plowing, herding cows, carrying wood and water, while boys helped mothers wash clothes and dishes. "I think the boys ought to do something," explained one mother. Just as responsibilities of the sexes overlapped in the adult world, so, too, did they in the children's world. But as time passed and children grew, sex distinctions were stressed. Daughters recalled mothers clarifying appropriate female behavior. Both sexes acquired knowledge of sexual boundaries, as records show. One reminiscence tells of "Margaret Isabell's sons, . . . teenagers . . . [who] had held their mother up so she could milk the cow. She was still weak from the birth of the baby, but milking a cow was 'woman's work' so they would not do it." Girls recalled their introduction to domesticity as they acted as a "mother's right hand." This was an apprenticeship for marriage, as Amanda Gaines explained. "I assist Mother in house-hold duties which are various. She is preparing me for a Farmer's wife." Another daughter wondered whether she had any existence aside from the domestic routine, for her life was "so prescribed for me by my family environment that I do not know who I am."

She did know what she did, however: washing, cooking, and assisting "dear old mother." Even recreation could be sex-bound, with girls riding, visiting, and picking wildflowers, while the "boys swam with Father . . . and trapped animals."

Since the frontier family worked together, it was natural that women shared child care with their husbands, a departure from nineteenth-century theory, which assigned child care exclusively to women. Women expected and wanted assistance, not only because of the work involved, but because of the need to clarify standards. Women assumed that their husbands would introduce sons to the male world and take responsibility for their development at the appropriate time. This might occur relatively early in the child's development. As one woman explained, one of her boys was a problem. "His pa is gone so much that he is becoming a great deal of trouble to me I have often heard it said that little boys would not be industrious about everything under their mother's controll . . . I find it so, They become so accustomed to their mother's commands . . . that they get so they do not mind it." Her conclusion was predictably, "When the little boys become old enough to do some work they need a father to show them and to push them forward to make them industrious."

In the first few years following emigration to the West, frontier women helped create a new life for their families. The ways in which they went about their duties and the ways in which they related to other members of their families were influenced by their culture just as much as by the new environment. Tired and overworked as they were, many of them still seem to have had the energy to worry about standards and norms. Necessary modifications were, of course, made. The concept of gentility was clearly inappropriate on the frontier, as was the notion of woman as ornamental (an extension of the concept of domesticity much criticized by its advocates, like Sarah Hale). Child rearing demanded encouraging traits not usually stressed in safer environments. "Children here have to learn self reliance and independence as well as their parents," explained one parent.

But the truth was that female culture shaped the ways in which women perceived the frontier experience and provided a means of orientation to it. Even though frontier conditions forced them into manly pursuits and led them to modify some of their standards, they hardly pressed for a liberation from female norms and culture. For much of the "freedom" which women experienced was the freedom to work even harder than they had before, with dramatic results. "I am a very old woman," wrote twenty-nine-year-old Sarah Everett. "My face is thin sunken and wrinkled, my hands bony withered and hard." Why should women lay claim to male tasks in addition to their own? The domestic ideal was a goal toward which women could direct their efforts, the promise of a day when their lives would not be so hard, their tasks so numerous. Domesticity, with its neat definition of woman's place, helped women bear what they hoped were temporary burdens and reestablished their sense of identity and self-respect. It served as a link with the past.

Frontier women gave many indications of their desire to hold on to the conventions of female culture no matter how unfavorable the circumstances seemed. "Home," crude and impermanent though it might be, received the kind of attention which would have pleased the proponents of domesticity. Though the cabin or sod house might not be the cozy nook pictured in stories of Western life, women hoped to make it one as they papered their walls with old newspapers or tacked up cloth to make the house snug and cheery. Old rags became rugs, old dresses curtains. A keg might become a footstool, upholstered with an old pair of pants. Thread turned into lace doilies. Outside, women planted flowers and trees from seeds they had brought with them and generally tried to maintain the standards of domesticity and hospitality with which they had been familiar before emigration. Although they often wore rough and rugged clothing, even buckskin trousers, pioneer women found "all these things . . . dreadfully annoying." As one pointed out, "We were always wishing for enough money to buy better clothes." The interest in fashion and the attempts to dress in style were symbolic of the intention to remain feminine. The "career" of a mid-century Oregon pioneer is typical. "Although I had now been absent from civilization—otherwise Ohio—for more than a year," she wrote, "I was still considered an authority on the matter of dress and fashion. I was consulted and acted as adviser whenever a new cloak or gown was made . . . I trimmed hats, literally, for the entire neighborhood, and I knew less than nothing about millinery."

The determination to maintain ties to the traditional female world and to create a female community where, in fact, there was none, was apparent in the energy with which frontier women sustained old friendships and associations. Mrs. Coe remarked in a letter to a friend in 1863 that she had written hundreds of letters, so many "that my Diary has dwindled away to almost nothing—All my romance has become reality—and as for poetry—it has vanish'd, resolved itself into and, mingled with the landscape around me." Pioneer women wrote letters to female relatives and friends in the East, detailing their lives, providing all the vital information which was the basis for an intimate female dialogue. They enclosed material of their dresses, described dress patterns, sent pictures of their children; they asked scores of minute questions about the health of family and friends, marriages and deaths, fashion, religion. "The most trivial things that you can mention about each other have a great interest to us way out here," Mary Ann Adair explained to her mother and sister.

Bonds of affection sustained the dialogue between pioneer women and their Eastern friends and relatives, but that dialogue had emotional costs. Slow and irregular mails which could take up to a year contributed to the natural anxiety women felt for the health and well-being of those far away. "My dear mother," wrote one woman, "you do not know how miserable I feel about you, for I have not received a line from any of my family." And as years passed, a new fear appeared. "Everything has changed so much at home since I left, that I expect I should feel like a stranger now." And with time, it was also possible that those at home would cease to care. "I have waited almost a year and a half hoping to receive a letter from you," Elisabeth Adams wrote from Iowa to her sister. "Why do you do so? Do you not wish to have intercourse with me? Do you not *love me*? I am sure I love you, and the longer I live the more I feel the want of affection from others, the more my heart yearns for kindness and love from my own family, I mean my *father's family*."

A common theme runs through the correspondence. "I want you to come if you can and as soon as you can for no doubt I shal feel my self very lonesome." Women's letters are filled with urgent invitations to friends and relatives to emigrate. Often over a period of years, encouragement and advice about the trip poured out of the West in hopes that friends from the old life could become part of the new. "I want you all here, then I would be perfectly contented," explained Louise Swift, while another woman told her sister, "When we get together again we will not be parted so easy."

If relatives and friends did not come West, women sustained ties with them by nourishing hopes of an Eastern visit. Eventually this hope was realized for a lucky few; other women remembered that, in the end, all would meet in heaven. Although some of their discussions about a heavenly meeting sound strange to modern ears, the emotional well-being of many pioneer women was sustained by their faith that the network of friends and relatives could be eternal. There is, perhaps, no greater testimony to the importance women far in the wilderness placed on female culture than the conviction that parts of it would be replicated in heaven.

While many women on the frontier devoted considerable energy to keeping alive the home network, feeling, as one young woman put it, "'Tis true we may have friends among strangers; but, ah, they are not parents, brothers nor sisters," most naturally attempted to establish new ties with other women as soon as possible. The trip overland had provided one opportunity for a new beginning. "Ever since I saw you in camp at Iowa (in '54)," Anna Goodell told Mary Bozarth, "you have looked and acted like my good Auth Sarah."

Proximity (which was a relative term) also determined friendships. Although the nearest neighbor might be miles away, women made a special point of visiting one another. Reciprocity was understood. "Mrs. Terry came this morning," wrote Almira Beam in her diary. "She says she will not come again until I come to see her." Soon Mrs. Terry had become "the best neighbor I ever saw, or heard of." Although women might go for days or even weeks without visitors, when they came, they stayed. The visits provided a relief from work and the opportunity for mutual support and sharing experiences. Rebecca Ebey's diary revealed the many rewards of female friendship. "I have been busy all day ironing cleaning up and mend the children's clothes Mrs. Alexander came over this evening to spend the night I was very much pleased to see her and had been look[ing] for her for a long time. . . . Mrs. Alexander is very cheerful and makes me feel much better than I have done to be awhile in her company."

Yet creating the new web of friendships on the frontier was difficult. Distance was an obstacle, at least at first. And cultural or social differences, usually overlooked, could stand in the way of intimacy. "Oh how I pine for association [of] some kindred mind," a young widow in Arkansas reflected. "All of my neighbours are good honest kind people but they seem to have no idile beyond their little s[p]here of action they do not appear to have a feeling nor aspiration higher than the things of life satisfying their physical wants." Aware of such distinctions on the frontier, she decided, "I had rather be aloan for I feel aloan." Loneliness for another woman made "my mind meditate upon former scenes in my life when I had doting loving relatives all around me."

With time, however, the new network took shape. Ties became warm as marriage bound families together and family, relatives, and old friends emigrated to swell the circle of love. A recent study of kinship in Oregon suggests that this process could be relatively rapid. At least 40 percent of the households listed in the 1850 census had kinship ties with one other household

and perhaps more. Census figures can only suggest the emotional significance of these relationships.

Despite the trials the frontier posed for them, many frontier women continued to see themselves as women within the mainstream of nineteenth-century culture. Although their courage, persistence, and physical endurance seem extraordinary to a later time, none of these women viewed themselves as extraordinary. Their diaries and letters show they expected to labor hard and long to achieve their goals. Though notes of weariness often creep into their accounts, they appear to have grumbled very little, at least on paper. Some complained of the monotony of farming life, though others seemed to enjoy the fact that there was "no bustleling crowd as in City or town to marr our peaceful happiness." They expressed discontent if family fortunes wavered. But they did not see themselves as drudges. Comments about Indian women invariably contrasted their own lot with that of the long-suffering Indian woman, who toiled like a slave for her husband.

The attitude of women during the early period of settlement was conditioned not only by their belief in hard work but also by limited expectations for personal happiness. Writing to her mother about a young niece's birthday, one woman advised telling the girl to remain a child "as long as she can, for the troubles of a woman, will come upon her soon enough!" The phrase "troubles of a woman" suggests something of the female frame of reference. Nineteenth-century ideology promised women fulfillment through marriage and motherhood, yet most knew the physical pains and dangers associated with bearing children and the disruption of female culture which marriage so often signified. In a highly mobile society, they witnessed the anguished separations which so frequently parted family and friends for life. The disparity between ideology and reality made it risky to assume happiness in any setting. The religious knew, of course, that God assigned both blessings and trials in life; Christians had to expect both. With such a frame of reference, nineteenth-century women were equipped to deal with the realities of their lives on the frontier far more easily than women of the present era could.

Their letters to friends and families in the East are good evidence of their plucky attitude to pioneer life. "Tell father I am not discourage and am not sorry I came," wrote Kate Robins to her brother, while Kate Blaine told her mother, "I could not have believed that I should have been as well contented as I am situated and must needs be here. We are deprived of all the conveniences I had considered indispensable before we came." Although most women were candid about the work required (Kate said, "A woman that can not endure almost as much as a horse has no business here, as there is no such thing as getting help") and frankly acknowledged their homesickness, they often were satisfied with their situation. "If our friends were here, we should be very contented, notwithstanding as we are deprived of many conveniences and comforts we might have enjoyed at home," Kate explained. Domestic triumphs, home improvements, new clothes, preaching in the vicinity were duly described and appreciated in the context of creating culture in the wilderness. The ultimate objective of many of the letter writer was, of course, persuasion. Still, the satisfactions cannot be discounted, nor can the women's underlying assumption of steady progress on the frontier. The future was promising in the West. So Phoebe Judson recalled, "The letters written back to our eastern friends gave such glowing descriptions of our fair dwelling place that some of them were encouraged to make arrangements to cross the plains the following year."

Women also told friends of the beauty of the West, of its good climate and healthy way of life. They noted the disappearance of old ailments and the feeling of bodily well-being they derived from the activities of outdoor life. And to their single relatives they described the "western gallant" perhaps not "dressed up gentlemen" but perhaps "better than anything you ever saw or heard of before."

Of course, it was in the interest of these women to attract friends and family to the West to aid in the task of building society anew. "I promise you a hearty welcome to my house" was a refrain of female letter writers. Yet the lures were real. As Pop from Arkansas pointed out, "If she was back and new as much as she does she would endure as much more as she has to get back to Oregon."

18

"GOUGE AND BITE, PULL HAIR AND SCRATCH": THE SOCIAL SIGNIFICANCE OF FIGHTING IN THE SOUTHERN BACKCOUNTRY

ELLIOTT J. GORN

Violence was an integral part of everyday life in antebellum America. In the nation's cities, members of competing fire companies routinely fought one another for the right to put out fires, local sporting matches often turned into general brawls, and bearbaiting and cockfighting continued to be favorite popular pastimes. On the western frontier, white encroachment and Indian resistance regularly led to the shedding of blood, and in every community court dockets recorded an alarming number of assaults, batteries, and other forms of criminal violence. As antebellum reformers never tired of pointing out, unrestrained violence seemed to be an essential component of the American character.

But while violence was endemic to antebellum society, nowhere did it play such a crucial social role as in the American South. Since the colonial era, southern men were notorious for the frequency and ferocity with which they fought one another, often for seemingly insignificant reasons. To call someone a "Scotsman" or a "rogue" was enough to provoke a fray that might cost a combatant his eye, his ear, or even his life. In this essay, Elliott J. Gorn surveys the ubiquitous violence of the American South and attempts to explain this peculiar regional trait by pointing to three interrelated characteristics. According to Gorn, the undeveloped state of the market economy emphasized fierce loyalties to kin and locality while the hard life of the backcountry promoted drinking, joking, and fighting as forms of personal release. Status and reputation in this rough-and-tumble world accrued to those who took personal risks lightly and were willing to inflict pain and permanent injury without flinching. In the southern backcountry, Gorn suggests, violence was truly the measure of a man.

"I would advise you when You do fight Not to act like Tygers and Bears as these Virginians do— Biting one anothers Lips and Noses off, and *gowging* one another—that is, thrusting out one anothers Eyes, and kicking one another on the Cods, to the Great damage of many a Poor Woman." Thus, Charles Woodmason, an itinerant Anglican minister born of English gentry stock, described the brutal form of combat he found in the Virginia backcountry shortly before the American Revolution. Although historians are more likely to study people thinking, governing, worshiping, or working, how men fight— who participates, who observes, which rules are followed, what is at stake, what tactics are allowed—reveals much about past cultures and societies.

The evolution of southern backwoods brawling from the late eighteenth century through the antebellum era can be reconstructed from oral traditions and travelers' accounts. As in most cultural history, broad patterns and uneven trends rather than specific dates mark the way. The sources are often problematic and must be used with care; some speculation is required. But the lives of common people cannot be ignored merely because they leave few records. "To feel for a feller's eyestrings and make him tell the news" was not just mayhem but an act freighted with significance for both social and cultural history.

As early as 1735, boxing was "much in fashion" in parts of Chesapeake Bay, and forty years later a visitor from the North declared that, along with dancing, fiddling, small swords, and card playing, it was an essential skill for all young Virginia gentlemen. The term "boxing," however, did not necessarily refer to the comparatively tame style of bare-knuckle fighting familiar to eighteenth-century Englishmen. In 1746, four deaths prompted the governor of North Carolina to ask for legislation against "the barbarous and inhuman manner of boxing which so much prevails among the lower sort of people." The colonial assembly responded by making it a felony "to cut out the Tongue or pull out the eyes of the King's Liege People." Five years later the assembly added slitting, biting, and cutting off noses to the list of offenses. Virginia passed similar legislation in 1748 and revised these statutes in 1772 explicitly to discourage men from "gouging, plucking, or putting out an eye, biting or kicking or stomping upon" quiet peaceable citizens. By 1786 South Carolina had made premeditated mayhem a capital offense, defining the crime as severing another's bodily parts.

Laws notwithstanding, the carnage continued. Philip Vickers Fithian, a New Jerseyite serving as tutor for an aristocratic Virginia family, confided to his journal on September 3, 1774:

> By appointment is to be fought this Day near Mr. *Lanes* two fist Battles between four young Fellows. The Cause of the battles I have not yet known; I suppose either that they are lovers, and one has in Jest or reality some way supplanted the other; or has in a merry hour called him a *Lubber* or a *thick-Skull,* or a *Buckskin,* or a *Scotsman,* or perhaps one has mislaid the other's hat, or knocked a peach out of his Hand, or offered him a dram without wiping the mouth of the Bottle; all these, and ten thousand more quite as trifling and ridiculous are thought and accepted as just Causes of immediate Quarrels, in which every diabolical Strategem for Mastery is allowed and practiced.

The "trifling and ridiculous" reasons for these fights had an unreal quality for the matter-of-fact Yankee. Not assaults on persons or property but slights, insults, and thoughtless gestures set young southerners against each other. To call a man a "buckskin," for example, was to accuse him of the poverty associated with leather clothing, while the epithet "Scotsman" tied him to the low-caste Scots-Irish who settled the southern highlands. Fithian could not understand how such trivial offenses caused the bloody battles. But his incomprehension turned to rage when he realized that spectators attended these "odious and filthy amusements" and that the fighters allayed their spontaneous passions in order to fix convenient dates and places, which allowed time for rumors to spread and crowds to gather. The Yankee concluded that only devils, prostitutes, or monkeys could sire creatures so unfit for human society.

Descriptions of these "fist battles," as Fithian called them, indicate that they generally began like English prize fights. Two men, surrounded by onlookers, parried blows until one was knocked or thrown down. But there the similarity ceased. Where as "Broughton's Rules" of the English ring specified that a round ended when either antagonist fell, southern bruisers only began fighting at this point. Enclosed not inside a formal ring—the "magic circle" defining a special place with its own norms of conduct—but within whatever space the spectators left vacant, fighters battled each other until one called enough or was unable to continue. Combatants boasted, howled, and cursed. As words gave way to action, they tripped and threw, gouged and butted, scratched and choked each other. "But what is worse than all," Isaac Weld observed, "these wretches in their combat endeavor to their utmost to tear out each other's testicles."

Around the beginning of the nineteenth century, men sought original labels for their brutal style of fighting. "Rough-and-tumble" or simply "gouging" gradually replaced "boxing" as the name for these contests. Before two bruisers attacked each other, spectators might demand whether they proposed to fight fair—according to Broughton's Rules—or rough-and-tumble. Honor dictated that all techniques be permitted. Except for a ban on weapons, most men chose to fight "no holts barred," doing what they wished to each other without interference, until one gave up or was incapacitated.

The emphasis on maximum disfigurement, on severing bodily parts, made this fighting style unique. Amid the general mayhem, however, gouging out an opponent's eye became the sine qua non of rough-and-tumble fighting, much like the knockout punch in modern boxing. The best gougers, of course, were adept at other fighting skills. Some allegedly filed their teeth to bite off an enemy's appendages more efficiently. Still, liberating an eyeball quickly became a fighter's surest route to victory and his most prestigious accomplishment. To this end, celebrated heroes fired their fingernails hard, honed them sharp, and oiled them slick. "You have come off badly

this time, I doubt?" declared an alarmed passer-by on seeing the piteous condition of a renowned fighter. "'Have I,' says he triumphantly, shewing from his pocket at the same time an eye, which he had extracted during the combat, and preserved for a trophy."

As the new style of fighting evolved, its geographical distribution changed. Leadership quickly passed from the southern seaboard to upcountry counties and the western frontier. Although examples could be found throughout the South, rough-and-tumbling was best suited to the backwoods, where hunting, herding, and semisubsistence agriculture predominated over market-oriented, stable crop production. Thus, the settlers of western Carolina, Kentucky, and Tennessee, as well as upland Mississippi, Alabama, and Georgia, became especially known for their pugnacity.

The social base of rough-and-tumbling also shifted with the passage of time. Although brawling was always considered a vice of the "lower sort," eighteenth-century Tidewater gentlemen sometimes found themselves in brutal fights. These combats grew out of challenges to men's honor—to their status in patriarchal, kin-based, small-scale communities—and were woven into the very fabric of daily life. Rhys Isaac has observed that the Virginia gentry set the tone for a fiercely competitive style of living. Although they valued hierarchy, individual status was never permanently fixed, so men frantically sought to assert their prowess—by grand boasts over tavern gaming tables laden with money, by whipping and tripping each other's horses in violent quarter-races, by wagering one-half year's earnings on the flash of a fighting cock's gaff. Great planters and small shared an ethos that extolled courage bordering on foolhardiness and cherished magnificent, if irrational, displays of largess.

Piety, hard work, and steady habits had their adherents, but in this society aggressive self-assertion and manly pride were the real marks of status. Even the gentry's vaunted hospitality demonstrated a family's community standing, so conviviality itself became a vehicle for rivalry and emulation. Rich and poor might revel together during "public times," but gentry patronage of sports and festivities kept the focus of power clear. Above all, brutal recreations toughened men for a violent social life in which the exploitation of labor, the specter of poverty, and a fierce struggle for status were daily realities.

During the final decades of the eighteenth century, however, individuals like Fithian's young gentlemen became less inclined to engage in rough-and-tumbling. Many in the planter class now wanted to distinguish themselves from social inferiors more by genteel manners, gracious living, and paternal prestige than by patriarchal prowess. They sought alternatives to brawling and found them by imitating the English aristocracy. A few gentlemen took boxing lessons from professors of pugilism or attended sparring exhibitions given by touring exponents of the manly art. More important, dueling gradually replaced hand-to-hand combat. The code of honor offered a genteel, though deadly, way to settle personal disputes while demonstrating one's elevated status. Ceremony distinguished antiseptic duels from lower-class brawls. Cool restraint and customary decorum proved a man's ability to shed blood while remaining emotionally detached, to act as mercilessly as the poor whites but to do so with chilling gentility.

Slowly, then, rough-and-tumble fighting found specific locus in both human and geographical landscapes. We can watch men grapple with the transition. When an attempt at a formal duel aborted, Savannah politician Robert Watkins and United States Senator James Jackson resorted to gouging. Jackson bit Watson's finger to save his eye. Similarly, when "a low fellow who pretends to gentility" insulted a distinguished doctor, the gentleman responded with a proper challenge. "He had scarcely uttered these words, before the other flew at him, and in an instant turned his eye out of the socket, and while it hung upon his cheek, the fellow was barbarous enough to endeavor to pluck it entirely out." By the new century, such ambiguity had lessened, as rough-and-tumble fighting was relegated to individuals in backwoods settlements. For the next several decades, eye-gouging match-

es were focal events in the culture of lower-class males who still relished the wild ways of old.

"I saw more than one man who wanted an eye, and ascertained that I was now in the region of 'gouging,'" reported young Timothy Flint, a Harvard-educated, Presbyterian minister bound for Louisiana missionary work in 1816. His spirits buckled as his party turned down the Mississippi from the Ohio Valley. Enterprising farmers gave way to slothful and vulgar folk whom Flint considered barely civilized. Only vicious fighting and disgusting accounts of battles past disturbed their inertia. Residents assured him that the "blackguards" excluded gentlemen from gouging matches. Flint was therefore perplexed when told that a barbarous-looking man was the "best" in one settlement, until he learned that best in this context meant not the most moral, prosperous, or pious but the local champion who had whipped all the rest, the man most dexterous at extracting eyes.

Because rough-and-tumble fighting declined in settled areas, some of the most valuable accounts were written by visitors who penetrated the backcountry. Travel literature was quite popular during America's infancy, and many profit-minded authors undoubtedly wrote with their audience's expectations in mind. Images of heroic frontiersmen, of crude but unencumbered natural men, enthralled both writers and readers. Some who toured the new republic in the decades following the Revolution had strong prejudices against America's democratic pretensions. English travelers in particular doubted that the upstart nation—in which the lower class shouted its equality and the upper class was unable or unwilling to exercise proper authority—could survive. Ironically, backcountry fighting became a symbol for both those who inflated and those who punctured America's expansive national ego.

Frontier braggarts enjoyed fulfilling visitors' expectations of backwoods depravity, pumping listeners full of gruesome legends. Their narratives projected a satisfying, if grotesque, image of the American rustic as a fearless, barbaric, larger-than-life democrat. But they also gave Englishmen the satisfaction of seeing their former countrymen run wild in the wilderness. Gouging matches offered a perfect metaphor for the Hobbesian war of all against all, of men tearing each other apart once institutional restraints evaporated, of a heart of darkness beating in the New World. As they made their way from the northern port towns to the southern countryside, or down the Ohio to southwestern waterways, observers concluded that geographical and moral descent went hand in hand. Brutal fights dramatically confirmed their belief that evil lurked in the deep shadows of America's sunny democratic landscape.

And yet, it would be a mistake to dismiss all travelers' accounts of backwoods fighting as fictions born of prejudice. Many sojourners who were sober and careful observers of America left detailed reports of rough-and-tumbles. Aware of the tradition of frontier boasting, they distinguished apocryphal stories from personal observation, wild tales from eye-witness accounts. Although gouging matches became a sort of literary convention, many travelers compiled credible descriptions of backwoods violence.

"The indolence and dissipation of the middling and lower classes of Virginia are such as to give pain to every reflecting mind," one anonymous visitor declared. "Horse-racing, cock-fighting, and boxing-matches are standing amusements, for which they neglect all business; and in the latter of which they conduct themselves with a barbarity worthy of their savage neighbors." Thomas Anburey agreed. He believed that the Revolution's leveling of class distinctions left the "lower people" dangerously independent. Although Anburey found poor whites usually hospitable and generous, he was disturbed by their sudden outbursts of impudence, their aversion to labor and love of drink, their vengefulness and savagery. They shared with their betters a taste for gaming, horse racing, and cockfighting, but "boxing matches, in which they display such barbarity, as fully marks their innate ferocious disposition," were all their own. Anburey concluded that an English prize fight was humanity

itself compared to Virginia combat.

Another visitor, Charles William Janson, decried the loss of social subordination, which caused the rabble to reinterpret liberty and equality as licentiousness. Paternal authority—the font of social and political order—had broken down in America, as parents gratified their children's whims, including youthful tastes for alcohol and tobacco. A national mistrust of authority had brought civilization to its nadir among the poor whites of the South. "The lower classes are the most abject that, perhaps, ever peopled a Christian land. They live in the woods and deserts and many of them cultivate no more land than will raise them corn and cabbages, which, with fish, and occasionally a piece of pickled pork or bacon, are their constant food. . . . Their habitations are more wretched than can be conceived; the huts of the poor of Ireland, or even the meanest Indian wig-wam, displaying more ingenuity and greater industry." Despite their degradation—perhaps because of it—Janson found the poor whites extremely jealous of their republican rights and liberties. They considered themselves the equals of their best-educated neighbors and intruded on whomever they chose. The gouging match this fastidious Englishman witnessed in Georgia was the epitome of lower-class depravity:

> We found the combatants . . . fast clinched by the hair, and their thumbs endeavoring to force a passage into each other's eyes; while several of the bystanders were betting upon the first eye to be turned out of its socket. For some time the combatants avoided the *thumb stroke* with dexterity. At length they fell to the ground, and in an instant the uppermost sprung up with his antagonist's eye in his hand!!! The savage crowd applauded, while, sick with horror, we galloped away from the infernal scene. The name of the sufferrer was John Butler, a Carolinian, who, it seems, had been dared to the combat by a Georgian; and the first eye was for the honor of the state to which they respectively belonged.

Janson concluded that even Indian "savages" and London's rabble would be outraged by the beastly Americans.

While Janson toured the lower South, his countryman Thomas Ashe explored the territory around Wheeling, Virginia. A passage, dated April 1806, from his *Travels in America* gives us a detailed picture of gouging's social context. Ashe expounded on Wheeling's potential to become a center of trade for the Ohio and upper Mississippi valleys, noting that geography made the town a natural rival of Pittsburgh. Yet Wheeling lagged in "worthy commercial pursuits, and industrious and moral dealings." Ashe attributed this backwardness to the town's frontier ways, which attracted men who specialized in drinking, plundering Indian property, racing horses, and watching cockfights. A Wheeling Quaker assured Ashe that mores were changing, that the underworld element was about to be driven out. Soon, the godly would gain control of the local government, enforce strict observance of the Sabbath, and outlaw vice. Ashe was sympathetic but doubtful. In Wheeling, only heightened violence and debauchery distinguished Sunday from the rest of the week. The citizens' willingness to close up shop and neglect business on the slightest pretext made it a questionable residence for any respectable group of men, let alone a society of Quakers.

To convey the rough texture of Wheeling life, Ashe described a gouging match. Two men drinking at a public house argued over the merits of their respective horses. Wagers made, they galloped off to the race course. "Two thirds of the population followed:—blacksmiths, shipwrights, all left work: the town appeared a desert. The stores were shut. I asked a proprietor, why the warehouses did not remain open? He told me all good was done for the day: that the people would remain on the ground till night, and many stay till the following morning." Determined to witness an event deemed so important that the entire town went on holiday, Ashe headed for the track. He missed the initial heat but arrived in time to watch the crowd raise the stakes to induce a rematch. Six horses competed, and spectators bet a small fortune, but the results were inconclusive. Umpires' opinions were given and rejected. Heated words, then fists flew.

Soon, the melee narrowed to two individuals, a Virginian and a Kentuckian. Because fights were common in such situations, everyone knew the proper procedures, and the combatants quickly decided to "tear and rend" one another—to rough-and-tumble—rather than "fight fair." Ashe elaborated: "You startle at the words tear and rend, and again do not understand me. You have heard these terms, I allow, applied to beasts of prey and to carnivorous animals; and your humanity cannot conceive them applicable to man: It nevertheless is so, and the fact will not permit me the use of any less expressive term."

The battle began—size and power on the Kentuckian's side, science and craft on the Virginian's. They exchanged cautious throws and blows, when suddenly the Virginian lunged at his opponent with a panther's ferocity. The crowd roared its approval as the fight reached its violent denouement:

> The shock received by the Kentuckyan, and the want of breath, brought him instantly to the ground. The Virginian never lost his hold; like those bats of the South who never quit the subject on which they fasten till they taste blood, he kept his knees in his enemy's body; fixing his claws in his hair, and his thumbs on his eyes, gave them an instantaneous start from their sockets. The sufferer roared aloud, but uttered no complaint. The citizens again shouted with joy. Doubts were no longer entertained and bets of three to one were offered on the Virginian.

But the fight continued. The Kentuckian grabbed his smaller opponent and held him in a tight bear hug, forcing the Virginian to relinquish his facial grip. Over and over the two rolled, until, getting the Virginian under him, the big man "snapt off his nose so close to his face that no manner of projection remained." The Virginian quickly recovered, seized the Kentuckian's lower lip in his teeth, and ripped it down over his enemy's chin. This was enough: "The Kentuckyan at length *gave out*, on which the people carried off the victor, and he preferring triumph to a doctor, who came to cicatrize his face, suffered himself to be chaired round the ground as the champion of the times, and the first *rougher-and-tumbler*. The poor wretch, whose eyes were started from their spheres, and whose lip refused its office, returned to the town, to hide his impotence, and get his countenance repaired." The citizens refreshed themselves with whiskey and biscuits, and then resumed their races.

Ashe's Quaker friend reported that such spontaneous races occurred two or three times a week and that the annual fall and spring meets lasted fourteen uninterrupted days, "aided by the licentious and profligate of all the neighboring states." As for rough-and-tumbles, the Quaker saw no hope of suppressing them. Few nights passed without such fights; few mornings failed to reveal a new citizen with mutilated features. It was a regional taste, unrestrained by law or authority, an inevitable part of life on the left bank of the Ohio.

By the early nineteenth century, rough-and-tumble fighting had generated its own folklore. Horror mingled with awe when residents of the Ohio Valley pointed out one-eyed individuals to visitors, when New Englanders referred to an empty eye socket as a "Virginia Brand," when North Carolinians related stories of mass rough-and-tumbles ending with eyeballs covering the ground, and when Kentuckians told of battle-royals so intense that severed eyes, ears, and noses filled bushel baskets. Place names like "Fighting Creek" and "Gouge Eye" perpetuated the memory of heroic encounters, and rustic bombast reached new extremes with estimates from some counties that every third man wanted an eye. As much as the style of combat, the rich oral folklore of the backcountry—the legends, tales, ritual boasts, and verbal duels, all of them in regional vernacular—made rough-and-tumble fighting unique.

It would be difficult to overemphasize the importance of the spoken word in southern life. Traditional tales, songs, and beliefs—transmitted orally by blacks as well as whites—formed the cornerstone of culture. Folklore socialized children, inculcated values, and helped forge a distinct regional sensibility. Even wealthy and well-educated planters, raised at the knees of black mammies, imbibed both Afro-American and white traditions, and charismatic politicians secured loyal followers by speaking the people's language. Southern society was based more on personalistic, face-to-face, kin-and-community relationships than on legalistic or bureaucratic ones. Interactions between southerners were guided by elaborate rituals of hospitality, demonstrative conviviality, and kinship ties—all of which emphasized personal dependencies and reliance on the spoken word. Through the antebellum period and beyond, the South had an oral as much as a written culture.

Boundaries between talk and action, ideas and behavior, are less clear in spoken than in written contexts. Psychologically, print seems more distant and abstract than speech, which is inextricably bound to specific individuals, times, and places. In becoming part of the realm of sight rather than sound, words leave behind their personal, living qualities, gaining in fixity what they lose in dynamism. Literate peoples separate thought from action, pigeon-holing ideas and behavior. Nonliterate ones draw this distinction less sharply, viewing words and the events to which they refer as a single reality. In oral cultures generally, and the Old South in particular, the spoken word was a powerful force in daily life, because ideation and behavior remained closely linked.

The oral traditions of hunters, drifters, herdsmen, gamblers, roustabouts, and rural poor who rough-and-tumbled provided a strong social cement. Tall talk around a campfire, in a tavern, in front of a crossroads store, or at countless other meeting places on the southwestern frontier helped establish communal bonds between disparate persons. Because backwoods humorists possessed an unusual ability to draw people together and give expression to shared feelings, they often became the most effective leaders and preachers. But words could also divide. Fithian's observation in the eighteenth century—that seemingly innocuous remarks led to sickening violence—remained true for several generations.

Men were so touchy about their personal reputations that any slight required an apology. This failing, only retribution restored public stature and self-esteem. "Saving face" was not just a metaphor.

The lore of backwoods combat, however, both inflated and deflated egos. By the early nineteenth century, simple epithets evolved into verbal duels—rituals well known to folklorists. Backcountry men took turns bragging about their prowess, possessions, and accomplishments, spurring each other on to new heights of self-magnification. Such exchanges heightened tension and engendered a sense of theatricality and display. But boasting, unlike insults, did not always lead to combat, for, in a culture that valued oral skills, the verbal battle itself—the contest over who best controlled the power of words—was a real quest for domination:

> "I am a man; I am a horse; I am a team. I can whip any man *in all Kentucky,* by G-d!" The other replied, "I am an alligator, half man, half horse; can whip any man on the *Mississippi,* by G-d!" The first one again, "I am a man; have the best horse, best dog, best gun and handsomest wife in all Kentucky, by G-d." The other, "I am a Mississippi snapping turtle: have bear's claws, alligator's teeth, and the devil's tail; can whip *any man,* by G-d."

Such elaborate boasts were not composed on the spot. Folklorists point out that free-phrase verbal forms, from Homeric epics to contemporary blues, are created through an oral formulaic process. The singer of epics, for example, does not memorize thousands of lines but knows the underlying skeleton of his narrative and, as he sings, fleshes it out with old commonplaces and new turns of phrase. In this way, oral formulaic composition merges cultural continuity with individual creativity. A similar but simplified version of the same process was at work in backwoods bragging.

A quarter-century after the above exchange made its way into print, several of the same phrases still circulated orally and were worked into new patterns. "'By Gaud, stranger,' said he, 'do you know me?—do you know what stuff I'm made of? Clear steamboat, sea horse, alligator—run agin me, run agin a snag—jam up—whoop! Got the prettiest sister, and biggest whiskers of any man hereabouts—I can lick my weight in wild cats, or any man in all Kentuck!" Style and details changed, but the themes remained the same: comparing oneself to wild animals, boasting of possessions and accomplishments, asserting domination over others. Mike Fink, legendary keelboatman, champion gouger, and fearless hunter, put his own mark on the old form and elevated it to an art:

> I'm a salt River roarer! I'm a ring tailed squealer! I'm a regular screamer from the old Massassip! Whoop! I'm the very infant that refused his milk before its eyes were open and called out for a bottle of old Rye! I love the women and I'm chockful o' fight! I'm half wild horse and half cock-eyed alligator and the rest o' me is crooked snags an' red-hot snappin' turtle. . . . I can out-run, out-jump, out-shoot, out-brag, out-drink, an' out-fight, rough-an'-tumble, no holts barred, any man on both sides the river from Pittsburgh to New Orleans an' back ag'in to St. Louiee. Come on, you flatters, you bargers, you milk white mechanics, an' see how tough I am to chaw! I ain't had a fight for two days an' I'm spilein' for exercise. Cock-a-doodle-doo!

Tall talk and ritual boasts were not uniquely American. Folklore indexes are filled with international legends and tales of exaggeration. But inflated language did find a secure home in America in the first half of the nineteenth century. Spread-eagle rhetoric was tailor-made for a young nation seeking a secure identity. Bombastic speech helped justify the development of unfamiliar social institutions, flowery oratory salved painful economic changes, and lofty words masked aggressive territorial expansion. In a circular pattern of reinforcement, heroic talk spurred heroic deeds, so that great acts found heightened meaning in great words. Alexis de Tocqueville observed during his travels in the 1830s that clearing land, draining swamps, and planting crops were hardly the stuff of literature. But the collective vision of democratic multitudes building a great nation formed a grand poetic ideal that haunted men's imaginations.

The gaudy poetry of the strapping young nation had its equivalent in the exaggeration of individual powers. Folklore placing man at the center of the universe buttressed the emergent ideology of equality. Tocqueville underestimated Americans' ability to celebrate the mundane, for ego magnification was essential in a nation that extolled self-creation. While America prided itself on shattering old boundaries, on liberating individuals from social, geographic, and cultural encumbrances, such freedom left each citizen frighteningly alone to succeed or fail in forging his own identity. To hyperbolize one's achievements was a source of power and control, a means of amplifying the self while bringing human, natural, and social obstacles down to size. The folklore of exaggeration could transform even the most prosaic commercial dealings into great contests. Early in the nineteenth century, legends of crafty Yankee peddlers and unscrupulous livestock traders abounded. A horse dealer described an animal to a buyer in the 1840s: "'Sir, he can jump a house or go through a pantry, as it suits him; no hounds are too fast for him, no day too long for him. He has the courage of a lion, and the docility of a lamb, and you may ride him with a thread. Weight did you say? Why, he would carry the national debt and not bate a penny.'" The most insipid marketplace transactions were transfigured by inflated language, legends of heroic salesmanship, and an ethos of contest and battle.

The oral narratives of the southern backcountry drew strength from these national traditions yet possessed unique characteristics. Above all, fight legends portrayed backwoodsmen reveling in blood. Violence existed for its own sake, unencumbered by romantic conventions and claiming no redeeming social or psychic value. Gouging narratives may have masked grimness with black humor, but they offered little pretense that violence was a creative or civilizing force. Thus, one Kentuckian defeated a bear by chewing off its

nose and scratching out its eyes. "They can't stand Kentucky play," the settler proclaimed, "biting and gouging are too hard for them." Humor quickly slipped toward horror, when Davy Crockett, for example, coolly boasted, "I kept my thumb in his eye, and was just going to give it a twist and bring the peeper out, like taking up a gooseberry in a spoon." To Crockett's eternal chagrin, someone interrupted the battle just at this crucial juncture.

Sadistic violence gave many frontier legends a surreal quality. Two Mississippi raftsmen engaged in ritual boasts and insults after one accidentally nudged the other toward the water, wetting his shoes. Cheered on by their respective gangs, they stripped off their shirts, then pummeled, knocked out teeth, and wore skin from each other's faces. The older combatant asked if his opponent had had enough. "Yes," he was told, "when I drink your heart's blood, I'll cry enough, and not till then." The younger man gouged out an eye. Just as quickly, his opponent was on top, strangling his adversary. But in a final reversal of fortunes, the would-be victor cried out, then rolled over dead, a stab wound in his side. Protected by his clique, the winner jumped in the water, swam to a river island, and crowed: "Ruoo-ruoo-o! I can lick a steamboat. My fingernails is related to a sawmill on my mother's side and my daddy was a double breasted catamount! I wear a hoop snake for a neck-handkerchief, and the brass buttons on my coat have all been boiled in poison."

The danger and violence of daily life in the backwoods contributed mightily to sanguinary oral traditions that exalted the strong and deprecated the weak. Early in the nineteenth century, the Southwest contained more than its share of terrifying wild animals, powerful and well-organized Indian tribes, and marauding white outlaws. Equally important were high infant mortality rates and short life expectancies, agricultural blights, class inequities, and the centuries-old belief that betrayal and cruelty were man's fate. Emmeline Grangerford's graveyard poetry—set against a backdrop of rural isolation shattered by sadistic clan feuds—is but the best-known expression of the deep loneliness, death longings, and melancholy that permeated backcountry life.

At first glance, boisterous tall talk and violent legends seem far removed from sadness and alienation. Yet, as Kenneth Lynn has argued, they grew from common origins, and the former allowed men to resist succumbing to the latter. Not passive acceptance but identification with brutes and brawlers characterized frontier legendry. Rather than be overwhelmed by violence, acquiesce in an oppressive environment, or submit to death as an escape from tragedy, why not make a virtue of necessity and flaunt one's unconcern? To revel in the lore of deformity, mutilation, and death was to beat the wilderness at its own game. The storyteller's art dramatized life and converted nameless anxieties into high adventure; bravado helped men face down a threatening world and transform terror into power. To claim that one was sired by wild animals, kin to natural disasters, and tougher than steam engines—which were displacing rivermen in the antebellum era—was to gain a momentary respite from fear, a cathartic, if temporary, sense of being in control. Symbolically, wild boasts overwhelmed the very forces that threatened the backwoodsmen.

But there is another level of meaning here. Sometimes fight legends invited an ambiguous response, mingling the celebration of beastly acts with the rejection of barbarism. By their very nature, tall tales elicit skepticism. Even while men identified with the violence that challenged them, the folklore of eye gouging constantly tested the limits of credibility. "Pretty soon I got the squatter down, and just then he fixed his teeth into my throte, and I felt my windpipe begin to loosen." The calculated coolness and understatement of this description highlights the outrageousness of the act. The storyteller has artfully maneuvered his audience to the edge of credulity.

Backwoodsmen mocked their animality by exaggerating it, thereby affirming their own humanity. A Kentuckian battled inconclusively from ten in the morning until sundown, when his wife showed up to cheer him on:

So I gathered all the little strength I had, and I socked my thumb in his eye, and with my fingers took a twist on his *snot box,* and with the other hand, I grabbed him by the back of the head; I then caught his ear in my mouth, gin his head a flirt, and *out come his ear by the roots!* I then flopped his head over, and caught his other ear in my mouth, and jerked that out in the same way, and it made a hole in his head that I could have rammed my fist through, and I was just goin' to when he hollered: "Nuff!"

More than realism or fantasy alone, fight legends stretched the imagination by blending both. As metaphoric statements, they reconciled contradictory impulses, at once glorifying and parodying barbarity. In this sense, gouging narratives were commentaries on backwoods life. The legends were texts that allowed plain folk to dramatize the tensions and ambiguities of their lives: they hauled society's goods yet lived on its fringe; they destroyed forests and game while clearing the land for settlement; they killed Indians to make way for the white man's culture; they struggled for self-sufficiency only to become ensnared in economic dependency. Fight narratives articulated the fundamental contradiction of frontier life—the abandonment of "civilized" ways that led to the ultimate expansion of civilized society.

Foreign travelers might exaggerate and backwoods storytellers embellish, but the most neglected fact about eye-gouging matches is their actuality. Circuit Court Judge Aedamus Burke barely contained his astonishment while presiding in South Carolina's upcountry: "Before God, gentlemen of the jury, I never saw such a thing before in the world. There is a plaintiff with an eye out! A juror with an eye out! And two witnesses with an eye out!" If the "ringtailed roarers" did not actually breakfast on stewed Yankee, washed down with spike nails and epsom salts, court records from Sumner County, Arkansas, did describe assault victims with the words "nose was bit." The gamest "gamecock of the wilderness" never really moved steamboat engines by grinning at them, but Reuben Cheek did receive a three-year sentence to the Tennessee penitentiary for gouging out William Maxey's eye. Most backcountrymen went to the grave with their faces intact, just as most of the southern gentry never fought a duel. But as an extreme version of the common tendency toward brawling, street fighting, and seeking personal vengeance, rough-and-tumbling gives us insight into the deep values and assumptions—the mentalité—of backwoods life.

Observers often accused rough-and-tumblers of fighting like animals. But eye gouging was not instinctive behavior, the human equivalent of two rams vying for dominance. Animals fight to attain specific objectives, such as food, sexual priority, or territory. Precisely where to draw the line between human aggression as a genetically programmed response or as a product of social and cultural learning remains a hotly debated issue. Nevertheless, it would be difficult to make a case for eye gouging as a genetic imperative, coded behavior to maximize individual or species survival. Although rough-and-tumble fighting appears primitive and anarchic to modern eyes, there can be little doubt that its origins, rituals, techniques, and goals were emphatically conditioned by environment; gouging was learned behavior. Humanistic social science more than sociobiology holds the keys to understanding this phenomenon.

What can we conclude about the culture and society that nourished rough-and-tumble fighting? The best place to begin is with the material base of life and the nature of daily work. Gamblers, hunters, herders, roustabouts, rivermen, and yeomen farmers were the sorts of persons usually associated with gouging. Such hallmarks of modernity as large-scale production, complex division of labor, and regular work rhythms were alien to their lives. Recent studies have stressed the premodern character of the southern uplands through most of the antebellum period. Even while cotton production boomed and trade expanded, a relatively small number of planters owned the best lands and most slaves, so huge parts of the South remained outside the flow of international markets or staple crop agriculture. Thus, backcountry whites commonly found themselves locked into a semisubsistent pattern of living. Growing crops for home consumption, supplementing food supplies with abundant game, allowing small herds to fatten in the woods, spending scarce money for essential staples, and bartering goods for the services of part-time or itinerant trades people, the upland folk lived in an intensely local, kin-based society. Rural hamlets, impassable roads, and provincial isolation—not growing towns, internal improvements, or international commerce—characterized the backcountry.

Even men whose livelihoods depended on expanding markets often continued their rough, premodern ways. Characteristic of life on a Mississippi barge, for example, were long periods of idleness shattered by intense anxiety, as deadly snags, shoals, and storms approached. Running aground on a sandbar meant backbreaking labor to maneuver a thirty-ton vessel out of trouble. Boredom weighed as heavily as danger, so tale telling, singing, drinking, and gambling filled the empty hours. Once goods were taken on in New Orleans, the men began the thousand-mile return journey against the current. Before steam power replaced muscle, bad food and whiskey fueled the gangs who day after day, exposed to wind and water, poled the river bottoms or strained at the cordelling ropes until their vessel reached the tributaries of the Missouri or the Ohio. Hunters, trappers, herdsmen, subsistence farmers, and other backwoodsmen faced different but equally taxing hardships, and those who endured prided themselves on their strength and daring, their stamina, cunning, and ferocity.

Such men played as lustily as they worked, counterpointing bouts of intense labor with strenuous leisure. What travelers mistook for laziness was a refusal to work and save with compulsive regularity. "I have seen nothing in human form so profligate as they are," James Flint wrote of the boatmen he met around 1820. "Accomplished in depravity, their habits and education seem to comprehend every vice. They make few pretensions to moral character; and their swearing is excessive and perfectly disgusting. Although earning good wages, they are in the most abject poverty; many of them being without anything like clean or comfortable clothing." A generation later, Mark Twain vividly remembered those who manned the great timber and coal rafts gliding past his boyhood home in Hannibal, Missouri: "Rude, uneducated, brave, suffering terrific hardships with sailorlike stoicism; heavy drinkers, course frolickers in moral sties like the Natchez-under-the-hill of that day, heavy fighters, reckless fellows, every one, elephantinely jolly, foul witted, profane; prodigal of their money, bankrupt at the end of the trip, fond of barbaric finery, prodigious braggarts; yet, in the main, honest, trustworthy, faithful to promises and duty, and often picaresquely magnanimous." Details might change, but penury, loose morality, and lack of steady habits endured.

Boatmen, hunters, and herdsmen were often separated from wives and children for long periods. More important, backcountry couples lacked the emotionally intense experience of the bourgeois family. They spent much of their time apart and found companionship with members of their own sex. The frontier town or crossroads tavern brought males together in surrogate brotherhoods, where rough men paid little deference to the civilizing role of women and the moral uplift of the domestic family. On the margins of a booming, modernizing society, they shared an intensely communal yet fiercely competitive way of life. Thus, where work was least rationalized and specialized, domesticity weakest, legal institutions primitive, and the market economy feeble, rough-and-tumble fighting found fertile soil.

Just as the economy of the southern backcountry remained locally oriented, the rough-and-tumblers were local heroes, renowned in their communities. There was no professionalization here. Men fought for informal village and county titles; the red feather in the champion's cap was pay enough because it marked him as first among his peers. Paralleling the primitive division of labor in backwoods society, boundaries between entertainment and daily life, between spectators and participants, were not sharply drawn. "Bully of the Hill" Ab Gaines from the Big Hatchie Country, Neil Brown of

Totty's Bend, Vernon's William Holt, and Smithfield's Jim Willis—all of them were renowned Tennessee fighters, local heroes in their day. Legendary champions were real individuals, tested gang leaders who attained their status by being the meanest, toughest, and most ruthless fighters, who faced disfigurement and never backed down. Challenges were ever present; yesterday's spectator was today's champion, today's champion tomorrow's invalid.

Given the lives these men led, a world view that embraced fearlessness made sense. Hunters, trappers, Indian fighters, and herdsmen who knew the smell of warm blood on their hands refused to sentimentalize an environment filled with threatening forces. It was not that backwoodsmen lived in constant danger but that violence was unpredictable. Recreations like cockfighting deadened men to cruelty, and the gratuitous savagery of gouging matches reinforced the daily truth that life was brutal, guided only by the logic of superior nerve, power, and cunning. With families emotionally or physically distant and civil institutions weak, a man's role in the all-male society was defined less by his ability as a breadwinner than by his ferocity. The touchstone of masculinity was unflinching toughness, not chivalry, duty, or piety. Violent sports, heavy drinking, and impulsive pleasure seeking were appropriate for men whose lives were hard, whose futures were unpredictable, and whose opportunities were limited. Gouging champions were group leaders because they embodied the basic values of their peers. The successful rough-and-tumbler proved his manhood by asserting his dominance and rendering his opponent "impotent," as Thomas Ashe put it. And the loser, though literally or symbolically castrated, demonstrated his mettle and maintained his honor.

Here we begin to understand the travelers' refrain about plain folk degradation. Setting out from northern ports, whose inhabitants were increasingly possessed by visions of godly perfection and material progress, they found southern upcountry people slothful and backward. Ashe's Quaker friend in Wheeling, Virginia, made the point. For Quakers and northern evangelicals, labor was a means of moral self-testing, and earthly success was a sign of God's grace, so hard work and steady habits became acts of piety. But not only Yankees endorsed sober restraint. A growing number of southern evangelicals also embraced a life of decorous self-control, rejecting the hedonistic and self-assertive values of old. During the late eighteenth century, as Rhys Isaac has observed, many plain folk disavowed the hegemonic gentry culture of conspicuous display and found individual worth, group pride, and transcendent meaning in religious revivals. By the antebellum era, new evangelical waves washed over class lines as rich and poor alike forswore such sins as drinking, gambling, cursing, fornication, horse racing, and dancing. But conversion was far from universal, and, for many in backcountry settlements like Wheeling, the evangelical idiom remained a foreign tongue. Men worked hard to feed themselves and their kin, to acquire goods and status, but they lacked the calling to prove their godliness through rigid morality. Salvation and self-denial were culturally less compelling values, and the barriers against leisure and self-gratification were lower here than among the converted.

Moreover, primitive markets and the semisubsistence basis of upcountry life limited men's dependence on goods produced by others and allowed them to maintain the irregular work rhythms of a precapitalist economy. The material base of backwoods life was ill suited to social transformation, and the cultural traditions of the past offered alternatives to rigid new ideals. Closing up shop in mid-week for a fight or horse race had always been perfectly acceptable, because men labored so that they might indulge the joys of the flesh. Neither a compulsive need to save time and money nor an obsession with progress haunted people's imaginations. The backcountry folk who lacked a bourgeois or Protestant sense of duty were little disturbed by exhibitions of human passions and were resigned to violence as part of daily life. Thus, the relative dearth of capitalistic values (such as delayed gratification and accumulation), the absence of a strict work ethic, and a cultural tradition that

winked at lapses in moral rigor limited society's demands for sober self-control.

Not just unconverted poor whites but also large numbers of the slave-holding gentry still lent their prestige to a regional style that favored conspicuous displays of leisure. As C. Vann Woodward has pointed out, early observers, such as Robert Beverley and William Byrd, as well as modern-day commentators, have described a distinctly "southern ethic" in American history. Whether judged positively as leisure or negatively as laziness, the southern sensibility valued free time and rejected work as the consuming goal of life. Slavery reinforced this tendency, for how could labor be an unmitigated virtue if so much of it was performed by despised black bondsmen? When southerners did esteem commerce and enterprise, it was less because piling up wealth contained religious or moral value than because productivity facilitated the leisure ethos. Southerners could therefore work hard without placing labor at the center of their ethical universe. In important ways, then, the upland folk culture reflected a larger regional style.

Thus, the values, ideas, and institutions that rapidly transformed the North into a modern capitalist society came late to the South. Indeed, conspicuous display, heavy drinking, moral casualness, and love of games and sports had deep roots in much of Western culture. As Woodward has cautioned, we must take care not to interpret the southern ethic as unique or aberrant. The compulsions to subordinate leisure to productivity, to divide work and play into separate compartmentalized realms, and to improve each bright and shining hour were the novel ideas. The southern ethic anticipated human evil, tolerated ethical lapses, and accepted the finitude of man in contrast to the new style that demanded unprecedented moral rectitude and internalized self-restraint.

The American South also shared with large parts of the Old World a taste for violence and personal vengeance. Long after the settling of the southern colonies, powerful patriarchal clans in Celtic and Mediterranean lands still avenged affronts to family honor with deadly feuds. Norbert Elias has pointed out that postmedieval Europeans routinely spilled blood to settle their private quarrels. Across classes, the story was the same:

> Two associates fall out over business; they quarrel, the conflict grows violent; one day they meet in a public place and one of them strikes the other dead. An innkeeper accuses another of stealing his clients; they become mortal enemies. Someone says a few malicious words about another; a family war develops. . . . Not only among the nobility were there family vengeance, private feuds, vendettas. . . . The little people too—the hatters, the tailors, the shepherds—were all quick to draw their knives.

Emotions were freely expressed: jollity and laughter suddenly gave way to belligerence; guilt and penitence coexisted with hate; cruelty always lurked nearby. The modern middle-class individual, with his subdued, rational, calculating ways, finds it hard to understand the joy sixteenth-century Frenchmen took in ceremonially burning alive one or two dozen cats every Midsummer Day or the pleasure eighteenth-century Englishmen found in watching trained dogs slaughter each other.

Despite enormous cultural differences, inhabitants of the southern uplands exhibited characteristics of their forebears in the Old World. The Scots-Irish brought their reputation for ferocity to the backcountry, but English migrants, too, had a thirst for violence. Central authority was weak, and men reserved the right to settle differences for themselves. Vengeance was part of daily life. Drunken hilarity, good fellowship, and high spirits, especially at crossroads taverns, suddenly turned to violence. Traveler after traveler remarked on how forthright and friendly but quick to anger the backcountry people were. Like their European ancestors, they had not yet internalized the modern world's demand for tight emotional self-control.

Above all, the ancient concept of honor helps explain this shared proclivity for violence. According to the sociologist Peter Berger, mod-

ern men have difficulty taking seriously the idea of honor. American jurisprudence, for example, offers legal recourse for slander and libel because they involve material damages. But insult—publicly smearing a man's good name and besmirching his honor—implies no palpable injury and so does not exist in the eyes of the law. Honor is an intensely social concept, resting on reputation, community standing, and the esteem of kin and compatriots. To possess honor requires acknowledgement from others; it cannot exist in solitary conscience. Modern man, Berger has argued, is more responsive to dignity—the belief that personal worth inheres equally in each individual, regardless of his status in society. Dignity frees the evangelical to confront God alone, the capitalist to make contracts without customary encumbrances, and the reformer to uplift the lowly. Naked and alone man has dignity; extolled by peers and covered with ribbons, he has honor.

Anthropologists have also discovered the centrality of honor in several cultures. According to J. G. Peristiany, honor and shame often preoccupy individuals in small-scale settings, where face-to-face relationships predominate over anonymous or bureaucratic ones. Social standing in such communities is never completely secure, because it must be validated by public opinion, whose fickleness compels men constantly to assert and prove their worth. Julian Pitt-Rivers has added that, if society rejects a man's evaluation of himself and treats his claim to honor with ridicule or contempt, his very identity suffers because it is based on the judgment of peers. Shaming refers to that process by which an insult or any public humiliation impugns an individual's honor and thereby threatens his sense of self. By risking injury in a violent encounter, an affronted man—whether victorious or not—restores his sense of status and thus validates anew his claim to honor. Only valorous action, not words, can redeem his place in the ranks of his peer group.

Bertram Wyatt-Brown has argued that this Old World ideal is the key to understanding southern history. Across boundaries of time, geography, and social class, the South was knit together by a primal concept of male valor, part of the ancient heritage of Indo-European folk cultures. Honor demanded clan loyalty, hospitality, protection of women, and defense of patriarchal prerogatives. Honorable men guarded their reputations, bristled at insults, and, where necessary, sought personal vindication through bloodshed. The culture of honor thrived in hierarchical rural communities like the American South and grew out of a fatalistic world view, which assumed that pain and suffering were man's fate. It accounts for the pervasive violence that marked relationships between southerners and explains their insistence on vengeance and their rejection of legal redress in settling quarrels. Honor tied personal identity to public fulfillment of social roles. Neither bourgeois self-control nor internalized conscience determined status; judgment by one's fellows was the wellspring of community standing.

In this light, the seemingly trivial causes for brawls enumerated as early as Fithian's time—name calling, subtle ridicule, breaches of decorum, displays of poor manners—make sense. If a man's good name was his most important possession, then any slight cut him deeply. "Having words" precipitated fights because words brought shame and undermined a man's sense of self. Symbolic acts, such as buying a round of drinks, conferred honor on all, while refusing to share a bottle implied some inequality in social status. Honor inhered not only in individuals but also in kin and peers; when members of two cliques had words, their tested leaders or several men from each side fought to uphold group prestige. Inheritors of primal honor, the southern plain folk were quick to take offense, and any perceived affront forced a man either to devalue himself or strike back violently and avenge the wrong.

The concept of male honor takes us a long way toward understanding the meaning of eye-gouging matches. But backwoods people did not simply acquire some primordial notion without modifying it. Definitions of honorable behavior have always varied enormously across cultures. The southern upcountry fostered a particular style of honor, which grew out of the contradiction between equality and hierarchy. Honorific societies tend to be sharply stratified. Honor is apportioned according to rank, and men fight to maintain personal standing within their social categories. Because black chattel slavery was the basis for the southern hierarchy, slave owners had the most wealth and honor, while other whites scrambled for a bit of each, and bondsmen were permanently impoverished and dishonored. Here was a source of tension for the plain folk. Men of honor shared freedom and equality; those denied honor were implicitly less than equal—perilously close to a slave-like condition. But in the eyes of the gentry, poor whites as well as blacks were outside the circle of honor, so both groups were subordinate. Thus a herdsman's insult failed to shame a planter since the two men were not on the same social level. Without a threat to the gentleman's honor, there was no need for a duel; horsewhipping the insolent fellow sufficed.

Southern plain folk, then, were caught in a social contradiction. Society taught all white men to consider themselves equals, encouraged them to compete for power and status, yet threatened them from below with the specter of servitude and from above with insistence on obedience to rank and authority. Cut off from upper-class tests of honor, backcountry people adopted their own. A rough-and-tumble was more than a poor man's duel, a botched version of genteel combat. Plain folk chose not to ape the dispassionate, antiseptic, gentry style but to invert it. While the gentleman's code of honor insisted on cool restraint, eye gougers gloried in unvarnished brutality. In contrast to duelists' aloof silence, backwoods fighters screamed defiance to the world. As their own unique rites of honor, rough-and-tumble matches allowed backcountry men to shout their equality at each other. And eye-gouging fights also dispelled any stigma of servility. Ritual boasts, soaring oaths, outrageous ferocity, unflinching bloodiness—all proved a man's freedom. Where the slave acted obsequiously, the backwoodsman resisted the slightest affront;

where human chattels accepted blows and never raised a hand, plain folk celebrated violence; where blacks could not jeopardize their value as property, poor whites proved their autonomy by risking bodily parts. Symbolically reaffirming their claims to honor, gouging matches helped resolve painful uncertainties arising out of the ambiguous place of plain folk in the southern social structure.

Backwoods fighting reminds us of man's capacity for cruelty and is an excellent corrective to romanticizing premodern life. But a close look also keeps us from drawing facile conclusions about innate human aggressiveness. Eye gouging represented neither the "real" human animal emerging on the frontier, nor nature acting through man in a Darwinian struggle for survival, nor anarchic disorder and communal breakdown. Rather, rough-and-tumble fighting was ritualized behavior—a product of specific cultural assumptions. Men drink together, tongues loosen, a simmering of old rivalry begins to boil; insult is given, offense taken, ritual boasts commence; the fight begins, mettle is tested, blood redeems honor, and equilibrium is restored. Eye gouging was the poor and middling whites' own version of a historical southern tendency to consider personal violence socially useful—indeed, ethically essential.

Rough-and-tumble fighting emerged from the confluence of economic conditions, social relationships, and culture in the southern backcountry. Primitive markets and the semisubsistence basis of life threw men back on close ties to kin and community. Violence and poverty were part of daily existence, so endurance, even callousness, became functional values. Loyal to their localities, their occupations, and each other, men came together and found release from life's hardships in strong drink, tall talk, rude practical jokes, and cruel sports. They craved one another's recognition but rejected genteel, pious, or bourgeois values, awarding esteem on the basis of their own traditional standards. The glue that held men together was an intensely competitive status system in which the most prodigious drinker or strongest arm wrestler, the best tale teller, fiddle player, or log roller, the most daring gambler, original liar, skilled hunter, outrageous swearer, or accurate marksman was accorded respect by the others. Reputation was everything, and scars were badges of honor. Rough-and-tumble fighting demonstrated unflinching willingness to inflict pain while risking mutilation—all to defend one's standing among peers—and became a central expression of the all-male subculture.

Eye gouging continued long after the antebellum period. As the market economy absorbed new parts of the backcountry, however, the way of life that supported rough-and-tumbling waned. Certainly by mid-century the number of incidents declined, precisely when expanding international demand brought ever more upcountry acres into staple production. Towns, schools, churches, revivals, and families gradually overtook the backwoods. In a slow and uneven process, keelboats gave way to steamers, then railroads; squatters, to cash crop farmers; hunters and trappers, to preachers. The plain folk code of honor was far from dead, but emergent social institutions engendered a moral ethos that warred against the old ways. For many individuals, the justifications for personal violence grew stricter, and mayhem became unacceptable.

Ironically, progress also had a darker side. New technologies and modes of production could enhance men's fighting abilities. "Birmingham and Pittsburgh are obliged to complete . . . the equipment of the 'chivalric Kentuckian,'" Charles Agustus Murray observed in the 1840s, as bowie knives ended more and more rough-and-tumbles. Equally important, in 1835 the first modern revolver appeared, and manufacturers marketed cheap, accurate editions in the coming decade. Dueling weapons had been costly, and Kentucky rifles or horse pistols took a full minute to load and prime. The revolver, however, which fitted neatly into a man's pocket, settled more and more personal disputes. Raw and brutal as rough-and-tumbling was, it could not survive the use of arms. Yet precisely because eye gouging was so violent—because combatants cherished maimings, blindings, even castrations—it unleashed death wishes that invited new technologies of destruction.

With improved weaponry, dueling entered its golden age during the antebellum era. Armed combat remained both an expression of gentry sensibility and a mark of social rank. But in a society where status was always shifting and unclear, dueling did not stay confined to the upper class. The habitual carrying of weapons, once considered a sign of unmanly fear, now lost some of its stigma. As the backcountry changed, tests of honor continued, but gunplay rather than fighting tooth-and-nail appealed to new men with social aspirations. Thus, progress and technology slowly circumscribed rough-and-tumble fighting, only to substitute a deadlier option. Violence grew neater and more lethal as men checked their savagery to murder each other.

19

FACTORY, CHURCH, AND COMMUNITY: BLACKS IN ANTEBELLUM RICHMOND

JOHN T. O'BRIEN

The last decade of the eighteenth century and the first three decades of the nineteenth century witnessed an intense revival of religion in America. One of the most important aspects of this Second Great Awakening was the attempt by preachers—many of them lay men and women—to reach out and spread the gospel to those in the lower ranks of society. As the revival spirit spread from the North to the South at the turn of the century, this message of personal redemption was carried to the most oppressed of American peoples: the African-American slaves.

In the beginning, many southern slaveholders welcomed the revivalists, seeing in the conservative aspects of Protestantism a means to augment their control over their slaves. But as many slave owners quickly learned, revivalism was a double-edged sword. While Protestantism could communicate a conservative message of otherworldliness and reconciliation with one's lot in life, it could also transmit a radical message of equality and deliverance from oppression. In spite of slaveholder attempts to suppress the radical side of Protestantism, many southern revivalists preached the full gospel to slaves, including in their sermons tales of Moses, Daniel, and other biblical leaders who sought the liberation of their people. As slaves listened to the preachings of these revivalists, they began to construct their own interpretations of Christian religion, drawing parallels between their own customary African beliefs and the new message of Christian revivalists.

In antebellum Richmond, Virginia, one of the South's foremost industrial centers, this new African-American Christianity took the form of separate churches and benevolent societies that provided the institutional focus for the city's powerful and dynamic black community. As John T. O'Brien reveals in this essay, the unique working conditions of Richmond's slave and free black communities permitted their members a degree of autonomy unusual in southern society and reinforced the independence of their distinctive church and community life.

"Factory, Church, and Community: Blacks in Antebellum Richmond." Journal of Southern History, *XLIV (November 1978), pp. 509–536. Copyright © 1978 by the Southern Historical Association. Reprinted by permission of the Managing Editor.*

In the weeks following Richmond's capitulation to Union troops on April 3, 1865, city blacks availed themselves of freedom by welcoming their liberators, celebrating emancipation, seeking work, and reuniting families. Black groups began at the same time to take complete control of their African churches and in cooperation with northern teachers to establish free schools for over a thousand children. These first collective efforts surprised the teachers but were largely ignored by white Richmonders. The whites could not, however, ignore the black community's public demand for legal equality in June 1865. Responding to the brutal enforcement by the police and army of pass and curfew laws which were designed to expel thousands of blacks from the city, black leaders conducted a court of inquiry into official misconduct. Failing to win redress from local officials, they called a mass meeting for June 10 at the First African Baptist Church. The more than three thousand blacks attending the meeting approved a protest memorial and selected seven representatives to present it to the President of the United States. The delegation, which included a representative from each of the five African Churches and was financed by collections in churches, had an audience with President Andrew Johnson, who promised assistance. By the time the delegates returned and reported back to their constituents the pass and curfew laws had been repealed, the civilian government removed, and the offending army officers replaced.

These collective black activities, which profoundly influenced the subsequent course of Reconstruction in the city, raise questions about the community life and organizational structure of antebellum black Richmond. They pose in particular the question of how the blacks were able to muster the initiative and cohesiveness necessary to establish schools, take control of churches, and mount a sophisticated mass protest so soon after their liberation.

White observers, in response to these events, offered only superficial characterizations of the newly freed slaves. Northern teachers and missionaries claimed that they were the smartest in Dixie, while military and civilian officials described them as a lazy and ignorant people susceptible to outside troublemakers. The freedmen saw themselves differently. They stated in their memorial that theirs was a law-abiding community with several thousand literate and propertied members, over six thousand regular churchgoers, and a tradition of caring for the sick and the poor through clandestine benevolent societies. Their proved respectability and past loyalty to the Union had earned them humane treatment as free men, they explained, not the abuse and lowly status the army was according them. Their memorial revealed important aspects of their historical development as a community, a past that historians of urban slavery have often slighted by focusing on the disintegrating forces in southern cities that allegedly produced social disorder among slaves.

Recent studies of rural slave societies, of the culture of the quarters, and of the slave family have begun to reconstruct the world of the plantation slaves, but the interior life of urban slave communities still awaits serious study. The collective behavior of Richmond freedmen in 1865 was an expression of their prewar experience and an extension in time and into new conditions of an order the slaves and free blacks had created earlier. The sources of their behavior were deeply imbedded in the slave past and demonstrated the impact of the two largest institutions of the Richmond black world, the tobacco factories and the African Baptist churches.

Between 1820 and 1860 the population of Richmond more than tripled, reaching 37,910 on the eve of the Civil War and making Richmond the twenty-fifth most populous city in the nation. The number of whites rose from 6,445 in 1820 to 23,635 in 1860, of free blacks from 1,235 to 2,576, and of slaves from 4,387 to 11,699. The average percentage increase per decade over the forty years was 38.5 percent for whites, 28.3 percent for slaves, and 22.1 percent for free blacks. Industrial development sparked the city's growth in population. Richmond contained the South's most important iron-making and machine-building works, the two largest flour mills in the country, and the nation's largest tobacco-manufacturing industry. The output of these three industries and other shops and factories in 1860 made Richmond the thirteenth most productive industrial center in the United States. Its forty-nine factories turned out more chewing tobacco in that year than all other southern factories outside the state. The tobacco industry relied exclusively on black workers. Its rise was intimately linked to the growth of the city's slave population.

Tobacco manufacturing accounted for the unique demographic profile of Richmond's slave population which, unlike most urban slave communities, grew between 1820 and 1860 and consisted of more males than females. In 1820, when the industry was in its infancy, males made up 49.5 percent of the slave population, but by 1860, at the height of industrial prosperity, 56.7 percent of the slaves were males. Tobacco factories in 1860 employed 3,364 men and boys, most of whom were slaves, and in this year the entire male slave population of the city stood at 6,636. More than half of all employees counted in the industrial censuses of 1850 and 1860 worked in these factories. Tobacco factory operatives accounted for 69.8 percent of all workers in 1850 and 50.3 percent of the total ten years later. They worked in larger groups than most other white and black workers. The average number of laborers in tobacco establishments was 84 in 1850 and 69.4 in 1860. Over the decade the number of tobacco factories rose from thirty-one to forty-nine. By contrast, the average number of workers in shops and factories in the city whose output exceeded $500 million annually was 20.6 in 1850 and 26.1 in 1860. Tobacco factories were the major employers in Richmond and the chief users of male slave workers.

Most tobacco manufacturers owned some of their factory hands and hired additional workers when market conditions warranted. James Thomas, Jr., for example, owned 88 of the 178 slaves who worked in his factory in 1853. Ownership assured manufacturers of a steady supply of slave workers skilled in preparing tobacco for market and accustomed to the rhythms, disciplines, and conditions of the factories. The main disadvantage was that ownership required large capital outlays that proved increasingly burdensome to entrepreneurs who started or expanded operations in the 1850s, a period of rapidly rising slave prices. Many therefore turned to hiring slaves and free blacks to fill their labor needs, and by 1860 over half the Virginia tobacco workers were hired. As the demand for black hirelings increased the rates of hire soared. James Thomas, Jr., for instance, hired Edmund from William B. Towles for $100 in 1852, for $125 in 1853, and was asked to pay $140 in 1854. Thousands of bondsmen were sent to Richmond during Christmas week each year to be hired out. They came from planters and urban slaveholders with surplus workers, from widows and elderly persons who depended on the hiring out of slaves for their income, and from executors of estates seeking to earn money for the estates' heirs.

Several distinct hiring practices developed over the years. Manufacturers sometimes negotiated directly by letter with slaveowners for the services of their slaves. This method was often employed when employers and owners knew each other personally, when they had enjoyed prior, satisfactory dealings, or when owners sought to send young slaves to the city for the first time. In these negotiations the reputations of all parties counted heavily. John Y. Mason, in charge of hiring out three of his father's slaves, left the terms of their hire to James Thomas. "My father," he wrote, "leaves the hire of the boys entirely to you, whatever they are worth he knows you will pay." William B. Wyatt was more demanding in his negotiations. "I understand by letter from my son that you want Anthony for the present year. You can keep him at $150 which I think he must be worth from the prices I have been offered." Even in such direct negotiations the slaves could make their wishes known. Benjamin Fleet told Thomas in 1856 that "Charles is exceedingly anxious to go back to Richmond on account of its being so much more convenient for him to visit his wife from there, than here, and under the circumstances, I feel inclined to indulge him as I can but appreciate the feeling that seems to influence him." Other owners and factory managers, who perhaps had not built up extensive contacts, frequently employed hiring agents located in Richmond to place or find slave hirelings.

Most slave hirelings were placed for the year by their owners in face-to-face negotiations with employers, or they found work by bargaining directly with employers in the streets of the city during the annual Christmas-week hiring period. One newspaper observed at the close of 1853 that Richmond had been "thronged with negroes, hirers, owners and buyers, as is the annual custom. Thousands of dollars changed hands, thousands of negroes changed homes and masters." Main streets were generally so crowded with hirelings that merchants complained that holiday shoppers were frightened away. The heaviest criticism, however, was directed at the practice of permitting hirelings to find employers and bargain for the terms of their own hire.

Just before the 1853 hiring season the Richmond *Daily Dispatch* tartly predicted that "Main street will be converted into one vast unroofed intelligence office, and the owners, masters and hirers, in accordance with the annual custom, will briefly dance attendance upon their black attendants." The *Southern Planter* joined the attack on this growing custom, recalling that in years gone by "the owner himself exercised care in selecting a master for his slave . . . but now the negro is permitted to 'choose his master,' as it is called. . . ." Naturally, the slave "selects a master who he knows will indulge him, will exact but little labor, and grant him many privileges and a good deal of time for himself, or he is bribed by money, or the promise of privileges, to live with some one who, possibly from hope of a certain profit to accrue from a modicum of labor, is willing to take him on such terms. . . ." The indulgent employer, the *Southern Planter* warned, "plants the germ of rebellion in the contract for obedience, and stipulates himself into a certain amount of servitude." Repeated warnings of the social dangers of permitting slave hirelings to find their own employers failed to halt the practice.

The custom of allowing slaves to choose their masters flourished in the 1850s because owners and employers found it convenient and profitable. It freed owners from the chore of traveling to Richmond during the holiday or of paying a 5 percent commission to a hiring agent. Since slaves liked the freedom of bargaining power it gave them, their masters could grant it as a reward for faithful past service or offer it as a lure for continued good behavior. Slaves may have won the privilege either by promising to work harder and thereby making themselves more valuable or by offering their owners a sum higher than the market rate for their yearly hire, paying the extra amount out of their factory earnings. Once owners allowed the slave to "choose his master" employers had little choice but to bargain directly with him. Judge John Taylor Lomax was one of many employers who dealt with slave hirelings in the streets at Christmas. He sought a dining-room servant for a year, found a likely slave, and struck a bargain with him. Before concluding the agreement the slave went off to "inquire into the standing and character of the Judge." A local newspaper, outraged at the slave's impudence, fumed that similar incidents "occur with us every day during the Christmas week." They undoubtedly multiplied when demand for hirelings rose in 1852 as a result of the opening of five new tobacco factories.

For the hired slaves there were two matters of great importance. The first was whether or not they would have the opportunity to earn money for themselves. According to a white Richmonder "All slaves had perquisites of some kind. If called on to do extra work, or to serve at unusual times, or if they showed marked fidelity, they were generally recompensed." Dining-room servants, porters, and coachmen collected tips, while domestic servants and factory slaves often received cash instead of clothing. Slaves at the Tredegar Iron Works regularly earned small sums for lighting and cleaning furnaces after working hours. Nowhere was money payment more thoroughly part of the daily production process than in tobacco factories. All tobacco workers had to fill daily production quotas, and they received piece-rate bonuses for all production above the quota. Surviving factory records do not list bonus payments, but contemporary observers did make rough estimates. The *Daily Dispatch* guessed in 1852 that factory hirelings earned about $120 annually. Five years later the Richmond *Whig* claimed that "Many of the hired negroes in the tobacco factories in Richmond make from $8 to $12 per week, overwork, without any extraordinary labor." The *Whig*'s estimate was certainly too high, but earnings seem to have been considerable. Freed black tobacco workers complained in late 1865 that their total earnings were half of what they had been before the war.

The second significant point was whether or not they would be allowed to make their own arrangements for board and room. The practice of giving board money to slave hirelings and to slaves owned by the manufacturers had been rare in the 1820s but had become widespread in the industry by 1850. Many tobacco manufacturers adopted this practice to attract slave hirelings, to retain their services from year to year, and to cut expenses. Slaves preferred boarding out for the freedom of movement and privacy it afforded them. Manufacturers favored it because it freed them from the expense of building dormitories on factory premises and from the responsibility of policing the slaves after working hours. Moreover, they integrated the boarding-out system into their bonus-incentive plan by paying slaves niggardly board stipends, which in the 1850s usually amounted to less than a dollar a week, thus making the slaves use part of their bonus earnings to pay for their board. By keeping board payments low and bonus scales high manufacturers maximized the force of production incentives.

Critics of the board system, the payment of cash to slave workers, and the lax hiring practices frequently campaigned for reforms. They charged that boarding out shifted the employers' responsibility for controlling their slaves to the police and the public treasury, that bonus payments corrupted slaves by encouraging gambling and drinking among them, and that their bargaining power at hiring time made slaves haughty and impudent. Above all, the critics feared that these practices were actually concessions that employers had made to slaves out of a sense of dependence on them. The *Daily Dispatch*, for example, argued that manufacturers had been "compelled, in order to secure labor, first to purchase the consent of the negroes to live with them, and then to hire them of their owners, and in order to do so, have allowed the servants to dictate their own terms as to the amount of board money to be given, the extent of daily labor to be performed, and the price to be paid for such overwork as they may feel disposed to do." However, the critics overshot the mark. It is true that the manufacturers' reliance on slave labor, particularly when demand was high, had given slave hirelings an opening which they broadened over time, but it had never given them the power to dictate terms. Slave hirelings could bargain and maneuver only within the limited boundaries of the racial etiquette imposed by whites. In this extended bargaining they transformed the role laid down for them by slave law, but they did not reverse it.

Critics called on the City Council to abolish the "evils" that had developed in the factory slave-labor system. Responding to these attacks on the boarding-out system the council proposed an ordinance in 1852 that would have required owners and employers to board slaves on their premises. A majority of the tobacco manufacturers counterattacked. They argued that the board system had improved the health and demeanor of their slaves, they claimed that they could not afford to build dormitories for them on factory premises, and they warned that many of them would be forced to evade the law if it were passed. They also asserted that many rural and city slaveowners strongly favored continuing the boarding-out system. Faced by the combined opposition of the influential manufacturers, slaveowners, and boardinghouse keepers, the council backed down, but the controversy persisted.

The financial panic of 1857 weakened the manufacturers' resistance to reforming the board system. Most tobacco factories and other establishments in the city closed by October 1. Newspapers noted that destitution was stalking working-class neighborhoods and that many laborers, particularly free blacks thrown out of work at the tobacco factories, were turning to petty crime to survive. Among working people only slaves seemed untouched by the economic crisis, for they had "masters to supply their wants, however tight the times may be." Manufacturers were sorely pressed by having to provision their own slaves and their slave hirelings. Therefore, they listened intently as Robert A. Mayo, one of Richmond's leading tobacco manufacturers, declared at their December convention "that the practice prevailing in factories of giving light tasks, paying for overwork and furnishing board money, was ruinous to the servants in every respect, unjust to the manufacturers and injurious to owners." The *Daily Dispatch* warmly welcomed Mayo's speech but warned that "No one manufacturer can now say that he will not give board money and over work, and expect to hire a sufficient force to carry on his business; but, by a general understanding, all of them could say so, and the system could be broken up without the slightest inconvenience to themselves." When the City Council passed a new ordinance two weeks later, outlawing the old board system and the practice of permitting slaves to hire themselves out to employers, the manufacturers supported it. The new ordinance did not require owners and hirers to board slaves on their premises, the major stumbling block to earlier reform efforts. It merely directed them to pay board money to those who boarded their slaves instead of to the slaves themselves and required them to inform the mayor where the slaves resided. The victory, however, was more apparent than real.

Critics of the over-work and bonus system did not win even a cosmetic reform. The *Daily Dispatch* spoke for many white Richmonders in arguing that the over-work system was a "curse" to many valuable factory slaves, for "Money in their hands leads to drinking and gambling, and these, in their turn, to other vices and crimes." Paying slaves for work they ought to perform, when their basic material wants were already provided, was a "mere waste of means" that should be "suppressed," the paper reasoned. A few manufacturers agreed, but most demurred. The majority recognized that the lure of bonuses combined most effectively with the threat of punishment to maintain high production levels. However necessary coercion may have been for

slave labor, exclusive reliance on it could backfire. Harsh employers risked injuring valuable slave property, antagonizing owners of hired slaves, and repelling those slaves who found their own employers. Punishments unmixed with rewards provoked work slowdowns, worker demoralization, and such retaliatory acts as physical attack and incendiarism. The promise of bonuses reduced the need for coercion by making it the slaves' interest to labor efficiently and steadily. The promise, moreover, easily became a form of discipline, for employers could dock pay for lateness and unruliness and could cancel the rewards of those who tried to run away. Bonuses were simply too important in the hiring and productive processes to be abolished, despite what editors and elected officials said about their socially subversive consequences.

The range of choice open to slave hirelings narrowed after the hiring period, but their ability to shape their working and living conditions did not end after they entered the factory gates. A highly concentrated labor force averaging about seventy-five men and boys per factory, tobacco hands developed a sense of group interest as slaves and free blacks and as workers with wants and needs different from and occasionally opposed to those of their employers. As working groups have generally done, tobacco workers recognized some of their fellows as leaders and created ways of initiating newcomers into their company and of familiarizing them with the customs of the factory.

White overseers, many in their late teens and early twenties, were set above the workers. Theirs was a ticklish job. It required them to maintain order and high productivity, both of which depended upon cooperation from the workers. The overseers gave orders to slaves who, in many cases, were older, stronger, and more knowledgeable about making tobacco products than they and who had often seen several overseers come and go, had broken them in, and had learned to exploit their inexperience. The successful overseers learned to balance rewards and punishments, to command respect without provoking hatred, and to win cooperation without surrendering all authority. The unsuccessful frequently relied too heavily on the whip. William Jackson, a nineteen-year-old overseer, was killed by a young slave stemmer he was whipping for slovenly work. Another overseer, a hot-tempered lad with a penchant for whipping slaves while he was enraged, lost his job because, his employer said, "the negroes generally had antipathy against him. . . ." Manufacturers, however, usually defended their overseers. William Graenor remained steadfastly loyal to his overseer in the face of a threat by some of his slave workers to burn his factory if he failed to discharge the man. Many overseers began taking arms with them into the factories in 1852, which suggests that they wanted more than their employers' moral support.

The slaves' chief resource and defense as workers in the factories was not their capacity to retaliate against employers and overseers by attacking their persons and property, though this served to remind managers that their power was limited. It was, instead, the control slaves had of their own labor and, since no factory before the war had adopted power-driven machinery, of the pace and quality of production. Quotas, bonuses, and coercive measures channeled the slaves' energies into production, but they never fully succeeded in giving managers complete control of the slaves' labor and of the production process. Scattered evidence suggests that slaves might have regulated the work pace and thereby have had a hand in determining quota and bonus levels. It is conceivable, though ultimately unprovable, that they conspired after hours to set the tempo of work. More likely, because it rests on strong but ambiguous evidence, is the possibility that slaves used song to determine the work pace. Their singing constituted a minor tourist attraction in Richmond. James Grant's slaves sang "several beautiful hymns" for Julia Lord Noyes Loveland and her companions from the North. The manager of another factory told William Cullen Bryant that he encouraged his slaves to sing because "the boys work better while singing." But he could not command them to sing. "They must sing wholly of their own

accord, it is of no use to bid them do it." The slaves decided when to sing. The same manager remarked, "Sometimes they will sing all day long with great spirit; at other times you will not hear a single note." They also decided what to sing and worked in time to their music. Through singing slaves set the pace of work. Some slaves apparently believed they had outsmarted their employers. They bragged to their pastor that "they sometimes received on Saturday night more wages for themselves than they had earned for their masters."

Six days a week the slaves toiled in factories whose conditions they had partly shaped. On the seventh day many joined thousands of other slaves and free blacks in churches over which they exercised far greater influence. On that day the community turned out in its finery. Marianne Finch, an English visitor, observed that the blacks' weekday apparel was dull and ordinary. A black person, she noted, only "appears in full-bloom on Sunday, and then he is a striking object; whether male or female, whether in silks or muslins; or beaver and broadcloth." Another English visitor, finding himself seated with the choir of the First African Baptist Church, noticed that the men "were dressed *en grand toilette*, handsome black coats and trousers, white waistcoats, and white ties; the women in silks and muslins flounced *en dernière mode*, of the gayest colours, with bonnets and mantles to match."

For all the important differences that existed between Sabbath and weekday activities, between the church and the factory, the links connecting them were strong. They were but two connected parts of the life experience shared by thousands of Richmond blacks. The hymns of worship, for example, were frequently the songs of work. One visitor to the factories remarked that the workers "think it is dreadful wicked to sing anything but sacred music." Bryant's informant noted that "their taste is exclusively for sacred music; they will sing nothing else." The majority were regular churchgoers. "Most of them are of the Baptist persuasion; a few are Methodists," he added. The money they made in the factories helped finance their African churches. The group consciousness and modes or organization created in one institution were transferred and adapted to the other, but in the churches they were more clearly articulated and were afforded more room for expression.

The history of the spread of Christianity among Virginia blacks is generally divided into three periods. The first sustained missionary activity among them occurred between 1750 and 1790. The Baptists and Methodists were most successful because they enlisted numerous black preachers and exhorters and mixed antislavery sentiments with the Gospel. This activity flagged after 1790, but regained momentum as a white-directed, proslavery movement after Nat Turner's rebellion in 1831 and the subsequent debate over slavery in the Virginia legislature. Virginia chose to retain slavery and passed laws making it illegal to teach blacks to read and write, suppressing independent black churches, and outlawing black preaching. Virginia's evangelical sects, having lost their black preachers and having committed themselves to defend slavery, redoubled their efforts to attract black converts and to reform the most odious features of slavery. The religious history of Virginia after 1830 formed, according to Eugene D. Genovese, "part of the great thrust to reform slavery as a way of life and to make it bearable for the slaves."

Well before 1830 hundreds of Richmond slaves and free blacks had become Christians and members of Protestant churches in which, consigned to separate areas, they worshipped with their white coreligionists. Most became Baptists, and they easily outnumbered their white brethren. In 1823 ninety-one free black Baptists, complaining that existing churches could not adequately accommodate the nearly seven hundred black Baptists, free and slave, petitioned the legislature for permission to establish an African Baptist church. Although they promised to obey laws passed for the "proper restraint" of black persons and had the support of prominent local whites, their petition was rejected. By 1828 the First Baptist Church counted about 1,000 blacks among its 1,300 members. The Baptists' humble origins, the democratic and mildly antislavery appeals of their early evangels, and their rough,

emotional preaching contributed to the success of the church among Virginia blacks. Equally important to that success were the work of its black preachers and exhorters and its form of church government, which permitted members, even slaves, a degree of self-rule.

Baptist churches had regularly licensed black preachers and exhorters prior to the legislative ban on black preaching. This proved a troublesome duty, for several blacks with unorthodox views or without official sanction preached and exhorted. In 1828, for example, a white committee of the First Baptist Church inquired into the extent of the "evil arising from the exercise of public gifts by the coloured brethren not authorized by the church . . ." and recommended that the church formally reexamine all black preachers and exhorters. Only a third of the eighteen men who had preached and exhorted passed the test and received licenses. When the law silenced these men it created a severe shortage of ministers able or willing to conduct funerals and other religious services for blacks. Baptist churches with racially mixed memberships operated on a two-tier plan. White pastors and deacons elected by the white members were in command. Under them were black deacons elected by the entire church. These black deacons scrutinized black members, settled disputes among them, investigated reports of misconduct, and presented candidates for admission or readmission to the church. The entire church membership made final decisions after receiving the black deacons' recommendations. The authority of the black deacons was tightly circumscribed, but within a limited area bounded by white supervision the deacons and their black constituents decided with whom they would have "fellowship" and the standard of conduct they would demand.

The Baptist church acted both as a staunch supporter of the slave regime and as a subtle subverter of its underlying rationale. Committed to slavery, the church required that its slave members be obedient servants. Numerous slave members were expelled from the First Baptist Church for disobeying their masters and for attempting to run away, but masters were rarely punished for mistreating slaves. Only once between 1825 and 1830 did the First Baptist Church exclude a master. It expelled William Muse in 1825 for "breach of promise, toward a man formerly owned by him and sent to New Orleans without giving him an opportunity to get a master in this place, and for making misstatements to the church concerning the same." Although the church enforced moral standards that frequently overlapped the state's slave code, it also undercut the central premise of that code. In its view slaves were not mere property. They were, instead, persons whose souls God prized, and who, therefore, ought to be sober, properly married, taught Christian truths, and treated humanely by their temporal masters. For all the obvious weaknesses of exhorting masters to treat slaves in a decent manner as fellow human beings while simultaneously defending slavery and its inhumane racial mores and legal apparatus, the churches provided slaves with more psychological leverage, stronger moral claims, and greater protection in dealing with their masters than did either the law or racial theories. Baptist churches were socially conservative institutions, and blacks occupied subservient positions in them, but the churches did insist on the slaves' humanity and did provide them a small measure of self-government.

Despite legislative rebuffs Richmond's black Baptists continually pressed for churches of their own, and when success was achieved it came as much from the desire of white Baptists to separate from them as by their own efforts. The Baptist message of salvation was being received by far more blacks than whites. When Jeremiah Bell Jeter assumed that pastorship of the First Baptist Church in 1836 he found only 400 whites among its 2,400 members. Baptist success among blacks became embarrassing, for its churches were susceptible to being stigmatized as black churches and thus becoming unattractive to potential white converts. According to one white minister some fastidious whites "did not like to resort to a church, where so many colored folks congregated, and this was thought to operate against the growth of the white portion of the audience." White Baptists sat uncomfortably beneath galleries packed with poor, mostly illiter-

ate blacks and grew irritated with the blacks' style of worship, their tardiness, and, indeed, their close proximity. Ministers fretted over composing sermons that would engage whites and appeal to blacks. The small white minorities carried much of the responsibility for financing their churches. Many white members became convinced that trusted blacks could best control their black brethren. According to one white minister a large portion of the black congregation, "being slaves, could not be reached and disciplined, except by persons of their own color." The solutions to the problems created by the influx of black converts varied. White members of the Second Baptist Church ruled by 1843 that "no coloured members would be received except under peculiar circumstances." The white congregation of the First Baptist Church decided to build a new church for themselves and sell the old one to the blacks.

Before that decision could be effected the legality of establishing an African church had to be determined. White church officers consulted legal experts, who advised that the law would permit such a church provided a white preacher became its minister. Having settled the legal question, church officers sought to allay public hostility to the project by creating an eighteen-member white superintending committee drawn from three Baptist churches. The majority of committee members came from the First Baptist Church, which acted as the parent church for the proposed First African Baptist Church. Although the old church building was appraised at $13,500, the white congregation demanded far less from the blacks. It received slightly less than $6,500. Nearly $3,000 was raised by James Thomas, Jr., and other fund raisers from white citizens, particularly tobacco manufacturers and merchants. The black congregation contributed $3,500. Shortly after the First African Baptist Church opened in 1841, the First Baptist Church reaped the benefits of separation. In 1842 during a series of revivals that swept Richmond 170 whites joined the church, among whom, Jeter noted with satisfaction, were "heads of families, men of business and influence, who added greatly to its strength and efficiency."

The constitution of the First African Baptist Church, drawn up by Jeter, created a form of government that was "more presbyterial than congregational," in that the black congregation enjoyed less autonomy than was customary among Baptists. It stipulated that the pastor be a white minister nominated by the superintending committee and approved by the elected black deacons. The committee received the power to oversee the African church's affairs, to hear appeals from its decisions, and to rule on changes in the constitution, but it rarely exercised its constitutional authority. Committee members were obliged to take turns attending all African church services, but some, according to the church's pastor, honored the obligation only intermittently. They never had to rule on amendments and they acted on only three appeals between 1841 and 1865. The constitution did not depart totally from congregational government. It gave the congregation power to elect thirty deacons who, together with the pastor the congregation accepted, constituted the church's "permanent ruling power." The pastor and the deacons ruled the church for twenty-four years relatively unfettered by interference from the superintending committee.

The committee nominated, and the black members accepted, Robert Ryland as pastor. At the time of his nomination and for several years after Ryland also served as president of Richmond College, a Baptist institution of higher learning. Deriving most of his income from the college, Ryland required an annual salary of only $500 from the church. He had impeccable credentials as a safe southern minister, for he defended both slavery and the southern church's concern for slaves against abolitionist attacks. Though he defended the institution, he harbored misgivings about the morality of destroying slave families merely for the profit of their owners and of obeying state laws against black preaching and literacy, fearing that they retarded missionary work among blacks.

Ryland's defense of slavery, which he shared with Jeter and some other Virginia ministers, rested in part on the assumption that slavery was part of the divine plan to introduce enslaved Africans in America to Christ and to bring Christ to Africa through the agency of repatriated Afro-American missionaries. The laws silencing black preachers placed added obligations on white ministers, and Ryland, who felt keenly this obligation and wanted a city pastorate, eagerly welcomed the call from the First African Baptist Church. The prohibition of black literacy created a dilemma for ministers like Ryland. He and Jeter among others had opposed slavery as young men. During the 1820s and 1830s, however, they followed most white Virginians and embraced the institution. To justify their new commitment they anxiously searched the Bible for evidence supporting slavery and resolved that it was a divinely approved means for spreading the Word. State law threatened to thwart divine purpose. Torn between the conflicting claims of religious mission and secular law, Ryland opted for the former. He admitted on at least one occasion in the 1850s that he was encouraging blacks to read and was distributing Bibles and religious tracts among them.

Unfortunately, more is known about Ryland than about his congregation and the deacons it elected. The church began with 940 members and, also benefiting from separation, grew to 1,600 in a year. It had over 3,000 members by 1856. The status of the founding members is unknown, but slaves far outnumbered free persons among members admitted after 1841. Of 2,388 members added between 1841 and 1857, 1,203 were male slaves; 932, female slaves; 92, male free blacks; and 161, female free blacks. Free blacks, however, held most of the deaconships. The identities of twenty-four of the original thirty deacons have been established and eighteen were free men. Ten of the original thirty had long been active in church affairs, having served as deacons and committeemen in the First Baptist Church between 1825 and 1830. Most of the twenty-nine deacons elected between 1841 and 1859 were also free men, usually tradesmen and property owners. Their domination of the Board of Deacons did not go completely unchallenged. Three church members complained to the pastor in 1850 about "partiality" shown to "free persons in the administration of church matters." Their complaint touched off a heated debate which so divided the church that the superintending committee made one of its rare interventions. The settlement imposed by the committee did not noticeably diminish the free blacks' influence.

The First African, as the largest and most prestigious black Baptist church in Richmond, served as a model for three others founded before the war. Their constitutions, for example, virtually replicated its constitution. Most of the black congregation of the Second Baptist Church departed in 1845 to form the Second African Baptist Church. The First African built the Ebenezer or Third African Baptist Church in 1858 and sent several hundred of its members to form the new congregation. In 1860 black members of the Leigh Street Baptist Church began meeting as a separate congregation in the basement of their old church. Black Baptists outnumbered whites by a margin of at least two to one by 1860, and their four African churches claimed 4,600 members or about a third of the city's black adults. Only the records of the First and Ebenezer African churches are extant for the antebellum period, but because the First African and its pastor set precedents that the other churches followed and because these two churches claimed three-fourths of Richmond's black Baptists much of the history of the black Baptist community can be reconstructed through their records. The minutes of the First African, which span an eighteen-year period, reveal how the congregation worked with the pastor, deacons, and parent church and how it operated as a semiautonomous body within the restrictions laid down by secular white society.

The pastor and deacons formed the governing body of the First African, and their decisions were usually final. As governing officers they guided the congregation's affairs and scrutinized the members' conduct, but they were also responsible to the congregation. Candidates for the pastorship had to win majority support among the congregation. When support evaporated, as it did at the Second African in 1858, the pastor resigned. Deacons owed their positions even more directly to the constituents who elect-

ed them. Because they antagonized a large portion of the congregation two deacons of the First African had to retire, although one had strong backing from Pastor Ryland. Nevertheless, deacons exercised great influence. They disciplined members who broke Baptist moral commandments, arbitrated disputes between members, decided whether to admit new members and readmit penitent offenders, and conducted the church's financial affairs. Selected from all areas of the city and suburbs, deacons were the church's listening posts, its disciplinarians, and the guardians of its moral code.

When reports of misconduct reached the church the deacons residing near the parties concerned made investigations and alerted the parties to the church's interest in them. They later reported their findings to the monthly meetings of the pastor and Board of Deacons, who conducted a trial, heard the testimonies of the accused and witnesses, and rendered judgments as to their guilt or innocence. The pastor and deacons also convened special meetings to consider requests for readmission from expelled members. The constitution gave the pastor and deacons greater authority in disciplinary matters than their counterparts in white Baptist churches enjoyed, for the black congregation could not vote in such determinations. It was their exclusive control over membership in the most important institution in the black community that gave the deacons such impressive authority.

The moral code upheld and enforced by the black deacons was essentially the same as that white deacons enforced. It prized harmony and fellowship, love, charity, marital fidelity, sexual continence outside marriage, and sobriety as virtues, and it condemned fighting, fornication, adultery, drunkenness, stealing, gambling, and cheating as vices. For some infractions, such as stealing and adultery, convicted offenders were immediately expelled. For most other offenses the deacons were far more concerned with reforming offenders and conciliating quarrelsome parties than with expelling them. Only after reform measures and compromise settlements failed and only when the guilty parties failed to show sufficient repentance did the deacons resort to exclusion. Deacons frequently labored for months to save troubled marriages, to reform drunkards and forgive them if they promised to abstain from drinking, to reclaim gamblers who returned their winnings, and to postpone disciplining debtors if they showed even the slightest willingness to repay. Only after it became obvious that their efforts at reform had failed did the deacons exclude the offenders from the church. Later they might readmit those who demonstrated that they had been reformed.

Monthly disciplinary meetings functioned in two important ways for the community. First, they provided a type of judicial apparatus unavailable to slaves and free blacks elsewhere. In municipal court the admissibility of black testimony was severely circumscribed since blacks could not testify against whites. Slaves rarely initiated suits, and then only through white spokesmen. Most slaves and free blacks who appeared in the mayor's court were defendants picked up by the police for some infraction of the law. White men heard their cases and handed down verdicts that usually reflected their interest in maintaining the social order and black subservience. In their churches, however, slaves and free blacks brought their claims and complaints before peers they had elected, whose purpose was to reestablish Christian harmony as well as to uphold the moral code. Church disciplinary hearings were the black community's small-claims courts, offering a service that no other body provided. Second, although the black deacons enforced the moral code common to all Baptists, the social effects of their activities were different, as different as the economic, social, and political conditions of blacks were from those of whites. When, for example, deacons upheld slave marriages and punished members who violated norms of marital fidelity they honored a practice that had no legal standing and that was only intermittently recognized by whites. They counterbalanced through community action the disintegrating tendencies inherent in secular slave society. When deacons reconciled quarreling members or creditors and debtors they offered a regular, peaceable alternative to individualistic,

possibly violent, settlements in the streets or to employing white men as arbitrators. The deacons also modified white Baptist practice in at least two ways. They granted divorces and permission to remarry to slaves whose marriages had been broken by forced separation, and they thus adapted their moral code to the harsh realities of slavery. In addition they generally did not expel runaways as the white-dominated churches had done. In black Richmond, because of the relative absence of legal and institutional mechanisms for dealing with mundane personal and social problems, the pronouncements of the African churches, the only bodies over which blacks had considerable influence, resonated with extraordinary power.

The churches' charitable work must be viewed in the same light. The municipal government usually appropriated funds to provide food and fuel for the white and free-black poor over the late winter months and periods of recession. It felt no responsibility, however, for assisting needy slaves, whose upkeep was viewed as the responsibility of their owners. The African churches considered the slave and free-black indigent to be equally deserving of their charities. Each month the congregation of the First African contributed to the "Poor Saints" fund, which was distributed to the needy by a seventeen-member committee staffed by five deacons from each of the city's three wards, a secretary, and a treasurer. Through such church bodies and an unknown number of illegal benevolent societies the black community cared for many of its poor. The Poor Saints Committee of the First African distributed over $2,000 between 1849 and 1858. During eight of those years the smaller, wealthier, white Second Baptist Church raised little more than $700.

Most of the money raised to maintain the church, purchase the church building, and pay the salaries of the pastor and sexton came from the congregation in weekly penny collections. Pews were not rented as they were in white Baptist churches, and, therefore, seating arrangements did not reflect wealth distinctions. Another source of revenue came from renting the church building to political parties, entertainers, and lecturers. A third source of income was the church's popular choir, which gave concerts periodically for the general public. When the church undertook unusually expensive projects, such as building the Ebenezer African Baptist Church, it had the choir perform, and it appointed its most prominent members to solicit subscriptions in the white and black communities. Money derived from these sources paid salaries, insurance and maintenance costs, and the more than $9,000 owed for the First African and Ebenezer churches. In addition to these routine expenses, the church gave money to a number of Baptist enterprises and secular humanitarian causes. It joined other black churches in buying the slave deacon Thomas Allen and the slave families of two free-black preachers to enable the three to embark on missionary work outside the South. It donated entire collections to struggling black congregations in seven Virginia towns and in Detroit, Philadelphia, the District of Columbia, Savannah, and Buxton, Ontario. It contributed money to aid yellow-fever victims in Norfolk and Portsmouth and to feed the poor of famine-stricken Ireland. The deacons conducted the church's financial affairs with efficiency and skill. Ryland wrote in 1855 that he had never "discovered one instance of an attempt to defraud, or palpable negligence of duty, or a want of competence to the office assumed." Anyone who doubted the blacks' abilities or regarded them "as a set of simpletons," he added, would "very quickly transfer the charge of folly from them to himself."

Relations between the pastor and the church were generally cooperative and cordial because each accommodated to the other's needs, peculiarities, and traditions. Ryland, a college president and defender of slavery, preached submission and obedience, lessons some of his listeners rejected. A cynical free black told James Redpath, an abolitionist writer who visited Richmond, that he had heard Ryland state from the pulpit "that God had given all this continent to the white man, and that it was our duty to submit." He also heard one of his brethren reply:

"He be d———d! God am not sich a fool!" When Redpath asked whether Ryland always preached to suit slaveholders, his informant answered wearily that Ryland "wouldn't be allowed to preach at all if he didn't." Ryland attempted to inculcate habits of chaste living, sedate and mannered behavior, and punctuality through "didactic" preaching, which he admitted was unexciting and less popular than emotional appeals to his listeners' "passions." He claimed considerable success. He believed that their sexual habits had been elevated and that their religious notions had become more rational. Because of his efforts church members, he announced, "have less superstition, less reliance on dreams and visions, they talk less of the palpable guidings of the Spirit as independent of or opposed to the word of God." They were also learning to "avoid habits of whining, snuffling, grunting, drawling, repeating, hic[c]oughing, and other vulgarities in prayer. . . ." A stickler for punctuality, Ryland never succeeded in communicating its importance. An Englishwoman who visited the church in 1853 observed that it was thinly attended when services began but that afterwards members trickled in without disturbing services, "though they all shook hands with the friends near them, and nodded to the more distant. . . ."

If, as Ryland claimed, his preaching and example modified the behavior of many in his congregation, it is also true that the traditions and needs of his congregation shaped his ministry. Two traditions that some free blacks and more than a few slaves had developed and that the laws of 1831 had suppressed but not destroyed were literacy and preaching. Already troubled about these laws, Ryland easily and with good conscience distributed Bibles and religious tracts among church members and established an informal lending library for them. He also incorporated their preaching into religious services. After the war Ryland recalled that "There were several ministers of respectable gifts in the church, who, at the request of private families and by the connivance of the officers of the law, often attended funerals in the city and the adjacent country." By law they could not preach from the pulpit, "But, as a sort of recompense for this slight, they, and others, were called on to pray, several times, at each religious service." Their prayers, which were actually extemporaneous orations, "exhibited great fervency and power, and afforded the highest degree of comfort, both to those who offered them and to those who heard them." After regular services some blacks preached to those remaining, who responded in ways Ryland would have disapproved. A visitor noticed that "there was an amateur performance of singing and exhortation, in which a few old people got very much excited, swinging their bodies about, stamping their feet, and shaking hands frantically with everybody near them, myself among the rest." She noted that the "most active, were those who had slept during the sermon, though, to do them justice, these were few, generally they had been very attentive." Speaking of one of these preachers, Ryland admitted frankly that "he was heard with far more interest than I was."

At the monthly meetings conducted by Ryland and the deacons a majority of deacons usually voted with their pastor, perhaps because his arguments were particularly persuasive. Occasionally, however, his side lost, and his voted counted as only one of thirty-one. He also intervened periodically in matters where the deacons believed he had no business, and they were quick to tell him gently that his advice was unappreciated. At the death of Deacon Joseph Abrams, for example, they purchased a tombstone and pondered what epitaph to inscribe on it. "When I learned that an inscription was to be prepared for his grave," Ryland recalled, "in my simplicity, I offered my services to write it." His friends, however, "thought their own literary taste fully equal to the occasion, and declined my proposal." The funeral attracted eight thousand persons and "one of the largest processions ever seen in Richmond, including more than fifty carriages, followed the remains to the tomb." The congregation's independence sometimes embarrassed Ryland. When a South Carolina judge offended the congregation while delivering a temperance lecture their displeasure "was painfully evident by loud murmurs, and by their leaving the house in large numbers!"

Though compromise characterized the relations between the pastor and the deacons, the superintending committee's interventions allowed the deacons little maneuvering room. Twice the committee imposed settlements on a divided congregation, and it also acted once when the church overstepped the boundaries laid down by the white parent church. The last incident demonstrated the limits of the congregation's autonomy. As long as the deacons operated within the sphere whites believed proper for church government their control was almost complete, but beyond it submission was demanded. The incident arose when the church, having paid its debt for the church building, tried to name three free blacks and two whites as legal trustees of the property. After receiving the deacons' nominations the superintending committee withheld confirmation pending consultation with the Virginia attorney general on the legality of the arrangement. The attorney general ruled that the property would be best secured if all the trustees were white men. Ryland than asked the deacons to revise their choices, but they adamantly refused. The superintending committee broke the stalemate by unilaterally picking five white trustees. The deacons surrendered, but only after announcing that "we do not admit to the propriety of such a restriction." Nor did the matter rest there. At a subsequent meeting, which Ryland characterized as "exciting and somewhat disorderly," representatives of the committee appeared to assure the deacons that the new appointments guaranteed title to the church to the black congregation for its "exclusive and perpetual benefit." At this point the church could do no more than grudgingly accept the committee's terms, for to challenge them again would be to challenge white supremacy openly and perhaps trigger a dangerous white reaction. The church's survival depended on appearing to conform to the whites' rules while subtly broadening its area of autonomy.

The black church's relations with the larger white society were mixed. On the one hand, many whites, especially Baptists, supplied time, money, and public support. White officials, for instance, permitted black preachers to officiate at funerals if they paid or persuaded white men to attend them. On the other hand, many whites remained suspicious and critical of African churches, seeing them as nurseries of rebellion or at least of impertinent behavior, particularly during tense periods. For example, after Jane Williams, a member of the First African, confessed to having murdered two members of her master's family, editors and public officials wondered aloud whether the church pacified slaves or created rebels, and they demanded tighter police control over the church. A similar reaction occurred when the police discovered that runaway slaves were using a mailing system, set up in the church by Ryland for sending and receiving conduct references for members, to encourage others to run away to inform them of the best escape routes. The church survived these and other scandals because its white patrons defended it and, more important, because the church never openly criticized slavery or overtly challenged white dominance. Many of its members secretly criticized their bondage, but until slavery was destroyed they could not demonstrate their opposition without incurring murderous reprisals. They emphatically demonstrated their hostility on April 3, 1865.

Thousands of tobacco factory workers and African church members welcomed Federal troops to Richmond. For many the transition to the free-labor system came easily, for they had long been accustomed to finding work, bargaining with employers, and managing finances. They seemed far more eager to recommence working than did the disheartened Confederate veterans. They had already developed modes of self-help and collective action which they activated and redirected after emancipation. Their shadowy secret societies surfaced and proliferated at an astonishing rate, numbering over four hundred by 1873. They seized control of their churches by June 1865, named new pastors, and used church buildings for schools, employment offices, and staging areas for organizing public protests and celebrations. Not without reason did whites come to hate these churches. Incendiaries destroyed the Second African Baptist Church because it housed a freedman's school and because organizers used it to plan a massive celebration of April 3, 1866, the first anniversary of the black liberation and the white defeat.

Long membership in the churches had not won blacks over to their pastors' views on race and slavery nor to the claims that God sanctioned slavery. Cyrus Hughes had joined the First African in 1848 and remained a member and a slave until the soldiers arrived. Three days later he told his former mistress, who asked him to continue working without wages until the harvest, that he would not work for promises, that "there was to be no more Master and Mistress now, all was equal. . . ." For Hughes and thousands of other former slaves and free blacks, emancipation verified Scriptural truth and shattered the fetters that had wrongly held them in bondage. Black spokesmen frequently compared emancipation to conversion, the former being the temporal fulfillment of the latter. Conversion, the enslavement of one's soul and will to God, had not legitimatized one man's claim to another as his property. From the same pulpits where Ryland and his white colleagues had delivered countless sermons on servants' duties to their masters came a different message. Whenever freedom was mentioned in the churches, a northern newspaperman observed in April 1865, "emotion kindles over the whole audience, and repeatedly have I heard them quote in prayer the language of God to Moses: 'I have surely seen the affliction of my people which are in Egypt, and have heard their cry because of their taskmasters; for I know their sorrows, and I am come down to deliver them.'" Blacks brought notions about freedom, moral sensibilities, work habits, familial and communal ties, and modes of collective activity to the years of Reconstruction. Into that process of creating something new in a slaveless world they took a culture and organizational structure they had created as slaves and free blacks, as church members and factory workers.

20

ADVOCATE OF THE DREAM

STEPHEN B. OATES

No American president has been as mythologized as Abraham Lincoln. Whether revered as the savior of the Union or condemned as the cause of the Civil War and the subsequent decline of the South, the sixteenth president has appeared larger than life since he took the oath of office in 1861. In this reconsideration of the man behind the myth, Stephen B. Oates examines Lincoln's commitment to a moral vision of national prosperity and political equality open to all Americans. Oates suggests that the "American dream" of material reward for individual effort was Lincoln's guiding philosophy from his early days as a young politician in Illinois through his final days as leader of the victorious Union.

The greatest challenge to this dream of moderate mobility was the continued existence of slavery in the southern states, and it haunted Lincoln throughout his public life. From his unsuccessful senatorial campaign of 1858, during which he declared that the nation could not exist "half slave and half free," through his wartime emancipation of southern slaves, Lincoln dealt with the complex moral, economic, and political issues raised by slavery with a mixture of principle and pragmatism. Ultimately, Oates argues, it was Lincoln's creative struggle with the conundrum of slavery and individual liberty that ensured his greatness as a leader.

1. THE BEACON LIGHT OF LIBERTY

In presidential polls taken by *Life* magazine in 1948, the *New York Times Magazine* in 1962, and the *Chicago Tribune Magazine* in 1982, historians and political scholars ranked Lincoln as the best chief executive in American history. They were not trying to mythologize the man, for they realized that errors, vacillations, and human flaws marred his record. Their rankings indicate, however, that the icon of mythology did rise out of a powerful historical figure, a man who learned from his mistakes and made a difference. Indeed, Lincoln led the lists because he had a moral vision of where his country must go to preserve and enlarge the rights of all her people. He led the lists because he had an acute sense of history—an ability to identify himself with a historical turning point in his time and to articulate the promise that held for the liberation of oppressed humanity the world over. He led the lists because he perceived the truth of his age and embodied it in his words and deeds. He led the lists because, in his interaction with the spirit and events of his day, he made momentous *moral* decisions that affected the course of humankind.

It cannot be stressed enough how much Lincoln responded to the spirit of his age. From the 1820s to the 1840s, while Lincoln was growing to manhood and learning the art and technique of politics, the Western world seethed with revolutionary ferment. In the 1820s, revolutions broke out not only in Poland, Turkey, Greece, Italy, Spain, and France, but blazed across Spain's ramshackle South American empire as well, resulting in new republics whose capitals rang with the rhetoric of freedom and independence. The Republic of Mexico even produced laws and promulgations that abolished slavery throughout the nation, including Mexico's sub-province of Texas. In that same decade, insurrection panics rocked the Deep South, especially the South Carolina tidewater, as America's disinherited Africans reflected the revolutionary turbulence sweeping the New World. In 1831, in an effort to liberate his people, a visionary slave preacher named Nat Turner incited the most violent slave rebellion in American history, a revolt that shook the South to its foundations and cleared the way for the Great Southern Reaction against the human-rights upheavals of the time. In the 1830s, a vociferous abolitionist movement sprang up in the free states; Great Britain eradicated slavery in the Empire; and impassioned English emancipators came to crusade in America as well. In distant Russia, Czar Nicholas I established an autonomous communal structure for Russia's millions of serfs—the first step in their eventual emancipation two decades later. In the 1840s, while Lincoln practiced law and ran for Congress, reformist impulses again swept Europe. Every major country there had liberal parties that clamored for representative government, self-rule, civil liberties, and social and economic reform. In 1848, the year Congressman Lincoln denounced "Mr. Polk's War" against Mexico, defended the right of revolution, and voted against slavery expansion, revolutions again blazed across Europe, flaring up first in France against the July Monarchy, then raging through Italy and central Europe. These were revolutions against monarchy, despotism, exploitation by the few, revolutions that tried to liberate individuals, classes, and nationalities alike from the shackles of the past. In sum, it was an age of revolution, a turbulent time when people throughout the Western world were searching for definitions of liberty, fighting and dying for liberty, against reactionary forces out to preserve the status quo.

Out in Illinois, Lincoln identified himself with the liberating forces of his day. In fact, he became the foremost political spokesman for those impulses in the United States, a man with a world view of the meaning and mission of his young country in that historic time.

From earliest manhood, Lincoln was a fervent nationalist in an age when a great many Americans, especially in Dixie, were aggressive localists. His broad outlook began when he was an Indiana farm boy tilling his father's mundane wheatfield. During lunch breaks, when he was not studying grammar and rhetoric, Lincoln would peruse Parson Weems's eulogistic biography of George Washington, and he would day-dream about the Revolution and the origins of the Republic, daydream about Washington, Jefferson, and Madison as great national states-men who shaped the course if history. By time he became a politician in the 1830s, Lincoln idolized the Founding Fathers as apostles of liberty (never mind for now that many of those apostles were also southern slaveowners). Young Lincoln extolled the Fathers for beginning a noble exper-iment in popular government on these shores, to demonstrate to the world that a free people could govern themselves without hereditary monarchs and aristocracies. And the foundation of the American experiment was the Declaration of Independence, which in Lincoln's view pro-claimed the highest political truths in history: that all men were created equal and entitled to liberty and the pursuit of happiness. This meant that men like Lincoln were not chained to the conditions of their births, that they could better their station in life and realize the rewards of their own talent and toil.

A good example, Lincoln believed, was his political idol, Whig national leader Henry Clay of Kentucky. Born into a poor farm family, Clay lift-ed himself all the way to the United States Senate and national and international fame. For Lincoln, this taught a "profitable lesson"—"it teaches that in this country, one can scarcely be so poor, but that, if he *will*, he *can* acquire suffi-cient education to get through the world respectably." Thanks to the Declaration, which guaranteed Americans "the right to rise," Lincoln himself had acquired enough education to "get through the world respectably." Thus he had a deep, personal reverence for the Declaration and insisted that all his political sentiments flowed from that document.

All his economic beliefs derived from that document, too. Indeed, Lincoln's economics were as nationalistic and deeply principled as his politics. Schooled in the Whig doctrine of order and national unity, Lincoln advocated a strong federal government to maintain a prosperous, stable economy for the benefit of all

Americans—"the old and the young, the rich and the poor, the grave and the gay, of all sexes and tongues, and colors and conditions," as he would say. Thus he championed a national bank, inter-nal improvements financed by the federal gov-ernment, federal subsidies to help the states build their own canals, turnpikes, and railroads, and state banks whose task was to ensure finan-cial growth and stability. "The legitimate object of government," Lincoln asserted later, "is to do for the people what needs to be done, but which they can not, by individual effort, do at all, or do so well, for themselves."

Lincoln's national economic program was part of his large vision of the American experiment in popular government. By promoting national prosperity, stability, and unity, his economics would help guarantee his "American dream"—the right of all Americans to rise, to harvest the full fruits of their labors, and so to better them-selves as their own talent and industry allowed. Thus the American experiment ensured two things essential to liberty: the right of self-gov-ernment and the right of self-improvement.

Nor was the promise of America limited to the native-born. Her frontier, Lincoln said, should function as an outlet for people the world over who wanted to find new homes, a place to "better their conditions in life." For Lincoln, the American experiment was the way of the future for nations across the globe. A child of the Enlightenment, the American system stood as a beacon of hope for "the liberty party throughout the world."

Yet this beacon of hope harbored a monstrous thing, a relic of despotism in the form of Negro slavery. In Lincoln's view, bondage was the one retrograde institution that disfigured the American experiment, and he maintained that he had always hated it, as much as any abolitionist. his family had opposed slavery, and he had grown up and entered politics thinking it wrong. In 1837, his first public statement on slavery, Lincoln contended that it was "founded both on injustice and bad policy," and he never changed his mind. But before 1854 (and the significance of this date will become clear), Lincoln generally kept his own counsel about slavery and abolition. After all, slavery was the most inflammable issue of his generation, and Lincoln observed early on what violent passions Negro bondage—and the question of race that underlay it—could arouse in white Americans. In his day, slavery was a tried and tested means of race control in a South dedicated to white supremacy. Moreover, the North was also a white supremacist region, where the vast majority of whites opposed emancipation lest it result in a flood of southern "Africans" into the free states. And Illinois was no exception, as most whites there were anti-Negro and anti-abolition to the core. Lincoln, who had elected to work within the American system, was not going to ruin his career by trumpeting an unpopular cause. To be branded as an abolitionist in central Illinois—his constituency as a legislator and a U.S. congressman—would have been certain political suicide.

Still, slavery distressed him. He realized that it should never have existed in a self-proclaimed free and enlightened Republic. He who cherished the Declaration of Independence understood only too well how bondage mocked and contradicted that noble document. Yes, he detested slavery. It was a blight on the American experiment in popular government, the one institution that robbed the Republic of its just example in the world, robbed the United States of the hope it should hold out to oppressed people everywhere.

He opposed slavery, too, because he had witness some of its evils firsthand. In 1841, on a steamboat journey down the Ohio River, he saw a group of manacled slaves on their way to the cruel cotton plantations of the Deep South. Lincoln was appalled at the sight of those chained Negroes. Fourteen years later he wrote that the spectacle "was a continual torment to me" and that he saw something like it every time he touched a slave border. Slavery, he said, "had the power of making me miserable."

Again, while serving in Congress from 1847 to 1849, he passed slave auction blocks in Washington, D.C. In fact, from the windows of the Capitol, he could observe the infamous "Georgia pen"—"a sort of Negro livery stable," as he described it, "where droves of negroes were collected, temporarily kept, and finally taken to southern markets, precisely like droves of horses." The spectacle offended him. He agreed with a Whig colleague that the buying and selling of human beings in the United States was a national disgrace. Accordingly Lincoln drafted a gradual abolition bill for the District of Columbia. But powerful southern politicians howled in protest, and his own Whig support fell away. At that, Lincoln dropped the bill and sat in gloomy silence as Congress rocked with debates—with drunken fights and rumbles of disunion—over the status of slavery in the territories. Shocked at the behavior of his colleagues, Lincoln confessed that slavery was the one issue that threatened the stability of the Union.

Yet Attorney Lincoln had to concede that bondage was a thoroughly entrenched institution in the southern states, one protected by the U.S. Constitution and a web of national and state laws. This in turn created a painful dilemma for Lincoln: a system he deeply loved had institutionalized a thing he abominated. What could be done? Lincoln admitted that the federal government had no legal authority in peacetime to harm a state institution like slavery. And yet it should not remain in what he considered "the noblest political system the world ever saw."

Caught in an impossible predicament, Lincoln persuaded himself that if slavery were confined to the South and left alone there, time would somehow solve the problem and slavery would ultimately die out. Once it was no longer workable, he believed, southern whites would gradually liberate the blacks on their own. They would do so voluntarily.

And he told himself that the Founding Fathers—that Washington, Jefferson, and Madison—had felt the same way, that they too had expected slavery to perish some day. In Lincoln's interpretation, the Fathers had tolerated slavery as a necessary evil, one that could not be removed where it already existed without causing wide-scale chaos and destruction. But, Lincoln contended, they had taken steps to restrict the growth of bondage (had prohibited it in the old Northwest Territories, had outlawed the international slave trade) and thus to place the institution on the road to extinction. And he decided that this was why the Fathers had not included the words *slave* or *slavery* in the Constitution. When bondage did disappear, "there should be nothing on the face of the great charter of liberty suggesting that such a thing as negro slavery had ever existed among us."

So went Lincoln's argument before 1854. Thanks to the Founding Fathers, slavery was on its way to its ultimate doom. And he believed that southerners and northerners alike accepted this as axiomatic. The task of his generation, Lincoln thought, was to keep the Republic firmly on the course charted by the Fathers, guiding America toward that ultimate day when slavery would finally be removed, the nation righted at last with her own ideals, and popular government preserved for all humankind. It was this vision—this sense of America's historic mission in the progress of human liberty—that shaped Lincoln's beliefs and actions throughout his mature years.

Still, despite his passionate convictions about popular government and human liberty, Lincoln before the Civil War did not envision black people as permanent participants in the great American experiment. On the contrary, he feared that white Americans were too prejudiced to let Negroes live among them as equals. If it was impossible for blacks to be completely free in America, then he preferred that they be free somewhere else. Once slavery died out in Dixie, he insisted that the federal government should colonize all blacks in Africa, an idea he got from Henry Clay.

Of course, emancipation and colonization would depend entirely on the willingness of southerners to cooperate. Lincoln hoped and assumed that they would. Before the Civil War, he always sympathized with the mass of southern whites and thought of them inherently humane

and patriotic. After all, Lincoln himself was a native Kentuckian, and *he* loved the American experiment and tried to be a fair-minded man. He said of southern whites and slavery, "They are just what we would be in their situation. When it is said that the institution exists, and that it is very difficult to get rid of . . . I can understand and appreciate the saying." Yet he thought the great majority of southern whites "have human sympathies, of which they can no more divest themselves then they can of their sensibility to physical pain." Because of their human sympathies, he assumed that they would abolish slavery when it became necessary to do so.

Assumptions aside, though, Lincoln had no evidence that southerners would ever voluntarily surrender their slaves, voluntarily give up their status symbols and transform their cherished way of life founded on the peculiar institution. In 1832, the year Lincoln entered politics, Virginia had actually considered emancipation and colonization (in the aftermath of Nat Turner's insurrection), but had rejected colonization as too costly and complicated to carry out. And neither they nor their fellow southerners were about to emancipate their blacks and leave them as free people in a white man's country. As a consequence, they became adamantly determined that slavery should remain on a permanent basis, not just as a labor device, but as a means of race control in a region brimming with Negroes.

Yet Lincoln clung to the notion that slavery would eventually perish in Dixie, that southerners were rational men who would gradually liberate their blacks when the time came. And he clung to the belief that somehow, when the time did come, the Republic would pay out all the millions of dollars necessary to compensate slaveowners for their losses and ship more than three million blacks out of the country. And he assumed, too, that southerners would consent to the deportation of their entire labor force.

Students often ask me, "Was Lincoln serious? How could a logical and reasonable man like him embrace such fantastic notions?" I can only guess at the answer. Given the tenacious existence of slavery in Dixie and the white supremacist attitudes that prevailed all over his country, what other choices did Lincoln have? His whole idea of southern-initiated emancipation and federal colonization may seem chimerical to us. But in his view it appeared to be the only course short of war that had the slightest chance of working. And he *had* to believe in something. He could not accept the monstrous possibility that southern slavery might continue indefinitely. No, he told himself, it must and would die out as he figured. And so he said it 1852: if the Republic could remove the danger of slavery and restore "a captive people to their long-lost father-land," and do both so gradually "that neither races nor individuals shall have suffered by the change," then "it will indeed be a glorious consummation."

2. THIS VAST MORAL EVIL

Then came 1854 and the momentous Kansas-Nebraska Act, brainchild of Senator Stephen A. Douglas of Illinois. Douglas's measure overturned the old Missouri Compromise line, which excluded slavery from the vast northern area of the old Louisiana Purchase territory. The act then established a new formula for dealing with slavery in the national lands: now Congress would stay out of the matter, and the people of each territory would decide whether to retain or outlaw the institution. Until such time as the citizens of a territory voted on the issue, southerners were free to take slavery into most western territories, including the new ones of Kansas and Nebraska. These were carved out of the northern section of the old Louisiana Purchase territory. Thanks to the Kansas-Nebraska Act, a northern domain once preserved for freedom now seemed open to a proslavery invasion.

At once a storm of free-soil protest broke across the north, and scores of political leaders branded the Kansas-Nebraska Act as part of a sinister southern plot to extend slave territory and augment southern political power in the national capital. Had not the pro-southern Pierce administration and powerful southern politicians like Senator David R. Atchison of Missouri helped Douglas ram the measure through Congress? Had not every southern senator but two voted in favor of it? Were not Missouri border captains vowing to make Kansas a gateway for proslavery expansion to the Pacific?

There followed a series of political upheavals. The old Whig party disintegrated, and in its place emerged the all-northern Republican party, dedicated to blocking slavery extension, saving the cherished frontier for free white labor, and dismantling southern power in Washington. At the same time, a civil war blazed up in Kansas, as proslavery and free-soil pioneers came into bloody collisions on the prairie there—proof that slavery was far too volatile ever to be solved as a purely local matter.

No one was more upset about Kansas-Nebraska than Lincoln. In his view, the southern-controlled Democratic party—the party that dominated the presidency, the Senate, and the Supreme Court—had launched a revolt against the Founding Fathers and the entire course of the Republic as far as slavery was concerned. Now bondage was not going to die out in the South. It was going to grow and expand and continue indefinitely, as slaveholders dragged manacled black people across the West, adapting slave labor to mines and farms and whatever conditions they found there. Now southern leaders would create new slave states on the frontier and make bondage powerful and permanent in America. Now the Republic would never remove the cancer that afflicted its political system—would never remove a "cruel wrong" that marred her global image and made a mockery of the Declaration.

Lincoln plunged into the antiextension fight. He campaigned for the national Senate. He joined the Republicans and became head of the new party in Illinois. He inveighed against the "Slave Power" and its insidious "new designs" to place bondage on the road to expansion and perpetuity. He spoke with an urgent sense of mission that gave his speeches a searching eloquence—a mission to save the American experiment, turn back the tide of slavery expansion, restrict the peculiar institution once again to the South, and place it back on the road to extinction, as Lincoln believed the Founding Fathers had so placed it.

Still, he could not believe that the southern people were involved in the new slave policy. No, they were beguiled by scheming Democratic politicians—by Douglas and southern leaders in Washington and back in Dixie, who were out to enlarge slave territory under the guise of popular sovereignty, under the pretext that it was all "a sacred right of self-government." On the stump in Illinois, Lincoln engaged in a rhetorical dialogue with the southern people, speaking as though they were in his audiences. He did not fault them for the origin of slavery; he bore them no ill-will of any kind. He still believed in their intrinsic decency and sense of justice, still believed that they too regarded slavery as wrong—that they too felt there was humanity in the Negro. Do you deny this? he asked them at Peoria in 1854. Then why thirty-four years ago did you join the North in branding the African slave trade as an act of piracy punishable death? "Again," Lincoln went on, "you have amongst you, a sneaking individual, of the class of native tyrants, known as the 'SLAVEDEALER.' He watches your necessities, and crawls up to buy your slave, at a speculating price. If you cannot help it, you sell to him; but if you can help it, you drive him from your door. You despise him utterly. You do not recognize him as a friend, or even as an honest man. Your children must not play with his; they must rollick freely with the little negroes, but not with the 'slave-dealers' children. If you are obliged to deal with him, you try to get through the job without so much as touching him. It is common with you to join hands with the men you meet; but with the slave dealer you avoid the ceremony—instinctively shrinking from the snaky contact."

Now why is this? Lincoln asked southern whites. Is it not because your human sympathy tells you "that the poor negro has some natural right to himself—that those who deny it, and

make mere merchandise of him, deserve kickings, contempt and death?" He beseeched southerners not to deny their true feelings about slavery. He beseeched them to regard bondage strictly as a necessity, as the Fathers had so regarded it, and to contain its spread as those "old-time men" had done.

"Fellow countrymen—Americans south, as well as north," Lincoln cried, let us prevent the spirit of Kansas-Nebraska from displacing the spirit of the Revolution. "Let us turn slavery from its claims of 'moral right,' back upon its existing legal rights . . . and there let it rest in peace. Let us re-adopt the Declaration of Independence, and with it, the practices, and policy, which harmonize with it. Let north and south—let all Americans—let all lovers of liberty everywhere—join the great and good work. If we do this, we shall not only have saved the Union; but we shall have so saved it, as to make, and to keep it, forever worthy of the saving."

But Lincoln's entreaties fell on deaf ears in Dixie. Across the region, in an age of revolutionary agitation, proslavery apologists disparaged the Declaration of Independence and the idea of human equality as "a self-evident lie." They trumpeted Negro bondage as a great and glorious good, sanctioned by the Bible and ordained by God throughout eternity. They contended that Negroes were subhuman and belonged in chains as naturally as cattle in pens. Cranky George Fitzhugh even exhorted southerners to destroy free society (or capitalism), revive the halcyon days of feudalism, and enslave all workers—white as well as black. And he ranted at abolitionists for allying themselves with the "uncouth, dirty, naked little cannibals of Africa." Because "free society" was "unnatural, immoral, unchristian," the proslavery argument went, "it must fall and give way to a slave society—a system as old as the world." For "two opposite and conflicting forms of society cannot, among civilized men, co-exist and endure. The one must give way and cease to exist—the other become universal." "Free society!" shrieked one Alabama paper. "We sicken of the name! What is it but a conglomeration of greasy mechanics, filthy operatives, small-fisted farmers, and moon-struck theorists?"

Such pronouncements made Lincoln grimace. They convinced him that a contemptible breed of men had taken over in the South and "debauched" the public mind there about the moral right of slavery. "The slave-breeders and slave-traders are a small, odious and detested class, among you," he wrote a southern friend; "and yet in politics, they dictate the course of all of you, and are as completely your masters, as you are the masters of your own negroes." But to Lincoln's despair, proslavery, anti-northern declarations continued to roar out of Dixie. Worse still, in 1857 the pro-southern Supreme Court handed down the infamous Dred Scott decision, which sent Republicans reeling. In it, the court decreed that Negroes were inferior beings who were not and never had been United States citizens and that the Constitution and Declaration were whites-only charters that did not apply to them. What was more, the court ruled that neither Congress nor a territorial government could outlaw slavery in the national lands, because that would violate southern property rights as guaranteed by the Fifth Amendment. As Lincoln and other Republicans observed, the net effect of the decision was to legalize slavery in all federal territories from Canada to Mexico.

The ominous train of events from Kansas-Nebraska to Dred Scott shook Lincoln to his foundations. By 1858, he and a lot of other Republicans began to see a treacherous conspiracy at work in the United States—a plot on the part of the southern leaders and their northern Democratic allies to reverse the whole course of modern history, to halt the progress of human liberty as other reactionary forces in the world were attempting to do. As Lincoln and his colleagues saw it, the first stage of the conspiracy was to betray the Fathers and expand bondage across the West, ringing the free North with satellite slave states. At the same time, proslavery theorists were out to discredit the Declaration and replace the idea of the equality of men with the principles of inequality and human servitude. The next step, Lincoln feared, would be to nationalize slavery. The Supreme Court would hand down another decision, one declaring that states could not exclude slavery either because that too violated the Fifth Amendment. Then the institution would sweep into Illinois, sweep into Indiana and Ohio, sweep into Pennsylvania and New York, sweep into Massachusetts and New England, sweep all over the northern states, until at last slavery would be nationalized and America would end up a slave house. At that, as Fitzhugh advocated, the conspirators would enslave all American workers regardless of color. The northern free-labor system would be expunged, the Declaration of Independence overthrown, self-government abolished, and the conspirators would restore despotism with class rule, an entrenched aristocracy, and serfdom. All the work since the Revolution of 1776 would be annihilated. The world's best hope—America's experiment in popular government—would be destroyed, and humankind would spin backward into feudalism.

For Lincoln, the Union had reached a monumental crisis in its history. If the future of a free America was to be saved, it was imperative that Lincoln and his party block the conspiracy in its initial stage—the expansion of slavery onto the frontier. To do that, they demanded that slavery be excluded from the territories by federal law and once again placed on the road to its ultimate doom. In 1858 Lincoln set out after Douglas's Senate seat, inveighing against the Little Giant for his part in the proslavery plot and warning Illinois—and all northerners beyond—that only the Republicans could save their free-labor system and their free government.

Now Lincoln openly and fiercely declaimed his antislavery sentiments. He hated the institution. Slavery was "a vast moral evil" he could not but hate. He hated it because it degraded blacks and whites alike. He hated it because it violated America's *"central idea"*—the idea of equality and the right to rise. He hated it because it was cruelly unjust to the Negro, prevented him from eating "the bread that his own hands have earned," reduced him to "stripes, and unrewarded toils." He hated slavery because it imperiled white Americans, too. For if one man could be enslaved because of the color of his skin, Lincoln realized, then any man could be enslaved because of skin color. Yet, while branding slavery an evil and doing all they could to contain it in Dixie, Lincoln and his Republican colleagues would not, legally could not, molest the institution in those states where it already existed.

Douglas, fighting for his political life in free-soil Illinois, lashed back at Lincoln with unadulterated race baiting. Throughout the Great Debates of 1858, Douglas smeared Lincoln and his party as Black Republicans, as a gang of radical abolitionists out to liberate southern slaves and bring them stampeding into Illinois and the rest of the North, where they would take away white jobs and copulate with white daughters. Douglas had made such accusations before, but never to the extent that he did in 1858. Again and again, he accused Lincoln of desiring intermarriage and racial mongrelization.

Lincoln did not want to discuss such matters. He complained bitterly that race was not the issue between him and Douglas. The issue was whether slavery would ultimately triumph or ultimately perish in the United States. But Douglas understood the depth of anti-Negro feeling in Illinois, and he hoped to whip Lincoln by playing on white racial fears. And so he kept warning white crowds: Do you want Negroes to flood into Illinois, cover the prairies with black settlements, and eat, sleep, and marry with white people? If you do, then vote for Lincoln and the "Black Republicans." But *I* am against Negro citizenship, Douglas cried. I want citizenship for whites only. I believe that this government "was made by the white man, for the benefit of the white man, to be administered by white men." "I do not question Mr. Lincoln's conscientious belief that the negro was made his equal, and hence his brother"—great laughter at that—"but for my own part, I do not regard the negro as my equal, and positively deny that he is my brother or any kin to me whatever."

Such allegations forced Lincoln to take a stand. It was either that or risk political ruin in white-supremacist Illinois. What he said carefully endorsed the kind of racial discrimination then enforced by Illinois law. Had he not done so, as one scholar had reminded us, "the Lincoln of history simply would not exist." At Charleston, Illinois, Lincoln conceded that he was not and never had been in favor "of making voters or jurors of Negroes, nor of qualifying them to hold office, nor to intermarry with white people." There was, he said at Ottawa, "a physical difference" between the black and white races that would "probably" always prevent them from living together in perfect equality. And Lincoln wanted the white race to have the superior position so long as there must be a difference. Therefore any attempt to twist his views into a call for perfect political and social equality was "but a specious and fantastic arrangement of words by which a man can prove a horse chestnut to be a chestnut horse."

We shall probably never know whether Lincoln was voicing his own personal convictions in speeches like these, given the heat of political debate before all-white audiences. To be sure, this is one of the most hotly disputed areas of Lincoln scholarship, with several white historians siding with Bennett and Harding and labeling Lincoln a white supremacist. Certainly in the 1850s he had ambivalent feelings about what specific social and political rights black people ought to enjoy. But so did a good many principled and dedicated white abolitionists. When compared to the white-supremacist, anti-Negro attitudes of Douglas and most other whites of that time, Lincoln was an enlightened man in the matter of race relations. In those same 1858 debates, he consistently argued that if Negroes were not the equal of Lincoln and Douglas in moral or intellectual endowment, they *were* equal to Lincoln, Douglas, and "every living man" in their right to liberty, equality of opportunity, and the fruits of their own labor. (Later he insisted that it was bondage that had "clouded" the slaves' intellects and that Negroes were capable of thinking like whites.) Moreover, Lincoln rejected "the counterfeit argument" that just because he did not want a black woman for a slave, he therefore wanted her for a wife. He could just let her alone. He could let her alone so that she could also enjoy her freedom and "her natural right to eat the bread she earns with her own hands."

While Douglas (like the Supreme Court) empathically denied that the Declaration of Independence applied to Negroes, Lincoln's position held that it did. The Negro was a man; Lincoln's "ancient faith" taught him that all men were created equal; therefore there could be no "moral right" in one man's enslaving another. As historian Richard N. Current has said, Lincoln left unstated the conclusion of his logic: that there was no moral right in one man's making a political and social inferior of another on grounds of race.

In the debate at Alton, Lincoln took his reasoning even further as far as the Declaration was concerned. "I think the authors of that notable document intended to include *all* men," Lincoln said, "but they did not intend to declare all men equal in *all respects*. They did not mean to say all were equal in color, size, intellect, moral development, or social capacity." What they meant was that all men, black as well as white, were equal in their inalienable rights to life, liberty, and the pursuit of happiness. When they drafted the Declaration, they realized that blacks did not then have full equality with whites, and that whites did not at that time have full equality with one another. The Founding Fathers did not pretend to describe America as it was in 1776. "They meant to set up a standard maxim for free society," Lincoln said, "which should be familiar to all, and revered by all; constantly labored for, and even though never perfectly attained, constantly spreading and deepening its influence, and augmenting the happiness and value of life to all people of all colors everywhere."

By stressing "to all people of all colors everywhere," Lincoln reminded his countrymen that the American experiment remained an inspiration for the entire world. But he reminded them, too, as historian Current has noted, that "it could be an effective inspiration for others only to the extent that Americans lived up to it themselves." No wonder Lincoln said he hated Douglas's indifference toward slavery expansion. "I hate it because of the monstrous injustice of slavery itself," Lincoln explained at Ottawa. "I hate it because it . . . enables the enemies of free institutions, with plausibility, to taunt us as hypocrites."

Exasperated with Douglas and white Negrophobia in general, Lincoln begged American whites "to discard all this quibbling about this man and the other man—this race and that race and the other race as being inferior," begged them to unite as one people and defend the ideal of the Declaration of Independence and its promise of liberty and equality for all humankind.

Lincoln's remarks, however, aggravated a lot of common people in Illinois; they voted for Douglas candidates in 1858 and helped return Lincoln's rival to the Senate.* The historical Lincoln even lost Springfield and Sangamon County, because of his controversial views on slavery and the Negro, as one historian has argued, were too advanced for his neighbors. If we are to understand Lincoln's attitudes on slavery and race, it is imperative that we weigh them in proper historical context. We can learn nothing, nothing at all, if his words are lifted from their historical setting and judged only by the standards of another time.

3. MY DISSATISFIED FELLOW COUNTRYMEN

We return to why Lincoln still ranks as the best President Americans have had. In large measure, it was because of his sense of history and his ability to act on that. It was because he saw the slavery problem and the future of his country in a world dimension. He saw that what menaced Americans of his day affected the destinies of people everywhere. On the stump in Illinois,

---

*In those days, state legislatures chose U.S. Senators. Lincoln hoped to win by persuading Illinois voters to elect Republican rather than Democratic candidates to the legislature.

Ohio, and New York, he continued to warn free men of the heinous efforts to make bondage permanent in the United States. He would not let up on his countrymen about the *moral* issue of slavery. *"If slavery is not wrong,"* he warned them, *"nothing is wrong."* He would not let up on "the miners and sappers" of returning despotism, as he called proslavery spokesmen and their northern allies, and on the historical crisis threatening his generation, a crisis that would determine whether slavery or freedom—despotism or popular government, the past or the future—would triumph in his impassioned time.

Yet in the late 1850s Lincoln's goal was not the presidency. One of the more popular misconceptions about him was that he had his eye on the White House even in the Great Debates. Yet there is not a scintilla of reliable evidence to support this. What Lincoln wanted, and wanted fervently, was a seat in the national Senate, because in the antebellum years it was the Senate that featured the great orators of the day—men like Daniel Webster, John C. Calhoun, and especially Lincoln's idol, Henry Clay. The presidency, by contrast, was a mundane administrative job that offered little to a man of Lincoln's oratorical abilities. No, he preferred the national Senate, because in that august body he could defend the containment of slavery, defend free labor, defend popular government and the American experiment, in speeches that would be widely read and preserved for posterity in the *Congressional Globe*. As a loyal Republican, he would take any respectable national office that would simultaneously "advance our cause" and give him personal fulfillment. But throughout 1859 and early 1860, he kept his eye on Douglas's Senate seat in 1864.

So it was that Lincoln kept assailing Douglas for his role in the proslavery plot Lincoln saw at work in his country. And he reminded northerners of the republican vision of a future America—a better America than now existed—an America of thriving farms and bustling villages and towns, an America of self-made agrarians, merchants, and shopkeepers who set examples and provided jobs for self-improving free workers—an America, however, that would never come about if slavery, class rule, and despotism triumphed in Lincoln's time.

Meanwhile, he kept trying to reach the southern people, to reason with them about slavery and the future of the Union, to woo them away from their reactionary leaders. He observed how ironic it was that the Democrats had abandoned their Jeffersonian heritage and that the Republicans—supposedly the descendants of the old Federalists—now defended Jeffersonian ideals. He warned southerners that "This is a world of compensations; and he who would *be* no slave, must consent to *have* no slave. Those who deny freedom to others, deserve it not for themselves."

"I think Slavery is wrong, morally, and politically," he told southern whites at Cincinnati in 1859, still speaking to them as though they were his audience. "I desire that it should gradually terminate in the whole Union." But "I understand you differ radically with me upon this proposition." You believe that "Slavery is a good thing; that Slavery is right; that it ought to be extended and perpetuated in this Union." But we Republicans not only disagree with you; we are going to "stand by our guns" and beat you in a fair election. Yet we will not hurt you. We will treat you as Washington, Jefferson, and Madison treated you, and will leave slavery alone where it already exists among you. "We mean to remember that you are as good as we are; that there is no difference between us other than the difference of circumstances. We mean to recognize and bear in mind always that you have as good hearts in your bosoms as other people, or as we claim to have, and treat you accordingly. We mean to marry your girls when we have a chance—the white ones I mean—[laughter] and I have the honor to inform you that I once did have a chance that way."

But he cautioned southerners about their threats to disrupt the Union should the Republicans win the government in 1860. How will disunion help you? Lincoln demanded. If you secede, you will no longer enjoy the protection of the Constitution, and we will no longer be forced to return your fugitive slaves. What will you do—build a wall between us? Make war on us? You are brave and gallant, "but man for man, you are not better than we are, and there are not so many of you as there are of us." Because you are inferior in numbers, "you will make nothing by attempting to master us."

Despite Lincoln's reassurances, southern spokesmen derided the Republicans as war-mongering abolitionists out to destroy the southern way of life based on slavery. In October, 1859, they got all the evidence they needed that this was so. Old John Brown and a handful of revolutionaries—most of them young, five of them black—invaded Harpers Ferry in an attempt to incite a full-scale slave rebellion. Though the raid failed and Brown was captured and hanged, the South convulsed in hysteria, as rumors of slave uprisings and abolitionist invasions pummeled the region. For their part, southern politicians pronounced the raid a Republican conspiracy, a mad and monstrous scheme to drown the South in rivers of blood. During a tour if the embattled Kansas Territory, Lincoln denied such accusations and argued that hanging Brown was just. But he warned southerners that "if constitutionally we elect a President, and therefore you undertake to destroy the Union, it will be our duty to deal with you as old John Brown has been dealt with."

At Cooper Union the following year, Lincoln responded to continued southern imputations about the Republicans and John Brown. "You charge that we stir up insurrections among your slaves," Lincoln said. "We deny it; and what is your proof? Harpers Ferry! John Brown!! John Brown was no Republican; and you have failed to implicate a single Republican in his Harpers Ferry enterprise." But he saved his most eloquent remarks for his fellow Republicans. Since they intended southerners no harm and promised over and over to leave their slaves alone, what then was the dispute about? "The precise fact upon which depends the whole controversy" was that southerners thought slavery

right and Republicans thought it wrong. "Thinking it right, as they do, they are not to blame for desiring its full recognition, as being right; but, thinking it wrong, as we do, can we yield to them? Can we cast our votes with their view, and against our own? In view of our moral, social, and political responsibilities, can we do this?" No, the Republicans' sense of duty would not let them yield to southern demands about slavery. Nor would Republicans be frightened from their duty by threats of disunion and destruction to the government. "LET US HAVE FAITH THAT RIGHT MAKES MIGHT, AND IN THAT FAITH, LET US, TO THE END, DARE TO DO OUR DUTY AS WE UNDERSTAND IT."

Impressed by his impassioned oratory and firm commitment to party principles, and impressed too by his availability, the Republicans chose Lincoln to be their standard bearer in 1860, to run for President on their free-soil, free-labor platform. In the countdown to the Republican nomination, Lincoln insisted that he preferred the Senate to the White House. But as his chances for the nomination brightened he confessed that "the taste *is* in my mouth a little," and he let a cadre of zealous lieutenants work to secure his nomination. Contrary to a persistent popular misconception, they did not do so simply by making bargains with Republicans from other states, promising Cabinet positions and other offices if they would throw their delegations to Lincoln. Modern scholarship has thoroughly demolished this claim. While Lincoln's managers may have made conditional overtures (as any manager would do), they followed Lincoln's own instructions and did not bind him to any convention deals. Moreover, supporters of William H. Seward, the front-running candidate before the convention, had as many offices to disseminate as Lincoln's men. What won Lincoln the nomination was not the peddling of spoils but a hard decision on the part of the Republican delegates that Seward "could not win and must give way to someone who could," as one historian has phrased it. And that someone was Abraham

Lincoln, who was available, who was a loyal party man, who came from a crucial state, and who was more likely than any other candidate to carry the populous lower North, which was indispensable for a Republican victory.

Lincoln, for his part, accepted the nomination because he was as ambitious as he was deeply principled. While he preferred to serve the Republican cause on Capitol Hill, he would work for it wherever the party wanted to put him so long as it was a meaningful national office. And in 1860 that was the White House. In Lincoln, as it turned out, the Republicans chose a candidate more unbending in his commitment to Republican principles than anybody else they might have selected. As the Republican standard bearer, Lincoln was inflexible in his determination to prohibit slavery in the territories by national law and to save the Republic (as he put it) from returning "class," "caste," and "despotism." He exhorted his fellow Republicans to stand firm in their duty: to brand slavery as an evil, contain it in the South, look to the future for slavery to die a gradual death, and promise colonization to solve the question of race. Someday, somehow, the American house must be free of slavery. That was the Republican vision, the distant horizon Lincoln saw.

Yet, for the benefit of southerners, he repeated that he and his party would not interfere with slavery in Dixie. The federal government had no constitutional authority in peacetime to tamper with a state institution like slavery.

But southerners in 1860 were in no mood to believe anything Lincoln said. In their eyes, he was a "horrid looking wretch," another John Brown, "a black-hearted abolitionist fanatic" who lusted for Negro equality. There were, of course, a number of loyal Unionists in the South who pleaded for reason and restraint, who beseeched their fellow southerners to wait for an overt Republican act against them before they did anything rash. For most, though, Brown's Harpers Ferry invasion was all the overt action they intended to tolerate. For all classes in Dixie, from poor whites in South Carolina to rich cotton planters in Mississippi, Lincoln personified the

feared and hated *Yankee*—the rapacious entrepreneur, the greasy mechanic, the mongrel immigrant, the frothing abolitionist, the entire "free-love, free-nigger" element, all of whom in southern eyes had combined in Lincoln's party. In him, southerners saw a monster who would send a Republican army into Dixie to free the slaves by gunpoint and whip up a racial storm that would consume their farms and plantations, their investments, their wives and daughters. Even if the South had to drench the Union in blood, exclaimed an Alabama paper, "the South, the loyal South, the Constitutional South, would never submit to such humiliation and degradation as the inauguration of Abraham Lincoln."

For Lincoln, the slavedealers had indeed assumed leadership in Dixie, and he would never compromise with them over a single plank in the Republican platform. Anyway, he still refused to believe that the South's blustery spokesmen truly reflected popular sentiment there. "The people of the South," he remarked during the obstreperous 1860 campaign, "have too much good sense, and good temper, to attempt the ruin of the government." He agreed with his advisers that southern Unionism was too powerful for secession to triumph. Surely, he reasoned, the southern people shared his own sentiments about the future of the American experiment. Surely, like the powerful southerners who helped found the country, like Washington, Jefferson, and Madison, the southern people of his day believed in the Declaration of Independence, which was their charter of liberty as much as his own and that of the Republicans. Surely the southern people would reject the forces of reaction in the world and come around to Lincoln's view, to stand with those who sought the liberation and uplift of the human spirit.

On election day, November 6, telegraph dispatches across the country carried the crucial news: Lincoln had defeated his three leading opponents—John Breckinridge of the southern Democrats, Douglas of the northern Democrats, and John Bell of the Constitutional Union ticket—and was to be the sixteenth president. Lincoln had won, not because his foes were split, but because he carried California and Oregon and every northern state except New Jersey, which divided its electoral votes between him and Douglas. In the electoral college, where Lincoln gained his triumph, his total vote exceeded that of his combined opponents by a margin of 187 to 123. In popular votes, though, Lincoln was a minority President, with 1,866,452 ballots compared to 2,815,617 for his combined foes. Many factors were involved in this confusing and raucous contest, but the fact remains that the majority of Americans in 1860 regarded Lincoln as too radical and dangerous to occupy the White House. Of course, you don't learn about this in the story of Lincoln as Man of the People.

In the Deep South, newspapers screamed with headlines about Lincoln, and people thronged the streets of southern cities with talk of secession everywhere. "Now that the black radical Republicans have the power," asserted a South Carolinian, "I suppose they will [John] Brown us all." Of course, Lincoln and his party did not have the power. They had only won the presidency. The Democrats, though divided, still controlled the Supreme Court and both houses of Congress, and would have demolished any abolition bill the Republicans might have introduced there. But for southerners that stormy winter, the nation had reached a profound turning point: an all-northern party avowedly hostile to slavery had gained control of the executive branch of the government. In the Deep South, a white man reading his newspaper could rehearse what was bound to follow. With the North's supremacy in population and drift toward abolition and revolutionary violence, that party was certain to win the rest of the government one day and then attack slavery in Dixie. Better, then, to strike for southern independence now than to await the Republican blow. Thus, even before Lincoln could be inaugurated, the seven states of the Deep South—with their heavy slave concentrations—left the Union and established the slave-based Confederacy. As a South Carolina resident explained to President Buchanan: "Slavery with us is no abstraction—but a *great* and *vital fact*. Without it our every comfort

would be taken from us. Our wives, our children, made unhappy—education, the light of knowledge—all lost and our *people ruined for ever. Nothing short of separation from the Union can save us.*" The editor of the Montgomery *Mail* agreed. "To remain in the Union is to lose all that white men hold dear in government. We vote to get out."

In Springfield, President-elect Lincoln admitted that there were "some loud threats and much muttering in the cotton states," but insisted that the best way to avoid disaster was through calmness and forbearance. What reason did southerners have to be so incensed? What had the Republicans done to them? What southern rights had they violated? Did not southerners still have the fugitive slave law? Did they not have the same Constitution they had lived under for seventy-odd years? "Why all this excitement?" asked Lincoln. "Why all these complaints?"

With the border states also threatening to secede, Lincoln seemed confused, incredulous, at what was happening to his country. He seemed not to understand how he appeared in southern eyes. He kept telling himself that his advisers were right, that southern Unionism would somehow bring the errant states back. He could not accept the possibility that *his* election to the presidency might cause the collapse of the very system which had enabled him to get there. The irony of that was too distressing to contemplate.

In his Inaugural Address of March 4, 1861, Lincoln pleaded for southern whites to understand the Republican position on slavery. He assured them once again that he would not molest slavery in Dixie, that he had no legal right to molest it there. He even approved the original Thirteenth Amendment, just passed by Congress, that would have explicitly guaranteed slavery in the southern states. Lincoln endorsed the amendment because he deemed it consistent with Republican ideology. And in his conclusion he spoke personally to the southern people, as he had done so often since 1854: "In *your* hands, my dissatisfied fellow countrymen, and not in *mine*, is the momentous issue of civil war. The government will not assail *you*. You can have no conflict, without being yourselves the aggressors. *You* have no oath registered in Heaven to destroy the government, while *I* shall have the most solemn one to 'preserve, protect and defend' it.

"I am loth to close. We are not enemies, but friends. We must not be enemies. Though passion may have strained, it must not break our bonds of affection. The mystic chords of memory, stretching from every battlefield, and patriot grave, to every living heart and hearthstone, all over this broad land, will yet swell the chorus of the Union, when again touched, as surely they will be, by the better angels of our nature."

In Dixie, excitement was so great that men read in Lincoln's words, not conciliation, but provocation. The feverish Charleston *Mercury* even blasted it as a declaration of war. At that very moment, in fact, war threatened to break out in Charleston harbor, where hostile rebel cannon ringed Fort Sumter and its lonely Union flag. The Confederates had already seized every U.S. fort in Dixie except for Sumter and one other in the Florida Gulf. Now Sumter became a symbol for both sides, as the rebels demanded that Lincoln surrender it and angry Union men exhorted him to hold.

In the ensuing crisis, Lincoln clung to the belief that the southern people would overthrow the secessionists and restore the southern states to the Union. But he had little time to wait, for the Sumter garrison was rapidly running out of provisions. Should he send a relief expedition? But what if that betrayed southern Unionists and detonated a civil war? In "great anxiety" about what to do, Lincoln consulted repeatedly with his Cabinet and with high-ranking officers of the army and navy, but they gave him conflicting advice. Far from being an aggressive tyrant who forced the innocent South to start the war, the historical Lincoln vacillated over Sumter, postponed a decision, suffered terribly. He told an old Illinois friend that "all the troubles and anxieties" of his life could not equal those that beset him during the Sumter nightmare. They were so great, Lincoln said, that he did not think it possible to survive them.

Then a report from an emissary he had sent to Charleston smashed his hope that the crisis could be peacefully resolved. The emissary reported that South Carolinians had "no attachment to the Union," and that some wanted a clash with Washington to unite the Confederacy. Moreover, Unionism was equally dead everywhere else in Dixie, and the seceded states were "irrevocably gone." There was no conceivable way that Lincoln could avoid an armed collision with southern rebels: if he did not hold Sumter, he would have to stand somewhere else or see the government collapse.

It was a rude awakening for Lincoln, who had placed great faith in the potency of southern Unionism, who had always thought that southern white people loved the country as much as he and shared his faith in the American promise. Well, he had been wrong. Out of that sobering realization, out of everything he held dear about the Union, out of all his suffering, came a decision to stand firm. After all, he had won the presidency in a fair and legal contest. He would not compromise his election mandate. He would preserve the Union and the principle of self-government on which the Union was based: the right of a free people to choose their leaders and expect the losers to acquiesce in that decision. If southerners disliked him, they could try to vote him out of office in 1864. But he was not going to let them separate from the Union, because that would set a catastrophic precedent that any unhappy state could leave the Union at any time. For Lincoln, the philosophy of secession was "an ingenious sophism" southerners had contrived to vindicate their rebellion. This sophism held that each state possessed "some omnipotent, and sacred supremacy," and that any state could lawfully and peacefully leave the Union without its consent. "With rebellion thus sugar coated," Lincoln complained, southern leaders "have been drugging the public mind of their section for more than thirty years." Yet it was a preposterous argument. The Constitution specifically stated that the Constitution and the national laws made under it were the supreme law of the land. Therefore the states could not be supreme as the secessionists claimed; the Union was paramount and permanent, and could not be legally wrecked by a disaffected minority. The principle of secession was disintegration, Lincoln said. And no government based on that principle could possibly endure.

Yes, he would hold Fort Sumter. In that imperiled little garrison in Charleston Harbor, surrounded by rebel batteries and a hostile population, Lincoln saw the fate of popular government hanging in the balance. He would send a relief expedition to Sumter, and if the Confederates opened fire, the momentous issue of civil war was indeed in their hands.

And so the fateful events raced by: the firing on the fort, Lincoln's call for 75,000 troops, the secession of four border states, and the beginning of war. Deeply embittered, Lincoln grumbled about all the *professed* Union men" in Dixie who had gone over to the rebellion. And he looked on in distress as one supposedly loyal southerner after another resigned from the United States Army and headed south to enlist in the rebel forces. It depressed him immeasurably. He referred to Robert E. Lee, Joseph E. Johnston, John Bankhead Magruder, and all like

them as traitors. And in his public utterances he never again addressed the southern people as though they were in his audiences. Instead he spoke of them in the third person, calling them rebels and insurrectionaries—a domestic enemy engaged in treason against his government.

And so the Civil War had come—a war that no reasonable man in North or South had wanted. What began as a ninety-day skirmish on both sides swelled instead into a vast inferno of destruction with consequences beyond calculation for those swept up in its flames. For Lincoln, the country was out of control, threatening to annihilate everyone and everything, all promise and all hope, and he did not think he could bear the pain he felt. His election had provoked this madness, and he took it personally. Falling into a depression that would plague him throughout his embattled presidency, he remarked that the war was the supreme irony of his life: that he who sickened at the sight of blood, who abhorred stridency and physical violence, who dreamed that "mind, all conquering *mind*," would rule the world someday, was caught in a national holocaust, a tornado of blood and wreckage with Lincoln himself whirling in its center.

21

HEROES AND COWARDS

BELL I. WILEY

The drama and sacrifice of war have occupied an important place in the American popular imagination for more than a century. Ironically, this fascination with the travails of warfare exists despite the fact that Americans have seldom experienced warfare directly. The security offered by the Atlantic and Pacific oceans as well as the relative military weakness of this country's northern and southern neighbors have largely allowed Americans to escape the debilitating effects of wars fought on their own territory. Only in the Revolutionary War, the War of 1812, and the Civil War did Americans find their farms, towns, and cities turned into battlefields and the civilian population menaced by contending armies.

The greatest of these internal wars was the Civil War of 1861–1865. Not only did the war claim over 600,000 American lives, destroy millions of dollars in property, and end a whole way of life, but it was also the only war in which American fought American. In this essay, Bell I. Wiley takes us beyond the exploits of military leaders and the movements of whole armies to the gritty experiences of the ordinary Confederate soldier. Wars are a collection of battles, and it was the danger and anarchy of conflict that tested the resolve of the ordinary soldier. Some, as Wiley poignantly reveals, became heroes and others cowards in the process, but none escaped the experience of combat unchanged.

From The Life of Johnny Reb: The Common Soldier of the Confederacy *by Bell Irvin Wiley (Baton Rouge, LA: Louisiana State University Press, 1970), pp. 68–89. Copyright © 1970, 1971, 1978 by Bell I. Wiley. Reprinted by permission of Louisiana State University Press.*

While it may be granted that there were significant changes in the reactions of soldiers as they became accustomed to combat, the fact remains that the experiences and behavior of those taking part in Confederate battles followed the same general pattern. These more or less common characteristics must be described in some detail.

When an encounter with the Yankees was expected certain preliminaries were necessary. One of these was the issue of extra provisions, accompanied by the order to "cook up" from three to five days' rations, so that time would not have to be taken for the preparation of food during the anticipated action. This judicious measure generally fell short of its object because of Johnny Reb's own characteristics: he was always hungry, he had a definite prejudice against baggage, and he was the soul of improvidence. Sometimes the whole of the extra ration would be consumed as it was cooked, and rarely did any part of it last for the full period intended. About the same time that food was dispensed the general in command would address his men for the purpose of firing their spirit and inspiring them to deeds of valor. Soldiers en route to Shiloh, for example, were thus charged by Albert Sidney Johnston:

> I have put you in motion to offer battle to the invaders of your country. With the resolution and disciplined valor becoming men fighting, as you are, for all worth living or dying for, you can but march to a decisive victory over the agrarian mercenaries sent to subjugate and despoil you of your liberties, property, and honor. Remember the precious stake involved; remember the dependence of your mothers, your wives, your sisters, and your children on the result; remember the fair, broad, abounding land, the happy homes, and the ties that would be desolated by your defeat.
>
> The eyes and the hopes of eight millions of people rest upon you. You are expected to show yourselves worthy of your race and lineage; worthy of the women of the South, whose noble devotion in this war has never been exceeded in any time. With such incentives to brave deeds and

with the trust that God is with us, your general will lead you confidently to the combat, assured of success.

Presently each man would be given a supply of ammunition. This was delayed as long as possible, so that the powder would not become damped through carelessness of the men. If Confederates held the initiative, the issue of ammunition would take place the night before the attack; but if the Rebs were on the defensive, without any definite knowledge of the time of assault, the issue of cartridges had to take place at an earlier stage. The customary allotment to each fighter was from forty to sixty rounds, a round being a ball and enough powder for a single shot.

Prior to their issue lead and powder for each load had, for convenience, been wrapped in a piece of paper with the bullet at one end, the powder behind it, and the other end closed with a twist or a plug to hold the powder in place. This improvised cartridge was cylindrical in shape, somewhat resembling a section of crayon. When Johnny Reb loaded his gun—usually a muzzle loader—he bit off the twisted end so that the powder would be exploded by the spark when the trigger was pulled, dropped the cartridge in the muzzle, rammed in a piece of wadding and waited for the opportunity to draw bead on a Yankee. Surplus rounds were kept in a cartridge box—a leather or metal container that hung from the belt—or in a haversack, or in trouser pockets.

Knapsacks and other baggage not actually needed on the field were supposed to be left in the rear with the quartermaster, but officers always had trouble preventing their men from throwing aside their equipment at random. After Bull Run and Shiloh most soldiers did not have to be cautioned about their canteens, as the acute suffering from thirst experienced in those engagements was a sufficient reminder to carry well-filled water tins into subsequent fights.

The day of battle finally comes. The men are roused from sleep at a very early hour, perhaps two or three o'clock. The well-known call to arms is an extended beat of the snare drum known as the "long roll." After the lines are drawn up officers inspect equipment, giving particular attention to ammunition, to see that all is in readiness.

Then a few words of advice and instruction: Do not shoot until you are within effective musket range of the enemy; fire deliberately, taking care to aim low, and thus avoid the overshooting to which you have been so markedly susceptible in previous battles. If you merely wound a man so much the better, as injured men have to be taken from the field by sound ones; single out a particular adversary for your fire, after the example of your sharpshooting forefathers at Bunker Hill and New Orleans. When possible pick off the enemy's officers, particularly the mounted ones, and his artillery horses. Under all conditions hold your ranks; avoid the natural but costly inclination to huddle together under heavy fire. When ordered to charge, do so at once and move forward rapidly; you are much less apt to be killed while going steadily forward than if you hesitate or retreat; but in case you have to fall back, do so gradually and in order; more men are killed during disorganized retreat than at any other time; if your objective is a battery, do not be terrorized—artillery is never as deadly as it seems; a rapid forward movement reduces the battery's effectiveness and hastens the end of its power to destroy. Do not pause or turn aside to plunder the dead or to pick up spoils; battles have been lost by indulgence in this temptation. Do not heed the calls for assistance of wounded comrades or stop to take them to the rear; details have been made to care for casualties, and the best way of protecting your wounded friends is to drive the enemy from the field. Straggling under any guise will be severely punished. Cowards will be shot. Do your duty in a manner that becomes the heroic example your regiment has already set on earlier fields of combat.

Orders to march are now given, and to the waving of colors and the stirring rhythm of fife and drum the regiments proceed to their appointed place in the line of battle. As the dawn mist clears away, a scene of intense activity is revealed on all sides. Surgeons are preparing their kits; litter bearers and ambulances are ominously waiting. Arrived at their place in line, the men wait for what seem interminable hours while other units are brought into position. There is some talk while they wait, though less than earlier in the war. Comrades quietly renew mutual pledges to seek out those who are missing at the battle's end—for help if they are wounded and for protection of belongings and notification of homefolk if they are dead. A few men read their testaments, some mutter soft prayers—a devout captain is observed standing with the Bible in hand reading aloud to his Mississippians, but this scene is unusual. Here and there a soldier bites off a chew of tobacco and joins a host of comrades whose jaws are already working. Very rarely an officer or a private sneaks a swig of "How Come You So" to bolster his spirit for the ordeal ahead. Everywhere suspense bears down with crushing force, but is indicated largely by silence.

Presently the rattle of musketry is heard in front. Skirmishers must have made contact with enemy pickets. All are alert. A signal gun is fired and the artillery joins in with accumulating fury. At last the command—"Forward!"—and an overpowering urge to make contact with the enemy. Soon lines of blue are discernible. Comrades begin to fall in increasing numbers. Now the shout, lost perhaps in the din of battle—"Charge!"—accompanied by a forward wave of officer's saber and the line leaps forward with the famous "Rebel yell."

This yell itself is an interesting thing. It was heard at First Manassas and was repeated in hundreds of charges throughout the war. It came to be as much a part of a Rebel's fighting equipment as his musket. Once, indeed, more so. Toward the end of an engagement near Richmond in May 1864 , General Early rode up to a group of soldiers and said, "Well, men, we must change them once more and then we'll be through." The response came back, "General, we are all out of ammunition." Early's ready retort was, "Damn it, holler them across." And, according to the narrator, the order was literally executed.

The Confederate yell is hard to describe. An attempt to reproduce it was made a few years ago when Confederate veterans re-enacted battle scenes in Virginia. But this, by the very nature of things, was an inadequate representation. Old voices were too weak and incentive too feeble to create again the true battle cry. As it flourished on the field of combat, the Rebel yell was an unpremeditated, unrestrained and utterly informal "hollering." It had in it a mixture of fright, pent-up nervousness, exultation, hatred and a pinch of pure deviltry. Yelling in attack was not peculiar to Confederates, for Yanks went at Rebels more than once with "furious" shouts on their lips. But the battle cry of Southerners was admittedly different. General "Jube" Early, who well understood the spirit of his soldiers, made a comparison of Federal and Confederate shouting as a sort of aside to his official report of the battle of Fredericksburg. "Lawton's Brigade, without hesitating, at once dashed upon the enemy," he said, "with the cheering peculiar to the Confederate soldier, and which is never mistaken for the studied hurrahs of the Yankees, and drove the column opposed to it down the hill." Though obviously invidious, the general's observation is not wholly inaccurate.

The primary function of the rousing yell was the relief of the shouter. As one Reb observed after a fight in 1864, "I always said if I ever went into a charge, I wouldn't holler! But the very first time I fired off my gun I hollered as loud as I could, and I hollered every breath till we stopped." At first there was no intention of inspiring terror in the enemy, but the practice soon attained such a reputation as a demoralizing agent that men were encouraged by their officers to shout as they assaulted Yankee positions. In the battle of Lovejoy's Station, for instance, Colonel Clark cried out to his Mississippians, "Fire and charge with a yell." Yankees may not have been scared by this Rebel throatsplitting, but they were enough impressed to set down in their official reports that the enemy advanced

"yelling like fiends," or other words to the same effect.

Naturally a thing of such informal character as the Rebel yell varied considerably with the time and circumstance. Mississippians had a note quite different from that of Virginians. Rebs attacking Negro troops injected so much hatred into their cry as to modify its tonal qualities. A most interesting variant was that of the trans-Mississippi Indians organized by the Confederacy. Colonel Tandy Walker, commander of the Second Indian Brigade, reporting an action of his troops in Arkansas, said that when the Federals retreated Private Dickson Wallace was the first man to reach their artillery, "and mounting astride one of the guns gave a whoop, which was followed by such a succession of whoops from his comrades as made the woods reverberate for miles around."

But those Rebs who are now charging at the Yankees know that yelling is only a small part of their business. Yankee lines loom larger as the boys in gray surge forward. Now there is a pause for aiming, and the roar of countless muskets, but the individual soldier is hardly conscious of the noise or the kick of his weapon. Rarely does he have time to consider the effectiveness of his shot. He knows that scores of Yankees are falling, and his comrades as well, but he cannot attend to details of slaughter on either side. He drops to his knee, fumblingly bites off and inserts a cartridge, rams it home with a quick thrust of the rod, then rises and dashes forward with his fellows. On they go, these charging Rebs, feeling now that exaltation which comes after the fight gets under way. "There is something grand about it—it is magnificent," said Robert Gill of his experience under fire near Atlanta. "I feel elated as borne along with the tide of battle."

Presently there is an obvious slowing down of the advance, as resistance increases and attacking ranks become thin. Artillery fire comes in such force as to shatter good-sized trees, and men are actually killed by falling limbs. The lines of gray seem literally to bend beneath the weight of canister and grape, and yelling soldiers lean forward while walking as if pushing against the force of a wind. Slaughter becomes so terrible that ditches run with blood. The deafening noise is likened by one Reb to "a large cane brake on fire and a thunder storm with repeated loud thunder claps." The flight of shells (called "lamp posts" and "wash kettles" according to their size and shape) reminds Robert Gill of "frying on a large scale only a little more so"; and Maurice Simons thinks of a partridge flying by, "only we would suppose that the little bird had grown to the size of an Eagle." Some of the men, unable to confront this holocaust, seek the protection of rocks, trees, and gullies. Others of stronger nerve close the gaps and push onward.

The overwhelming urge to get quickly to the source of danger brings an end to loading and shooting. With one last spurt the charging troops throw themselves among their adversaries, gouging with bayonets, swinging with clubbed muskets, or even striking with rocks, fence rails and sticks. Presently one side or the other gives way, and the charge is over.

But not the battle. Before the day's fighting is completed there will be several charges, each followed by lulls for reorganization. And perhaps the conflict, as at Gettysburg, will extend to a second and third day, each characterized by repetitions of attack over various portions of the field; or perhaps the main action, as at Fredericksburg, will be defensive, staving off repeated Federal assaults.

Moving to the charge, though by far the most dramatic part of fighting, actually made up only a small portion of a soldier's experience in battle. There were hours of lying on the ground or of standing in line, perhaps under the heat of a boiling sun, while troops on other parts of the field carried out the tasks assigned them. Then there was endless shifting, to bolster a weak spot here, to cut off an enemy salient there, or to replenish ammunition. These and many other activities, coupled with repeated advances on enemy positions, took a heavy toll of the soldier's strength.

As the day wore on he was increasingly conscious of exhaustion. Though accustomed before the war to long hours of labor on the farm or extended jaunts in pursuit of game, he found fighting the hardest work he had ever done. Fatigue was sharpened by the fact that rest and food had been scarce during the days before the battle. By midafternoon his strength was often so depleted that he could hardly load and fire his gun, if indeed he was able to stand at all. Those who fought at Shiloh may have joined in the postwar criticism of Beauregard for not pushing the battle as Sunday's sun sank in the west, but officers' reports made soon after the fight show that most of the men were so exhausted that further aggression was impossible.

Increasing with the combatant's fatigue came intolerable thirst. Sweating in the grime and dust, he had emptied his canteen early in the day, hoping to refill it from some stream. But rarely was there any such chance. If he were lucky enough to reach a pond he was apt to find it so choked with the dead and wounded as to be unfit for use. But even so, that soldier considered himself lucky who could sweep aside the gory scum and quench his thirst by greedy draughts of the muddy water underneath.

If the battle happened to be in winter, as at Murfreesboro, Fredericksburg, or Nashville, the suffering from thirst was not so intense. But the exposure to cold was hardly less severe. Discomfort was increased by damp weather, scarcity of clothing, and the inability to make fires. At Murfreesboro, for instance, soldiers lay in line of battle for nearly a week under a cold rain without fire.

When the combat extended over several days, as was frequently the case, hunger was added to other discomforts. At Gettysburg Washington Artillerymen became so famished that a captain sent a detail to gather food from the haverstacks of Federal dead. Many other hungry soldiers were not so fortunate as to have this opportunity.

The coming of night usually brought a rest from fighting, but not from suffering. The disorganization which characterized Confederate battles often separated the soldier from his regiment. The command of duty, plus a desire to know the lot of his friends, would cause him, tired to the point of prostration though he was, to set out on a tedious search for his fellows. When he found the scattered remnants of his company he would probably discover that some messmate, committed to his care by mutual pledge before the battle, was missing. Then he must make a round of the battlefield and the emergency hospitals, inquiring patiently, calling out the name of his friend, and scanning by candlelight the ghastly faces of dead and wounded. The quest might end in happy discovery, but more likely it would prove futile. At last the weary soldier would fall down on the ground. And in spite of the piteous cries of the wounded he would sink at once into heavy slumber.

The morrow of a battle, whether its duration was for one or several days, was in some respects more trying than the conflict itself. Scenes encountered in the burial of the dead were strange and appalling: there a dead Yankee lying on his back "with a biscuit in his hand and with one mouthful bitten off and that mouthful still between his teeth"; here "the top of a man's Skull Hanging by the Hair to a Limb some 8 or 9 feet from the ground"; yonder another "man Siting behind a large oak tree his head . . . shot off"; to the right a small, whining dog curled up in the arms of a dead Yankee, refusing to be coaxed from its erstwhile master; to the left a lifeless Reb sprawled across the body of a well-dressed Federal, the gray-clad's hand in the Northerner's pocket—a gruesome warning to those who are tempted to plunder during battle; farther on, the field is strewn with nude figures blackened and mutilated by a fire that swept across the dry foliage in the wake of the fight. One of the burying party working in Federal-traversed territory is shocked to find that before his arrival "the hogs got a holt of some of the Yankey dead." In any direction one chances to gaze lie heaps of disfigured bodies; to rural-bred Georgian the scene following Fredericksburg suggested "an immense hog pen and then all killed."

After a prolonged summer encounter the task was unusually repulsive. Wrote a soldier who

helped in the burial of the Gettysburg dead:

> The sights and smells that assailed us were simply indescribable—corpses swollen to twice their original size, some of them actually burst asunder with the pressure of foul gases and vapors. . . . The odors were nauseating and so deadly that in a short time we all sickened and were lying with our mouths close to the ground, most of us vomiting profusely.

While some were burying the dead, others were walking about picking up spoils. Trinkets of all sorts, such as Yankee letters, diaries, photographs and pocket knives were much in demand as souvenirs to be sent home to relatives. "I am going to send you a trophie that come off the battlefield at Gettysburg," wrote a Reb to his sister. "I got three pictures out of a dead Yankees knapsack and I am going to send you one. . . . The pictures are wrapped up in a letter from the person whose image they are. . . . She signed her name A. D. Spears and she lived in Main somewhere, but I could not make out where she lived." Occasionally Rebs laughed over the sentimental contents of such letters. Some soldiers profited financially from their plundering of battlefields. Following the Franklin engagement of December 1864 George Athey wrote:

> I got agood knapsack fuol of tricks whitch I sold $4.5 dolars worth out of it and cepe as mutch as I wanted.

Articles essential to personal comfort were eagerly gathered up. After the Seven Days' Battles a Reb wrote exultantly:

> We have had a glorious victory with its rich Booty A many one of our boys now have a pair of Briches a nice Rubber cloth & a pair of Blankets also a pair or more of Small Tent Cloths.

The avidity with which an impoverished Confederate might pounce upon the riches left in the wake of Federal defeat, as well as the unhappy consequence of overenthusiasm, is evidenced by an entry in a Tennessean's diary following the battle of Seven Pines:

> I awoke quite early yesterday morning, and everything seemed very quiet, I went over the field seeing what I could see. Here were Sutlers' tents, filled with luxuries, oranges, lemons, oysters, pineapples, sardines, in fact, almost everything that I could think of. My first business was to eat just as much as I possibly could, and that was no small amount, for I had been living on hard tack for several days. I then picked out a lot of stationary, paper, envelopes, ink, pens and enough to fill one haversack, then I found a lot of puff bosomed linen shirts, and laid in a half dozen together with some white gloves and other little extras enough to fill another haversack. Then I filled another with nuts and candies and still another with cheese. With this load, I wandered around picking up some canteens to carry back to the boys. Then adding to my load such articles as a sword, an overcoat, etc. . . . I quickened my pace and before I had gone twenty steps, the Yankees opened fire . . . and the balls whistled around me in a perfect shower. I had about two hundred yards to go before reaching my regiment and by the time I reached it, I had thrown away all my plunder.

If the battle ended in defeat, falling back might be so hurried as to leave the dead and wounded in Federal hands. This, added to the increased hardships of retreat and the disappointment of being whipped, caused the soldier's cup to overflow with bitterness.

But whether victorious or not, Johnny Reb began within a remarkably short time to recall and to enjoy the interesting and humorous detail of the combat. Campfire groups must have delighted in teasing Private Joseph Adams about losing his pants when a shell exploded near him at Murfreesboro; and there was doubtless plenty of laughter when M. D. Martin told how a shell cut off his two well-stocked haversacks and scattered hardtack so promiscuously that "several of the boys were struck by the biscuits, and more than one thought he was wounded."

James Mabley could always get a good laugh with his story of the Reb at Chancellorsville who while in the act of drawing a bead on a Yank was distracted by a wild turkey lighting in a tree before him; the Federal was immediately forgotten, and in an instant the crack of this Reb's gun brought the turkey to the ground.

The men of Gilmor's Battalion never tired of asking their colonel after a valley engagement of 1864 "if spades are trumps"; for during this fight a ball went all the way through an unopened deck of cards that he was carrying in his inside coat pocket, stopping only at the last card, the ace of spades.

Almost everyone could tell of a "close shave" when a bullet hit a knapsack, perforated a hat, or spent itself by passing through a bush immediately in front, to fall harmlessly to the ground in plain view. One soldier marveled at hearing through the din of battle the cry of John Childress as he fell: "I am killed, tell Ma and Pa goodbye for me."

Then someone may have mentioned the tragic case of Jud and Cary Smith, Yale-educated brothers from Mississippi. While in the act of lying down under fire, the younger, Cary, putting his hand under his coat, found his inner garments covered with blood; and with only the exclamation "What does this mean?" he died. Jud was so overwhelmed with grief that he spent the entire night muttering affectionate words over his brother's corpse. He passed the next day and night in unconsolable solitude. The third day was that of Malvern Hill, and when the first charge took place Jud kept on going after his comrades fell back under the murderous fire, and he was never seen or heard of again. After the father learned of the fate of his two sons he joined Price's army as a private soldier; when his regiment charged at Iuka, he followed the example set by Jud at Malvern Hill, and he likewise was never heard of again.

But there was not much lingering on tragic notes. It was more pleasant to talk of how Jeb Stuart at Second Manassas beguiled the Yankees into exaggerated ideas of Rebel strength by having his men drag brush along the roads to stir up huge clouds of dust; or of how the Yankee General Banks was duped into abandoning several strong positions during his Red River campaign by such Confederate ruses as sending drummers out to beat calls, lighting superfluous campfires, blowing bugles, and "rolling empty wagons over fence rails"; or of how George Cagle, while lying on a ridge at Chickamauga, kept at work four or five muskets gathered from incapacitated comrades, and as Yankee bullets whistled overhead he simulated the activity of an artillery unit, giving such commands as "attention Cagle's Battery, make ready, load, take aim, fire"; of how Sergeant Nabors scared nervous Yankee prisoners who asked him at Atlanta if he were going to kill them by replying, "That's our calculation; we came out for that purpose."

By no means was all of the fighting in the open field. Warring in trenches—Johnny Reb usually called them "ditches"— made its appearance in the spring of 1862 on the Virginia peninsula where Magruder's army was entrenched for a month. At Vicksburg, where Pemberton's troops were under siege for forty-seven days, soldiers spent most of the time in earthworks along the line, or in caves to the rear. During the Atlanta campaign Rebs of the Army of Tennessee saw considerable trench warfare. But by far the longest stretch of this sort of campaigning was done by Lee's troops, who spent the greater part of the war's last year in ditches around Petersburg.

Occasionally the routine of trench fighting was broken by an assault of one army or the other, but the time was mostly spent in desultory exchanges of artillery and musket fire. The Federals, being the besiegers and having vastly superior resources, did the larger part of the firing. So unlimited, indeed, were their supplies of ammunition that they could make the countryside reverberate with repeated discharges of their heavy cannon.

The defenders of Vicksburg were subjected to heavier fire than any other trench fighters in the war. Back of them lay the Mississippi, dotted with gunboats, and before them were the troops of Grant and Sherman well equipped with artillery. The besieged were deficient in both guns and ammunition. Hemmed in thus by supe-

rior forces and equipment, conscious of their inability to give effective retaliation, living on ever dwindling rations, suffering from a shortage of drinking water and cut off largely from their friends, they were subjected day after day and night after night to a cannonading that was so severe at times as to make heads ache from the concussion. One of the defenders wrote in his diary at the midpoint of siege:

> The fighting is now carried on quite systematically . . . in the morning there seems to be time allowed for breakfast, when all at once the work of destruction is renewed. There is about an hour at noon & about the same at sunset, taking these three intervals out the work goes on just as regularly as . . . on a well regulated farm & the noise is not unlike the clearing up of new ground when much heavy timber is cut down! Add to that the nailing on of shingles by several men & one has a pretty good idea of the noise. It might be supposed that a score of villages had sprung up all round him & that the inhabitants were vieing with each other to see who could be the most industrious.

The caves dug in the hillside were poor protection against the heavy shells that came screeching through the air with varying notes of terror. If one lifted his head ever so little above the earthworks, the crack of a sharpshooter's rifle, followed instantly by a dull thud, would announce the doom of another Reb. A man who was slightly wounded in the trenches stood in considerable danger of being more seriously injured, if not killed outright, as he traversed the open space between battle line and hospital. Life under such conditions became a torturing ordeal, and the situation was not helped by jesting speculation as to the prospective comforts of Johnson's Island, Camp Chase and Camp Douglas.

In the trenches before Atlanta and Petersburg existence was not so perilous nor so gloomy as at Vicksburg. Common to all, however, was the intolerable heat of the summer sun. Some men sought alleviation by building little brush arbors along the trenches. The sultriness of the ditches became so unbearable at night that some of the men resorted to sleeping on the edge—and when the Federal batteries opened they would simply roll over to safety. But immunity from danger in the Atlanta and Petersburg trenches was only comparative. The killing and wounding of men by Federal sharpshooting and artillery fire were of such common occurrence as hardly to elicit notice save by the company to which the casualty belonged.

The number of killed and wounded would have been much greater but for the skill of the men in side-stepping arched shots. "The mortars are thrown up a great height," wrote an Alabamian from Petersburg, "and fall down in the trenches like throwing a ball over a house— we have become very perfect in dodging them and unless they are thrown too thick I think I can always escape them at least at night." He added that the dugouts which they contrived at intervals along the trenches and which they were wont to call bombproofs were not impervious at all to mortar shells, and that "we always prefer to be out in the ditches—where by using strategy and skill we get out of their way." So confident did the troops become of their ability to escape these lobbed shots of the Yankees that they would keep up a derisive yelling throughout a bombardment.

During periods of truce ladies from Petersburg made several visits to the lines, walking down the ditches in their cumbersome hoop skirts to see how bombproofs were made, climbing upon the parapets to get a look at the Yankees, giggling and oh-ing at the strange sights confronting them. Both Federals and Rebs enjoyed these interludes in crinoline but some of the latter could not refrain from mischievously expressing the wish that the Yanks would throw a few shells over to see if the fair visitors would shake with terror or raise the Rebel yell.

But these tantalizing glimpses of Petersburg belles afforded only brief respite from the terrible filth, the smothering heat of summer and the cold of winter, the rain and mud of all seasons, the restricted movement and the countless other deprivations that made trench warfare the most unpleasant aspect of Confederate soldierhood.

Open fighting with all its dangers was immeasurably preferable to such existence as this.

But what of valor and of cowardice on the field of battle? There were numerous manifestations of both, though many more of the former than of the latter. Deeds of Rebel bravery, individual and collective, were of such common occurrence as to be quite beyond all estimation. A few definite instances will serve as examples of the glory that lighted up the fields of Manassas, of Shiloh, of Antietam, of Gettysburg, of Spottsylvania—and of countless others.

At Shiloh Private Samuel Evans refused to go to the rear when a ball passed through both cheeks, "but remained and fought for a considerable length of time, cheering on the men and loading and shooting as fast as he could." An officer who saw his men reduced from twenty-eight to twelve as he led them into the ravaging fire at Seven Pines cried out as he fell pierced through the heart, "Boys, I am killed, but you press on." Private Ike Stone was severely wounded at the beginning of the Murfreesboro fight, but he paused only to bind up his injuries, and when his captain was incapacitated Stone took charge of the company and led it valorously through the battle, this despite a second wound. In the thick of this same fight Sergeant Joe Thompson was overwhelmed with the impulse to take a prisoner; leaping ahead of his comrades he overtook the retreating Federal column, seized a Yank and started to the rear with him; but this man having been shot down in his grasp, Thompson ran back to the still-retreating lines, seized a second Federal and brought him away safely. When Private Mattix's left arm was so seriously injured that he could no longer fire his musket, he went to his commanding officer and said, "Colonel, I am too badly wounded to use my gun but can carry the flag; may I?" Before this three standard-bearers had been shot down in succession, but when the requested permission was given him, Mattix seized the staff, stepped boldly in front of the regiment, and carried the colors throughout the remainder of the contest.

In his official report of Second Manassas Major J. D. Waddell, commanding Toombs'

Georgians, said that he "carried into the fight over 100 men who were barefoot, many of whom left bloody foot-prints among the thorns and briars through which they rushed, with Spartan courage and really jubilant impetuosity, upon the serried ranks of the foe." Colonel E. C. Cook of the Thirty-second Tennessee Infantry reported after Chickamauga that one of his men, J. W. Ellis, who had marched for six weeks without shoes, "went thus into battle and kept up his company at all times till wounded."

At Chickamauga Private Mayfield was wounded in the thigh by a Minié ball and at the same time dazed by a shell. Litter bearers picked him up and were carrying him to the rear when he recovered from the shock and sprang to the ground with the remark, "This will not do for me," and rushed back to continue the fight. In this same engagement Private McCann fought gallantly until his ammunition was exhausted; then he picked up cartridge boxes of the dead and wounded and coolly distributed ammunition among his comrades. When the colonel commended his heroic conduct McCann asked that his bravery be cited in the official report of the battle. Shortly afterward he received a mortal wound and as he was borne dying to the rear, he turned smiling to his colonel and reminded him of the promise of honorable mention.

Of all the brave those who were entrusted with the colors had the most consistent record. Almost every official report of regimental commanders mentions the courageous action of standard-bearers. To keep the flag flying was a matter of inestimable pride, and its loss to the enemy was an incalculable disgrace. Consequently men vied with each other for the honor of holding the cherished emblem aloft in the thickest of the fight. The Federals, knowing the close association of morale and colors, and being easily able to single out standard-bearers because of their conspicuousness, were wont to concentrate an unusually heavy fire upon them. Literally thousands of those who aspired to the honor of carrying and guarding the flags paid for the privilege with their lives.

"In my two color companies," reported Colonel Jenkins of the Palmetto Sharpshooters after Seven Pines, "out of 80 men who entered 40 were killed and wounded, and out of 11 in the color guard, 10 were shot down, and my colors pierced by nine balls passed through four hands without touching the ground." At Antietam the First Texas Infantry lost eight standard-bearers in succession, and at Gettysburg, the Twenty-sixth North Carolina lost fourteen. At Antietam also, the flag of the Tenth Georgia—which regiment lost fifty-seven per cent of its men and officers in this one engagement—received forty-six shots. The standard of Lyle's Regiment was torn to tatters at Corinth, and color-bearer Sloan when last seen by his comrades was "going over the breast works waving a piece over his head and shouting for the Southern Confederacy."

Color Sergeant Rice of the Twenty-eighth Tennessee Infantry, downed by a bullet at Murfreesboro, still clung to the flag, holding it aloft as he crawled on his knees until a second shot brought death and delivered him of his trust. On another part of this bloody field Color Sergeant Cameron advanced too far ahead of his comrades and was captured. He tore the flag from its staff, concealed it on his person, carried it to prison with him, escaped and brought it back to be unfurled anew above its proud followers.

Murfreesboro likewise afforded the setting for perhaps the most extraordinary of all color-bearer feats. While this contest raged at its greatest fury the opposing lines came very near each other in that portion of the field occupied by the Nineteenth Texas Cavalry (dismounted). A Yankee standard carrier stood immediately to the front of the Texas Color Sergeant, A. Sims, waving his flag and urging the blue column forward. Sergeant Sims, construing this as something of a personal insult, rushed forward, planted his own flag staff firmly on the ground with one hand and made a lunge for that of his exhorting adversary with the other. At the moment of contact, both color-bearers, Yankee and Rebel, "fell in the agonies of death waving their banners above their heads until their last expiring moments." The Texas standard was rescued, but not until one who rushed forward to retrieve it had also been shot down.

Confederate authorities sought to stimulate the men by offering medals and badges to those who were cited by officers. Unable to supply these emblems, Congress passed an act in October 1862 providing for the publication of a Roll of Honor after each battle which should include the names of those who had best displayed their courage and devotion. Such lists were read at dress parades, published in newspapers and filed in the adjutant general's office. As a further inducement commissions were offered to those who should distinguish themselves, and special inscriptions were placed on flags of those regiments that captured artillery or gave other proof of unusual achievement. But the most effective incentive was probably that of personal and family pride. This was strikingly evidenced by the remark of a Georgian to his brother after Franklin: "I am proud to say that there was no one between me and the Yankees when I was wounded."

Cowardice under fire, being a less gratifying subject than heroism, has not received much attention from those who have written or talked of the Confederate Army. Of the various sources of information on this obscure point the most fertile are the official reports of battles by commanders of units ranging from regiments to armies. But the most numerous of these reports—those submitted by regimental commanders—are characterized by a reluctance to admit wholesale cowardice because of possible reflections on the conduct of the commanders themselves. This reluctance sometimes resulted in misrepresentation of the rankest sort, as in the following case: After the attack on Battery Wagner, Morris Island, South Carolina, July 18, 1863, Colonel Charles W. Knight, commanding the Thirty-first North Carolina Regiment, said in closing his report, "It is useless to mention any officer or man, when all were acting coolly and bravely." In the body of his report he mentioned being repulsed, but there is absolutely no suggestion of bad conduct on the part of the regiment. But when Knight's superior, General William B.

Taliaferro, reported the battle, he said: "The Thirty-first North Carolina could not be induced to occupy their position, and ingloriously deserted the ramparts. . . . I feel it my duty to mention . . . [their] disgraceful conduct."

In the reports of higher ranking officers, who could admit bad conduct of portions of their commands with more impunity than colonels, and in the wartime letters and diaries of the common soldiers, much testimony on the subject may be found. This evidence shows clearly that Confederate soldiers were by no means immune to panic and cowardice.

At First Manassas a few Rebs fled into the woods when shells began to fly. There was disgraceful conduct at the beginning of McClellan's peninsula campaign, when General D. H. Hill wrote that "several thousand soldiers . . . have fled to Richmond under pretext of sickness. They have even thrown away their arms that their flight might not be impeded." At Seven Pines there were a few regiments that "disgracefully left the battle field with their colors." General W. H. C. Whiting in reporting the battle of Gaines's Mill said: "Men were leaving the field in every direction and in great disorder . . . men were skulking from the front in a shameful manner; the woods on our left and rear were full of troops in safe cover from which they never stirred." At Malvern Hill, General Jubal Early encountered "a large number of men retreating from the battle-field," saw "a very deep ditch filled with skulkers," and found a "wood filled with a large number of men retreating in confusion."

Men ran, skulked and straggled by the hundreds at Shiloh. A Tennessee regiment took fright during an advance, ran back on supporting lines crying, "Retreat! Retreat!" and caused great confusion; but they were rallied and set in motion toward the Federal position; again they were overcome with fear, and this time they rushed back so precipitately that they ran over and trampled in the mud the color-bearer of the regiment behind them. A Texas regiment behaved in the same manner; placed in line of battle it began firing, but before the guns had all been discharged, "it broke and fled disgracefully from the field." An officer who attempted to bring back the fugitives and threatened to report them as "a pack of cowards" was told that "they did not care a damn" what they were called, they would not follow him. When General W. J. Hardee tried to rally another demoralized regiment he was fired on by its members. Some of the straggling for which Shiloh was notorious was due to circumstances that exonerate those involved, but there can be no doubt that a large part of those who found various pretexts for leaving the firing line were playing the coward. Said Colonel O. F. Strahl in his official report: "On Monday morning we . . . had a great number of stragglers attached to us. The stragglers demonstrated very clearly this morning that they had strayed from their own regiments because they did not want to fight. My men fought gallantly until the stragglers ran and left them and began firing from the rear over their heads. They were then compelled to fall to the rear. I rallied them several times and . . . finally left out the stragglers." General Beauregard clinched this evidence in his official report: "Some officers, non-commissioned officers, and men abandoned their colors early in the first day to pillage the captured encampments; others retired shamefully from the field on both days while the thunder of cannon and the roar and rattle of musketry told them that their brothers were being slaughtered by the fresh legions of the enemy."

General Bushrod Johnson reported that at Murfreesboro troops on his right became demoralized and "men of different regiments, brigades, divisions, were scattered all over the fields," and that he was almost run over, so precipitate was their fight. Captain Felix Robertson said that he had never seen troops so completely broken as those demoralized at Murfreesboro. "They seemed actuated only by a desire for safety," he added. "I saw the colors of many regiments pass, and though repeated calls were made for men of the different regiments, no attention was paid to them."

At Chancellorsville and Gettysburg the conduct of the soldiers seems to have been exceptionally good. This may have been due in some part to vigorous efforts of General Lee and of the War Department early in 1863 to tighten up the discipline of the Army of Northern Virginia. The fighting before Vicksburg was marred by shameful conduct in the action of May 16, 1863, of which General Pemberton said: "We lost a large amount of artillery. The army was much demoralized; many regiments behaved badly," and Colonel Edward Goodwin reported of a small number of troops immediately in front of him:

> At this time our friends gave way and came rushing to the rear panic-stricken. . . . I brought my regiment to the charge bayonets, but even this could not check them in their flight. The colors of three regiments passed through. . . . We collared them, begged them, and abused them in vain.

The wholesale panic which seized Confederate troops at Missionary Ridge was as notorious as it was mystifying. A soldier who took part in the battle wrote in his diary, "In a few minutes the whole left gave way and a regular run commenced." After a retreat of several hundred yards, this Reb's battalion rallied momentarily, "but it was in such a confused mass that we made but a feeble resistance, when all broke again in a perfect stampede." His conviction was that the troops acted disgracefully, that they "did not half fight."

General Bragg in his official report of the fight said that "a panic which I had never witnessed seemed to have seized upon officers and men, and each seemed to be struggling for his personal safety, regardless of his duty or character." He added that "no satisfactory excuse can possibly be given for the shameful conduct of the troops on our left in allowing their line to be penetrated. The position was one which ought to have been held by a line of skirmishers against any assaulting column, and wherever resistance was made the enemy fled in disorder after suffering heavy loss. Those who reached the ridge did so in a condition of exhaustion from the great physical exertion in climbing, which rendered them powerless, and the slightest effort would have destroyed them." What stronger indictment could there be of any soldiery by its general-in-command!

But the woeful tale is not ended. In connection with Early's campaign of 1864 in the Shenandoah Valley occurred some of the most disgraceful running of Confederate history. After an engagement near Winchester on July 23, General Stephen Ramseur wrote his wife:

> My men behaved shamefully—They ran from the enemy. . . . The entire command stampeded. I tried in vain to rally them & even after the Yankees were checked by a few men I posted behind a stone wall, they continued to run all the way to the breastworks at Winchester—& many of them threw away their guns & ran on to Newton 6 miles beyond. They acted cowardly and I told them so.

On September 19, 1864, during another hard fight near Winchester, a panic of unprecedented proportions struck the ranks of Early's army. Regiment after regiment broke and fled back toward the town. General Bryan Grimes, appalled by the demoralization and fearful that his brigade would succumb to it, threatened "to blow the brains out of the first man who left ranks," and then moved over to confront the fugitives, waving his sword and giving many a Reb the full weight of its flashing blade. But fleeing regiments, increasing now in number, could not be stopped. They poured into the town, out of the valley pike, and some continued their disordered course for miles beyond. "The Ladies of Winchester came into the streets and beged them crying bitterly to make a stand, for their sakes if not for their own honor," wrote a captain who witnessed the rout; but "the cowards did not have the shame to make a pretense of halting."

A month later at Cedar Creek, plunder combined with cowardice to inflict upon Early's veterans one of the most shameful defeats of the war. In the morning, by brilliant action, the Confederates pounced upon the Federals and drove them from their camps. As the Southern lines advanced large numbers of soldiers and officers turned aside, against positive orders, and began to ransack the rich stores abandoned by the foe. While the victors were absorbed in pillage, the Federals rallied, and in the afternoon they counterattacked. The disorganized Confederates broke first on the left, and then all along the line. Efforts of division commanders and of others who attempted to stay the tide of panic was to no avail, and the field was utterly abandoned.

"It was the hardest day's work I ever engaged in," Grimes said, "trying to rally the men. Took over flags at different times, begging, commanding, entreating the men to rally—would ride up and down the lines, beseeching them by all they held sacred and dear, to stop and fight, but without any success. I don't mean my Brigade only, but all."

Price's Missouri expedition of 1864 was marked by an instance of large-scale panic. When the Federals attacked the Confederate rear on October 25, near Carthage, Missouri, demoralization set in. As Price rode rapidly to the point of danger he "met the divisions of Major-Generals Fagan and Marmaduke retreating in utter and indescribable confusion, many of them having thrown away their arms. They were deaf to all entreaties or commands, and in vain were all efforts to rally them."

While the Atlanta campaign seems to have been remarkably free of demoralization under fire, there were at least two instances involving a considerable number of men. In a skirmish on June 9, 1864, a Texas cavalry unit that had a distinguished record in battle broke upon slight contact with the Federal cavalry, and fled in a manner described as disorderly and shameful by General Ross. Later, in the Battle of Jonesboro, August 31, 1864, an advancing brigade of Confederates halted without orders when it came to the Federal picket line, the men seeking shelter behind piles of rails. They seemed "possessed of some great horror of charging breastworks," reported Colonel Bushrod Jones, "which no power of persuasion or example could dispel."

The last instance of large-scale panic during the war was at Nashville, December 16, 1864. On this occasion the division of General Bate, when assaulted about four o'clock in the afternoon by the Federals, began to fall back in great confusion and disorder. In a few moments the entire Confederate line was broken, and masses of troops fled down the pike toward Franklin. All efforts to rally the troops proved fruitless. General Bate in his official report leaves the impression that the rout, due to extenuating circumstances, cast little if any reproach upon his men. But General Hood, in chief command, was evidently of contrary opinion, as he says that Confederate loss in killed and wounded was small, implying that withdrawal took place without much resistance. He says further that the break came so suddenly that artillery guns could not be brought away. Captain Thomas J. Key says in his diary that "General Bate's division . . . shamefully broke and fled before the Yankees were within 200 yards of them," and that there "then ensued one of the most disgraceful routs" that it had ever been his misfortune to witness."

There were innumerable cases of individual cowardice under fire. When men are assembled in such large numbers, especially when many of them are forced into service, a certain proportion are inevitably worthless as fighters. Some of those who fled wanted earnestly to act bravely, but they had not the power to endure fire unflinchingly. This type is well exemplified by the Reb who covered his face with his hat during the battle of Fredericksburg, and who later, when told that his turn at the rifle pits was imminent, "made a proposition that he would go out from camp and strip" and let his comrades "get switches and whip him as much as they wanted" if they would obtain his release from the impending proximity to Federal fire. A similar case was encountered by Colonel C. Irvine Walker. A man had been reported for cowardly behavior on the field. Walker called him to task and told him that he would be watched closely during the next engagement. When the time came the colonel went over to check his performance as the regiment advanced. "I found him in his place," reported Walker, "his rifle on his shoulder, and holding up in front of him a frying pan." The man was so scared that he sought this meager protection, yet he moved forward with his company and was killed.

Another case of infamy converted to valor was cited by Colonel William Stiles, of the Sixtieth Georgia Infantry. During a charge this officer saw a robust Reb drop out of line and crouch behind a tree; the colonel slipped up and gave him a resounding whack across the back with the flat of his sword, and shouted, "Up there, you coward!"

The skulker, thinking evidently that he was the mortal victim of a Yankee shot, "clasped his hands, and keeled over backwards, devoutly ejaculating, 'Lord, receive my spirit!'"

After momentary bafflement, Stiles kicked the prostrate soldier violently in the ribs, exclaiming simultaneously, "Get up, sir! The Lord wouldn't receive the spirit of such an infernal coward."

The man sprang up with the joyful exclamation, "Ain't I killed? The Lord be praised," grabbed his musket, rejoined his comrades, and henceforth conducted himself with courage.

Other officers had less success. Men who had no shoes were often excused from fighting, and a good many soldiers took advantage of this rule by throwing away their shoes on the eve of conflict. Others left the field under pretext of helping the wounded to the rear, and this in spite of strict orders against removal of casualties by anyone except those specifically detailed for the purpose. Still others feigned sickness or injury. A favorite ruse was to leave one's own regiment during the confusion of battle, and then to evade duty by a pretense of endless and futile searching for the outfit intentionally abandoned.

Infuriated officers would curse these shirkers, beat them with swords and even threaten them with shooting, and on occasion carry out their threats on the spot. Commanders would place file-closers in the rear with instruction to arrest, and in some instances to shoot down, those who refused to do their duty. Courts-martial sentenced great numbers to hard and disgraceful punishments. Private soldiers covered spineless comrades with scorn and ridicule. But these measures were only partially effective.

There can be no doubt that they trying conditions under which Confederate soldiers fought contributed to the bad performance of some on the field of battle. Men often went into combat hungry and remained long under fire with little or nothing to eat. Sometimes, as at Antietam and Gettysburg, they fought after exhausting marches. Many of those who participated in the routs at Chattanooga and at Nashville were without shoes. Often the Confederate artillery protection was inadequate. The superior number of the Federals made Rebel flanks unduly vulnerable,

and flank sensitiveness was the cause of more than one panic. Casualties among line officers were unusually heavy, and replacement with capable men was increasingly difficult after 1863.

When all of these factors are considered, it is rather remarkable that defection under fire was not more frequent than it actually was. Those soldiers who played the coward, even granting that the offenders totaled well up in the thousands, were a very small proportion of the Confederate Army. Taken on the whole of his record under fire, the Confederate private was a soldier of such mettle as to claim a high place among the world's fighting men. It may be doubted that anyone else deserves to outrank him.